Foreword by Former Secretary of the Navy Richard Danzig
Afterword by Dr. Robert Norton of Auburn University

Elementary... the Art and Science of Finding Information

Achieving More "Knowledge Advantage" through OSINT

Revised and Expanded Edition
Original Title: *What You Don't Know....*

Miguel Fernandez, Alan Millington, Mark Monday and Dr. Emil Sarpa

BookLocker
Saint Petersburg, Florida

Library of Congress Cataloging in Publication Data
Elementary... the Art and Science of Finding Information by Miguel Fernandez, Alan Millington, Mark Monday and Dr. Emil Sarpa
Library of Congress Control Number: 2019917913

Published by Boolocker.com, Inc., Bradenton, Florida.

BookLocker.com, Inc.
2019

Revised Edition

About the Authors

Miguel Fernandez is tenured Composition and Literature faculty, and Faculty Liaison for Student Veterans, at Chandler-Gilbert Community College, in Arizona. He has received several teaching awards, including the 2012 Gilbert Chamber of Commerce Community College Educator of the Year, a 2013 League of Innovation's Roueche Excellence Award, and was a recipient of the 2015 Maricopa Community Colleges Foundation Recognition Award for his work with student veterans. He graduated Valley Leadership Institute, Class 38. He currently teaches Freshman composition with a focus on OSR/OSINT research techniques to detect and decipher bias and fake news. He is a 2019 ISPPF Fellow and a 2019-2020 Maricopa Institute of Learning Research Fellow, focusing on credibility literacy. He is also Director of Human Countermeasures for Ronin Consulting.

Alan Millington has a diverse intelligence background that covers the last decade. He began his career in intelligence with the United States Marine Corps as a signal's intelligence marine. After two deployments and 5 years with the military, he attended Auburn University in the state of Alabama. While attending Auburn he worked at the Open Source Intelligence Laboratory, where he was introduced to OSINT and its diverse applications to military, law enforcement, government, and private industry. After completion of his degree, he entered the cybersecurity field where he focused on helping organizations understand their attack surface and its associated risks by applying OSINT from an adversarial perspective. He has also served in a cybersecurity engineering role and as a competitive intelligence program manager.

Mark Monday covered a variety of beats and was an investigative journalist at the *Arizona Republic* before moving to the *San Diego Tribune*. He spent two decades there investigating such things as the foster care system, a probe that brought legislative hearings and new laws and earned him a resolution from the state assembly. He investigated attempts by the Gambino crime family to take over local businesses and governments, coverage that resulted in a grand jury investigation. He also shared in the 1979 Pulitzer Prize staff award for best general local reporting. On the side he published two international journals on terrorism and insurgency. Leaving journalism to join a firm associated with the US Navy SEALS, Mark practiced Open Source Intelligence (OSINT) and wrote and edited SEAL manuals, including the tactics manual. After the events of 9/11, he worked with the Department of Energy doing open source intelligence, tracking radiological materials usable for a "dirty bomb." He served a stint as a researcher for the Afghanistan Human Terrain Reachback Team at Ft. Leavenworth, Kansas, then returned to Arizona to write doctrine at the US Army Intelligence Center at

Ft. Huachuca. For six years he taught and developed OSINT classes at the Fort. He wrote five books dealing with security and military matters and has three small collections at the Hoover Institution of War Revolution and Peace at Stanford University.

Emil J. Sarpa was from Ohio and was a school teacher at several schools, the last being Shaker Heights High School after graduation from The Ohio State University (BS) and Bowling Green State University. After winning fellowships (John Hay Whitney fellowship (U. of Oregon), National Science Fellowship (Western Michigan U.), and a National Defense Education Fellowship (Stanford U.) the result was a PhD. He spent five years at Stanford as Human Resources Director and Labor Relations Negotiator and three years as a private consultant. He then joined The Intel Corporation for five years and Sun Microsystems for 23 years as Director of External Research. He was a private consultant after Sun was purchased.

Dedication

To you, the reader and user. And to those others who know who
they are.

Foreword To
Original Edition

By Richard Danzig
Former Secretary of the Navy

Our virtues imprison us. Cultures, institutions and individuals all have special strengths. They invest and reinvest in developing, routinizing and indeed exalting these strengths and wind up overlooking, undervaluing, indeed actively resisting, whatever is perceived as inconsistent or irrelevant to the virtues esteemed as heroic. Thus, doctors envision medicine as paradigmatically surgery and police build an image of professionals who confront criminals, fire weapons and make arrests. They resist prioritizing prevention; the medical profession devalues maintenance and amelioration; and police officers, many of whom will never fire a gun, give little priority to training to improve their skills at what they do most: handling domestic disputes.

Our intelligence agencies were born and proudly brought to maturity as masters of stealth, secrecy and covert operations. So it should be no surprise that they have had problems assimilating the subject of this book, Open Source Intelligence. Despite special programs and institutions grafted onto the body of intelligence agencies, open source generates more anti-bodies than admiration. At best it is an adopted smaller sibling, marginally nourished in most of the houses of our intelligence establishment.

In three ways this is a problem. First, digital information systems, sensors, communications capabilities and analytic tools have proliferated while secrets are surely not comparably growing (some would argue they are contracting). Accordingly, to understand the world it is increasingly necessary to access the mass of open source material. To do otherwise is to take a stand like those ancient Greeks who felt that all that mattered could be memorized, that written material distracted, and that memory, the traditional tool, was alone sufficient – indeed it was optimal – for securing knowledge and understanding. But the new tool had too much power as an instrument for mastery. The old methods had to make space for the new. If today, an analyst accesses only secret information he is blinkered and sometimes blinded.

Even were this not true, a second factor demands attention to what is not secret. That is the high likelihood that opponents will be using just such public material. Even an individual or a small group can now use Open Source to muster an arsenal of tools that would have done credit to any twentieth century intelligence service: satellite photos, data banks, data analytic tools, the ability to track social communication, etc. Open Source lets us see the world as our opponents see it. When we understand it we can influence it. Who could deny that benefit?

Were this not alone sufficient, a wise analyst recognizes a third factor: his policy-making principals will commonly consciously or unconsciously strive to integrate an analyst's insights with those the policy-maker derived and derives from open sources. It is not just that our current President assiduously watches TV. It is that all laymen swim in a sea of open source information. If an analyst would proffer a different view, he had better be prepared to understand what is out there and how to establish the value of his view as against what can be inferred from the public record.

In this light it is a problem three times over if analysts do less than a premier job in mining open source materials. But in the opinion of their seniors, they often fail to meet this standard. The authors note this deficiency. But their achievement begins with the fact that they do not spend time admiring the problem. Instead they provide the tools to address it. This is a book filled with invaluable practical advice.

The authors offer so many useful metaphors about their subject that I hesitate to offer another one. (And I recognize that I have offered a number already!) But I cannot help but think of myself and readers of this work as novices learning to fish in unfamiliar waters. As novices we might think the trick is simply to put a line in the water, look at what emerges, toss back what's unappealing and make a meal of what remains.

But skilled fishing isn't like that and neither is harvesting the bounty from the sea of facts and opinions accessible in this "Information Age." Good information harvesting, like good fishing, consists in first knowing where to look, then in how to choose your bait and cast your line. It requires knowing when you can be nonchalant and when (and how) you must disguise what you are doing. It requires principles of selection, skills in preservation and artistry in preparation for consumers who care about the results but little if anything about the methods used to produce them. It even requires being aware that some of what you take in may be poisoned. And information harvesting against nation states can be more like dealing with Moby Dick or the great white shark in Jaws – you may be struggling with powerful adversaries who bite back.

In this situation, who would want to fish simply with an uneducated intuition? But that's what many of us do. A few are burned by the experience. A number find it unproductive. Most of us think we're pretty good, but in fact we're mediocre. In these pages, the authors teach us how to be better. Much better.

They also teach something else – something even more valuable. That is that the critical variables are not so much in mastering machines and information sources. They are in mastering ourselves. Accordingly, the authors remind us of our inclinations to confirm our presuppositions, to disproportionately value secret over open information, to fall into habits of search instead of refashioning our methods to suit our purposes, to organize teams that suppress rather than reward independent analysis, etc. Above all, they are concerned to help us, even force us, to develop our skills. Many books like this explain the world to you. This book compels the reader to be an actor. It assigns tasks designed to develop skills, abilities to access, synthesize and analyze secret information, the authors empower us to transcend ourselves. True to their subject, they "open" our apertures and teach us how to be comfortable, creative and appropriately mindful of what our improved insight can provide us. Even the Greeks most resistant to reading would, I think, like this book. So will you.

Table of Contents

Acknowledgements

Beyond my family and wife, I would like to thank the inspirational role model of sixth grade teacher Byron Broderick, a WWII war-fighter turned public school teacher in Harlem, NYC. Finding this veteran and educator, 31 years later, with no address, no leads, a man who never had an email address, was an early application of OSR techniques that became a TED TALKS BLOG story and seeded a reunion, student and teacher, that lasted as friendship until his death in 2015.
This link to the man I refer to is summarized here:
https://www.lib.washington.edu/support/endowments/broderick

And the 'prized student expressed the impact Byron had upon his life in a TED Blog' is, well, me:
https://blog.ted.com/finding-mr-broderick-how-a-ted-talk-launched-my-search-for-the-teacher-who-changed-my-life/

Miguel Fernandez

***

I'd like to thank Dr. Robert Norton and Dr. Greg Weaver. Without their guidance and willingness to find and share opportunities with students, I would never have been exposed to open source intelligence. I truly owe them my greatest gratitude for helping me find my calling and career. Finally, I would like to thank my beautiful wife Heather Millington. Many of my accomplishments would not be realized without her love and encouragement.

Alan Millington

***

Many people have played a role in this effort over the years – but, of course, I take full responsibility for all errors – and inevitably there are some. I am particularly appreciative of the chance to learn from many people such as Christiaan Triebert, who has helped elucidate the Bellingcat concept, Dr. Robert Norton, Fabian Hinojosa, Dr. Christopher Callahan, Neal Hanley, Dr. Randolph Hock, Jaimi Dowdell, Stephen Stock, Catherine Wyman, Lt. Gen Patrick Hughes USA (Retd), E. Ben Benavides, Steve Capps, Larry Panther, S. E. Foster, Jesse Woodruff, Joseph L. Smith, Tom Smith, Alijandra Mogilner, C. M. Miner, Vee Herrington, Kyle Conley, Morgan Clements, Thomas Liffiton, and Kristy Westphal. Others who had a profound effect that finally resulted in this text include my journalism mentors, Jack West and C. Logan McKechnie, Dr. Don Kalick, Alexander Moser, Ron Hutcherson, Jan K. Bennett, John Engels, Lisa Miller, Elizabeth Brooks, M. V. Riley, Phyllis D. Vosbeck, John Edgington, Michele Davis, David Wheeler, Col. Joshua J. Potter USA, Clifton Reed, Tony Scotti, Lee F. White-Marsh, and

Robert Fessler as well as the late Owen Muldoon, James Profitt, Dr. J. Bowyer Bell, Dr. Norman White, M. L. Greenwell, N. H. Nemeth, Anna B. Riley, Engwald C. Olberg, Lena Pondelek, Victor Bucher, and Jimmy Thornton. Undoubtedly I have left some out, for which I apologize.

My late parents, Albert and Ann Monday, pushed me into computer research decades ago at a time when most of the world was still changing typewriter ribbons. Without that loving shove – and the many other wonderful things they did for me – I would have missed good things, and much knowledge, in life. My sister, Blaise Pope, and her husband William, also have had a pervasive influence in my life's direction.

My wife Anne Callahan Monday, an excellent open source researcher in her own right, has put up with much in the development of the manuscript while teaching me many things about techniques. I am grateful for her partnership in life.

My thanks to all of them.

Mark Monday

***

I wish to acknowledge the influence of the individuals in my career in education and technology. Andy Grove, Bob Noyce and Gordon Moore of Intel, Scott McNealy and James Gosling of Sun Microsystems, Richard Lyman and Bill Miller of Stanford provided support and direction. I have worked with Mark Monday since the '70's in different aspects of our careers. Mark and I have experiences that tracked technology and development. We sought to influence the future in the nation's security. This book will further develop the conceptual framework that gives the information from different sources a base from which to influence present and future action. I am honored to have worked with Mark Monday in this exciting project.

Dr. Emil Sarpa

Preface

"Knowledge is of two kinds. We know a subject ourselves, or we know where we can find information upon it. When we enquire into any subject, the first thing we have to do is to know what books have treated of it. This leads us to look at catalogues, and at the backs of books in libraries." — **Samuel Johnson, as quoted in Boswell's** *Life of Johnson*)

You, and everyone now living in what has been dubbed "The Information Age," have an ever-growing need to know how and where to snag essential information. Samuel Johnson, living in another age, long before the Internet, understood that useful knowledge – stacks of it – had already been collected, catalogued and was now available to anyone who wanted it. *However, they had to go get it.*

You have to do the same today.

How to snag useful material from the cascade of information? In three letters – OSR.

These three stand for Open Source Research. OSR may not answer every question, but it can answer many needs and simultaneously show where the gaps in knowledge exist.

OSR is the real deal.

OSR is open source information that has been collected, massaged, and managed to meet a specific need. OSR answers the unique questions and the individualized needs of a person or organization.

The US Congress, in PL 109-163 § 931, defines open sources as "Publicly available information anyone can lawfully obtain by request, purchase or observation." That definition is simple and straightforward, even if somewhat incomplete.

3

Crucially, the Internet is never mentioned. The Internet is not mentioned because essential information is found in many places besides the Internet.

What is OSR?

OSR is practiced everywhere, even by people who do not know they are doing it. It is not necessarily deep thinking, deep knowledge – certainly it is not yet wisdom. OSR is the process of finding, sorting through, and quantifying important variables and facts – ultimately using them to make decisions. OSR creates a tapestry of facts.

OSR provides knowledge, the fuel which allows users to act in the best way, in what they see as their own best interest. It is a way of bringing in light to dispel the intellectual gloom.

OSR depends on the senses: vision, hearing, touch, smell, and taste. For the most part, the first two of these predominate. Touch, smell, and taste are only occasionally used in OSR.

OSR uses Open Sources: Anything that is said, released, published, broadcast, or is otherwise available for general public consumption, hearing, viewing, or legal purchase. The very breadth of the information stream makes this research type challenging. OSR deals with the breathtaking mass of information that can be lawfully observed or heard by a casual observer, or any information made available at a meeting open to the general public. OSR material may also be information or data that becomes available when requested by a member of the general public.

It may also be purchased. Open source research material is not necessarily without costs.

Remember, whether for a fee or for free, information is valuable.

The accidental or unintentional release of information to the public, perhaps through a failure to understand computer coding or the way a system works, is usually considered Open Source. Even purloined information, posted in a public place by a hacker for all to see, is considered fair game for information mavens.

However, if the information is contained in something like a clearly-closed social media profile it is not open source.

OSR does not achieve its goals by hook or by crook; it observes definite left and right limits.

Open Source Research thrives on 720° thinking. Consideration has to be given to the central issue, the right, the left, what is above and what is below, things that are loosely linked and those that are tightly bound.

OSR is always an intellectual feat, a puzzle to be solved. It is a game of hide-and-seek played out in the information universe. Open sources provide snippets of facts can be juxtaposed to provide a comprehensive view. The mosaic's parts may be text, images, video, voice or some combination of those, provided they are publicly and legally accessible.

OSR professionals collect scraps of information from open sources and merge these data tidbits with other pieces of information. OSR professionals commonly compare their process to completing a picture puzzle. The resulting research product is usually a compilation, one providing greater understanding through a review of the sum of its parts. Researchers create a knowledge package that provides an otherwise-unobtainable picture, one assuring information supremacy in whatever field they are involved with.

OSR has a long history. Some techniques were practiced more than four millennia ago – and probably much before that. In any event, the first solid written evidence of OSR techniques is Biblical. It is found in Numbers 13, the story of Moses sending spies into the Land of Canaan.

The Book of Daniel (5: 1-31), a millennium later, contains yet another story about what might well be termed open source research. When king Belshazzar of Babylon throws a feast, using looted cups, a hand appears and writes "MENE, MENE, TEKEL, UPHARSIN" on a wall. The event scares the king and assemblage, but no one can read the message until Daniel, the wise man, is called. He berates Belshazzar for the theft of the cups and reads the message that is there for all to see, interpreting it as a message of impending disaster for king and kingdom – and that night Belshazzar was killed and his realm is taken over by the Persians.

Observation – whether through seeing, listening, or touching – and the understanding of what was observed have always been a major part of the OSR technique. They remain so today.

Open information sources have been used throughout history, but the advent of technology has increased their importance to the point that success in today's world often depends on how well the open sources are ferreted out and then used.

Technological advances and newly-developed talents and skills do not decrease the workload of a researcher. They improve capabilities and increase the ability to accomplish tasks while providing many more roads to travel before reaching a destination.

There Are Steps

Essential information is out there for those who know where, and how, to look. However, developing an effective OSR program from scratch is an overwhelming prospect unless you approach it cautiously, thoughtfully, and step by step – exploring what you want and how deeply you want to delve into the myriad methods and techniques.

Improving an existing program may be even harder than starting from scratch because habits and methods that are already baked in may have to be altered. Old habits die hard, if they can be changed at all. That may be truest in some corners of the intelligence field, where "old school" thinking about information collection remains rampant.

But the leaders of even change-resistant fields know that the OSR effort – to gather information widely and winnow it down – has to be made soon.

The United Kingdom's Chief of Defence Intelligence (CDI), Lieutenant-General James Hockenhull, said in September of 2019 that: "Publicly available data is the future backbone of situational awareness." According to the CDI leader "we need significant change in the way we do business." He warned that in the future access to readily-available open source knowledge resources could be the "difference between winning or losing future conflicts."

A former director of the US Defense Intelligence Agency, Lt. Gen Samuel V. Wilson, highlighted the importance of open source investigation saying: "Ninety-percent of intelligence comes from open sources. The other ten percent, the clandestine work, is just the more dramatic. The real intelligence hero is Sherlock Holmes, not James Bond."

Sherlock Holmes may have been only a creature of the mind of Sir Arthur Conan Doyle, but the realistic words of Holmes and his sidekick, John H. Watson, M.D., sparked a transition in the public's thinking about information, how to gather it, and the logic of using it. His words – whoever that "he" may be – have become "simply common sense" today.

The 19th Century words of Doyle, Holmes and Watson are the elementary outlines for successful use of OSR in the 21st Century.

Modern OSR comes straight from the pages penned by Sir Arthur Conan Doyle.

In *The Sign of the Four* "he" outlined the method and codified some of the steps in the Holmesian approach, which is also the OSR process of calculated reasoning, observation, and inference.

Collection comes first. Sherlock Holmes is quoted in *The Adventure of the Copper Beeches* as pleading for information. "'Data, data, data' he cried impatiently. 'I can't make bricks without clay'"

Holmes also enunciated the idea of collecting data, but theorizing only after listening to what the data said and where it led. "I have no data yet. It is a capital mistake to theorize before one has data. Insensibly one begins to twist facts to suit theories, instead of theories to suit facts," he admonished in *A Scandal in Bohemia*.

Theory must fit the data, not be shoehorned in the other way around, Holmes said. The Watson-Holmes view found in Doyle's stories was set down long before the Information Age or the Computer Age (it first developed in the age of gas lights). The Holmes stories have now become a compendium of basic OSR tactics and techniques.

The Holmes sagas shed a laser light on the best ways to think about and use OSR today.

Holmes, in *The Adventure of the Blanched Soldier,* clearly stated the mantra of Open Source researchers everywhere: "It is my business to know things. That is my trade."

OSR investigators, just like Holmes, smoke out the facts and then connect them like rail cars. They create a coherent train of thought that answers a question. That sums up the trade of OSR researchers.

Today's information need can be as uncomplicated and obvious as locating a car part, finding a restaurant in Paris that caters to your taste, or tracking down a high school friend. The needs can be as complex and hidden as teasing out leadership shifts in the North Korean hierarchy, identifying whose face is in a crowd picture on the news, or unearthing the building plans for the structure where terrorists are holding hostages. All these problems have been successfully solved using OSR methods.

Successful people share a common trait with Sherlock Holmes – they learn the facts before they act. They know that *a priori* decisions are dangerous. Holmes, in *The Velley of Fear*, stressed that "the temptation to form premature theories upon insufficient data is the bane of our profession."

That idea was reiterated during a back and forth conversation with Watson in the literary adventure known as *The Naval Treaty*. Holmes stressed the need to be wary of coming to conclusions too early.

"You suspect someone," Watson asked.

"I suspect myself."

"What!"

"Of coming to conclusions too rapidly." Holmes said.

Holmes knew conclusions had to be based on facts. He understood that it took time and effort to assemble the factual underpinning for any action.

OSR turns ideas or the facts held by others into accomplishments for you. OSR is a way of candling the information egg. It is focused. It drives decision making. OSR is not mere curiosity, although those who perform the intricate dance of modern research are certainly curious. Scoundrels, cheaters, deadbeats, and con-artists try to use ignorance of facts as a cloak. You, and those you work with, need "the facts." To get those facts in the modern world you also need increased digital sophistication.

We wrote this book with a simple idea in mind: to help you and other curious people develop and operate an effective, sophisticated research program, one capable of exploring virtually any field. Your information operation may fulfill a variety of personal, commercial, governmental, or organizational needs.

We started the project looking at a number of specific fields that use the varied techniques of OSR. We then sought a way to concatenate the best techniques and resources of the various fields.

That was when we had an epiphany, or maybe it actually was a slow-motion conversion. It became apparent to us that everybody functioning in modern society needs to be able to use the information-gathering techniques of OSR, not just those in the handful of areas we initially investigated.

Yes, we wanted to improve their professionalism of those five areas. But we also realized that many other people needed the same capability. Parents who are asked questions by their children could begin teaching even their preschoolers about some basic OSR with the injunction to "look it up," providing any needed help. Students in middle school could learn how to do better research, From high school to the university's post-doctoral level the mantra is "look it up." And in every stage of life thereafter the lessons of effective research must be practiced daily. "Look it up" increasingly gives way to "I'll find out."

While it was certainly not our initial objective, we saw that proficiency in OSR can be used by parents to help protect their children from the iniquities of the Internet and the criminals and liars who roam its precincts. We also know that every adult can find out many things they need to know by using OSR techniques.

10

Some of those things may be deep knowledge, but many are far more pedestrian.

With fake news and alternative facts becoming more prevalent the ability to discern truth from fiction, the ability to ferret out the truth and identify the important data pieces, becomes a vital talent for every voter.

We saw that OSR is one of the keys to life-long learning. Whether you are five, seven or 75, in all the years of your life you will need the information that flows through the many channels of OSR. The more channels you can use intelligently and efficiently the better chances you have of achieving your goals and living a fruitful life. The younger anyone starts mastering the complexities and changes of OSR the more useful information they can corral over the months and years of their lives.

We also saw Internet users grow more vulnerable to various attacks, seemingly by the hour. We know that many of the OSR techniques can provide a layer of protection that is otherwise unavailable to most Internet users. Even people who are not planning on doing research on the Internet can use the tactics outlined in this book to better protect themselves, we decided. We strengthened the security sections.

It would be an understatement to say that the OSR field grows exponentially. This book started three years ago as an unpublished manuscript of 150 pages. Less than two years later the first edition topped out at 350 pages of must-know information. Now it has grown to 600 pages of key life-long learning information. There are also a thousand sources, in print and on the web, that will teach the details and attributes of the resources, sites, and techniques referred to in these pages.

We wanted to craft a step-by-step learning program, one that prompts users to create their own organization or method of doing research. We saw that learning program should be general enough to be usable by a wide swath of people but adaptable enough that people will develop a program that meets the unique challenges they face. We also understood that just as no single blueprint for a house meets the needs and desires of everyone, no one information program will properly serve every reader or user.

We know that no one needs to include everything in their information toolkit, but everyone needs a passing familiarity with all the major tools and techniques. It is better for people to reject the ones they don't want or need rather than miss some useful ones they didn't know about.

Knowing that the needs of readers will be as wide as the population, we brainstormed a wide variety of sites and programs to meet the many different needs, knowing that some sites and techniques will not initially – at least – be used by everyone.

"Choice" became our mantra in selecting sites for you to explore.

Choose ones that help you in your work and give you useful starting points. But take the time to look at them all and consider how or whether you might use each one.

Many modern methods of OSR are free or low-cost. The basic ideas are simple, and many of the lessons are amazingly easy. But there are many, many lessons and methods. We try to make the field inexpensive, the complexity easier to navigate. But we won't try to fool you. OSR does have some expensive resources and complex techniques.

While we have included some so-called "premium" sites in the book, we strongly suggest that researchers always exhaust the no-cost options and sites before relying on paid sites. It's not that we have an aversion to people making money from the information they provide. Rather, in many cases the free sites will return about as much information as the premium sites do. More importantly – most importantly – every time you pay for information you leave a financial trail that speaks directly to your interests. Paying money for information, usually through a charge-card, can become a serious security problem.

We have provided information about a wide range of resources so that you can choose the ones that best suit your own needs. We know your precise needs are unquantifiable, but we selected about 1,000 Internet sites and dozens of techniques to give you choices, to provide a jump start when developing your personalized research program that will serve your needs over a lifetime.

While we cannot know your unique needs, or whether you will occasionally have to pay for information, we designed a creative program to solve your individual needs in an ever-evolving information universe. To use it you don't need to start out as tech-savvy, or be part of the Internet generation. Importantly, we don't want you to continually reinvent the wheel as you enter the new age of on-demand information access.

We looked carefully at the programs and texts that are already available – and we know there are some good ones because we have taken them ourselves, or read them. Why write hundreds of pages more?

Most of the others, we thought, start somewhere in the middle. The first steps are assumed. Which is fine if the initial steps are in place, and are working well already.

Most books and programs concentrate on the "what" and "how" – what programs to use and how to use them. They are about programs, hardware, and apps.

This book's authors wanted to start from the very beginning, to concentrate on the "why" before moving into the "what" and "how."

Moreover, we reasoned that in many cases the "how" changes so rapidly that books and educational programs cannot keep pace with the changes.

The digital world, the Internet, and video sites like YouTube provide a much better, more complete, more up-to-date "how."

We also recognized that the "why" is different for almost everyone who picks up this book, or follows our program. When you, as a reader and user, answer the "why," the "what" immediately changes dramatically. What programs, techniques, approaches, apps, and sites you will use depend on your unique "why." Moreover, the "how" to use those programs or approaches differs for everyone depending on what they plan on doing. And "plan" becomes a crucial part of the equation because too many other highly-useful educational resources never touch on planning at all.

Effective research doesn't just happen. There are steps, though the content of those steps may be different for everyone. Open Source researchers need to know what is possible so they can put the best tools in the top drawer of their tool chest, but still store knowledge of the less-useful ones somewhere, even if they are put out of the way.

At the same time researchers need to start with a wide variety of useful and useable sites and tools available to them from Day One. They will add to that personal tool chest, of course, but a wide variety of possibilities is needed at the start. That is why we offer so many choices – hundreds – throughout these pages. Find the ones that work best for your needs; ignore those you won't need in your particular approach. Just remember they are there if you need them later.

The truths that the very real Samuel Johnson and the fictional Sherlock Holmes recognized have not changed, although the information techniques and storehouses have evolved. Knowledge still wins. Facts matter.

Research capabilities are better today than last year and they will continue changing as resources and methods are modified. Modern researchers will face new challenges. They will solve new problems while they continue to improve their methods and techniques.

Information professionals can travel anywhere in the world, in fact anywhere in the universe. They can do so in the today, a million years hence, or in the moments after the Big Bang. They can go anywhere on the Web or even ethically burrow into some special spaces usually kept private and unseen by outsiders. Fact and even fiction are theirs for the taking. Facts about anybody and anything are increasingly available, but that information is available only to people who know how and where to look. The wealth of understanding and perspective is provided only to those who master the ins-and-outs of information acquisition.

But understand that OSR never promises omniscience. Some things always remain unknowable. While OSR may be imperfect, it gives you the "information edge" when it is time to go look something up, time to find out, time to act.

And "act" is the key. Possession of the best information without action, or the ability to act, is useless. Knowing that the gun pointed at you is .357 Magnum is valueless when you are leaning on your hands against a wall. OSR, to be effective, is only the precursor to action. If information cannot or will not be acted upon, there is no reason to do any of it. Unused or unusable research is an exercise in futility.

The Internet has become the great equalizer, an engraved invitation to knowledge, offering unprecedented information capabilities to a global audience. The Internet is a smorgasbord of perspective and data. It provides a measure of intellectual equality to those who use it wisely, filling the appetite for facts and illuminating areas that are in the shadow. From woodworking to North Korean politics, from cooking eggs to the first milliseconds after the Big Bang, research into questions – simple or complex – has become easier and more effective. Data and information are stored everywhere, in many forms and formats.

The plethora of resource types forces today's researchers to adopt the outlook of the fictional Holmes, considered by many to have originated modern open source research thought and techniques. Holmes the harbinger is quoted in *The Musgrave Ritual* on the need to work unceasingly to acquire expertise "in all those branches of science which might make me more efficient." Standout OSR operators, like Holmes, must be indefatigable in their use of every available tool and technique. They must continually meet the many evolving changes in, and challenges of, OSR.

Knowledge and acuity in "all those branches," multiple dimensions, and among the ever-growing myriad resources and processes is far more complex today than in Holmes' time. The still-unperfected, but constantly improving, resources and processes of OSR seem to evolve almost hourly.

We have tried to make the key aspects of Open Source Research less convoluted, stripping away much of the confusion and artificial complexity. Whether you are starting out in the field and need a baseline to work from or are already in the information business and want to improve your work, we designed this book to conform to your particular needs.

This book can serve either as a training manual or reference compendium. Or both.

We worked to simplify research, not to dumb-down the process. The knowledge advantage process is scalable to the need, but the process must be formalized, systematic, and continuous. It is not a hit-and-miss, once-in-a-while activity.

To be useful, the processes you employ must be consistent with your available resources and time. Always balance the time windows and asset pressures against probable results. Research should be efficient, if not always fast, but sufficiently in-depth to capture the nuances.

This book was never intended to provide you everything you will need to know in your career, but it will teach you how to set yourself, your employer, or your family up for success. It provides knowledge about the modern skills needed in the information age.

Those skills are many.

Skills and capabilities are layered. They often rely on what came before. An open source researcher needs one set of skills and capabilities to support other skills. Layering of abilities and skill brings success. The authors have tried to give you an arsenal of tools to build a solid but flexible first and second layers and guide you in building even third and successive layers.

This book is not a magic bullet. Neither is OSR. Beware of magic bullets and their salespeople. While accurized weapons are a reality, magic bullets don't exist. Don't let anyone convince you that they have a secret recipe; the only secret recipe is the one that works for you. The challenge for you is to find that recipe; that challenge is great because the stakes are often high.

OSR is an evolutionary force. OSR is the process of locating, collecting, storing, analyzing, and finally using or distributing useful information. These are all differing activities, skills that must be both mastered and merged.

OSR is essentially an ecosystem, where one technique, method or resource works alongside, and sometimes depends, on other methods, techniques, or resources. OSR is often considered to be the creatively "applied science of understanding."

OSR legally and ethically gathers, analyzes, and allows someone to act upon, information.

Science or Art?

OSR is both science and art. Some consider it to be scientifically managed artistry; others see it as artistically controlled science. In any case the exact proportions of art and science will always vary, depending on the project and the players.

Just as in art, where there are a variety of tools. Pencils and charcoal must be mastered for line drawings, oil paints for portraits, plaster for frescos, lead for stained glass windows, and precious metals for jewelry design. The range of tools and resources for OSR is wide. OSR artistry requires wide knowledge and extensive skills, but often leads to some specializations.

As with art, seldom is there instant gratification when researching open sources. Slap-dash never works. Fanatical efficiency does. But the OSR process does not offer immediate knowledge or wisdom, only a better opportunity to find the accurate information you need. It is a process of hope, failure, new hope, more failure and – usually – final success.

But there are Alamos in the information quest; the most heroic efforts cannot always produce hoped-for results. Failure is also part of OSR

Researchers face problematic surprises. They need flexibility and the ability to think quickly. They must be undeterred by deep, dry, holes. Good researchers must be able to meet man-killing demands and schedules, complicated search situations, and dizzying contingencies.

Open Source Research, we know, is believed by many to be as exciting as doing trigonometry problems. But as a researcher you actually will pry open many informative and interesting spots. Open Source researchers live in a renaissance world.

The Information Age is a double-edged dagger. Some like it; others bemoan its excesses and even existence. Names like Open Source Intelligence, Opposition Research, and Competitor/Competition Research sound slightly smarmy to many people. While some may call their activity "social discovery" others will term it "stalking." Information Literacy, and Computer-assisted Reporting, on the other hand, leave a neutral or perhaps positive impression.

Whatever the reputation of the field, the future is open to those who understand its capabilities today and its promises tomorrow. Those who remain mired in another time – the era before the Information Age – are destined to fall behind.

As an information provider your talents and abilities are on display with every report you write, with every factoid you send a client – and most of all with the result of every decision that you or someone else makes that is based on the research.

Today's OSR may be a game-changer, but it is not always easy to use. The "information superhighway" is as smooth as a wagon train's route on the Oregon Trail and is just about as easy to navigate. Technology changes are complicated and may not always be an unalloyed advance. Modern technology also provides the best information – but sometimes the best surveillance methodology – ever available. It provides information regarding all manner of things, including information about you, to those who know how to employ its techniques.

Moreover, it is easy to drown in today's information sea. Like ocean water, most of what we find is worthless to drink in. Anything you can think of is there. And while we live amid an information ocean it is simultaneously a knowledge desert. The nuggets of important information are often obscured by an eclectic mix that contains annual reports, corporate government filings, press releases, libraries of useless information, social media information on people you don't care about, the Dark Web, a plethora of associations and publications, and conferences you won't attend. These all vie for your time and attention. The whole of the Web, useful and useless, all comes at you like flying monkeys. Glynda, the good witch, is not another name for the Internet.

While tidal waves of useless data threaten to drown us, the thirst for precise knowledge, the need to drink in correct and personally useful information, grows.

In the era of false news, alternative facts and phony data there is an ever-greater need to locate, gather, evaluate, and use only the valuable information that applies to us, our lives, and those we work with. An incredible amount of ridiculous and, yes, cockamamie information is floating around. Garbage in; garage out.

People have a voracious need for relevant results; we all need insight, not the information stew we are often presented.

Information overload is always a threat to accurate OSR results. The dichotomy of research is the need to narrow searches and the search results while, concurrently, scraping up every bit of available on-point information. Filtering the cascade of information is the balance, the yin and the yang of OSR.

Successful prospectors seek gold wherever – in a swift-flowing river with a gold pan, in the crusty earth with a pick and shovel. A good prospector knows where to look, uses many tools, and tries many tricks of the trade. Good prospectors know the value of their finds. They understand the difficulties they will encounter in finding gold. They know well that the golden flakes are mixed with dirt, sand and pebbles. They are cognizant that the most-valuable vein is concealed beneath tons of non-descript rock.

The best researchers know that in many cases – such as when using search engines – it is often wise to use more than one tool that gathers the same type of information, comparing and contrasting the results. If the results are too divergent or appear incomplete the best researchers will use another tool of the same type until they have confidence they have they have exhausted the supply of available data. The name of the game isn't search; it is discovery. For researchers, and prospectors, the "desired result" is the payoff at the end of any information trek.

Some compare the process of finding information to the difference between window shopping and working as a purchasing agent. Purchasing agents sometimes window shop, but when they are serious about their purchases they apply much more sophisticated techniques to optimize their results.

Whatever analogies seem best to you, the fact is that you are looking for something of value, locating it, and then moving it to a place you can use it. That, in a nutshell, is Open Source Research.

Many roads lead to Rome – there is no single "right" way to do the research, but there are also many "wrong" ways. Often the most baffling part is where to begin and what road to travel along. When that happens, and it will, it often pays to start locally and use the "digital back fence." Expand from there. Remember, as an example, that information on a fatal traffic accident in Kansas City probably isn't going to be found in the *New York Times* but is likely to merit mention in the pages of the *Kansas City Star.*

Sometimes smaller community-based resources are helpful. So-called "shop and swap" postings may be useful in certain types of local searches. Hyper-local groups often are useful for another reason. People in them often know one another and don't suspect that "outsiders" might be looking at their postings. Local people who make good – or become infamous – and nearby events may be talked about over this digital "back fence."

In OSR uniqueness counts. An email address, a driver's license number, or an airplane's tail number are more likely to provide information about the search subject than are a person's first name, their choice of cars, or the type of aircraft.

OSR is practical work, research conducted in multiple dimensions. It is thoughtful work, unlike most people's information searches which are usually mercurial, conducted at high velocity, and without thoughtful direction. Planning and practicality can be supplemented by passion in OSR work, but strategic vision is always needed. Properly used, OSR provides answers and information with a speed, scope, and accuracy undreamed of even a few years ago. It provides a value-added product – the result usually becomes greater than the sum of the parts.

Make no mistake, the work is hardly glamorous or fun. Challenging, always; both lugubrious and satisfying, often; fun, seldom. The groundwork and the need for granularity often take much time and effort. There is always the need to make haste, but often even that takes frustrating amounts of time. Progress often has to be made at a persistent crawl. Nebbishes quickly fail. Inveterate researchers seize leads and turn them into successful searches. Open Source Research can slake the thirst for knowledge and feed the appetite for accomplishment.

Over the last few decades the advances in technology, techniques, and procedures have produced a real revolution in information acquisition and management. The advances have supplemented, not superseded, traditional means of research. The functions of books, newspapers, magazines, television, radio, mail, and even movies have been rolled up into the Internet. Digital has become a prime communications channel of the new millennium. The ever-evolving technology has changed the world in ways we never imagined. It often empowers us but also threatens us at those times when the power is misused.

OSR research today is headed in at least two different directions. Like the difference between an MD and a DO, the directions are not, by any means, mutually exclusive but they should be understood and taken into account as you plan and perform your information searches. They are:

- Documentary/textual based
- Image/Geo-based.

Documentary and textual searches touch many areas, from reports to social media and news. In this type of search, researchers primarily seek written information and textual data. Concept, historical, or economic searches – for instance – are highly likely effective using this type of search.

On the other hand after-the-fact image- and geo-based research, as practiced by the enthusiasts of the Bellingcat collective, starts with pictures and videos. It relies heavily on searching eyes poring over visuals and probing reams of geo-data. Central to this type of research are location-based questions and those that begin with a visual record such as a video or picture.

Some may feel there is competition between the two search types. Most books or training stress one direction over the other. Complete research employs both; competent researchers use a mixture of both and adjust their search plan to the direction that is most useful and reliable for their particular tasking or need. The initial research plan may take both search types into account, or the research plan may be created along lines that place a far-heavier emphasis on one or the other. A final plan might involve jumping between the two types at different times. Ruling out the tools and techniques of either search type at the start of a project is self-defeating.

Yes, OSR is complicated and time-consuming for those who really want to do a professional quality job. Groundwork is grunt work; it often takes a long, excitement-poor time.

Information intelligence specialists answer questions. They gather, organize, and analyze data – then they develop reliable analytic products that improve situational understanding, provide support for plan development, and answer the information requirements of decision makers. The efforts of an infoshop may be aimed at immediate situations or they may work with an eye to having long-term impacts on operations, emerging situations, or planning, as well as personnel and capabilities.

The best OSR specialists are capable of researching, reviewing, evaluating, and integrating Open Source data. They possess the prowess to contribute to and produce Open Source assessments. They are able to identify and analyze problems and generate possible solutions. OSR operators need writing and presentation abilities since they will develop reports and conduct briefings, etc. They often provide their clients with direct customer support and sometimes alternate between independent work and operating as part of multi-discipline teams. OSR professionals multi-task, adapt to short-notice tasking, and accomplish their goals with limited supervision.

But remember – no researcher or research desk knows everything or has mastered every technique or resource. Such comprehensive knowledge is beyond any single person's ability.

The OSR process may seem ragged initially, but as time goes on researchers become more proficient at fluidly and quickly finding the information they or others need.

Learn, in detail, the fine points of every site you visit, the breadth of information available. Master the site's filters. Those filters, the way you get to "the good stuff" and eliminate the "noise," are roads to success.

Learn to use the arsenal of tools available on the Internet to answer those questions about research that do crop up. People post the answers to your quandaries on YouTube, Google, and other web services because these are quandaries they also have faced. Books will often provide the nuts and bolts of various systems and programs. Materials are available when you need advanced knowledge. They can help you squeeze out success despite limited resources and knowledge. Valuable information is provided everywhere on the Web, or in a library. Do a search if you really want to solve a research problem or learn about an information asset. Any blank spots in your knowledge are generally there because you have not had to value that particular technique or resource before. You can track the answer down!

Our purpose is to guide you step-by-step as you develop a plan, your own plan, and help you acquire needed competencies in information gathering. We urge you to develop a research plan that fits your specific needs.

You need a standard operating procedure (SOP) for your research efforts. We are mindful of the need to apply security procedures in research, the need to plan, to gain proficiency in a variety of search techniques and resources, and of the importance of evaluating, validating, and presenting your findings. These things will probably all have a place in your SOP.

We have worked to avoid jargon, making the meaning clear to non-techies, but we also want to let you know that the jargon exists and familiarize you with it. Jargon can always be easily researched on the Internet.

Our challenge has been to simplify and clarify. The task we saw was to make knowledge about effective research techniques available to all, and usable by everyone who wants to develop their talents and improve their knowledge.

Many books touch this subject. Any of them are quite good in what they strive to do. What makes this book different from others is that it sets up a form and format to follow from the very beginning, but accepts the reality that there is no real end. While others may parcel out their knowledge without any discernable order or goal this book is designed to develop your personal research prowess step-by-step.

From the start it was clear to us, as it is to you, that all searches are individual. There is no one-size fits all technique, nor does even one-size fit many. Information requirements are seldom the same. Moreover, we foresaw the danger of getting locked into instructions related to todays (or yesterday's) technology and techniques, to slavish detailing of instructions that are bound to change within months, weeks, days or even hours.

With few exceptions we decided not to provide detailed instructions on specific programs or sites. We do not explain how to use every technique, program, or site within these pages, much less how to optimize them. Had we done so the book would have been 3,000 pages deep, unusable for most people, too heavy to lift, and so expensive that only companies on the Dow 30 – and they are not our target readers – would be able to afford the tome. Besides such a book would have been too unwieldy to even open. Many online sites and programs have instruction, "about us," or "how to use" areas. They are usually granular and up to date. If these don't answer your needs, we assumed most researchers would use the collective intellect of the Internet. There is little about anything associated with the Internet that does not have some supplemental explanation or instruction posted elsewhere.

We opted to focus less on the *minutiae* of how to do something, instead emphasizing the "what and why to do." Useful "how to's" are found everywhere on the Web and are available readily through good search engines. Text and YouTube-type videos generally keep up with, or even race ahead of, changes in technology. Information about the ever-widening range of techniques and resources to use in your research – importantly what to use when solving your unique problem – is available across the Web. Books and print articles can also explain the "how-to's" once you have decided on the "what and why to do it."

We have tried to break down this complex field into understandable pieces; the concepts within each chapter tend to be granular. We intended the book to be read at your own pace, and the parts digested in any order you deem best. We believe the order we chose may be good for an average researcher, but know you are not "average." You have your own interests and needs.

Yes, we simplified. Simplifying is not dumbing-down. For those who are satisfied by putting a couple of words in the search box this book is useless. Nor is it your cup of tea if you want infallible checklists that will give you the right answer every time. Lists of enumerated tasks, search scripts, are often useful – but they are only helpful as a starting point. Most cookie-cutter investigations are insufficient. Tailored searching plans are required for every project.

This book is written for those who know enough that they intend to learn more, much more. It is for those who intend to progress beyond the last chapter, the final appendix, of this book.

It is written for those who seek structure to their learning and the research process. It is intended for those trying to mold observations and unstructured data into meaningful information and finally create understanding and knowledge. This book is for those who understand that the authors don't – and cannot – know everything in the vague infinity of the information universe. Nor can they peer into the future.

This is written for those who understand that what the authors know and will impart is only a first step, a foundation, a floorplan to build up from. The walls, roof, and furnishings are yours to design and add. This book only starts, rather than completes, the process. You will – and should – consult other books, learn from other web sites, and perhaps even change your approach to suit your particular needs in the future. We seek only to provide a foundation for you to build on.

We are painfully aware how baffling building that foundation can be. Sometimes it seems like trying to lay a foundation in the Everglades, searching for hard facts but finding lots of mush and an occasional snapping 'gator for your efforts.

Hope for, but don't rely on, help from others in this field. Some online researchers are obsessively secretive about their techniques. Some husband their resources, technologies, and capabilities. They may treat their capabilities as dark secrets, like voodoo – incapable of being replicated by others. Some treat research as some sort of magic that only they can perform. Some don't want others to understand what they do nor how they do it, what techniques and technical capabilities contribute to their success, or what spoils their efforts. For many, but fortunately not all, practitioners the best techniques and methods must remain a great secret. We chose not to take that path.

The authors of this book only want to start, but do not pretend to end, your personal growth in mastering the twists and turns of the Information Age. College courses, certificate courses, seminars, journals, the Web, articles, and other books promise to provide additional growth opportunities. Today's researcher or research desk – you – has to be adept at adapting. In this book we want to employ the best teacher for what you are hoping to accomplish.

That teacher is you.

No single "correct" process, method, or technique will ever serve everyone. Individual results *will and must* vary! You need to choose the "correct" processes, methods, resources, and techniques – the ones that meet your specific research needs.

Assume there are no "experts." The field is too large; techniques and capabilities change too often to allow anyone to know how to use or do everything. No one can truthfully say they know and can impart everything you need to know. Even peer-reviewed journals, a former gold standard for research, have faced scrutiny, falsification and the problem of information agents and sock puppets. RetractionWatch.com, a website that tracks retracted peer reviews articles because of false or poor data, exists because of the continuing problems with research, especially in the digital age.

This book presents some alternatives, but you need to understand how to "Target Holes In My Knowledge." You will need to think out of the box and extemporize throughout this book, and into the future. When things aren't quite right you will have to ferret out expeditious expedients that quickly get you where you want to go, that get you the information you need. You will become expert at selecting and rejecting resources among the many processes, methods, and techniques that are available. Not everything in this book is precisely right for you or your research needs at this moment. You have to select the tools and alternatives that are most likely to fill the hole in your knowledge. You will reject things that don't work for you. You have to adjust the lessons of this book to your own needs.

This book was written to help you bring the facts out of the shadows, to make you a leader in the Information Revolution. We attempt to provide encyclopedic knowledge of the research field. Encyclopedic knowledge is not necessarily expertise. Encyclopedias provide a useful knowledge baseline, a foundation, a working familiarity with the area under discussion. They give information on important resources; they link similar areas. Once you acquire encyclopedic knowledge you need to know how to quickly improve your ability in, and knowledge of, the particular processes, methods, or techniques in those research fields that serve your needs.

We did not write this book to make you an expert; we wrote it to put you solidly on the path to expertise. We created an extensive and eclectic set of links – some that are helpful to you, some that may be more helpful to others – but all are included to illustrate an idea, make a point, and help you to find the resources that resolve your needs.

You will rise beyond encyclopedic knowledge in areas that are important to you, achieving the better-than-baseline ability that you will build on later as needed.

OSR is an entryway into many parts of the tech and information world. You may even decide that your niche is in a related area such as penetration testing or search engine optimization. But you will find that your experience with open source research will pay off throughout the coming years and decades.

Good researchers are the kin to Sherlock Holmes, observing, finding the important points, connecting the key elements, and reaching sound conclusions based on the totality of the available information. "Observation" is a major technique you can use on your information voyage. Sherlock Holmes chided Watson about his lack of observational skills, noting that the good doctor had climbed the steps at 221B Baker Street often but did not know how many stairs there actually led from the streets. "You see, but you do not observe. The distinction is clear," he intoned in *A Scandal in Bohemia.* "I know there are 17 steps, because I have both seen and observed."

OSR operators are not Internet spies; they are modern Sherlocks. "My name is Sherlock Holmes. It is my business to know what other people don't know," he said in *The Adventure of the Blue Carbuncle*. And his business is the business of everyone in this information-intensive field. But that ability to know what others do not doesn't come automatically.

Information wizardry is not a matter of waving a wand. No author or instructor can hand it to you. The edge you need, the information supremacy that precedes success, always requires your personal participation. To gather pertinent information and put it in a usable form requires your knowledge, study, observation, and attention. But it should not be convoluted or scattered. You need to operationalize the programs and techniques that best serve your search needs. You must develop expertise in those things that meet your own requirements.

Searches have to be target-directed. There is much of general interest that doesn't apply to a researcher's needs. In *The Adventure of the Bruce-Partington Plans* Watson observed: "I was aware that by anything of interest, Holmes meant anything of criminal interest. There was news of a revolution, of a possible war, and of an impending change of government; but these did not come within the horizon of my companion." Similarly, OSR practitioners must be careful to stay in their lane.

Researchers must also be aware of impending changes in their world.

We recognize that it is no easy task to remain current on changes and advances – and that not all changes are advances – in information access. The text of the book is static; we cannot change that. But we always try to update you, through **our website** at http://www.opensourceresearch.net. Developments and changes are covered there as they occur, or are discovered.

In these pages the authors have addressed about a thousand potential sites and research resources to give you wide choice as you build your information search machine. Unfortunately, we know, not all of them will be available when you crack these pages.

This book was error-free only in the first minutes it was written. Internet changes do not wait for the dawn of a new day or the publishing of the next book. Each tick of a clock brings changes that may – make that will – outdate or alter parts of this book. Sites and resources we have used for years suddenly disappeared on us, along with the useful capabilities they provided. Things changed even as we wrote these words. Text had to be ripped out; new paragraphs added. And it will happen to you. We know that of the hundreds of sites cited here, some will disappear into the ether by the time you read this.

At the same time the information world is so large, chaotic, and changeable that new things pop up even as old ones are consigned to the trash bin. The OSR waters are turbid and muddled, to say the least. This has particular importance when the programs or software you have been using on the Web, and those you planned to use today, suddenly disappear. You are confronted with the ugly fact that the capability, the service, or the software site has vanished. The crowd-sourced **AlternativeTo:** https://alternativeto.net/ site may be an answer to this problem, providing links to programs that are similar to any suddenly-missing services or information sources.

We Emphasize the Internet

We understand, and presume, you probably already know a great deal about the Internet, but there is always more to learn. (For those who feel a need to review some of the computer basics we suggest Appendix A, Internet Basics).

We concentrate much, but by no means all, of our attention on the Internet and Web. Since many searches are commonly conducted through a Windows operating system we act as if that is what you are using. We know many of you may be using some other computer operating system but we also have confidence that if you are using something else you probably have the knowledge to convert our information to make it compatible with your operating system.

In today's connected world you need to know all the parts of a system or program, how they are connected, and how to use them. Never assume programs or parts of the Internet are intuitive; they seldom are.

If you are going to use a program or site you should learn it in detail. Learning all the bells and whistles of any program you use is best. It is the professional way. But learning only what you need to get you through your project at hand may be what you need to do when timelines close in.

We did not want to make this a user manual for any particular platform, tool or program. We did not write this book for people who wanted to know details about particular programs, or to explore in depth the specialized resources some professionals use. There are already books, videos, and classes that drill down to minute technical details. We decided people need the broad outlines of how to acquire knowledge in the Information Age. We wanted to provide the "Big Picture," a solid foundation that you could build on. Simultaneously we looked to individualize the experience, knowing your needs are unique; that they are different from those of others.

For you, we decided to handle this difference by having you write your own personal guidebook. We wanted you to create a living document, a personalized standard operating procedure (SOP) that includes the information, tools, and techniques that you find apply to your particular needs. You have to know and memorialize the ins and outs of all programs, apps or sites that you use. You have to create, and write down, your own SOP for using those resources. And you need to explore the nooks and crannies of those resources.

You have to know what the resources are capable of, what they can do for you, what they cannot do to you, and where you can get in trouble with them. All of these can and should be part of your SOP.

An SOP organizes your work. One of the major labor-saving elements of OSR is organization. Organization issues are important in every phase of OSR, from security and collection through analysis and distribution. If you are not organized, if you carry out research by the seat of your pants, you may score an occasional success but it will probably be bookended by a string of "fails." Organization does not mean a slavish obedience to the SOP or anything in it, but it does mean that the SOP meets your needs and successfully guides you in most cases. SOPs are designed and intended to be followed – unless and until there is a good reason to deviate.

We do not expound about some rigid organizational method. The text will outline an SOP you could follow – "could" not "should." Your SOP is yours alone. It is not the authors', not anyone else's. It is meant to help you organize your own work and assure the results will be uniformly positive. It's what works for you but the thinking about what goes into it has to start somewhere.

Your SOP will change over time; it must never become static. It is a living document that will grow more personalized as you meet the challenges and changes of the Information Age. The SOP will become more effective and efficient the longer you use it, the more you massage its contents. Your research process will evolve to meet ever-changing conditions and needs. Your SOP will improve as your experience, training, and the technology improve.

This book concentrates heavily on the start-up and implementation phases of OSR. We do not intend to, and cannot, detail everything that someone will ever need to know about the process. We can provide the outline, the basics of what you need to know. You will provide, now and throughout your career, those details that apply specifically to you.

Expect to learn more from your own experiences rather than from this, or any, book, video or talk. Top researchers are not just well-trained, they are experience-trained by responding to the continuing challenges of OSR. That doesn't happen in a week or two

Those who promise instant or unvarying success are charlatans. Completing a paint-by-numbers picture does not make anyone an artist; mastery of the drawing tools in each of the genres, doing the work freehand, that is what makes someone an artist. It is much the same with research. Mastery of each tool with gratifying vigor, in each type of research, is what produces the journeyman researcher.

The book you write for yourself, your own work plan, your SOP, your arsenal of skills, will be useful far beyond us and the last chapter of this book. As you acquire skills and knowledge you will continually and carefully add new tools and capabilities to your SOP. Always be on the lookout for additional training, whether in a classroom or on YouTube. Good people in the field sometimes help; let them if they are willing. OSR is a journey without end and you never know who your traveling companions will be. You will, and should, learn from others and your own experiences as well as from us.

And hopefully you will pass on your knowledge.

Many people, some of them our competitors, offer valuable information. You need to be aware of all their capabilities and resources. Some Open Source link sites to explore, for various reasons and materials, include:
- **Bellingcat Guides:**
  https://www.bellingcat.com/category/resources/how-tos/
- **Bellingcat Online Investigation Toolkit:**

https://docs.google.com/document/d/1BfLPJpRtyq4RFtHJ
oNpvWQjmGnyVkfE2HYoICKOGguA/edit
- **Citizen Evidence Lab (Bellingcat-type tools):**
  https://citizenevidence.org/
- **Mario's Cyberspace Station:** http://mprofaca.cro.net/
- **Netbootcamp (Videos and links):**
  https://netbootcamp.org/osinttools/
- **ONSTRAT (Randall Hock):**
  http://www.onstrat.com/news/
- **OSINT Framework:** http://osintframework.com/

Learning and using new skills is a life-long requirement. Today it starts before grade school and continues into the 30s, 40s, 50s and beyond. It wasn't always so vital, perhaps. But times, they are a'changin.

Aspects change, some faster than others perhaps, but all situations eventually change. You need to be knowledgeable of the altered pathways. You will change things in your own SOP book because you will discover new methods. You will find new tools tomorrow that work better than those of yesterday and today. Sometimes you will eliminate things from your SOP as your experience, abilities, and expertise grow.

The *Projects* at the end of each chapter are designed to help you develop your unique SOP. They are broken into small, achievable, tasks designed to motivate researchers and ultimately help you in the creation of your personalized plan. The projects, along with the text, enable readers to identify and master the core skills that apply to the their particular information needs.

And the skills, resources, and sites to master are many.

Your toolbox should never be locked. New products and concepts appear; occasionally some disappear. But you will know the best ways to find the information you need – *and you will do it your own way.* We don't presume to tell you what you need. While we have outlined some *Projects* for your SOP, you are likely to come up with your own ideas for customizing your individualized plan. You will refresh your skills, improve your swiftness, and amplify your performance. Add any information or ideas to your SOP that you believe will help your work. Create new chapters and sections of the SOP. Change any part of your personal SOP at any time you wish.

The OSR effort may seem small but the results are potentially vast. As Sherlock Holmes was alleged to have said in *The Adventure of the Red Circle,* "Education never ends, Watson. It is a series of lessons with the greatest for the last."

***

Project:
Create, on your computer, a directory or section titled Online Research.

Project:
In the online research section you just made, create a word file folder named "My Research SOP." In that file create sub-folders titled:

- Overview
- Technology
- Techniques
- Digital Library
- People, Software, and Equipment
- Browsers
- Security and Legal Issues
- Planning
- Search Engines and Directories
- Links to look at
- Web 1.0, Web 1.5, Web 2.0
- News Media
- Deep Web and Dark Web
- Databases, Gray Literature and Ephemera
- Pictures, Videos and Audios

- Translations
- Analysis, Evaluation, Vetting and Production
- Things I need to learn
- Future projects.

Project:
In the Overview section of your SOP write at least five, and no more than 10, sentences explaining what you want to accomplish once you have improved your research capabilities through OSR. Remember that any part of an SOP can be changed later if you find a better method of handling material. Most think it best to add ideas now and refine and revise those, or even eliminate them, in future versions as their knowledge and understanding changes.

1. Introduction and Overview

Knowledge is power. That is elementary!

That's what this book is about: Gaining the knowledge that gives you the power.

We supposedly have lived in, or perhaps through, "The Information Age," not that anyone would know it. There are understandable fears we have "progressed" to "The Post-Information Age," where the noise that humans attach to data and information has drowned out its utility.

Yes, we have tons of data and information available. But data is unprocessed facts, figures without context. Information is the actionable facts or figures that are presented in a meaningful context; they are the things that bring insight, that transform mere knowledge into power.

Despite all the ballyhoo, in too many cases the readily available data and information of the Internet and libraries have yet to be sculpted into insight. Insight is valuable; it leads to good decisions and guides you away from many bad ones. Insight gives you the edge you need, the knowledge that is power, the information supremacy that makes your success more likely. But information supremacy, for now, remains tantalizingly out of reach for many.

There is often more haystack than there are needle-points of insight. One of the first problems for OSR investigators may be finding out which – of the many haystacks in the field – to look through in order to gain insight.

OSR is a practical way to gain insight. There is a need for OSR in today's world. Too few people know how to actually use OSR to their benefit. But when properly used, it can be remunerative.

Sherlock Holmes allegedly said it best more than a century ago in *A Study in Scarlet*: "Yes, I have a turn both for observation and for deduction. The theories which I have expressed there, and which appear to you to be so chimerical, are really extremely practical — so practical that I depend upon them for my bread and cheese."

In today's world OSR is at once a profession, a talent, and a necessary life-skill. Hunch, deduction, or planning – all may work in finding essential information. But planning and an effective SOP offer a better chance to find you the facts you don't know, but need.

'
What you don't know can hurt you.

What you don't know may make a tremendous difference.

What you do know can help you. What you do know, or can learn, will make you money and provide greater satisfaction in life.

Facts and truth matter because they drive decisions and beliefs. Successful people learn, know, use, and value facts. But too often people rely on information sorcery and magical thinking rather than reliable information sources. There is a vast amount of data and information, but a paucity of people who know the rough – let alone finer – details about gathering, vetting, and using the available data or information to gain insight.

Marginalia can be more important in an information search than many people understand.

There is both positive and negative evidence to reap. While most people are aware of the former; fewer can see that the lack of something can also be indicative. Sherlock Holmes understood the concept of negative evidence and explained it in *The Adventure of the Three Gables.* "I don't think we shall find him in the directory," Holmes says of a businessman whose card provided no contact information. "Honest business men don't conceal their place of business."

Good information shops, the ones that recognize what is missing and then turn that knowledge into insight, are all too rare. The process of elimination, using negative evidence, can be powerful but many researchers forget it in their search for positive information.

Also rare are the researchers who understand the capabilities of Archimedean thinking – the ability to use one set of facts or queries to substitute in information searches for other facts which remain hidden or undiscovered. Commonly employed by better researchers today, it was used during WW II when Allied forces wanted to know how effective air attacks on the French railway system were, but lost too many spies looking at the tracks. Instead they used the prices of transported goods as a guide – if those prices went up, the railways were effectively interdicted, when prices went down freight trains were getting through. In much the same way researchers can keep an eye on employment by a competitor, and whether a new shift is being added in a factory, by counting the cars in the parking lot even when they cannot access the actual hiring figures.

Those who can access and assess reliable knowledge – those who have the tradecraft to operate in the Information Age and Post-Information Age – will thrive and prosper. They will be able to, at the least, detect when someone if trying to fool, manipulate, or direct them. They can make informed choices rather than be socially engineered by the information and the hidden human factors that frame a medium and a message.

Those who fail to understand and properly use the tools, techniques, and the massive amounts of available data will drown in the information tidal wave or die of the thirst for knowledge in what seems like an information desert.

OSR is the gateway to other cyber activities and digital activities. It promises to become a major employment field of the next three decades.

Yes, OSR work can be tedious and even wearisome at stretches but it is exciting to those who weather their way to the end.

OSR uses the best lessons, tools, and the methods that have proved useful in many major research fields.

OSR's steps often combine largely-secret methods and break-through technology with simple, well-known techniques. OSR incorporates and combines the skills, techniques, and procedures learned from many different, but technique-related, research areas. It improves and optimizes knowledge acquisition.

OSR serves more than one master. It is based on the techniques of many. Primary contributors to OSR are the fields of Computer-assisted Research (CaR) in Journalism, Open Source Intelligence (OSINT) in Government, Information Literacy (IL) in Library Science, Opposition Research (OPPO) in Political Science, and Competitor/Competition Intelligence (CI) in Business.

These fields all seek highly-specific, usable, and timely information about someone or something – whether it is a person, company, group, enterprise, activity, or nation. The sources of that information may be people such as experts, leaders, followers, employees, or suppliers. The collected information often leads to actionable ideas.

But the methods of these various research areas are not well-integrated. Moreover, all the individual fields are seriously deficient in ways. They share common threads in their research techniques but they are not congruent.

Each field has strong points, weak points, and some areas that are total blanks. OSINT, for instance, tries to protect sources and methods so thoroughly that the security issues often hinder it in actual use. OSINT's regulations may hinder meaningful and practical social media exploitation; IL is extremely light on security. Some of the information fields rely almost exclusively on execution scripts and automatically-collected databases of others rather than on humans and their thoughtful search strategies.

However, when you concatenate the techniques and practices of all these areas, choose the best parts of each, recognize the weaknesses, fill in blank spaces, and integrate the best methods and capabilities of them all, you come up with bleeding-edge knowledge about current open source research methods and techniques.

The strengths of one field fill in the weaknesses and faults found in other leading research areas. All of the fields hold major pieces of this Information Age puzzle. At the same time all the fields lack pieces and ideas that other areas have.

The more-complete research area known as OSR is in fact a constantly growing, transformational, and integrated system of systems. The indispensable eyes and ears of many fields, OSR techniques offer the advantage that only information research can provide – the knowledge advantage.

OSR takes in the wide picture. It gathers others' knowledge into one place. It tries to integrate all the puzzle pieces so that you, as a knowledge consumer, can go where you need to go, get the information you need when you need it, analyze it for its usefulness, and apply it to the things in your life, your concerns, and your business. OSR is driven by data and analytics. It is an immediate, essential, urgent, critical, and vital need in today's world. It can provide answers – and occasionally pose new questions – rapidly, accurately, and in a wide scope.

Today's information needs have become a voracious vortex. People require more information today than yesterday; tomorrow they will need more than they did today.

Finding and using useful publicly-available information has become an essential life skill in the Information Age; it is a skill set that flows into every aspect of life. But is that a skill that people and institutions have or use effectively? A few do; many do not.

Not everyone does competent research.

OSR is a means to an end. It is not the end itself. There are steps.

Important parts of OSR include planning, information gathering, management, analysis/assessment, and production. Executing on the knowledge advantage you gained is essential, but is not part of the OSR schema unless you are researching for your own needs.

Some components of OSR are well-known; other parts remain obscure.

Competency requires the knowledge of, and ability to use, a wide variety of systems that apply to the user's needs. Integrated multi-dimensional research – not just popping a word or two into a search engine – produces results rather than failure.

That is not to say results will appear magically. Sometimes all you can do is trudge forward, slogging through the miasma of fact, misinformation, and off-point data that the Internet offers. There are times when open source research seems too much like scutwork and drudgery. Researchers seldom find themselves boiling along; inevitably it is a slow grind to get the information needed. The speed of any search is controlled by boundless energy and an unwillingness to waste any of that most precious commodity, time. Making progress relentlessly, even if at a crawl, is a principle guiding OSR.

Many workable and surprisingly effective research options and avenues are widely available. Some will work well for you; some miss your unique needs today. But some of the options you don't need today will be required next week. Cocktail lounges stock a full bar, including some ingredients their bartenders may only use once or twice a year. And while bartenders are adept at mixing the common drinks, they also have a manual that tells them how to mix what they need to craft when faced with unusual customer requests. OSR works much the same way.

OSR is about knowing and having access to the options; operators need familiarity with every research area and all types of techniques in order to mix and match them to the ever-changing requirements. Only with that how-to knowledge can OSR users choose wisely from the research smorgasbord. At the same time, just as at a smorgasbord, seldom will anyone need everything available on the resource table. Researchers learn to pick and choose at the information table, just as at a restaurant.

The "Fields" of OSR
Different contributing fields offer a variety of "flavors" to OSR.

Information literacy (IL)) is strong on storage and retrieval of information, particularly from databases and anything found in fiber-based materials. Knowledge of IL helps a researcher in filing and retrieving the information collected elsewhere. IL is also particularly good when it comes to using online databases and non-digital materials. It is not particularly strong in dealing with some other research techniques or security.

Opposition research (OPPO) has proven its strengths through many election cycles. Its techniques are wide-ranging, but they focus largely on individuals. That laser-focus, and the fact that the most effective OPPO techniques tend to be close-held, mean some of this field's special techniques remain largely unknown and often unused by other information professionals.

Competitor intelligence, or competition intelligence, (CI) are widely used in the business community to provide the facts and background needed by many corporate decision-makers. Competitor intelligence focuses solely on competitors, their activities or plans. Competition intelligence adopts a wider view. It takes into account any aspect that affects the field and all business opportunities, anything that provides insight to business leaders. Another way to look at this field is to assume competitive intelligence is focused on specific targets and there is another term, market intelligence, which focuses on an industry or market segment. CI has a long history of use and success but, again, many of the techniques and resources needed for this work remain close-held.

Computer-assisted Research (CaR) is an extension of journalistic techniques. It has great strength in gathering information from social media and excels in webscraping, analysis, and interpretation. CaR, like many other research fields, tends to be light on security and safety.

Open Source Intelligence (OSINT), is used by intelligence, military and police organizations. It features extensive penetration of the Web, use of specialized databases, and is heavier on security than virtually any other research type.

Many people, in the past, associated OSINT with "spying." It had a theatrical aura, one of mystery and even hushed-up notoriety that made many people wary of it and its practitioners.

Worth noting, this term is increasingly being used to refer to almost any type of open source research, not just the investigations in the intelligence field. The term "OSINT" is becoming more popular in the commercial world, especially in the cyber field. There are now multiple commercial cyber security certifications focused on OSINT and its applications. There is also a strong and growing "OSINT" community of hobbyists, security professionals, and world-event followers. The adoption of the term by the cyber security community has also created many open source tools and techniques to help enable new forms of data collection and analysis.

When used in the newer meaning, OSINT is synonymous with OSR.

When OSINT is used in its more restrictive sense – the research conducted by intelligence, military and police organizations – the emphasis on security is positive for the safety of the researcher. But the rigidity of OSINT's numerous – and often-draconian security rules – can interfere with the research process and severely limit results.

Other fields are just starting, in ways that are large and small, to use the ever-expanding methods of research that OSR offers.

What OSR Does

OSR combines the best of the five contributing fields to balance the problems of each with solutions that the others provide. OSR offers an information advantage to those who master the integrated techniques and the tools it uses.

Business, schools, universities, libraries, political organizations, the media, and security organizations world-wide are investing in the equipment and resources needed for information exploitation, under whatever name. Information shops combine and balance the best technology, processes, and people in their quest for information.

All fields, all students, all people, badly need to acquire the talents required to do the research.

Many fields are putting a foot in the water; some have already advanced to swimming. Some use outsourced services to fill their information needs; others employ their own dedicated personnel and equipment. All are looking for OSR-capable people.

The need is already there for people knowledgeable in areas such as:

- Open Web information
- Information gathering
- Analysis and interpretation
- People, equipment, and programs
- Location-based research
- Social media monitoring and analysis
- Deep Web and Dark Web capabilities
- Database use and Big Data capabilities
- Use of webscrapers and offline browsers
- Multi-media acquisition and video/visuals analytics
- Visualization tools and instruments
- Cyber-security and red-teaming.

The explosion in social networks, groups, forums, multi-media resources, and user-generated sites – and the plethora of material these often provide – also drives the need for capable researchers.

"Capable" is the key word. Some people think of themselves as information gurus because they know how to put a word or two in a website's search box. That's it. And that's magical thinking! They believe they have mastered information searches. In reality, such people are in the pre-kindergarten of the OSR discipline.

Others try OSR but quickly become disgusted with information searching. They find that putting a few words into a search engine just doesn't do it. They quit trying when the reality of their search efforts doesn't match the information promise they anticipated. The reality of the search simply doesn't match the aspiration level when you don't know the tradecraft to get you there. There is more, much more, to obtaining and using quality data.

Very few people have been taught the best ways to explore their information environment. Only a handful know how to get what they need by using integrated information tactics. Fewer still know how important it is to learn and map the structure of key sites, explore subdomains, and find or copy the important folders.

Professionals in the information business learn these, and other, *minutiae.*

They often find the fine details on the Internet. They learn by exploring the filters and quirks of the key sites they use consistently. The pros know how their key sites operate, and how to use them to their best advantage.

Such knowledge and ability is not developed in an hour or two, or even in a month or two. It doesn't come from reading a dozen paragraphs in this, or any, book.

Many of the tools and resources, often the best ones, are anything but intuitive. Search-box-type simplicity may be found on search engines, but it is rare with other tools and techniques. The ways to use advanced tools and techniques – even those available on search engines – have to be researched, learned, and practiced. A fan in the stands understand what a baseball bat is used for and the basics. It takes a professional touch to swing a home run out of the many bits and pieces of knowledge that go into a professional understanding of the bat's use. OSR professionals need to develop that same level of understanding about their tools and techniques, and they need to practice their swing before coming up to the plate.

Learning how to achieve in the Information Age is seldom simple, not when you consider that the Internet and computers are overlaid by an extensive matrix of other, older, information resources which remain both usable and useful. Nor is it made any easier by the determination of many who know how to harvest information to keep their knowledge of that capability to themselves. There is often a demonstrated reluctance by professionals to share even the simplest techniques that are needed to exploit the wide world of information. Competition is unwelcome to some.

OSR Resources

Web search engines, rightly or wrongly, are believed by many to be the 21st Century successor to Samuel Johnson's library. While the search engine is one information source, it is not the only – nor is it always the best – resource. Some useful resources are found on the Internet; many are not. Research is always a work in progress; new techniques and fresh resources appear all the time. Older resources still prove valuable, as well.

Important information resources include products of academia, from courseware to research papers. Other resources include commercial and public information services that provide news and special reports. Some of these resources are expensive but they are often available cost-free to library patrons. Groups and individuals produce everything from leaflets and graffiti to letters and posters; getting on mailing or emailing lists helps in collecting information for medium- and long-term projects. Email information can sometimes be useful. Social media postings and even overheard street-corner discussions can qualify as open source information resources.

The resources for information gathering are almost inexhaustible for those who want to mine the knowledge trove, who understand how to use the instruments of OSR.

OSR Phases

"Common knowledge" holds that there are three distinct phases of OSR research:

- Acquire or "find"
- Process
- Distribute.

That is the short view: There are always collection, processing and presentation steps. OSR, in reality, is more complicated; what seem like three simple steps are actually composed of many parts:

- Collect
- Secure and preserve information
- Process
- Verify and validate
- Analyze
- Interpret
- Review and polish
- Publish.

The SOP you create while reading these pages takes all the phases into account.

Although all stages of the process are important, the researcher or research desk must first collect the information before it can be turned into the finished product, turned into insight. Until information has been collected no other phase exists.

Seldom do you know with any certainty what will, or won't be, valuable. For that reason expert researchers save a lot of material, even things that don't appear useful at first. They know that things which initially seem to be peripheral may become important later.

The rule is collect widely early, winnowing the information during the analysis and report writing phases.

Asked about what to do with a particular piece of information in *The Adventure of the Six Napoleons*, Holmes answered in the way every good researcher would: "To remember it – to docket it. We may come on something later which will bear upon it." The Holmes of literature understood that solutions are based on a mélange of ideas and facts, not one only, and that all must be put in a safe place for possible later use.

Researchers need to designate a repository such as **Hunchly ($$$$, Web capture):** https://hunch.ly/ where they can squirrel away all the bits and pieces of information they collect on the way to developing an insightful report.

As you build your personal or team SOP, remember that most research plans include:
- Preliminary search strategy
- Research plan
- Security plan
- Research tools selection
- Assignment of research tasks
- Research phase
  - Documentation and research preservation
  - Revision of research plan
  - Continued research
- Validation of information and sources
- Analysis
- Vetting and drafting of the product
  - Finalization of the product
  - Distribution of the product.

Physical Assets

The physical assets needed for a modern OSR project can range from a laptop computer connected to the Internet and a library card to specialized servers and use of the pricey, but commercially available, software that some intelligence agencies use.

Arguably the most important assets are the human senses. OSR has been carried out through the millennia with nothing more than the senses. (In Occupied France during WW II, Allied agents were taught to take note of the smell of coffee brewing as they walked down the street; that normally indicated they were outside a building housing high-level members of the Nazi Occupation.)

Little things mean a lot in OSR. Windshield wipers are a desirable feature on cars, but most Moscow cars didn't have them at the height of the Cold War. Soviet surveillance vehicles were well-equipped with them, however, and CIA agents routinely checked the traffic around them for cars with windshield wipers to see if they were being followed.

See, smell, hear – the senses are the OSR sensors.

Predictive, Current, Reactionary?

Research can be predictive, current, or reactionary. OSR may try to see what is ahead (predictive), know the present situation (current), or understand what has passed (reactionary).

The tools and techniques of greatest use to you will depend on what type of research you are doing. You must look over the collection of tools and techniques, master those that are most useful to you, and include them in your personal SOP. No two Christmas trees look precisely alike though each may be beautiful; no two search plans should be the same, either.

The OSR craft constantly changes – sometimes borrowing things from others, at other times developing useful new techniques. You need to do the same. People in the infoshop practice a craft that is working its way toward, but has yet to become, being an industry.

Successful researchers develop, over time, their own matrix of skills, assets, resources, and techniques. These are similar to those used by investigative journalists, reference librarians, post-graduate scholars, business leaders, intelligence operators, and law enforcement officers. Learning how "these people" do their job – through books, manuals, information posted on the Internet, and personal contacts – are among the ways to constantly improve your qualifications and achieve better research results. But books on how to be a private detective or reporter, while they may provide useful ancillary tips, do not make anyone a successful information collector.

Moreover, no one starts the first chapter of any book as a novice and emerges an expert in the field by the final chapter. Information professionals grow into the field; they are not born into it.

Mastery of the techniques and tradecraft comes automatically to few, if any. Most people find help and guidance more useful than learning by mistakes, when blasphemies abound. This book tries to guide you around some of the common missteps. But in the final analysis success using the tactics of OSR does not come from this book or any other resource. Success derives from practice, from the experience gained by selectively applying resources and techniques to specific situations.

If there is one piece of advice that should be kept in mind, it is this: Use your experience and your gut feelings when responding to the challenges. Avoid cookie-cutter approaches. Allow intuition to guide you. Give it free reign. Think outside the box. Train the brain to defy the orthodox. Conservative, by-the-book thinking (and searching) is often far from the ideal in OSR. Control the process; don't be controlled by it. No research system works flawlessly all the time. Use your intuition to find those pathways to success that neither this nor any other book or class can provide.

Good results are far more important than slavish adherence to any checklist. The spirit of initiative should never be squelched. User drive, brainstorming, time-outs for thinking, and even some unconventionality are often as valuable as any thought-through search script. The success of all research rests primarily with the individuals doing the work.

Your SOP book will be unique to you, designed specifically for your needs and purposes. Good personal notes on what worked for you, what didn't, and what might work better, become your best manual. These will give you the edge.

You will get out of this effort what you put into it! Nothing less; nothing more.

***

Project:
If you haven't read the Preface – and many of us skip that part of a book – go back and review it before moving forward. It contains important information.

Project:
In the overview section of your SOP define the current audiences you are now serving, including yourself and family, and the types of information you are likely to need to provide. Also select an audience you are not currently serving, but would like to work with, and the types of information you would likely need to provide that audience.

Project:
In the digital library section you recently made, search the Internet and then download these book files:
- NATO Open Source Intelligence Handbook.pdf
- NATO Open Source Intelligence NATO Reader.pdf
- Intelligence Exploitation of the Internet.pdf
- Untangling the Web.pdf
- Desktop OSINT Handbook.pdf
- Exploring Social Media Web Sites.pdf

- 2oolkit on the Go.pdf
- Army OSINT Manual/US Army ATP 2.22-9.pdf

Save these documents to the digital library section of the SOP you have created on your computer. Review them and make note in your SOP of any helpful material. This project will come up again.

2. OSR Sources and Resources

Open Source Research techniques – when properly used – provide quality information quickly, at a relatively low cost, in an ever-changing environment. The OSR information product can be easily shared and stored.

OSR is a straightforward method of collecting publicly available information from one or several open sources, then weaving the information strands together to understand a situation and accomplish a goal. Knowledge, and the ability to quickly and effectively acquire and utilize that information, is the precept of success.

OSR provides usable information about individuals, groups, businesses, institutions, and governments. It delves into a wide range of events, habits, lifestyles, interest, abilities, and contacts. OSR may delve down to the molecular level or it can encompass a universe. It seeks to answer any query and, in some cases, poses new questions.

Answers to the questions about Who, What, When, Where, Why, and How are central to any search for information. The search for those answers is the first half of OSR. A second part, which is essential to verification of the purported answers, is the examination of sources through information flow theory.

Understanding information flow is important at every step in OSR. It is an essential element of the edge needed to gain information supremacy. Understanding information flow is critical throughout OSR, but it is particularly important toward the end of the process, when you need to assess what you have collected.

However, as you go along, from the start, keep in mind the seminal work of Harold Lasswell. He broke message flow into five parts. When collecting and analyzing Open Source materials it is essential to keep each of those five parts in mind.
They are:

- Sender
- Message
- Medium
- Audience
- Result or desired effect.

When thinking of Senders be aware of who is sending the message, what their interests are, and who may be supporting or financing their effort.

The issues to be considered about the Message itself include what the wording is; how the message is constructed; if there is any agenda, either obvious or implied?

The Medium used to carry the message may affect the sense of authoritativeness, the message's accessibility, and the impact the message is likely to have.

When considering the Audience, ask questions about who watches, listens, or reads, and who can see, read, or receive it.

The Purpose of any message is to have some result or desired effect. What is that purpose? Is the true purpose clear or hidden?

Correctly applying Lasswell's information flow theory when assessing information usually provides a sound basis to decide whether to believe and act on the data.

Where is Information Found?

Information collectors think in broad terms, not only the Internet. Knowledge is found in many places, even in places that are not obvious. Both the analog and digital worlds host various types of Open Source information.

Useful non-Internet materials and resources include:
- Libraries
- Printed media
  o Books
  o Newspapers
  o Magazines and periodicals
  o Annuals
  o Leaflets
  o Pamphlets
  o Journals (covering specialized areas)
- Electronic media, including radio and television
- Motion pictures
- Loudspeakers
- Novelties
- Posters
- Maps and geographic imagery
- Clothing
- Food and drink
- Speeches, forums and sermons
- Conversations in public places
- Talk shows
- Non-governmental releases
- Research reports
- Dumpster diving
- Banners, posters and billboards
- Flags
- Graffiti
- Tattoos
- Educational materials
- Theses and dissertations
- Conference proceedings

- Census and social data
- Advertisements
- Government releases and public documents
- Jewelry and wearable emblems

And the list goes on from there.... All of these – and many other things – are, and remain, potentially helpful information sources.

As you go along you will create your own stash of information resources, one that is unique to you and the intricacies of your own work. (See Appendix B, Your Reference Library.)

Parts of your library may be fiber-based; much will be digital. The Internet has made open source research more complex and widened the range of resources, but any type of observation or resource can contribute to knowledge and understanding.

Many people believe the Internet and the Web are synonymous with OSR. They are not. These were not available in times past and they are not necessarily the best sources today. Observation and listening remain viable techniques, particularly in areas and among people where computers and the Internet are rare or uncommon. The Internet is only one of the tools that information professionals use.

The time period you are searching has important implication in the choice of materials and the resources to search, as well.

Information about things that happened in the digital age may well be stored in digital formats as a routine matter and may be accessible with a computer. But things that happened in 1938, or 1983, are probably more fully noted in a written or electronic format – books, documents, magazines, television news reports, film, or tape. Many things saved originally in other formats are being, or have been, converted to digital formats. These include census records, passenger lists of ships carrying immigrants, land records, etc. But the conversion process is hit and miss, often depending on available funds as well as urgency of need. Old newspapers may be stored on microfilm or microfiche. City directories may still be in paper formats.

Many researchers make it a practice to assume, unless they have information to the contrary, that anything being researched before 1995 is probably preserved in some format other than an easily readable computer format or digital language. In those circumstances they look first to resources other than their computer.

Professional-grade practitioners consider all resources when drafting their personal playbook. For example, the US government publishes many manuals, reports and instruction pamphlets covering a variety of fields, fields that include every area that the government touches. Many resources are public, some are free, and many documents are available on the Internet in pdf format. In researching some subjects a careful look around government sites pays big dividends.

The variety of information, having the widest useful variety, is more than the spice of OSR. It is the very essence. When a competitor suggested he did not need to know the history of their location. Sherlock Holmes, in *The Velley of Fear*, stressed that getting as much information as possible, from as many places as possible, is essential. "Breadth of view, my dear Mr. Mac, is one of the essentials of our profession. The interplay of ideas and the oblique uses of knowledge are often of extraordinary interest," Holmes shot back.

The Internet Parts

Some Internet parts, some non-Internet resources, might not be used often – in fact some are probably never used by the average OSR collector – but professionals know that they exist and be prepared to use them when they appear to be useful.

Such preparations, even for the unlikely eventualities, are necessary. Being prepared for the unlikely is vital, as Sherlock Holmes said in *The Problem of Thor Bridge*. "Holmes waved his hand toward some papers on a chair. 'I had no idea that the case was coming my way or I should have had my extracts ready,' said he."

Today "extracts" may be thought of as parts of the Internet.

The Internet is often conflated with the Web and email – the latter so often accessed through a web browser that it is commonly thought of as part of the Web although it is actually a separate service. The Web is undoubtedly central to modern research and to the operations of a viable information shop. But there are many parts to the Internet. It is, after all, a system of systems. Like a car, the Internet has many moving parts, each one of which often has other moving parts. The Web is only one part of the Internet, and it is a part that itself has many other moving parts.

Many of the Internet systems other than the Web and email have been bypassed or fallen into disuse over the years. Those other parts of the Internet theoretically, and some cases actually, may be used on your information voyage if they are remembered and accessed. Not all the parts are particularly useful or even current, but the professional researcher keeps in mind that the Internet includes:

- Archie
- Email
- File Transfer Protocol (FTP)
- Finger
- Gopher
- Internic
- Telnet
- WAIS
- World Wide Web (WWW or Web).

Most of the various Internet parts are potentially exploitable in one way or another. For some workups, useful information from ages ago may still reside in those mostly-forgotten reaches of the

Internet. Even today crafty communicators may utilize the largely-disused parts of the Internet that are seldom known, much less visited, by most people.

Sometimes parts of the Internet are exploited in unique or unusual ways. Most people do not see email as being highly useful in OSR – it cannot be ethically read, so it is often ignored as a research tool. Yet the email address of a person or organization is far more personal than a name. There are many people of the same name; an email – in almost all cases – is uniquely attached to a person or organization. It is also written on many documents, web pages, and is found throughout the Internet, It can be picked up from Internet search engines.

Some researchers, particularly those who research or contact a variety of people, prospects and organizations, create their own databases of email addresses. Sales professionals and online marketers seek out, extract, and save many email addresses – as well as other types of contact information they find – including them in a database. While people in sales are among the most consistent of people who use these tool types, police and security professionals also find it useful to have large email databases.

Email extractors include:

- **Email Harvester:** https://www.abbulkmailer.com/email-harvester-free.php
- **Hunter:** https://hunter.io/
- **Mail-Biz ($$$$):** https://appv2.mailbiz.co/
- **WindowsReport:** https://windowsreport.com/email-extractor-software/.

Email addresses are also found on many open Internet databases where hackers post them – often for sale but sometimes for free. They are often used for sales pitches. A simple search for "stolen email address" is revealing. Passwords are often included in the data. The hacked email addresses are usually considered open source; the passwords that go with them are not.

The Web

The World Wide Web (WWW or Web) is undoubtedly central to modern research and any viable information shop. The Web can be conveniently divided into three parts. (OK, really two, but who's counting.)

The most familiar part is what we usually call simply "The Web," "The Open Web," or "The Surface Web." The second part is "The Deep Web" or "The Hidden Web." The third portion – some can properly claim it is actually a subsection of the Deep Web – is the "Dark Web."

The "Surface Web" is the part that is patrolled by search engines. It is the portion that is readily available to any web searcher. The surface web is essential to much of today's research.

The Surface Web can be subdivided into Web 1.0, which is largely webmaster-to-user communication, Web 1.5 which presaged the next step, and Web 2.0 – interactivity between and among both users and webmasters. A major part of Web 2.0 is social media. Web 3.0 is more promised than promising; it has not yet become a significant resource for OSR operators.

The Surface Web is perhaps one, or most-generously two, percent of everything posted on the Web. Some Surface Web resources may be high-tech, but in the final analysis most are low-value.

The Deep Web is often more likely to contain useful information, or to provide leads to better-quality information. The Deep Web, or as it is sometimes called the Hidden Web, is the second part of the WWW. There is much value in the Deep Web. It is the portion that search engines are not proficient in accessing. This part may or may not be purposely hidden from searchers, but the efficient use of it requires specialized knowledge and advanced techniques. Putting key words into a search engine is not much help to the user who wants to access the Deep Web because whatever information is stored there is largely hidden from, or by, search engines and their databases. For the most part Deep Web sites are relatively innocuous, though there are certainly exceptions.

The Dark Web is the Wild West part of the WWW – and like the Surface Web, is numerically only a tiny part. Secrecy thrives in the Dark Web. Everything that passes through the Dark Web is encrypted. Darknet aficionados often make an important distinction by referring to the Open Web or Surface Web as the "Clearnet" because it is not encrypted.

The Dark Web may be used for good, and sometimes for things that are truly evil. It is the part of the Web that is intentionally hidden from prying eyes, whether those are the gaze of governments, police forces, or the scrutiny of the general public. It is the part used by democracy advocates in countries where there is no freedom; by sellers of drugs, guns, and other humans, as well as by people who simply want to go "under the radar" of governments, hackers, or society in general. Organized criminals, organized patriots, and unorganized individuals rub elbows on the Dark Web. Patriots use the Dark Web to strive for freedom; criminals use the Dark Web for nefarious purposes. Governments – whether criminal enterprises or democratic paragons – would like to shut down the Dark Web, or at least know more about what goes on there.

Exploiting the Internet

Information professionals are aware of, and are able to exploit, each of these subdivisions of the Web as well as the other parts of the Internet that have fallen into disuse. Exploitation of any part of the OSR field – including any part of the Internet – requires knowledge, attention to detail, practice, and experience.

Yet another way of seeing the Surface Web is to look at what various parts do. Open Web resources can usually be roughly grouped into a number of categories such as:

- News and public affairs sites
- Blogs and opinion sites
- Social media sites
- Chat rooms
- Newsgroups
- Citizen journalism sites
- Business sites
- Entertainment sites
- Government sites
- NGO sites
- Gaming sites
- Databases
- Gray (Grey) Web sites.

It would be nice if that was a Web hierarchy, particularly if it had some relationship to the quality of the information on a given type of site. Unfortunately no type-ranking provides help in vetting sites or evaluating the material available on those sites. Site type does not determine information accuracy or quality. Only the capabilities and intent of the people who put the material together are determinative.

Drawbacks and Blindspots are Expected

Understand from the beginning that any research effort has drawbacks. OSR does not solve every problem or situation. It cannot definitively answer all questions. Sometimes OSR cannot answer a question at all.

The location, or indeed the existence, of the Lost Dutchman gold mine cannot be answered through OSR. The location of Atlantis will never be revealed by any open source research, no matter how intensive, enthusiastic, or detailed. Even the very existence of Atlantis will always remain dubious.

Someone must have known and publicly revealed information before it can be accessed by an open source operator. Archimedean research techniques used by open source researchers can suggest – based on publicly available information – whether a new element could be created because there is a gap in the atomic table, or whether there is the possibility of a new planet being discovered because of known wobbles in another planet's path. Often, however, open source research is limited to making intelligent projections and suggesting possibilities. To that extent, OSR could suggest only that the Lost Dutchman Mine, if indeed it ever existed, was probably somewhere in central Arizona.

Besides the light drizzle of reliable information in some cases, the data deluge in other searches becomes a severe limitation. A researcher or research desk can be overwhelmed by the flood of information that must be processed and analyzed when there is no search plan or the plan is not followed. For this, and a number of other reasons, planning – particularly in establishing policies and adhering to time windows – is an important preliminary step.

There are other serious problems in Internet research. Only a small percentage of the material available on the Open Web is actually valuable, factual content. While things are improving in Webworld, studies show that much of the Web is either data movement, opinion, or pornography. Moreover, the Internet is only a relatively small part of the information universe. Perhaps 25 percent of the information contained in the world's libraries can be found on the Internet. No matter how much information is available, inevitably something will be missing. Information gaps are common.

The Secrecy Heuristic

The Secrecy Heuristic is a major minefield for OSR professionals. Cassandras seeking to deny the value of open source research insist that if information isn't secret it is valueless.

Despite the millennia of utility, OSR is bedeviled and devalued by what is today called the "secrecy heuristic." Long before it was named as such, the secrecy heuristic has affected the acceptance and use of open source research discoveries. In the time of Moses, his spies came back, told what they saw, but were not believed because their results were obtained openly. Intelligence professionals are perhaps the premier purveyors of the secrecy heuristic message, but the thinking is pervasive throughout society.

The secrecy heuristic is the widespread – perhaps naturally ingrained – human attitude that secret information is far more valuable than open source information. Studies seem to imply the secrecy heuristic holds true even when the secret information is clearly wrong and open source or public information is obviously correct. Conspiracy theories, which are simply secrecy on steroids, often are given far more currency than is afforded provable facts.

People acquire a heightened sense of self-importance and keen pleasure from belonging to some "special" class" that has access to privileged information, secret information, which others do not have available or cannot get.

Open Source information – by definition information that anyone may get – fails to provide that same sense of importance or pleasure.

What is missing from this equation is the difference between "can" and "may." Open Source information may be available to any who know how to look. But many – in some cases, most – people do not know *how* or *where* to look. In the end much OSR information is effectively available only to the few. Open Source researchers do belong to a special class, that class of people who routinely access privileged information which most others don't know how to dig out. And the people who receive that information, likewise, are privileged. The secrecy heuristic really should never apply to OSR techniques.

Sherlock Holmes, like many modern researchers, apparently saw and understood the impact of the secrecy heuristic though he may not have known the term. He seemed disinclined to speak about his own methods, fearing that their very simplicity would render them valueless in the eyes of others. "'I begin to think, Watson,' said Holmes, 'that I make a mistake in explaining. *'Omne ignotum pro magnifico,'* you know and my poor little reputation, such as it is, will suffer shipwreck if I am so candid"' he mused in *The Red-Headed League.*

He reiterated his concern that people – once they understood how he used open, available, information to reach his conclusions – just passed his talent off. In *The Stock-Broker's Clerk* Holmes lamented "'I am afraid that I rather give myself away when I explain,' said he. 'Results without causes are much more impressive.'"

There is little, beyond recognizing that the secrecy heuristic exists and that it actually doesn't apply to OSR in given situations, that can be done to counter it.

Confirmation Bias

As threatening as the Secrecy Heuristic may be to good research, another factor can be even more pernicious in OSR: confirmation bias.

People hear or see what they wish, or expect, to hear or see. They accept whatever supports their thinking, rejecting anything that does not. Confirmation bias thus creates a feedback loop that reaffirms whatever was expected. Confirmation bias also strengthens an erroneous or questionable belief.

Confirmation bias becomes a major threat to collection, analysis, and interpretation. People look for the information that they expect to see in those places that they expect to see it. They do not seek contrary evidence. In fact they tend to reject contrary information when it is thrust upon them. Confirmation bias is a normal human behavior, but unchecked it is a behavior that poses potential problems for anyone trying to do proper open source research.

Sherlockians will understand the great detective's concern about the taint of confirmation bias as he expressed it in *The Sign of Four:* "It is of the first importance not to allow your judgment to be biased by personal qualities. Emotional qualities are antagonistic to clear reasoning," Holmes said.

Sherlock Holmes again stressed the dangers of Confirmation Bias in *The Adventure of Black Peter.* There he chided Watson, saying "we all learn by experience, and your lesson this time is that you should never lose sight of the alternative."

Confirmation bias is obviously dangerous during the analysis phase because it obscures the less-favored answers to any question, but it may even be more problematic during the collection phase. When confirmation bias is allowed free reign during the collection phase there is no opposing thought to even consider in the analysis phase. Information laying out alternative possibilities is never collected when confirmation bias reigns unchecked. Alternatives never make it to the analysis and interpretation phase.

Adjusting thinking to minimize confirmation bias is essential to effective research. Trying to find a contrarian view in research can mitigate the more pernicious effects of confirmation bias. But good researchers never overdo that either – the earth is not flat and there is no scientific evidence that dinosaurs were taken down by arrows!

Evaluation and Assessment

Collecting information is a major part of Open Source work, and in some cases raw data may be all that a client requires or wants. However, usually the Open Source professional will be asked to assess the collected material and make some sense of it, to draw conclusions and evaluate the collected information. Skepticism about information, no matter where it is collected, is healthy.

Sherlock Holmes stressed the need to evaluate facts, at every stage, this way: "It is of the highest importance in the art of detection to be able to recognize, out of a number of facts, which are incidental and which vital. Otherwise, your energy and attention must be dissipated instead of being concentrated" he said in *The Reigate Puzzle*.

OSR Roles

In large organizations the varied roles of Open Source professionals may be distinct. The work may be assigned to people known by job titles such as collectors, managers, librarians, analysts, disseminators, or researchers. In real-world operations a single person often handles two, three, or perhaps all these roles. In this book the people who conduct any of the steps may be simply referred to by such terms as information professionals, operators, researchers, the team, or the cell.

A project may have many people assigned to it, or it may be worked by a one-person shop. Whatever the size of the operation, there are distinct roles that people play. In a one-person shop the roles will be performed by a single individual. In a multi-person environment the roles have to be carefully apportioned. These roles often are divided as:

- Manager
- Collector
- Analyst.

The manager focuses on four main areas: collection, tradecraft, the analysis and interpretation process, and production. Managers:

- Oversee the entire operation and work on the basis that "the buck stops here."
- Identify trends in tradecraft or equipment
- Identify any tradecraft or analysis deficiencies and take corrective action
- Are knowledgeable about, and stay current on, the tools of the trade including hardware, software, and techniques
- Train new personnel, when needed

- Oversee the development and upkeep of the SOP
- Provide or develop remedial training, or needed education about changes in technology, equipment, and tradecraft
- Assist in the management and coordination of collection requirements
- Review products before they are sent to a customer
- Oversee customer acquisition
- Encourage customer feedback in order to improve overall capabilities
- Oversee promotional efforts.

Collectors:
- Follow the directions of the manager
- Are knowledgeable in various programs and the techniques that they must use
- Specialize in finding, collecting suitable material, and filling the project library.

Analysts:
- Follow the directions of the manager
- Study the information collected in the project library to develop an assessment
- Produce the final product for dissemination.

More-detailed information on parts of the OSR personnel process will be included later.

To do OSR you will need:
- Equipment
- Software
- People
- Data sources
- Digital
- Non-digital.

Equipment and software will likely be your biggest initial expense; if you hire people, or even count your own time into the mix, people will likely be the largest ongoing cost.

Your information voyage will involve three main activities: the collection of raw material and data; analysis, interpretation and determination of the material's meaning and usefulness; as well as publication of the analyzed material to those who need to know. During all of these phases the researcher or research desk must navigate among numerous known elements and unexpected problems that crop up.

Your Personal Library

In addition to the project library that will contain all the relevant information you or the team finds, you also need to create a personal library where you keep all your OSR-related materials. Your personal library is likely to be both fiber-based – books and paper records – and digital. (See Appendix B, Your Reference Library for additional information and potential downloads.)

Mishaps and attacks occur. They don't even have to be the result of an antagonist's efforts. Today malware, ransomware, or simple computer problems can easily wipe out weeks or months of research and background effort. The digital part of your personal library should be stored on a separate production computer, or on the drive you hang on, where it is safer.

It should not be stored on the computer you use to access the Internet. Why? Because if someone is able to penetrate the safeguards you have in place on the research computer they can see, or even destroy, all your good work. They can piece together what you are looking for, why you want to find the information, what you are doing with the information, and even who you are working with or for. That may not be information you want to share, much less share with a computer hacker.

In the time of Sherlock Holmes physical records and books were important in any open source investigation. Researchers, including the famous detective, didn't live by their memory alone. They kept good records, and used them. "Sherlock Holmes sat moodily at one side of the fireplace cross-indexing his records of crime...." Watson noted in *The Five Orange Pips*. Holmes was apparently meticulous in his care for already-collected knowledge. You need to be just as careful about your own records.

Items in your own basic library should include all the things you will need for production. These include dictionaries and thesauruses in all the languages you will be searching in, glossaries, spelling manuals, almanacs, encyclopedias, atlases, gazetteers, as well as business guides and other research books appropriate to your searching needs. These may be in either digital or fiber format. Depending upon the work being performed by the researcher, organizational directories are useful. These directories may cover groups, members, a trade or business, or alumni.

Your library should also include publications and manuals that will be useful when conducting your research. Depending on your needs that might include books as well as online manuals or instruction sheets about programs and methods you are using. Any information on specific ways to do good research in your particular area of expertise should also be saved to your library.

Paper files – well categorized ones so that you can find things rapidly when necessary – may fit in a drawer or you may need locking file cabinets; in the most sensitive probes you will need a government-level security safe. On the other hand, you may decide that color-coded loose-leaf binders, each with an index to tell you what is where, may be sufficiently secure.

What you include in your personal library will be determined by what you are researching, your security needs, and the ways you will acquire information.

Archiving is important, as Sherlock Holmes alluded to when he boasted in *The Lion's Mane* case that "I hold a vast store of out-of-the-way knowledge, without scientific system, but very available for the needs of my work." Every researcher needs to keep similar vast stores of knowledge to call upon when they are needed, but most would question one part of Holmes' view. Systemizing it would have made it an even more useful storehouse of information.

Despite the belief that nothing ever disappears from the Web, things do vanish – or at least they cannot be found again easily, if ever. News articles are swiftly replaced on the Internet as time moves on. Social media posts are often removed, particularly when they are noteworthy or controversial. Sites may take down posts or articles they consider to be at odds with their rules; entire sites may disappear at the whim of the owner or the Internet providers.

Make certain you archive valuable material – whether it is your own archive or one of the online archiving sites. Always archive anything (and everything) you think you might use in the future. Archiving preserves material if it is later removed from a website, proving its existence in the form and at the time you claim. Even if the material is not controversial you still want to have access to it so that you can refer back and refresh your own memory.

Consider saving likely material immediately and then reviewing it off-line rather than spending hours poring through the material while online.

Archive complete sites with your offline browser when the site has much good information about your subject. Pages may be saved to your own computer as well as to archive locations such as the Wayback Machine. If the latter, make certain that the preserved dates cover all the information you need.

Interactive sites pose a preservation problem. They may not be saved anywhere by anybody; they can completely disappear because of the problems involved in saving the wide range of formats and materials in a single coherent file.

It is one thing to find and save material you plan to use later. It is quite another to locate that useful nugget when you want to use it sometime – maybe months – later. To eliminate the problem before it develops, there are several ways that, taken together, will ease the rediscovery process.

First, keep all your information downloads in a single computer folder that is often backed up. Don't spread downloads out across the computer. You can certainly maintain subfolders within the key folder, but keep all your research products together.

Capture everything you could conceivably want on your first pass at a site. The preferred way is to save it the best way you can on your own computer. Mark the saved files with the date, time, location (URL), and downloader's identity. Make certain the information is named and saved in a location so that you can find it again quickly. When you use an off-line browser your dwell time on a site may be a security consideration.

Screenshots, saved pages, and material saved to your own computer are quite acceptable for your own use and reference. Additionally, you can save it to archive locations where you have no ability to change anything, a consideration if it is likely to be scrutinized in any court. Sites like this include:

- **Archive.org (aka Waybackmachine):** https://archive.org/
- **Archive today:** http://archive.is.

When the material saved is likely to become a piece of evidence presented at any legal proceeding it is always best to talk with an attorney about the way a judge or hearing officer would find the saved item admissible.

Archive.org runs the Waybackmachine/Internet Archive as part of a larger program. It began saving webpages in 1996 and makes periodic visits to download the sites it has chosen, or to those sites that users have asked it to copy. Archive.org may not be as useful or functional in saving material from some social media sites. However the Waybackmachine records, overall, are thought to be the most extensive on the Web.

On the left hand side of their page, at the top, they have easily-overlooked symbols showing the types of savings from the Web: These can be text such as books, videos, audio recordings, software, and images.

Archive.today is probably better for saving material from social media sites but its use may be banned or blocked in some nations. Material in archive.today is submitted solely by users who copy or type the URL of the page to be saved into a box. There is no automatic retrieval of sites, such as archive.org carries out.

Hunch.ly ($$$$): https://hunch.ly/ is a Web-capture plug-in that captures and preserves all the webpages visited during a research session. Some professionals use it as a backup to their archiving effort; others may use it as their primary, or sole, collection and preservation resource.

Information professionals who are collecting audio-visuals may need the original files and the URL where they were found as well as the text of any audio, and at least keyword descriptions of the visual parts, for later reference and use.

Audio-visual libraries are complex to set up and can be difficult to keep up-to-date. If A-V libraries become part of your need, consider using the **Kodi** site for home theater software at https://kodi.tv/ or at https://fileforum.betanews.com/detail/Kodi-for-Windows/1423598543/1.

If Kodi proves insufficient, research the way television stations and networks develop and maintain their film clip files.

Try to get and keep the original video files posted since these are likely going to have the highest resolution – the quality only goes down from there – and it is also important to know where the file originated. Reposts are never as good as originals for researchers.

Think through the archiving process before starting to set up your research system; thinking now will prevent later frustration with a kluge setup that is likely to bring on a blast of blasphemies. Remember, there is no single system that is "best." There is only one that is best for you. Be aware of how important things like chain of custody may be in your research and if there are any legal ramifications attached to the information you are collecting.

Consider getting, installing, and using a desktop search engine that will scour your own computer. Programs like **Copernic Desktop Search:** http://www.copernic.com/ can be found by typing terms like "desktop search engine" into your usual search engine.

Simply typing in the right key words will usually help find the article you want when you are using a desktop search engine, but winnowing down the list that any desktop search engine presents can be daunting unless you develop a naming convention for files. It helps to have your files named in some consistent way, one that makes sense to you. There are any number of solutions. You may decide that subject, location, people, or date may come first in a file name. Many who are researching a single issue and saving to a single folder will choose to title items by date because that provides an instant time line.

Develop your own naming format for saved files. For instance you might: Put the year first, then the month, and finally the date in a two-number increment – year-month-date. This will make a search for a particular time frame easier. 190101 will always come before

191231 and that will come before 200704; all dates in between will be sequential.

That date number may be followed or preceded by the subject, a country, personal names, or all of these. Leave no spaces in the file title. Spaces often will be filled with a "%" sign. That makes both reading and searching difficult. Type everything in lower case; do not use capitals since a mixed-case line makes searches more difficult. The subject/country/name may be run in with date, or be separated by an underscore (_). The saved file may now have a name like 190101venezuelaeconomy or 190631_usstamps.

Additional key words, or even codes you develop to identify the material, may be added but try to keep the naming format file name as short as possible. Then put in a hyphen. Do not use a hyphen prior to this. The hyphen is used to signal that everything after it is the original URL, allowing you or another researcher or research desk to get back to the original item on the web. The saved file now has a name like 190101venezuelaeconomy-url or 191231_usstamps-url.

The result is a file name that is identifiable, dated as to download, and has an attached working URL linked to it so that you or another researcher can return to the original page, whenever necessary.

Audio-visual files can be saved in the same file folder, or in separate ones created for the need. The same can be said of saved offline browser files, which are likely to be larger, much larger, than other files.

How you save files, and how you name them, is your individual choice. The important thing is that you are able to smoke out the material when you want, without hours of frustrating search time. Thoughtful consistency in naming and saving files pays dividends.

Web Reference Report

As an adjunct to your archives and reference resources you may want to create web reference reports about important sites that you want to keep information on. They may be used in deciding where to look, where not to search, or as references in analysis. In the chaos of the Internet, the anarchy of the Web, your reference reports can help guide you to reliable resources. Web reference reports can be digital or they may be placed in a binder. Digital ones may be saved in databases. Web reference reports often contain the following information:

- Web Reference Report on (site name)
- Website-Provided Name (If not in English):
- Link:
- Type: (news, blog, etc.)
- Primary Language:
- Other Language Versions: Yes/No.
- Date of founding if known: YYYY/MM/DD
- Available on Waybackmachine Yes (earliest date) or No.
- General quality of material:
- Known or obvious biases:
- Picture of Web header:
- Background and key information: (Information about the site, including short historical info, location, operators etc.)
- Names and descriptions of internal links prominently located (where) on the site:
- Overall site contents: (well-developed, little or no content etc.?)
- "Home Page" contents and outside links: (describe)
- Major Sections of Website: (name and describe)
- On-site Search Engine: Yes or No
- Membership Registration: Yes or No
- Reader Comments: Yes or No
- Associated Blogs/Forums/Message Board/BBS: Yes (name and description) or No
- RSS available: Yes or No

- Twitter: Yes and address/URL or No
- Facebook: Yes and address/URL, or No
- Other Social Media Links:
- Site registration: Where, When, by Whom, Address etc.?
- Contact Information:
- Email:
- Skype:
- Physical Address:
- Postal Address:
- Comments and observations.

***

Project:
Research Lasswell's work, either on the Internet or in a book, and include a section of no less than five and no more than 10 sentences in the overview section of your SOP describing whether and how you would use Lasswell's work in your own research effort.

Project:
Consider whether you want to create a form that would allow you to keep message flow information about the individual resources and sites you find in your research. If you believe such a form would be useful, create it and save it in your personal book. Remember, you can always modify anything you write, remove things later, or add things back later.

Project:
In your SOP mark down the general steps you will take in developing your product and doing research. These may include Tasking, Collecting, Saving, Analyzing and Evaluating Information, Validating Sources, Disseminating and Integrating. The general steps may also include steps that are unique to your situation and needs.

Project:
In your SOP write down the various parts of the Internet you plan on using and why. Most people will at least mark the Web and

Email. Do quick research on the other portions of the Internet and note why, or why not, you plan to use them.

Project:
Decide which of the Web parts you will use: the Open Web, the Hidden Web, or the Dark Web. In your SOP write at least three sentences about how you plan to use any of these, or why you will not use them, for your projects.

Project:
The Open Web is loaded with venues, so loaded that you must consider what type of venue will provide the information you are seeking. In the SOP you are creating for yourself make sections for the traditional Internet media (Web 1.0) and new or emerging media (Web 2.0), including social media. Write down under those the categories and types of media you plan on using at this time.

Project:
Think through the non-Internet resources you will want to use for your research and list them in the "where to look" section of the SOP document. List them in the order you feel will be most useful to you and your work.

Project:
In the "links to look at" section of your SOP list any found above, or later in the book, that you feel will be useful to your research. List the types, sources, and media you will use to find open source information. Be specific, list the exact tools, programs, sites, and sources you plan to employ. You may want to create categories of, and add notations to, those links which you feel will be useful. Consider this an ongoing project throughout your work in the field.

Project:
Go to a job search site of your choice and find three positions that would require the use OSR or OSINT work in the job duties. Select one of the jobs and write out a sample search someone would undertake in that position.

Project:
In the SOP list all of the libraries you have access to, their contact information, addresses, URLs, and a short description of the services available or any people you know who work at those libraries.

Project:
In your SOP indicate whether you will you use or create Web Reference Reports. If so decide whether they will be digital or fiber based, then create and store any format you plan to use.

Project:
In the SOP, under the library heading, describe the naming format you will use to save material and quickly find it again when needed. If you opt not to use a uniform naming format explain what system or systems you plan to use to find downloaded materials.

3. People

The human dimension remains the most important part of any, and every, information shop.

In the Information Age it is people who think through the search process; they develop the work at every stage. OSR operators cannot rely on today's technology, or hoped-for improvements in the future, to relieve them of the punishing pressure inherent in OSR searches. Automating parts, even large portions, of research is possible but the human factor remains essential. The spirit of initiative and imagination are vital in research. No computer can supply either of them.

Computers are be wonderful at supplying the disciplined attention required in OSR work, but they lack the temperament of an artist or the free-spirited approach that is common among effective OSR operators.

OSR "Personalities"

Choosing the people who possess the talents, the tradecraft, and the "knack" to do OSR, is important. Whether you are thinking about going into the field, or hiring others, you should consider how people interface with the OSR world.

OSR is not a field for everyone. People either can happily do the job or they are temperamentally unfit the work.

No one should be shoehorned into it. People who are not inquisitive, who are uninterested in OSR, people who are inept, are incompetent, or those who are otherwise unsuitable for the work are poor fits. Dabblers need not apply. Unfortunately sorcerer's apprentices do get into the field. Fortunately they seldom last long.

Individualism and inquisitiveness are a plus for any successful researcher but those alone are not enough. Dull drudgework sessions are depressing. Slogging through projects, seeking tenuous clues that have no personal interest is all-too-common for professionals. The ability to overcome tedium and to work through the dull, boring stretches that are endemic to all online research is a must. It is acceptable to be dismayed; it is not acceptable to be discouraged. Diligence leads to success. Clarity of thought is not optional, but lurching incompetence among amateurs is all-too-common in research work.

Nothing guarantees success. But some things weigh more heavily for good results. Some things are clearly problematic. It may be impossible to quantify or assess in advance the likelihood that someone will be an OSR standout. Nonetheless there are tells, traits that suggest when someone will be good, or at least competent, in the research process.

Researchers often have useful experience through previous work in a library, employment in the mass media, or experience writing papers in higher education. Many highly qualified people may have none of that background, however. People who may be green about techniques can be successful if they are also keen about learning and using the OSR processes.

Inherent inquisitiveness, consistency, and diligence are always the virtues of any researcher. Researchers, above all, must be curious almost to the point of obsession. Some make fanatical efficiency their virtue.

The ability to think "outside the box," a capability to remain organized in the midst of online chaos, and strong analytical skills are highly-desired. People who are nonplussed by uncertainty and revel in quietly wading through constantly-changing circumstances seem to perform better in OSR.

Information professionals have to be innovative, conscientious, goal-directed, and action-oriented to find and retrieve information through ways and in places that originally may not have seemed fruitful. Imagination and creativity count. Eccentricity is always acceptable but reliability and efficiency are required. Efficiency and eccentricity often work well in tandem while the lack of imagination and initiative is often fatal in OSR.

Without people and their human input, without the ability and willingness to rethink unproductive approaches, effective research is unlikely

Searchers must have an experienced, specially trained, mind that does not shy away from extemporizing when necessary. Adeptness, versatility and the willingness to find and adopt new skills and techniques are valuable personal assets for researchers. Within their own specialization area the top researchers display what some might even characterize as a mysterious, almost eerie, certainly uncanny, ability to locate pertinent information amid the miasma of online confusion. But OSR isn't voodoo. It is based on the application of an ever-evolving, but learned, technique.

Effective researchers often develop their own personal variations of OSR techniques. They are never confined by slide-rule thinking. Failure of imagination seriously limits any researcher.

Sherlock Holmes clearly understood the need for imaginative thinking. Lecturing a police inspector in *The Adventure of the Retired Colourman,* he advised "You'll get results, Inspector, by always putting yourself in the other fellow's place, and thinking what you would do yourself. It takes some imagination, but it pays."

Seeking hidden information is hard work, hard mental work. Besides imagination, important aspects are patience and knowledge of how and when to deftly select and use appropriate core skills.

Knowledge of the intricacies of the information universe and the possible variations of search techniques to suit the particular project are important to success.

Open Source Research has many moving parts. Knowledge tendrils grow one way and suddenly turn in a different direction. The researcher has to be aware of any changes in direction and be ready to act on them.

There are no guarantees in OSR, despite the tub-thumpers of the field who promise unfailing results. Knowledge of the field, efficiency, and intelligent guesses may be equally responsible in producing a positive final report. But sometimes nothing anyone can do will turn up the information you seek. The needed information is often, but is not always, "somewhere out there." Perspicacity and promise do not always turn into performance. The prospect of failure always looms. Only good researchers can reduce that prospect to acceptable levels. Only confident researchers, those who know others could do no better, can accept or explain any limited or failed outcomes. And in the final analysis only patient researchers will prevail.

Effective open source researchers seldom look for notoriety. And that is probably a good thing. OSR tends toward inconspicuous success but obvious failures. Even researchers' most successful efforts are often accepted with a barely-appreciative shrugs. Success is expected, a given, always and in all ways.

Tedium, rather than theatrical reveals, is a constant in OSR work. The researcher is driven to carry on nonetheless, often with a show of enthusiasm that belies the actual situation.

The best researchers may not have obsessive-compulsive disorder, but many are so concerned with missing a key fact that they seem to be afflicted by OCD when working. They seek their personal "Eureka" moments despite the drudgery of any search.

Successful researchers need the internal discipline to pay strict attention to detail and, importantly, the judgement needed to avoid disappearing down rabbit holes.

Imagination is a must. OSR operators "see" solutions vividly through the mind's retina rather than the eye. Low-grade researchers can be turned out by some assembly-line, one-size-fits all, instruction program. But that is something better used for car production or military indoctrination than individualized training. Information professionals are challenged to think out of the box. Assembly-line thinking fails fast in OSR.

Be cautious of checklist fanatics. Many people who are actually unsuitable for OSR collection and interpretation work see checklists as their salvation. They rely on checklists. They feel that by ticking off the checklist's items their work is done. For them a checklist excuses any failure or shortcoming. They checked the boxes, found nothing, and now it is time for them to move on.

Check marks on checklists are never a substitute for results.

The ability to run through a pre-flight checklist does not mean someone can keep a plane in the air or return it, and the people aboard, back to the ground in one piece. Checklists are only a jump-off point for the professional-grade researcher. Those who use checklists for the totality of their search procedure are violating an important rule of all phases of life: Know not only what you are doing but understand why you are doing it.

Checklists, no; scripts yes.

Scripts differ from checklists. They are only starting points. Scripts get rewritten, often on the fly. The players who deliver their lines on stage may even alter their scripts while performing; changes are made as inspiration and events demand. Researchers, too, find that changing conditions and new facts or developments demand changes in the scripts they are using.

Goals, skills, and roles differ widely from search to search. The reasons, depth, and the needs of any research project all differ. Every search is unique so information specialists develop niche talents and capabilities to fill those special needs. No one-size-fits all; specialization becomes crucial. Skill sets are going to differ, and they should. The skill set of any researcher or research desk should be slightly larger than whatever research the investigator is likely to be called on to perform.

While no one knows everything, good researchers know their own field, whether it is narrow or wide. They understand where to find their special type of information, and how to use the programs, the sites, and the skills needed to access that information.

They also know their limitations. And researchers have definite limits.

Information cannot always be revealed with machine-like precision or perfection. Research today has many moving parts - so many that much depends on the skill, tools, and knowledge of the researcher.

Few people know even most of the tools and skills. Beware of anyone claiming to possess all the answers, talents, or capabilities. Generic researchers who can do anything and everything are unicorns. They do not exist. No one knows everything or has a process that solves all problems, except – perhaps – snake oil salesmen. Many people who hold themselves out to be information professionals are not. They don't know the width and depth of their own field. Many talk the talk but far fewer can walk the walk.

As an example, there are those who will claim any research is inadequate or doesn't deserve to be called proper work unless every possible last resource has been explored. But a requestor's time constraints and LTIOV (Last Time Information of Value) may mean that a 75 percent search, or even a 35 percent review, is all that can be done. A range of needs and time windows apply to different research problems. That is something the true professional knows but the *poseur* is ignorant of. Sometimes the time just isn't there. Insistence on perfect research conditions inevitably damages the good. OSR professionals do everything they can, but they do it within whatever limits are imposed on them. They do what they can, with the tools they have, in the time they are allotted.

But as far as the results you provide – in whatever time frame – there is only one standard, and that is perfection. Whatever the name the researcher goes by, exactness and accuracy are musts.

Information specialists call themselves many different names, including business intelligence executive, oppo research specialist, analyst, or computer-assisted investigator. Titles mean little. The best people in the field are usually the jacks of all trades and masters of many.

When looking for qualified researchers there does not seem to be any way of assuring, in advance, whether someone will be an asset or a flop. Performance can only be measured by – actual performance. There are tells, but no one can bet the farm on them. The best route is to give applicants a chance – often two chances because some projects are just impossible. But relieve non-performers after two failed tries. Not everyone is cut out for OSR.

The need for knowledge of where and when new resources and techniques become available means information specialists are wise to devote some part of each work day or week to improving their own knowledge and skills. No one knows everything, but the successful researcher or research desk is the one who learns, in detail, the resources and techniques they and their clients need most – now and in the future. The best researchers become adept with tools and sites before they are needed, not on the fly.

The Team and Crowdsourcing

The OSR producer may be an individual or a team, so any SOP planning may apply not only to you, but to any team you develop.

Crowdsourcing can bring valuable results to many OSR projects. Bellingcat has made good use of the technique, getting a variety of people with differing talents to contribute in areas where they excel. Even when crowdsourcing is not technically available because of security or other issues, teamwork responses can be substituted to gain many of the same advantages.

Both crowdsourcing and teamwork bring more eyes on a subject. They concentrate brainpower on knotty problems. They improve creative efforts. They can speed up the successful completion of OSR projects. Crowdsourcing and team efforts are, like open source research, usually greater than the sum of the parts.

Information teams are composed of specialists. Since no one can know everything about the information universe all members must be competent in general searches but each researcher should also specialize in a select area or field of knowledge.

Teamwork means different things to different people.

In general, the business use of the word "teamwork" seems to have little or no relation to fellow workers and their skills. While almost everyone demands teamwork, too often the word is used simply to imply unwavering support to an employer or an organization. That type of teamwork seldom produces good research results.

Teamwork is not a one-way street of support and approval, of cheerleaders and pom-poms. But that is often the way companies and organizations see, and present, the issue.

When the team concept is actually brought into play, a collaboration model rather than a top-down model usually is the preferable way to promote organization effectiveness.

Teamwork means functioning as an organism, each part playing its role. Eyes may help you choose what to eat, but they don't digest the food and extract the needed nutrition; blood may carry the oxygen but the oxygen first comes in through the nose and mouth.

Teamwork means determining what each person does well, or best, and having each person perform in their best fields. But no one does everything well; a no-hitter pitcher may well be a mediocre catcher or shortstop.

Teamwork, in the best sense, even goes beyond functioning as part of an organism. On a good team the members try to help others improve their skills and abilities. Pinch-hitting and learning how to play the other person's position marks a good team. So team members learn from each other, acquiring new specialties, capabilities, and talents to spread the workload. If you are the only one with the skill you will always be doing the same thing. By the same token, if you lack the particular skill you cannot do the project, or you will do it badly.

At the same time researchers, even those who are good team players, are individually responsible and capable of making thought-through decisions without outside direction or prompting. Individuality doesn't mean that collaboration isn't important.

While there is always a team leader, in the collaboration model the team members cooperate, meet often, and make suggestions which are discussed and dissected during team meetings. Then the team leader passes judgement on what is effectively the joint suggestion of the team members.

Coordination of efforts rather than the coincidence of individual achievement is a major goal of team research.

When the team concept is required, team members agree on how the collaborative effort will be carried out. They make certain that there is clarity about the end product and the way the team will reach the common goal. It is important to get all team members into a collaborative mindset, one where members feel positive about giving and receiving new ideas but also recognize that any critiques of their proposals are not personal attacks.

Team members in an information shop discuss security, what levels of protection are needed, and how to achieve safety for themselves, team members, and others who could be negatively affected.

The team sets clear internal timelines.

Whenever possible, "stop and review" and sharing sessions are planned to make certain the research effort remains on track. Team members freely share both resources and information. They try to make "the other guy's" work easier and more efficient. When working with others they are more likely to provide URLs – direct knowledge – rather than headlines or titles that must be searched for.

The multiple mind-power of the team focuses on the problems and the glitches that inevitably arise. Sometimes the team will identify, predict, and resolve difficulties even before they surface.

Teamwork is built on a willingness to share, trust in the people you are working with, and constant communication between team members. Egotism is tamped down. It's critical that everyone read off the same sheet of the music from the start. Someone has to lead, but even that person – perhaps especially that person – has to project a collaborative state of mind to lead effectively.

Identifying the leader from the outset is important, but in complex research issues the leadership roles may shift as the investigation, and team members' expertise, dictates. All such leadership shifts should be planned and announced well before any changeover.

Accept that team disagreements as inevitable. People will often agree on the result they seek but diverge on how to get there. In some cases team leaders may do well to create alternative paths, effectively setting up a race to the finish.

Project outlines – the left and right limits – must be understood by all team members. Clarity of purpose and process is important.

Teamwork, whether as a leader or member, requires the willingness to both give and receive, to be receptive to new ideas that the team develops or receives along the way. Common goals, and deadlines are important.

Shirking either work or responsibility inevitably puts an extra load on other team members. It seriously upsets the team's sense of collaboration.

Team training expands the capabilities and cohesion. It starts with the individual training of members, overseen by the team leader who focuses on tools and capabilities. It then progresses to integrate sections of the team such as researchers and analysts. It finishes by molding the group so that they help each other while developing new and improved ways to accomplish their tasks.

Large, established, information shops may have a worry that small ones seldom do – bureaucracy. Older, larger, organizations often become stultified, developing teams where seniority is king. Talent and prowess may be ignored. Inertia takes control. Work progresses slowly, cautiously, unimaginatively. Even stupidly. Bureaucratic organizations isolate themselves from new ideas or new techniques. Such organizations forget, or perhaps have never heard, a researcher's mantra: Get it first, but get it right.

Computer Help

Closely related to the "bureaucracy in the office" problem is one that has little to do with you or your team, but has everything to do with the capabilities of you or your team to actually do the work. Computers work long and hard. Then they or the programs inside break down. They usually break down at the worst possible time, in the worst possible situations. They often break down far beyond the capabilities of you or the staff to get them working again. What do you do to get them working again?

If you have to take a computer to a service owned by a large commercial company you have no control over the security of anything on that system. Likewise, you have no assurance about the capabilities of the individual workers who are charged with fixing the computer, or their dedication to their work. These may vary greatly. But you have no way of choosing who works on your system. Large companies that repair computers are often set up on an assembly line basis, something that works well when you are building a computer or a car, but is hardly the ideal in repair work and certainly not in OSR.

Since you cannot predict when computer failures will happen it is important to identify your repair personnel in advance. There are many qualified people – some of whom may work at big box stores and some of whom may have small shops, or even do the work on the sidelines.

Ask around, but put your reliance on people, individuals, rather than a store name. Talk to them before you need help; select someone who will assist in setting up the system you use and can be relied on to solve its problems with minimal down time. People repair; stores sell. Keep that difference clearly in mind. Identify, and use in advance, the hardware specialists you will need later.

It's one more thing to do. That's as clear as it is annoying, but planning for repairs in advance of any problems reduces far greater annoyance later.

Identifying repair people in advance may be only the first step for a highly-capable OSR operation, whether it is an individual or a team. The same person who keeps your computers working may also be a coder, capable of writing script.

Bringing on such dual-threat people, whether as a member of the store team or a part-time contract helper, offers the additional abilities that can bring your operation to a pinnacle of capability.

Good coders are almost indispensable for OSR providers who are going to do any type of webscraping. The techniques involved in webscraping usually demand some knowledge of, and proficiency in, coding to be able to find, download, and edit the material.

Beyond that, and perhaps even more crucially, a good coder can create unique search tools. Smart coders who understand a problem can develop proprietary machine language that make it possible to do things that programs or applications that are currently available on the Internet cannot do, or cannot do well. An in-house capability to develop unique machine-language answers, solving difficult problems, may be the apex of any OSR operation.

***

Project:
In the SOP write down the traits you think would be useful in OSR work. List those factors you would use when evaluating people to work in a team.

Project:
In your SOP indicate whether you plan to develop an OSR team, and if so how you would manage the team and help develop the capabilities of individual team members.

Project:

Go to the SOP and write in the name, phone number, and cost per hour of a computer expert – the guru – you plan to consult in the event of a computer breakdown. In the SOP detail the process(es) you will use when dealing with computer crashes.

4. Equipment, Software, and Storage

EQUIPMENT

Information professionals can use an array of devices, from multi-core systems working in parallel to cell phones, but the most useful and commonly used are probably desktop or laptop computers, ones loaded with the programs that will be needed.

Equipment and software are tools, tools that are generally divided into hardware and software classes. A third set of semi-tools, discussed later, is sites.

Constantly consider what the best tools are likely to be for your investigations, what tools you will use in your information shop to locate and gather the information you need.

Tools, of course, change over time as new ones are developed. The tools in the chest must be up-to-date, sharp, and well-oiled. Keeping current with the newest of tools, and using them properly is important as Sherlock Holmes pointed out in *The Adventure of the Retired Colourman.* Holmes didn't have today's latest gadgets, of course, but he had and used what was new in his time. In some ways his comments presage computers and the methods of using the tools available for today's open source research. Instructing Dr. Watson, Holmes said "Thanks to the telephone and the help of the Yard, I can usually get my essentials without leaving this room."

While modern phones and mobile devices can be and often are still used in research, for everyday work most serious rely on computers because they allow easy downloads and exports, support extensive suites of capabilities, and provide better security. Keyboarding on a cellphone is tiresome and difficult for many, as well.

That does not mean, however, that researchers ignore the research avenues that cellphone use opens. This is particularly true in developing situations where people on the scene are reporting, using their phone, about what they see around them.

In real-time and near-real-time searches, time-limited or streaming cellphone messaging may be good sources. Potential resources include:
> **Periscope:** https://www.periscope.tv/
> **Snapchat**: https://www.snapchat.com/.

In some cases, particularly with some social media sites that operate exclusively over mobile phone platforms and provide no means of computer-based access, researchers must be prepared to cross-platform and use a cellphone or something that simulates such a phone in their probes.

Since cellphones provide virtually no way of saving captured material for later use and analysis, it is imperative in some research to use phone emulators on a computer system. Phony phones can be the software answers to the need for a cellphone in OSR. Emulators are virtual phones, phones without the hardware and often without actual access to the telephone network. While they may not be useful for calls they do allow researchers to access some social media sites that effectively shut out computers.

Setting up a phone emulator for OSR needs can be dicey. The best way is to reverse engineer what you need. Decide, first, what sites you may need to access. That will tell you what apps you need to put on your phony phone, which in turn will suggest where to get the apps, and then what workarounds you need to use to get those apps. Setting up an emulator is not always easy but when you need the capability the effort is worthwhile.

Phone emulators, often used by gaming enthusiasts, include:
- **Android Studio:** https://developer.android.com/studio/

- **BigNox:** https://www https://bignox.com/
- **BlueStacks:** https://www.bluestacks.com/
- **Droid4x:** https://droid4x.en.uptodown.com/windows
- **Genymotion:** https://www.genymotion.com/#!/
- **KoPlayer:** http://www.koplayer.com/.

Over the past two decades advances in the tools used to acquire information have sparked a revolution. Today's variety of tools is large and varied. Like auto mechanics who know that a single wrench or screwdriver is insufficient for their work, information professionals familiarize themselves with all the classes of tools and the tools that are available within each class.

The selection of the individual instruments and the mastery of those tools is the responsibility of OSR practitioners.

Expect that today's tool choices will have to be changed tomorrow or the day after, but some basic decisions must be made at the outset. Remember that OSR is a system of systems. Setting up your work system requires clear thought.

Computers, the ironmongery of Internet research, must be individualized to serve both the needs of the OSR collector and the likely projects.

Generally a system with plenty of power, good storage, and backup capacity is preferred. But start-up organizations and individuals often do quite well with systems that are not top-of-the-line. Inventiveness makes up for limitations in hardware and software.

You will probably use other tools as well, but the Internet-connected computer will often be the research workhorse.

In the best of situations, information professionals use either a single computer equipped with a Virtual Machine (VM) program or two-computer systems.

Virtual Machine programs use a simulated electronic computer, one that is contained within the main computer. A Virtual Machine is software, not hardware. Virtual Machines act as though they are independent of the actual computer they are loaded on.

While any downloaded material can be exported from the Virtual Machine to the host system, when a properly-configured Virtual Machine is shut down everything in the electronic computer disappears. That includes any malware or bugs picked up during research. Antagonistic site operators cannot bypass the virtual machine and enter the host system, either, when a Virtual Machine is used. Virtual Machine software, when configured properly, provides a high degree of safety.

Few people have Virtual Machine software on their computers, however, and for them a two-computer solution works just as well. (In some cases people use three – one of them being a throw-away clunker computer to employ on the Internet whenever you are concerned you might pick up viruses. A fourth, emergency backup, computer is useful for anyone who can afford the outlay.)

For security's sake, divide the work between "outside" and "inside" computers, or as they may be called the "research" and "production" computers. Use the computers in tandem.

You will always need a research system – the "outside" system – with high speed Internet connections and the ability to safely transfer information. The research computer is the one used for locating and downloading material. This part of the system is designed for heavy lifting. It carries out search strategies.

The "inside" or production computer is used for holding and manipulating the information after it is collected, for analysis and assessment, and for producing reports. The "inside" machine is restricted to those purposes. The "inside" computer is never directly exposed to the Internet for day-to-day searching.

All computers, both systems, should have the strongest anti-virus program(s) available. When you are using two computers in tandem, one might have a different anti-virus program than the other so that any chinks in one program will be covered by the other.

Check around for expert opinions about your choice of anti-virus software.

The most-popular anti-virus programs are exactly, and only, that. They are popular. They may not be the most effective answer to your particular situation; they may not meet your need. Anti-virus programs with big advertising budgets don't necessarily translate into top-flight security.

In the free or inexpensive category of anti-virus programs, versions of Avast and AVG are considered standouts by many researchers. Their full-featured software does almost everything that is needed except cook breakfast.

All computers are also loaded with the software types required to carry out their particular role.

The "outside" system is used to access the Internet and conduct research. For the safety of the OSR operator and the security of the client, this system is set up minimally.

Security issues are always important, but they are foremost with the "outside" system. This research system should have an innocuous name like "my computer," certainly nothing that would identify its origin, ownership, purpose, or use. Too often bureaucrats are inclined to name their computers in such a way that they can be readily identified as government or corporate machines. Knowledgeable system operators (sysops) at any site you visit can quickly identify visitors and, if they wish, thwart their research. Sysops often know more about the people knocking on their doors than you do about visitors at your home. Like you, they can balk at opening the door. They even have ways of ordering you off the property or, in extreme cases, of attacking you.

Be assured that, other than possibly at hobbyist websites, sysops are watching carefully at every site and the sites' users are monitored to see who is using it and how it is being used.

The research computer, mobile hybrid device, or tablet should have all of the programs and capabilities that are needed to access, and download from, the Internet. Since sysops and others on the Internet are usually able to see what you are doing, and even what programs or information are on your system, you want to keep any resources there as spare as possible. You will also want to move what you collect on the "outside" system to another, safer, location as quickly as possible. All information storage, analysis, and report production should be done on the other computer – the "inside" or production machine that is disconnected from the Internet.

The production system is used to process whatever things were originally downloaded onto the research computer. The production machine is used during the analysis phase and for creation of reports. Virtually everything done following the collection searches is performed on the production system. While it may occasionally have limited access to the Internet – perhaps for sending and reading materials, messages or reports – the production machine is never used to collect information from the Internet.

Information collected on the research computer is "airgapped" to the production machine, providing security. Airgapping is a safer way of moving material from one computer to another. Information to be transferred from the research computer is first saved to a disk or thumb drive. The disk or thumb drive with the collected information is then put into the production machine, run through an anti-virus program, and the saved information is transferred to the production machine's memory. When you are certain the material is safely on the production machine, the saved material can be safely erased from the research computer.

This method reduces the possibility of getting bugs and viruses on the production machine. More importantly, since the production machine is not connected to the Internet, hackers and snoopers can neither see what is on it nor can they break into it.

Storage Systems

In addition to two computers, you should have at least one, and preferably two, large drives to attach to the production computer for information storage. You will probably want to save your collected materials somewhere in addition to the production computer. If you are serious about the work you are doing, save your results to a backup drive that you keep in a secure place away from the production machine.

Since drives sometimes crash and the information on them cannot be recovered, having two external drives which mirror each other is the safest and most professional route. Navy SEALS have a saying – "One is none and two is one." Their math may be a little off, but they know what they are talking about. Your data needs to be kept securely in a central location and backed up someplace – also securely.

Some people in the field believe that storing files in the cloud is the – read that as THE – answer. Cloud computing – storing your documents and files on someone's mainframe somewhere else – is safe for most people. Probably. The stored material is backed up so there is relatively little chance of permanent loss. Probably!

It is not enough to caution researchers about using the cloud, users must know the reasons. Walking away from something that everyone else is touting – like the cloud – is hard to do. You have to understand why you should not use it. And why, if you are doing OSR, the cloud is a wonderful asset for searching, particularly when you are looking for other people's documents and the important information contained in the cloud.

First, understand that there is really no cloud. The cloud is a convenient lie. It is simply another computer system, connected to the Internet, with a huge storage capacity. The cloud is useful to hackers for a number of reasons that most people never consider. Any time you store material with someone else you are sending it to, and through, a system where it can be intercepted and traced back to you. If you are gathering any information for others, whether for government or a private concern, you want to reduce the chance of interception to zero. Even if the cloud machine you are using has first-rate security, your data is exposed to interception during movement. "Perimeter security" on the cloud is minimal to non-existent. VPNs are too-often not used when working in the cloud, making interdiction more likely. Your information becomes vulnerable to interception or even malware infection during transit. This threat exists at every node your information passes.

Because cloud-based applications and programs could be theoretically be installed and configured without the close-held permitting authority found on a single computer or system, and because many applications are "buggy," may contain undetected "zero day" threats, or simply give wide-ranging access permission, traditional safeguards are often considered weaker than on a well-secured personal system.

Besides the concerns about the inherent security of cloud servers, there are as-yet-undetermined legal questions about the ownership of some material in the cloud. Whether or how governments can legally demand access to anything, or everything, stored there also remains unresolved.

The proliferation of mobile phones, and their ease of use with cloud applications where the paucity of security is endemic, makes cloud use doubly dangerous. Technologically the cloud is often considered to be a breakthrough; from a security standpoint the cloud simply may be a bad break.

People like using the cloud because things posted there can be accessed from anywhere in the world – someone in London can have people in New York and Singapore look at the document, make comments or changes, provide input. It allows users to carry lighter, slimmer, devices. Cloud users don't need the digital horsepower of larger computers. In some cases cloud users don't have to purchase programs to do their work – they simply go to the cloud and use programs there. No muss, no fuss, nothing saved on their own systems.

In theory material stored on the cloud can be created and stored safely. But people make mistakes in proving or denying access, they mislabel things. In some cases they violate all the safety protocols they ever learned. Moreover, people who hack into others' sites often use anonymous cloud sites to post and distribute purloined proprietary documents. Rule of thumb: When the CIA starts using cloud sites to process, hold, and manage its most-important documents the cloud will be safe enough for OSC use.

Searching cloud storage systems, particularly for documents, can be highly useful. The cloud, because it is often thought of as a storehouse for documents of all kinds, can be usefully exploited.

People post many documents on the cloud that they wouldn't want to be public so that others of their team can edit or contribute to them – bad judgment. Some post to share with friends or co-workers, sending an e-mail to alert them of their posting. They believe their documents would never be found in the miasma of uploads – more bad judgment. Some may neglect to take their documents down after they have been viewed and massaged by co-workers – bad memory. It all adds up to bad security.

Often documents can be found in the backwaters of cloud websites by using the "site" command (explained later) and appropriate keywords. The "site" search is a mainstay of OSR operators.

Terms such as "confidential," "secret," "business confidential," "restricted," or "FOUO" (For Official Use Only), used along with a descriptive word or sets of words, in a site search can produce information that the people who wrote the documents never intended the public to see.

Site-type searches for "resumes," "curriculum vitae," or "CV's" usually have contact information. They can provide the types of personal history and information that a researcher could otherwise spent hours or even days compiling.

Other key words that can provide useful information are the identifiers of document types such as "doc," "docx," or "sdw" for documents, "pdf" for portable document files, "xls," "ods," or "sdc" for spreadsheets, and "ppt" or "odp" for presentations.

Storing the name and phone number of your favorite restaurant in London on the cloud is fine, but you have to ask yourself if bosses or clients would be happy if you stored their sensitive information there.

For researchers, the cloud is far less secure than keeping your downloaded material on your own disk drives. Of course, to prevent loss through fire, flood, theft or other disasters you will want to keep backup disk drives stored apart from one another, in safe places.

Sites, whether in or out of the cloud, can provide useful information when searching for information about resumes, businesses, technical subjects and much more. Document-rich sites are not always easy to search. Many site managers try to secure their sites and keep them safe. But even then, mistakes made by uploaders can reveal information that should be private. Some sites have a search bar; others do not, making searches difficult. In either case a "site:" type search is wise.

Key cloud areas to be searched include:
- DropBox: https://www.dropbox.com/
- GoogleDocs: https://www.google.com/docs/about/
- Scribd ($$$$): https://www.scribd.com/.

Another area to search for documents is the scores of pastebin-type sites. For this search some use **The Paste Bin Search Tool** at https://netbootcamp.org/pastesearch.html#gsc.tab=0&gsc.q=osint&gsc.sort=.

Others prefer to go to the various text storage sites and search them individually.

Some paste-type sites try hard to prevent random searching, others are used extensively by hackers who anonymously paste their stolen information online for the world to see. Familiarity with the quirks of paste-type sites pays good dividends.

Storage Systems (Programs)

Not everyone believes long-term information storage is important. Decide that for yourself. In making decisions about storage there are at least three questions you will need to answer:
- Who might want to see and use the information, as this impacts what information you want to store?
- What would be the best method for sharing, as this will impact the format in which you store the information?
- How long do you anticipate storing the information, or at what intervals will you delete stored information?

However you choose to retain your research, the metadata and any tags you attach are sometimes as important as the found content.

The ability to backtrack, cite, and date your research sometimes becomes essential.

Whatever their interest area, many OSR professionals find that saving information about important files – particularly multi-media files – to a database or spreadsheet eventually saves time during analysis and production. That database or spreadsheet may show:

- File name in your system
- Country/area of origination
- Subject
- Source
- Original name of file
- URL of item
- Type of file format
- Content (Short description)
- Origination date
- Collection date
- Language, if foreign, subtitled or translated
- Speaker(s) or narrator
- Clip duration
- Password protected Y/N, password if yes
- Text associated with the clip
- Comments of collector
- Pictures (1, 2, 3)
- Media metadata.

When there is any possibility the material will be used in court proceedings or similar legal situations you will probably want to save entire dated pages, with operating links. In this situation always consult the client to make certain that formats, proof of authenticity, and chain of custody will be acceptable to your client and the court.

SOFTWARE

The software mix on any computer reflects its intended use. Software on a computer either limits your search and production capabilities or opens the Internet for wide exploitation.

The research computer setup should be heavy on programs that will aid in finding, downloading, and saving the needed material. The research computer should generally stand alone, be independent, and should never be part of any client's network. There are very practical reasons for this. No matter how careful you are, the possibility exists you will get some kind of "bug" on the research machine. If malware gets into your system it can propagate to the client's entire network. It has happened that superiors have ordered "you must use our computer setup" only to find days or weeks later that their entire system has been compromised and dozens or even hundreds of computers are riven with bugs.

Also, when you are going through any business or government network the opposing sysops often can see who you are and pinpoint where you come from. It doesn't take a genius to tie your queries and the network you are using together. An intelligent sysop, or even an inspired one who is not that bright, can make educated guesses what you are doing and why.

Commercial Internet access for the research computer is a must in most cases. If any antagonist sysop is able to see – and even not-so-good ones can – that your search is coming from a government location or a competitor's corporate site that may be a major security problem for you, and for your client.

Whenever you are concerned that the sysops of any site you are going to, or through, might know who you are or what you are doing you should always be coming from a commercial ISP and appear to be browsing innocently. This might also be the time to use a throwaway computer or Virtual Machine ware and take strong security measures, such as using VPNs.

Anti-virus, anti-malware

Virus protection is an obvious need. Your anti-virus program must be robust. You need the best protection you can get. The same goes for firewalls.

The best anti-virus programs are not necessarily the most popular or widely-known. Check with your local computer gurus for advice on the anti-virus programs they find best; look for information about the outstanding ones on the Internet. Learn from those who have used them. And remember that just because someone in the IT shop insists on using a particular brand, that doesn't mean it fits your security needs. Your security needs may be much higher than the company's. Decisions about what anti-virus program to use may have been made by supervisors who know little and have researched the subject even less. All-too-often security decisions such as this are based on cost or the effectiveness of TV commercials. Bad protection is never a bargain.

You will also be well-advised to have an anti-spyware capability, one that will find and remove malware programs. Malware is a shorthand way of saying malicious software. There are different kinds. Some malware is only highly annoying while other types are highly dangerous.

Malware may track your interests and searches. That kind is as common as air. Less common types may allow others to access your computer system. Some malware takes over part or all of your computer, changing the search engine, or automatically displaying irritating pop-ups. Any kind of malware on your computer is an unacceptable security issue

Anti-malware capability is not always provided by even good anti-virus programs. You may have the best anti-virus program on the block yet be completely vulnerable to malware downloads. Your computer can sometimes be infected with malware – unknown to you – several times in a single day of searches.

While your anti-virus program may sit quietly in the background and will yell to you when it spots a potential problem, many anti-malware programs are much different. They often don't tell you when malware is being downloaded; instead they will find it and allow you to erase it only when you run the anti-malware program.

Beware of Internet pop-ups that suddenly appear, warning that your computer is infected with malware and if you will only download their free anti-malware program they will remove it. Some malware installers use that scare tactic to get you to download their own brand of malware, not an anti-malware program.

Using a Virtual Machine (VM) eliminates or reduces the malware threat, but for those not using VM ware many professionals, out of an abundance of caution, wipe their research computer clean with anti-malware programs daily, and in some special cases after each search.

Look up the available programs on the Internet with key words such as "anti-malware." Download anti-malware programs only from sites that have a good reputation.

VPNs

The research computer often also needs some cloaking capability – programs or methods that make your identity and location invisible, or at least uncertain. Virtual Private Networks, also known as VPNs, proxies, or anonymizers are intermediate sites designed to protect your identity. They change the network IP address from the one you are using to their own. Look them up on the Internet but be aware they do not all have the same capabilities. The best VPNs offer a variety of locations, particularly various countries around the world, where a researcher can seem to come out of on the Internet and where the person will appear to be located. This factor can be crucial in some international searches where sites restrict access to – or from – certain countries. Most VPNs require payment, though many offer the limited use of free versions. Some VPNs include:

- **Anonymizer Universal ($$$$):** https://www.anonymizer.com/
- **Anonymouse:** http://anonymouse.org/anonwww.html
- **Anonymouse Email:** http://anonymouse.org/anonemail.html
- **CyberGhost VPN ($$$$):** https://pro.cyberghostvpn.com/
- **Express VPN ($$$$):** https://www.expressvpn.com/
- **HideMyAss ($$$$):** https://www.hidemyass.com/
- **Hotspot Shield:** https://www.hotspotshield.com/free-vpn
- **Ipredator ($$$$):** https://www.ipredator.se/
- **Ironsocket ($$$$):** https://ironsocket.com/
- **JonDonym ($$$$)** https://anonymous-proxy-servers.net/
- **NordVPN ($$$$):** https://nordvpn.com/
- **PersonalVPN ($$$$):** https://www.personalvpn.com/
- **Private Internet Access ($$$$):** https://www.privateinternetaccess.com/pages/buy-vpn/
- **Private VPN ($$$$):** https://privatevpn.com/bestvaluevpn/
- **Private Tunnel ($$$$):** https://portal.privatetunnel.com/apps
- **Proton ($$$$):** https://account.protonvpn.com/signup
- **Proxify ($$$$):** https://proxify.com
- **ProXPN ($$$$):** https://secure.proxpn.com/
- **PureVPN ($$$$):** https://www.purevpn.com/
- **SaferVPN ($$$$):** http://www.safervpn.com
- **Strong VPN ($$$$):** https://strongvpn.com
- **Surf Anonymous Free:** http://download.cnet.com/Surf-Anonymous-Free/3000-2144_4-75300270.html
- **SurfEasy ($$$$):** http://www.surfeasy.com
- **Tunnel Bear ($$$$):** http://www.tunnelbear.com
- **Windscribe ($$$$):** https://windscribe.com
- **ZenVPN ($$$$):** https://zenmate.com/.

Browsers

Browsers are essential software. Without them you cannot access the key parts of Internet, particularly the Web. There are a variety of browsers in popular use.

Many researchers give little, if any thought to their browsers. They use whatever comes pre-loaded on their computer. For a number of reasons it is vital to have a variety of browsers – at least three to five – available. OSR professionals often install multiple web browsers on their research machines and use all of them interchangeably.

Firefox, Internet Explorer, Opera, Edge, Brave, and the Tor Bundle are among the popular choices for general browsing. Some browsers – among them Firefox, Tor, and Brave – are designed specifically to provide various levels of security. They limit or eliminate the amount of information being spewed out about you as you travel around the Internet. Specialty browsers have also been designed for other parts of the Internet, such as Newsgroups.

Decide what you want to use as your primary web browsers only after preliminary research, and always know why you are choosing whatever you are choosing. Articles that may help are easily found by looking up "web browser reviews" on the Web. But beware of articles and advice that appear to be marketing ploys by a browser provider.

Customize the browsers you choose to use, increasing their utility and security with add-ons. Whenever setting up a browser carefully set the preferences – choose the preferences that will make it best meet your needs, provide protection, and make your work easier.

Switch browsers during searches. Your identity, present location, searches, and interests can be determined by webmasters and others based on the information available to them, courtesy of your browser. Changing browsers between site visits makes identification of you more problematic.

You can also search for "user-agent switcher" on the Web and download an add-on that will spoof a variety of mobile devices, desktop browsers, and operating systems. That allows the researcher to "mix it up" and seemingly come at the same site from many different directions, from many different devices, using different operating systems and browsers.

Different browsers have different native capabilities. Many browsers allow add-ons, small programs that increase the utility of that browser. Add-ons, also called extensions or plug-ins, can make searching easier, more efficient, and more enjoyable. But add-ons can also be used by system operators trying to identify you.

A very few add-ons have been written to surreptitiously snag information from you. The spy types are not the biggest problem, however. The major difficulty is that extensions are often crafted by people with good intentions, people who have a smattering of programming knowledge but little security sense. Extensions are seldom written with security in mind. Too many add-ons have flaws that allow others to exploit the extension, thus exploiting the user.

Download and use add-ons understanding the trade-offs and possible consequences of using any particular one. A good idea, if not a perfect defense, is to check around the Internet for information on any extension you plan to use. Someone may have deconstructed it and reviewed it for possible security flaws.

Add-on icons, after they have been downloaded, can usually be found in the upper-right corner of the browser so they can be easily accessed and used.

Other Needs

On your research machine install all appropriate software needed to download, save, store, and play back the various text and non-text format types you expect to encounter. Web browsers may play or display a particular file, but that browser may not necessarily allow you to properly save the material for later use. Programs to capture or save material often include:

- **7-Zip:** https://www.7-zip.org/download.html or similar program to unzip files
- **Adobe Reader:** https://get.adobe.com/reader/ or similar program
- **CamStudio:** https://camstudio.org/, **Movavi Screen Capture:** http://www.movavi.com or similar program
- **CCleaner:** https://www.ccleaner.com/download or similar program (essential for security and keeping the system clean) such as
  BleachBit: https://www.bleachbit.org/download
- **Duplicate File Finder** or similar program (to keep your file system clean): https://www.ashisoft.com/
- Free Online OCR optical character reader, **SodaPDF** or similar programs to create searchable documents from PDFs https://www.sodapdf.com/
- **Libre Office:** https://www.libreoffice.org/download/download/, **Open Office**, https://www.openoffice.org/download/, Word, or similar word processing program
- **Libre Office Base:** https://www.libreoffice.org/discover/base/, Access, or a similar database program
- **PhotoShop ($$$$):** https://www.adobe.com/products/photoshop.html (to crop or sharpen pictures) or alternatives such as **GIMP:** https://www.gimp.org/
- Spreadsheet program such as those in **Libre Office:** https://www.libreoffice.org/download/download/
- Presentation program such as **Open Office Impress:** https://www.openoffice.org/product/impress.html
- **Swiff Player**, or similar program: http://swiff-player.findmysoft.com/
- **VLC Media Player** or similar player: https://www.videolan.org/vlc/download-windows.html

- **Windows Media Player:**
  https://support.microsoft.com/en-us/help/14209/get-windows-media-player.

In the event that you do not have a program on your computer that will allow you to read a particular document type, the **Online Document Viewer** at https://onlinedocumentviewer.com/Welcome/ may resolve the problem.

Investigate and use other useful programs, techniques, and sites for researching, such as:

- **Malwarebytes** or similar program for thwarting malware: https://www.malwarebytes.com/mwb-download/
- **WinRAR** (almost essential for viewing a variety of video types): https://www.win-rar.com/download.html?&L=0
- **Java:** https://java.com
- **JavaScript:** https://www.javascript.com/
- **BurnAware,** or similar program (to burn disks): http://www.burnaware.com/download.html
- **LogMeIn ($$$$),** or similar "rescue" program with "long-distance repair over Internet" capability, but make certain your computer guru also uses the same one. https://www.logmein.com/
- **HTTrack Website Copier:** https://www.httrack.com/
- **Downforeveryoneorjustme** is a site that checks to see whether a site is actually down, whether you are being excluded by the system operator, or if the page cannot be displayed for other reasons https://downforeveryoneorjustme.com/.

Depending what browser you are using, look up "turn off browser referral" to prevent any site you are accessing from learning who you are and what you using.

If you do not feel you have enough information or sufficient experience with OSR to know what you need in setting up your own research machine, there are a number of programs and sites that include the information, set-ups, or Web reconnaissance links you might need. They can provide you with a head start. And even if you are confident about your own setup, they are worth reviewing to see how they might supplement your own system:

- **Awesome OSINT:** https://github.com/jivoi/awesome-osint
- **Bellingcat's Online Investigation Toolkit:** https://docs.google.com/document/d/1BfLPJpRtyq4RFtHJ oNpvWQjmGnyVkfE2HYoICKOGguA/edit
- **Citizen Evidence Lab (Bellingcat-type tools):** https://citizenevidence.org/
- **CentralOps (Internet utilities):** https://centralops.net/co/
- **Freeality:** http://www.freeality.com/
- **Maltego ($$$$):** https://www.paterva.com/web7/
- **OSINT Framework:** https://osintframework.com/
- **OSINT Tools Comparison:** https://docs.google.com/spreadsheets/d/18U1qcaPaqIF8ER VLI-g5Or3gUbv0qP_-JUtc0pbEs0E/edit#gid=0
- **OSIRT (Law enforcement only):** http://www.osirtbrowser.com/
- **Recon-ng (Reconnaissance tool):** https://bitbucket.org/LaNMaSteR53/recon-ng
- **Sam Spade 1.14:** https://sam-spade.en.lo4d.com/
- **Spiderfoot**: https://www.spiderfoot.net/download/
- **Splunk ($$$$):** https://www.splunk.com/
- **StartMe:** https://start.me/p/wMdQMQ/tools
- **ToolboxToolbox (Everything for everybody):** http://www.toolboxtoolbox.com/
- **YouGetSignal (Multiple testing tools):** https://www.yougetsignal.com/.

The production computer's setup is somewhat different from the research computer because this one performs a different function. The production system requires storage and indexing programs for research, as well as programs to produce reports based on any material you might airgap from the research computer. Some of these programs will duplicate those on the research system.

Virus and anti-spyware protection remain a must on the production computer, even if it is never connected to the Internet. You are transferring material that was on the Internet. If it is buggy you do not want the production machine, and certainly not the files you send to a client or boss, to be infected by malware or spyware.

Microsoft's Word, a clone, or some similar multi-featured word processing program, is usually at the heart of the production system.

Commercial file indexing programs, like **Copernic Desktop Search ($$$$)** at http://www.copernic.com/en/products/desktop-search/, is useful in helping to find files on the computer or drive. There are few things more frustrating than remembering that sometime last month you downloaded and saved the exact information you need, but cannot now find it.

Develop a consistent system for naming your files to make it easier to find files. To eliminate the computer inserting a % sign between words of the file name, do not separate them with spaces when naming files. Instead use an underline/space (_) symbol if you decide to separate the words of the file title in the folder or, even better, runthemtogetherlikethis. Use all lower case letters, avoid capital letters. Use the actual URL for the last part of the address when saving to your computer; put your own title in front of the URL, separated from the URL by a hyphen. Develop, and be consistent in using, a standard format such as:
- country_group_date_source-url
- author/publisher_title-url.

Other highly-useful programs for the production computer include:
- **CCleaner:** https://www.ccleaner.com/download or similar program (essential for security and keeping the system clean) such as

BleachBit: https://www.bleachbit.org/download
- **Duplicate File Finder** or similar program (to keep your file system clean): https://www.ashisoft.com/
- Free Online OCR optical character reader, **SodaPDF** or similar programs to create searchable documents from PDFs https://www.sodapdf.com/
- **PhotoShop ($$$$):** https://www.adobe.com/products/photoshop.html (to crop or sharpen pictures) or alternatives such as **GIMP:** https://www.gimp.org/
- Spreadsheet program such as in **Libre Office:** https://www.libreoffice.org/download/download/
- Presentation program such as **Open Office Impress:** https://www.openoffice.org/product/impress.html
- **Swiff Player**, or similar program: http://swiff-player.findmysoft.com/
- **VLC Media Player** or similar player: https://www.videolan.org/vlc/download-windows.html
- **Windows Media Player:** https://support.microsoft.com/en-us/help/14209/get-windows-media-player.

In less-than-ideal situations, when you have only a single computer and don't have a Virtual Machine installed, consider an alternative that is relatively safe: Employ a hang-on hard disk drive connected to your research computer and use it in place of the production machine.

When you have only a single machine make doubly certain that all security programs and mechanisms on your computer are in place and operating. Clear the memory and run an anti-virus program; do an anti-spyware search often throughout the research sessions, particularly before going from one site to another and always after visiting an adversary's site.

When using only a single computer with a hang-on drive, completely disconnect the computer from the Internet at the conclusion of your research session. Run anti-virus and anti-spyware programs. Connect the hang-on hard drive. Move (do not copy) all of the downloaded research material to the separate hard drive. Then do all your analysis and production from, and on, that separate disk drive.

When finished with the analysis, report, or the other production activity, back up the material – perhaps to another hard drive, thumb drive, or disk depending on the situation. Remember that two is one and one is none if and when you suffer a disk failure. Thoroughly clean the hang-on hard drive with a suitable program. Then physically disconnect the hang-on drive before cleaning the computer and its internal hard drive with a suitable program. Finally, run your anti-virus and anti-spyware programs prior to reconnecting to the Internet.

At the end of the day wipe all empty space at least three times using a suitable program, such as:

        CCleaner: https://www.ccleaner.com/download

        BleachBit: https://www.bleachbit.org/download.

Your Local Library

Not long ago, libraries were a place to house a collection of shelved information. Librarians have since expanded their specialized field of Information Literacy. Libraries are now are part of a world-wide information resource network. Some skill sets in using a library are now undergoing changes and expanding because of the changes in technology, but most of the research methods used by information seekers 100 years ago remain highly useful.

Library cards, and at least a passing acquaintance with both the research staff and the holdings of nearby libraries, are essential.

Research librarians are not there to do your work, but they can be immeasurably helpful in getting you on track when the path seems dim, or the road has disappeared altogether. They can be helpful in solving knotty problems. Like you, they have to be familiar with out-of-box thinking and ways to get information quickly. Consider them to be important consultants in your work.

Libraries today have access to everything from documents and books to databases and multi-media. It is essential to become familiar with both the extent and the limits of your library's holdings. But understand local limits can be overcome. Interlibrary loans will stretch the resource possibilities of any library worldwide, far beyond even the best local resources.

Many professional researchers develop extensive knowledge of, and contacts in, at least two local libraries – often a community library and college one. Some add a third library, one that specializes in their specific field of interest.

Knowledge of a library's reference section is critically important. Walk through and see what is there for the asking.

For those who find trade journals and associations useful, check out *The Standard Periodical Directory*. This resource is helpful for finding topic-specific trade journals. Trade associations may provide much information and sponsor events. Libraries often have books like *The Encyclopedia of Associations* by Gale Publishers at http://www.gale.com. Books such as this can provide information on trade associations. Many business-oriented researchers find there is value in publications such as the *National Trade and Professional Associations Directory,* which can be found at https://www.associationexecs.com/National-Trade-and-Professional-Associations-Directory. Photocopy applicable listings of association catalogs and trade journals.

Get to actually know, and talk to, the reference librarians. They have deep knowledge in many areas, particularly as it relates to their geographic or specialty area.

At the same time be aware of special libraries, whether near or far, that may focus their collections on your subject area. Special libraries may be private or government libraries, or libraries within corporations. When you can identify the special libraries that deal with your subject it makes sense to see how, or whether, you can work with them and access their collections. Ask. The worst answer you can get is "no."

***

Project:
In your SOP write down the Web browsers you will use and why you feel those are best for your purposes. Search for and download information on all browsers you will use to the Browsers section of your SOP.

Project:
In your SOP, list factors you will use when choosing equipment, software and storage. Write down any programs and add-ons you plan to use for your computer(s). Decide where various programs and research materials will be stored on your computer.

Project:
In the SOP list the programs you will use on your research computer, including the reasoning on why you will use them. If there are major types of programs you plan to avoid explain in a few sentences why you do not want to use them. Look at the categories above such as anti-virus, anti-malware, anonymizers, audio-visual and download storage in making your choices.

Project:
As part of the SOP write down libraries you will use and any special materials you may want to use, their hours and phone numbers.

Project:
In the SOP list the programs you will use on your production computer, including the reasoning on why you will use them. If there are major types of programs you plan to avoid, explain in a few sentences why you do not want to use them. Look at the categories above such as anti-virus, anti-malware, anonymizers, audio-visual and download storage in making your choices.

5. The Tradecraft of Security

The Information Age requires us to be informationally daring, to accept reasonable risks as we garner the information that we and those around us need. But daring is the same as foolish.

Security should never be a bet or a gamble, a reliance solely on luck. Professional bettors are not gamblers; they know the odds, watch for tells, and understand how to count cards. What some call luck can often be controlled, even manipulated. Know-how and the mastery of the key techniques are skills that often masquerade as "luck."

Tradecraft removes much, but never all, of the need for luck in security – just as it does in gambling. Tradecraft alters the odds in any gamble, making a move a calculated risk.

The Internet, by concentrating public and private communications in a single pipeline, has become a surveillance and attack apparatus *par excellence*. Whatever you are doing may interest anyone from garden variety snoops, hackers, political parties, criminal groups, and corporate giants to law enforcement and even intelligence agencies of unfriendly foreign powers. The latter groups may be using mass surveillance techniques to invade your privacy. They want to pick up and save every 1, every 0, of yours that crosses the Internet. They do that, not necessarily because they now suspect you of anything nefarious or are particularly interested in what you are doing and thinking. Rather they want to save everything they can acquire because they never know whether, eventually, in some indefinable future, they may be interested in you, your associates, or your beliefs and activities. Their interest may be "just in case."

If there is a Golden Rule of security tradecraft it is this: Avoid attracting attention to yourself or to your information sources!

Virtually every facet of security tradecraft comes back, in one way or another, to this golden rule. Make yourself less visible and you will also be less vulnerable, less open to compromise by those who would harm you or your sources. Particularly when the research is about anyone's adversary – whether your own or a client's – the standard is to conduct only surreptitious sorties for information.

Your identity or the identity of your employer, once revealed, cannot be put back in the toothpaste tube. Anonymity, once lost, is irrecoverable. You must practice security from the start, or even before you start searching, for maximum effectiveness. While it is hard to break anything on the Internet, poor security procedures when using the Internet are guaranteed to break your anonymity.

A result vs. risk equation always exists on the Internet, or wherever you do research. The important question is how to improve the result and optimize the opportunity to find information, but reduce the risk while doing so.

In the constantly evolving war between Internet users and Internet snoopers, assume that technology – by itself – is not the answer to providing security. It would be nice if you could put some program on your computer that would eliminate all risks, but you cannot. In many cases, the more you put on your computer the more direct the threat.

Tradecraft that layers technology and techniques is a more reliable solution to the basket of risks that grows exponentially over the years.

Tradecraft is lessons learned, often by hard-won experience, that are passed from one professional to another. Tradecraft has proved effective, often over many generations. While tradecraft rules are occasionally broken successfully, they should only be ignored for good reason and with full knowledge of the dangers of non-observance. Compromise on security tradecraft and, sooner or later, your own security will be compromised!

Tradecraft tries, through various means, to keep you invisible, to assure that you and your work are unseen – or at the very least misunderstood – by your opponents. Sherlock Holmes certainly understood the need to remain unseen and misunderstood, saying in *The Adventure of the Speckled Band* "...I only trust that our little friend will not suffer from her imprudence in allowing this brute to trace her."

Security tradecraft:
- Minimizes risk to ourselves and everyone we deal with
- Protects our families
- Protects our important sources and their families
- Protects materials, plans, and procedures
- Denies opponents any information about **our own** vulnerabilities.

Security tradecraft is not like a guarantee on a car; it is more akin to proper maintenance – do it and the chances of major problems are lessened.

Threats are diminished by tradecraft; they never vanish completely, no matter how good the security plan or tradecraft. There is no perfect security plan, a reality that makes security planning highly challenging.

In reality the "one-percent of the one-percent" – intrusions by capable national security agencies – are difficult, and in some cases impossible, to effectively defeat. Standard, even enhanced, security techniques may be insufficient in the face of national treasuries and secret technological powers. If you are faced with that level of scrutiny you will need something beyond this book to beat back a dedicated government or criminal intrusion. But for the majority of adversaries a thought-though defense suffices.

Security is extremely individualized. The problems facing one person are different – in most cases far different – than those facing another researcher.

People may try to sell you a "one size fits all" security plan; no such plan actually exists. Needs range anywhere from being discreet to being totally secret.

From the outset you must tailor your own protection, crafting one based on your unique circumstances and your situation.

Nothing you see in this chapter should be considered "doctrine." Rather, think in terms of "best practices" for conducting investigative searches. What follows are "thinking points."

You must decide early-on what dangers you and your information shop face and whether you want to try for online anonymity – there are often very obvious reasons to be anonymous – or if you will instead settle for some degree of privacy when doing research on the Internet and elsewhere.

There is a marked difference between privacy and anonymity. A reasonable privacy level – there are many levels of privacy – is relatively easy to achieve. True anonymity is difficult, perhaps even impossible, for the average user. Anonymity means no one – NO ONE – is able to see what the user is doing and then tie that activity back to the user's identity.

Anonymity does not mean that no one can see or record what is being done, rather that no one can connect you or your IP address to whatever activity they do see.

Information professionals usually strive for anonymity but expect that in many cases they will probably only achieve a high degree of privacy, one hopefully at a level approaching anonymity.

That said, don't be lulled even by the word "privacy" and what seems like promises of digital privacy.

"Privacy modes" on browsers often simply disable some cookie collection features and prevent the gathering of information about websites that you visit. Engaging browser "privacy modes" does not prevent the internet service provider (ISP), search engines, or the sites you visit from seeing you and recording your activity. Still, never reject offers of any privacy-producing feature or technique. Protecting your privacy always goes part way toward increasing your security, but never make the mistake of equating privacy with anonymity.

Security falls into one of three levels:
- Basic security takes into account all major threat types.
- Enhanced security covers basic security, plus threats based on known specific actors.
- High security covers both Basic and Enhanced security plus likely threats from organizations, governments and adversaries you may not know about or have anticipated.

Many parts of your life and work need protection:
- Notes, downloads, searches, and other resources
- Identity of the sources and people you deal with
- Families – yours and the families of sources
- Plans
- Day-to-day activities and operations.

People are important. Many people may need protection:
- You
- Your clients and associates
- Information sources
- Anyone with knowledge of your activities
- Anyone considered close to you, your client, or your sources.

As you go along you will discover the unpleasant truth: Others who have no skin in the game may nonetheless insist they have the decisive voice in setting **your** security level.

Often you are denied the final word about your own security and safety in your work. Organizations you work for, or are associated with, often insist that they will determine your security plan. They want to decide what level of security you will have, based on whatever they deem to be "safe enough." They can easily shortchange you and your safety.

When others have a hand in setting your security level, even before beginning to draft your own security plan, it is wise to develop – at least in the back of your mind – some idea of how you will deal with any differences between your actual needs and your needs as perceived by your organization. You may end up following their path, you may change or augment their program, or ...?

If you don't think you need any help or improvement in your security, just look at one area which we will expand on later – your own computer. Can the managers of those sites you contact tell much about you when you are on their pages? If they can identify you or tell where you are, you are vulnerable.

Unfortunately your Internet *persona* identifies you as an individual among the millions of Internet users. It speaks about your computer, where you are from, where you are going, what you are doing, and even your methods of searching.

Why is this true?

Your computer and any system that you contact exchange detailed information about the hardware and software available on your system. The other system needs to know the best way configure the information it sends so that it will display properly for you. It asks question; your system gives the answers.

System operators take advantage of this information exchange. By triangulating the characteristics and the information gleaned from a user's browser such as operating system, screen resolution, and computer model a SYSOP can identify individual visitors. Some studies have shown that Web operators can identify a single user up to 99 percent of the time.

Although it seems intellectually incomprehensible, there are enough "tells" that out of the millions of Internet users it is often possible to build an accurate user profile and boil down the identity of the site user to a single person.

Some call that online profile or *persona* a footprint; think of it as a fingerprint. Maybe you can't prevent yourself from leaving a fingerprint, but you can smudge the fingerprint by turning off – or on – features of your browsing so that you become less of an individual and more like a generic visitor.

Many useful sites will check for elements of the online *persona* for you, but they do not all cover the same areas. It is wise to use several such checking sites to see what information you are leaking before going to any research location, or doing any online work – particularly if you plan to visit adversarial sites. Decisions about the security level depend on the need for secrecy and for deniability about the search.

Useful tools, ones that will tattle on the ways your own browser and your computer tell tales about you, include:
- **Am I Unique:** https://amiunique.org/fp
- **Browserleak:** https://browserleaks.com/
- **Browserleak Social Media Detection:** https://browserleaks.com/social
- **Browser Mirror:** http://browserspy.dk/headers.php
- **Browser Spy:** http://browserspy.dk/
- **Check Your Persona:** http://navigators.com/cgi-bin/persona.pl

- **DigiCrime:** http://www.digicrime.com/noprivacy.html
- **Evercookie:** https://samy.pl/evercookie/
- **IP Check:** http://ip-check.info/?lang=en
- **IPchicken:** http://ipchicken.com/
- **IP Leak:** https://ipleak.net/
- **IP Leak Privacy Test:** http://ipleak.com/full-report/
- **IP Location:** https://www.iplocation.net/
- **MrWhoer:** https://whoer.net/
- **My IP Info:** http://myipinfo.net/
- **Panopticlick**: http://panopticlick.eff.org/
- **Personna Tips:** http://www.navigators.com/persona.html
- **UniqueMachine:** http://uniquemachine.org/
- **What is My IP Address:** https://whatismyipaddress.com/.

Your computer use is only one of many areas where your security may be at risk. (See Appendix D. Tradecraft of Security, for more information.)

The Basic Security Level

At the most basic level there are three security threats:

- **Environmental** – Fire, flood, power disruptions, natural disasters, and temperature extremes are always threat possibilities. Solution: Take standard precautions and back up research results. Make certain the backup copy is in a location where any threat won't destroy the backup as well as the original.

- **Mechanical** – Disk failure and power surges happen. Solution: Use a surge protector, know what to do when you encounter signs of hard disk disintegration such as grinding sounds. Back up new material to secure locations daily.

- **Human** – Sites, site administrators, webmasters, hackers, search subjects, governments, or insiders can all be threats. All of these can steal information, see what you are doing, or attack back. Solution: Take good security precautions and employ proper procedures.

Successful security plans are based on a security mindset, a way of thinking that may be uncommon among most Internet users but is not paranoid either. "Normal" people seldom concern themselves with intensified security when using the Internet. They sign on, expect their anti-virus to work, look for information, and sign off with scant thought about any danger. Researchers are not "normal users."

For any researcher, ignoring the need for proper security can be dangerous. At the same time over-concern about security can immobilize the research effort. A security mindset allows you to take a realistic approach. It allows you to find solutions that fit your actual security situation.

When the environmental and mechanical threats have been met, it is time to solve the thorniest problem, the human concern.

Business and large online services are considered by many to be the biggest snoopers; firms try to achieve targeted advertising. If they can improve their profits by tracking you, your individual interests, your likes, dislikes, monetary habits, and searches, be assured that those businesses and online services will be among the first to try to collect, buy, and sell information about you. They, governments, and even hackers have effective toolkits designed specifically to shred your anonymity and privacy.

The would-be trackers of your activity are legion. Governments, from China and Russia to the United States, want to collect and save a record of everything everybody does on the Internet. Hackers, some of whom are employed by other sinister characters or have bad motives of their own, also have interests in the material that researchers see or collect. Hackers may work for governments, business, or their own interests.

Trackers and intruders of all kinds pose a threat. Beat the snoopers at the outset and, as a general rule, you are well on your way to achieving online security. Where possible, avoid sites known to be dangerous. Look-up sites that rate the security of many Web locations include **SafeWeb** at https://safeweb.norton.com/.

Some add-ons to your browsers can boost security when properly selected and consistently used.

A Firefox add-on that gives you a security rating about the sites you visit is **WOT:** https://www.mywot.com/.

Make it difficult or impossible for snoopers to watch you while you are going to websites. Make your site requests over the Internet more secure with **HTTPEverywhere** at https://www.eff.org/https-everywhere. This add-on encrypts your requests, making it unlikely or impossible for anyone ay intermediate locations to see where you are going and what you have asked for from a website.

Ghostery, found at https://www.ghostery.com/, **UBlockOrigin** at https://ublock.org/, and **NoScript** at https://noscript.net/, are add-ons that can identify and block tracking threats.

The **Privacy Badger** of the Electronic Freedom Foundation at https://privacy-badger.en.softonic.com/ can help solve many cookie problems.

Disconnect at https://disconnect.me/ blocks your computer from signing on unbeknownst to you and sending back information to trackers that are associated with a web page you are visiting.

Your Defense
A good defense is a planned defense, one based on knowledge about your critical information, the risk, the threat, your vulnerability, and your possible countermeasures. Understand these components of security, your own security. They are the foundation you need when building a security structure tailored to your unique needs.

- **Critical Information** – Information that could harm a researcher, the organization, its work, or any of the other people you identify as needing protection
- **Risk** – An event that could cause damage
- **Threat** – Any adversary who has both hostile intent and capability
- **Vulnerability** – Any weakness of yours which could be exploited
- **Countermeasure** – A procedure to reduce vulnerability.

Start writing your security plan by answering these questions:
- Who are your adversaries, or potential adversaries?
- What do they want?
- How do they get it?
- How could you thwart them?
- What else can go wrong?

Understanding the identity, desires, and capabilities of adversaries or potential adversaries, is critical. So is an understanding of how to thwart them. Sometimes "what else can go wrong" is knowable – often it is not.

With an understanding of the adversary, it is time to look at your own situation. Use a handful of inward-looking security steps:
- Identify critical information to be protected (What do I need to protect?)
- Analyze threat avenues (What are they?)
- Analyze vulnerabilities (What are my weaknesses?)
- Assess risks (How great are the dangers?)
- Apply countermeasures (How do I reduce the risks?)

The information that an adversary needs to prevent your success – Critical Information – includes:
- Your interests
- Your limitations

- Your specific plans: who, what, when, where, why, how
- Your products and capabilities
- Your client information
- The identity of your personnel and families
- The identity of any contacts and their families
- Your security steps and methods.

Countermeasures

Adversaries can be stopped by "countermeasures" such as:
- Communications protection techniques
- Policies
- Alertness and awareness
- Reasonable suspicions.

Countermeasures are woven into researchers' way of life. Consider the possible threat whenever you use the computer or phone, answer a stranger's questions, discuss your work in public places, or engage in social networking.

Security issues are complex. They vary from resource to resource, and require both time and study in order to implement adequate safety measures. We strongly recommend that anyone doing information intelligence read the Security Overview in Appendix D. Researchers need to look religiously into both the level of threat they face and the ways they can resolve any real, potential, and serious, problems.

***

Project:
Identify and list in your SOP the environmental, mechanical, and human threats you face.

Project:
In the security section of your SOP list your critical information, risk, threat, vulnerability, and countermeasure assessment.

Project:
After considering the security issues outlined above, and those in Appendix D, detail your own security plan in your SOP and confirm that you have carried out all parts of it to this point.

Project:
Determine and list in your SOP the browser add-ons you will use to prevent snoopers from seeing your online activities. Download the add-ons.

Project:
In the SOP identify a legal resource you would consult when questions arise about your own research activities. Include phone numbers, addresses, and current fee schedules.

Project:
In the security section of your SOP download, save – and read – a copy of every EULA or Terms of Service Agreement that you accepted. You never know when you may need to refer back to an original copy of the agreement you signed or agreed to.

6. Planning For Your Success

Overview

Amid the inevitable confusion of the Internet it's easy to start research projects with more velocity than direction, to just jump in and "git goin.'" At the same time, at the outset of a project, it often seems like you are engaging in a nebulous guessing game. But neither manic abandon nor abandoned hope gets the researcher very far.

While serendipitous success does happen, carefully planned and orderly research are more likely to tear the needed information from the disorder of the Internet.

Planning refines and defines the workflow. It imposes order on the anarchy of the Internet. Effective searches are usually systematic. They are structurally comprehensive. Improvised or impulsive searches seldom lead to balanced conclusions.

There are defined steps in OSR. Each one is an inflection point.

Sherlock Holmes was a staunch advocate of defined steps. He was always methodical, reminding his sidekick in *The Adventure of the Crooked Man,* that "'you know my methods, Watson. There is not one of them which I did not apply to the inquiry. And it ended by my discovering traces, but very different ones from those which I had expected.'" Holmes stressed in that story that any research work should be conducted in a defined order. In that case, long before the time of computers and the Web, he went down his own list in the case. "Always look at the hands first, Watson. Then cuffs, trouser-knees, and boots." Holmes' list from that case will not work for today's researcher, but it leaves us with a clear idea of the value of both planning and sequencing.

The "5 Ps of Success"– Proper Planning Prevents Poor Performance – apply everywhere. In research, the observance of those 5 Ps certainly pay off.

Good research is not carried out by the seat of the pants or "b'guess and b'god." In reality, any failure to plan is often the same thing as planning to fail. When searches are unplanned the searcher careens around the information universe enroute to "destination: failure." The researcher ends up feeling, and actually being, frustrated and ineffectual.

Plans are starting points. They start somewhere promising and let you know what you are going to do next, and at the step after that. Plans allow you to go to lunch without wondering where you will pick up. They allow you to sleep at night counting sheep rather than ruminating about where to begin the next day's work. But plans are not carved in marble. They have limitations. In real life plans sometimes have to be changed on the fly as the research proceeds. Some plans will need to be changed in big ways, others in small matters.

Strictly mechanical approaches fail, either quickly or eventually. Researchers cannot go on autopilot if they hope to succeed. There is much truth in the saying that "no plan survives the first contact with the enemy."

Flexibility is always essential. Plans are seldom static. They may, and probably will, change. Threadbare ideation is no match for constant and continued rethinking of the needs, the time window, and the assets that are available. Static plans fail; they fail quickly.

Progress requires a constantly-moving review. In a real sense, there are three days that matter on OSR. They are:
- Yesterday
- Today
- Tomorrow.

Yesterday requires cognizance of what parts of the project has already been done and where the material is being safely held.

Today requires an understanding of what needs to be carried out immediately to move the project along and what resources and techniques have to be used next.

Tomorrow requires a review of the work of yesterday and today to see if the current plan should be followed or if alterations and improvements are needed in light of what has been discovered, whether that is hard information or holes in understanding.

Effective research is often Medusa-headed. Amateurs will ineptly flail about because it is not unusual for several directions to present themselves simultaneously. What road to take then? What seemed to be so simple a minute ago is suddenly turned into a skein of complexities.

Facts are where you find them, and you find them scattered amidst many search strands. For that reason good research is planned to cover the many filaments of a successful search. Achieving critical mass of factual information is more difficult than many think because that critical mass is composed of so many strands. Planning to achieve critical mass involves knowing what information you need, for whom, from whom, where to find it, meeting deadlines, what assets you will use, as well as right and left limits – all the while keeping the entire process friction-free.

Creative skills are needed to achieve the goals, organize and ladder the many resources, and develop inventive methods of acquisition. A pre-defined process allows unstructured data to be turned into useful information through the manipulation of all of those factors, and others. Concrete research structures and the use of well-defined processes help promote success in information gathering. They prevent information myopia and eventually bolster self-confidence.

The overall research process involves three major steps:
- Collect and store information
- Analyze the stored information
- Produce and distribute actionable information/report.

The role of "time" throughout the process is nothing short of challenging. All the steps must be accomplished in an often-fixed – and occasionally reasonable – time window.

OSR is almost always time-bound. Thinking through the entire process, and the individual steps, prior to starting collection allows accurate setting of the time parameters. While "getting right down to business" often seems to be the most attractive alternative, in the final analysis that approach is often a time-waster. It is far better to spend some of that most-precious commodity, time, in planning your approach to each research project.

Planning is not an extra step; it saves more time than it takes.

Know exactly what you are searching for – that's obviously a key thing. But then figure out where the information is, who has it, and how you can obtain it. If you have been following a particular subject for an extended period and are collecting documents in your own library you may discover that the information you need is buried among your already-saved materials. Never overlook obvious sources, including your own resources. Spend time strategizing.

Know exactly what you are searching with. Consider your search assets. It makes sense, when developing your plan, to check the reputation of online resources before adding programs, utilities, or sites to your SOP. Crowd-sourcing may be useful in some cases. The community can be a useful arbiter on the utility and security of virtually any part of, or anything on, the Internet.

Many top-flight researchers create a table that includes – under a heading that lists the problem statement and learning goals – information on:

- What is already known
- What must be found out
- What resources, tools and methods will be used
- What you hope to learn.

Scope and Focus must be kept in mind. Both are closely related to the time issue.

Think scope.... How extensive do you want the research to be? Will your time window allow an extensive scope that looks at everything touching your subject?

Think focus.... What kinds of information do you want? Unless you are researching a new subject every day, think in terms of finding a number of good sites or information resources that deal extensively with your subject. But never forget the non-Internet portion of the information spectrum and the sources there that specialize in your field.

Understanding the search structure of the web sites you visit is often essential to success. Learn how each website you use is structured and how the results are filtered, whether it is a tool you use or a resource to search. Know the ins-and-outs of your commonly used websites and resources; develop expertise in the use of each one, not just an ephemeral ability. Understand the structure and the details of their operation and use. Learn to read the ripples.

When you are looking for information on a person, typing the name, email or phone number into a search box might seem like a reasonable starting point. But if you are dealing with a concept or product, think organizationally. Laser-like focus, concentration on the subject alone, is sometimes required but accept that sometimes such a strict focus can be self-defeating. The periphery of a subject can prove to be as, or more, important than the individual, group, or organization.

Going further afield is not necessarily going astray. Knowing the associates, friends, supporters, workers, and business or financial interests and contacts – presently and in the past or foreseeable future – may be key. In some cases consider if there are online, or even off-line, groups or "organizations" that deal with the subject, or which a person may be a member of.

Is it likely someone wrote a university paper on the subject? Are there organizations devoted to the subject? Do government agencies play any role? Who are the major players in the field and do they have web pages or post somewhere on social media? Sometimes even bit players in a field may unintentionally leak things on social media; it may be worthwhile keeping one eye cocked for any such verbal meanderings, particularly on social media.

Depending on the amount of time available – and the centrality of the person, group, concept, or organization to your information goal – you have to decide on the depth and breadth of your search. Everyone and everything aren't equal. Decide, in advance, how much time, expense, and energy you can afford to devote to any individual, concept, group, or organization. Stick with that decision unless you have a reason, one that is clear enough to put down on paper, to change it. Nonetheless, don't be afraid to alter your time allocation when new information changes the equation.

Get organized before you begin your project. Plan how and where to stockpile records and information. Even material that doesn't hold promise at the moment can become important later. Create folders and subfolders, both digital and fiber-based, even before you know what to name them or how you will fill them.

Spreadsheets are useful for many things, including creating time lines, contact lists etc.

Collect resumes and biographies; see when anything changes by using cached copies and setting up change alerts.

Develop link diagrams.

Create a separate planning spreadsheet. Use it to measure your own progress and to serve as an outline of any planned future research. Effective organization now saves time and frustration later.

Virtually any subject can be expertly "covered" by good OSR specialists. Even rust could be developed as a full-time specialty.

But always be careful. Gold mines and rabbit holes sometimes look alike at first glance.

Never be afraid to explore new and promising areas that come up while exploring. The "look-around rule" applies to any page, site or resource you visit. Always look around to see if there is anything useful and related. There may be embedded links or report titles in the copy, there may be organizations cited at the bottom. Look around carefully, but always have the courage to say "stop" when the focus shifts away from your research topic. It's far too easy to get "out of focus." Rabbit holes, no matter how arresting the information in them, are not useful to you. Think directly about your subject and the search requirements. Avoid any unremunerative information expeditions.

Develop a list of sites related to the research subject, people to call or write, or whose names and work you could research. Know how to reach key people through the mail, social media, email, phone, or any other communication medium. Develop and keep resource lists. When sites or resources appear to be particularly valuable keep Web Reference Reports on those locations, as described earlier.

Information-mining researchers often find resources that must be "guarded" – visited often, perhaps daily – to get a baseline. After all, you have to know what is usual before you can determine what is abnormal. Other locations to be guarded are useful sources that appear likely to provide valuable information in the future. They must be monitored continually with "Alerts" or visited at defined periods, looking for any website changes, new postings, or information.

Use Appendix F to brainstorm. Take the time to physically write out your generic search plan, perhaps similar to the one in Appendix G, and follow it. But remember, plans should always be adaptable. No plan should be considered strictly linear. Plans are not checklists. Change the plan when necessary, but only for good reasons.

When you follow a search plan the things you should be doing or looking at are far less likely to be overlooked or to slip through the cracks.

Use the Internet, but in lengthy projects make at least one trip to any libraries where you have access and see what books and other resources may be available to you there. Photocopy useful book or magazine pages and those that list thought-leaders in the field or other major players, whether people or institutions.

It is important to have patience with long-term projects, no matter how soon the results are desired or demanded by others. Information comes at its own rate, and that is seldom gazelle-speed. The more obscure the information is, the longer it takes to find it. Tech-savvy targets or those large enough to afford a large digital online team may be better equipped to hide the information you need.

Learn the structure of whatever you are studying, see how the pieces fit together, learn who the important people are, why they are important, and what they think.

The "go to" people may not be listed in any table of organization. Contacts – whether people, groups, books, or web sites – are often important. If you are not restricted from developing contacts as part of your own infoquest, the "contact and exchange ideas" part may take longer but will probably be worthwhile. Knowledgeable people are often part of a closed circle that may be suspicious of outsiders seeking information. At the very least people in that circle are often chary because they don't want to take the time to explain the real meaning of their information – the facts behind the facts – that the closed circle understands but outsiders seldom comprehend. "Making friends" doesn't happen overnight, nor with a single email.

The structure, not only generally but of any individual site, is important. Intuit what you cannot see. Look for any sensitive directories as you explore a site that seems useful. Many things, particularly addresses, on the Internet are often rigid or stylized. Once you understand the style or format used on a site, after some study, you can use that information to find information you don't know. Email addresses are a simple example. If you are looking for an email address of John Smith at XYZ Company, after studying the XYZ site you may determine that their email format is usually lastnamefirstinitial@xyz.com. Now you will be able to contact smithj@xyz.com. Titles, forms of address, salutations, and similar stylized, socially-fixed, or rigid resources can sometimes be used in locating difficult-to-access information.

Learn the "lingo." Every subject area, each field, has terms of art. The language you encounter may be obscure, but that may be the easiest problem to deal with. For you the most dangerous terms of art are those that sound like ordinary language. They are the terms you think you understand but don't know that they really have a specialized meaning for those in the particular field. This is the classic case of not knowing what you don't know! Do some online searches for buzz phrases or key words, both as part of the lingo lessons and occasionally to see what's new.

Every field is made up of many sub-parts. Get the broad picture as you focus on your true information needs. Define the center of the field and work around the periphery as you develop your search pattern. Always keep in mind what your center actually is. Be aware of changes in your central area; that's where alerting services such as **Visual Ping** https://visualping.io/, ones that specialize in noting website changes and sending you an email alert, come in handy.

Remember too that government agencies involved in your subject area – no matter how tangential their role may be – often have valuable information. Many types of information are available from government agencies. Some agency information can be used to track people, understand connections between people and entities, or determine compliance with laws and regulations. Almost every government database or record contains vital information such as names or addresses.

Sherlock Holmes slyly hinted at the value of government records when he said to Watson, in the adventure known as *The Naval Treaty*, that "I have no doubt I can get the details from Forbes. The authorities are excellent at amassing facts, though they do not always use them to advantage."

You can use government records to your advantage. Governments collect huge amounts of data and information, whether at the local, state or federal level. Much of that information is available to anyone who asks – maybe "demands" is a more appropriate word – for it.

Some governmental resources are oft-used by journalists and opposition researchers, but many are overlooked. The list below is not meant to be comprehensive, but is intended only as a "thinking point" about what information might be available and some of the resources you might use in your own information search.

- Annual reports
- Appointment calendars
- Audit reports
- Budgets
- Building, occupancy, and other permits
- Call records of government officials who use publicly-provided cell phones or calling cards
- Contracts and contract-letting records
- Deeds, mortgage information, and liens
- Delinquency records, anything from taxes to parking tickets
- Departmental reports
- Disclosure forms
- Docket pages
- Financial information about incomes, expenditures, and payees
- Flight logs of government aircraft and repair information
- Franchise tax reports
- Government property records
- Government employees' identities and salary information, including overtime
- Health and other inspection records
- Legal opinions and case records and filings
- Licenses
- Meeting records
- Mileage and gas records
- Non-profit tax reports
- Official documents, or lists of documents, filed in archives
- Perquisite information
- Phone directories and logs
- Police incident logs
- Political campaign contribution records and databases

- Public comment letters on proposed legislation
- Tax records and liens
- Transcripts.

Don't expect anyone in government to smile as they turn over the information when you ask. They may, or they may not. Too often government officials, at all levels, have a proprietary view of "their" information. Moreover, it requires the time of "their" staff to find the information for you. There is a high likelihood you will have to file a Freedom of Information Act form (FOIA request if you want to be nice; FOIA demand when nice doesn't work) or fill out an Open Record Act form.

While journalists are often thought of as the users of these demand forms, any member of the public can use the FOIA or the various Open Records Acts to ferret out key information. **MuckRock** at https://www.muckrock.com/ is a site that helps activists, just plain citizens, researchers, and journalists get governmental information. It also makes the information public so that not only do the people who used the FOIA process get the information. Those uncovered facts are also available to the public. More information on FOIA and open records act techniques is available at:
- **Access Reports:** http://www.accessreports.com/
- **FOIAdvocates:** http://www.foiadvocates.com/
- **MuckRock:** https://www.muckrock.com/about/
- **National Freedom of Information Coalition:** https://www.nfoic.org/
- **RCFP Letter Generator:** https://www.rcfp.org/foia.

Specialized journals and newsletters dealing with, or likely to deal with, your subject should have a place in your search plan.

Consider how multi-media and audio-visuals might fit into the mix, as well.

Information dealing with your person or business subject – almost everything involves money somehow – may be found on state corporation pages, investor pages, or business sites such as:

- **CorporationWiki:** https://www.corporationwiki.com/
- **Experian ($$$$):** https://www.experian.com
- **OpenCorporates:** OpenCorporates.com.

Develop, as you go along, a list of sites (and types of sites or resources) that have proved useful. Separate them into sections, sites, or things to check – daily, weekly, monthly, or irregularly. Try to understand the posting schedule of any site you visit routinely – how often they update or change information. Schedule your own review of such sites accordingly and supplement your in-person reviews with automatic updating resources such as Alerts.

Find and list sites that may have statistical or other data that can be downloaded, scraped, and analyzed.

As you develop your own research SOP, consider this chapter and the information in Appendices F and G. They may be useful to you while you create a basic search plan that is crafted to meet your unique needs.

You may profit from signing up to mailing lists that are linked to your subject.

Blogs – perhaps those written or followed by people in the field, key players, or identified thought leaders – are important to watch.

Depending upon the subject, Usenet sites might also prove to be a valuable resource.

Don't forget observational note-taking when circumstances warrant.

Consider this book to be an instructional device, and your reading time to be a learning period. It is a time for testing both your current knowledge and the variety of new assets needed to do open source research. You will have to add to, weed out, and find and correct defects in your planning and procedures. But by the conclusion of the book you should be ready to research any areas you have selected for study.

Every day, set aside some time to prepare yourself for those crisis searches that are inevitable. There will always be those times where you have to produce results "yesterday." You can master the tools, a few minutes at a time now, which you are sure to need when that crisis occurs.

Explore sites and research methods that are of potential, but not immediate, value at a time when no crisis looms. If you prepare in advance you will have the skills, access, and knowledge to act immediately whenever the inevitable occurs. When you prepare consistently – a few minutes every day that you do research – you will quickly master the new resources of the information spectrum that you may soon need at short notice. Nothing, including this book, replaces practice and experience. You learn best from your own experience. As the saying goes, "practice makes perfect."

***

Project:
In your SOP outline the planning techniques you will use in your work. Appendices F and G may be helpful.

Project:
Determine whether you will have occasions to use FOIA requests. If so, include in your SOP those resources you might utilize in your information quest.

Project:
In your SOP set down whether you will block out a regular time – and how much, when – to learn techniques, tactics, and resources that you are now unfamiliar with but may need in the future. If you

plan on a self-education program write down up to three priority areas and specify possible sites or methods you could use for at least the first learning project.

7. The Research Process

Research often seems far more frustrating than productive. Because of that sense of frustration many people seek formulaic answers – checklist responses that they think (or hope) will never fail to provide an answer.

Regimented checklist-type thinking always shackles the researcher because it excludes the intangibles. Hidebound, rule-book researching often leads to wretched performance and picayune results. A soupcon of knowledge, techniques, experience, and resources goes into successful research. Cookbook-style searches may be considered adequate by some, but it is the carefully guarded "family recipe" that stands out. It requires a pot of sources and resources, and a deft hand with the burners, to cook up an information broth that suits the tastes of research customers.

We don't know of any checklist or formula that works infallibly, nor does anyone else despite the overblown claims of some. However, avoiding deadly conformity doesn't mean reinventing the wheel each time you start your information quest. Rather it implies that you should have and use a general search pattern. That is a script that you rethink before each search session, tailoring it to the details of the specific question and problem area before you.

You will consider all techniques and resources, and additionally use your "sixth sense" in planning. You must also be willing to alter your plan and regroup in the middle of research when events and results require. Persistence and perspicacity help.

You might also want to look at appendices F and G as you write your search plan. They provide some thought provoking points that could be useful to you if you insert them into your overall search plan.

Consider drafting a companion log that will recount what you did when, and why. The written analysis of all the tactics, techniques, and procedures you used, the successes, as well as the problems you encountered, highlights your professionalism and helps you uncover any flaws in the OSR search.

In most cases the successful generic research plan follows an overall pattern that looks much like this:

First (Initial Planning) Phase

The importance of laying solid groundwork and planning thoroughly before starting the research process is highlighted by a widely-known quote – a quote that is almost certainly apocryphal – attributed to Albert Einstein. "If I had only one hour to save the world, I would spend fifty-five minutes defining the problem, and only five minutes finding the solution." Apocryphal or not, thinking a project through is never wasted time. Not doing so squanders time and opportunity.

It is important to determine in advance what tasks are required, implied, or essential to the research. Define all critical facts and any assumptions at the outset.

In the Initial Planning Phase most OSR practitioners find their personal SOP invaluable to build upon.

Understand the details of any request for information and the actual needs, whether the research is for yourself or others. Make certain you are working with a carefully- and closely-defined objective.

There is no single "best place to start." That will vary, depending on your project. Review the capabilities and assets available. Determine how these relate to the objective. Identify what you or the requestor already know, and what is unknown. Many researchers begin with what is already known, expanding from there.

At the same time, start thinking about problems or constraints you will face during the search for information.

Determine the type of information resources you need to answer the question that was posed. That may be books; that may be search engines to find pdf files. That may be an online discussion with an expert, if that type of contact is permitted by your search procedures.

Determine the search techniques you think will be most productive. Determine what kind of research methods you plan to use, broad ones or narrow ones.

Factor in any constraints, such as time and expenses. Every search has some limitations. Crucially, determine what time is available for each element, such as research and product production. Set your schedule accordingly. Avoid overly-intricate or rigid timelines but don't make them so flexible that they can stretch forever. All too often an open-ended search timeline produces little – not even bunnies from the rabbit holes you will end up going down if you do not factor in time constraints.

Clear objectives limit confusion, reduce the temptation to go down rabbit holes, and guide collectors to the proper resources.

Formulate the actual research question based on the original request for information, making certain it will fully answer the real need. Often, on rethinking what information is actually needed, the real query turns out to be quite different from the question initially asked. Customers often define their information needs incorrectly. Careful engagement can help identify the real question. When clarifying the real request, determine the context of any request. Tailor production to the intended audience. Learn and understand:

- What the customer wants (the request)
- What the customer needs (the real need)
- When the customer needs it (the timeline)
- Why the customer needs it (the context).

Understanding the context of the customer's request before you get too far into the research process is important. It saves time and money for client. It also saves time – not to mention exasperation – for information collectors. Any failure to understand the context of the request often foreshadows the failure of the search.

Make certain you examine and understand your own capabilities, both positive and the negative:
- What assets do I have? (knowledge/capabilities)
- What assets do I need? (resources/tools/help)
- What information can I get in time? (deadline)
- Where can I get it? (search capabilities and collaborative network)
- What can't I do? (search limitations and legal boundaries).

As you start every plan, write out the key information so you can refer to it later. Written plans keep the collection process on track.
- Context: the user's actual need
- Wording of the question to be answered
- Who, What, When, Where, Why, and How elements
- Priority – Is time more important than detail level?
- LTIOV – Last time information is of value
- WENTK – Who else needs to know?
- Product type – Desired format, as this often drives the collection methods.

Then flesh out the collection plan:
- Identify what is known and who knows it.
  - How much do I know about the subject?
  - Has this question been addressed previously by others?
    - If so, by whom?
    - If so, where is that information?
    - If so, can I get it there?
  - Select the data sources.
    - What available sources are most appropriate?

- Are they non-Internet, government domains, free web, commercial, other sources?
- Frame the constraints on timeline and level of detail.
- How much time is available to answer the question?
- What level of detail is required?

Framing the timeline is an important challenge because the minutes slip away to hours and the hours can become days for the researcher who wants to do a thorough job. There is always one more place to search, and yet another location after that! Time is more limited than the possible places to search. Your plan has to anticipate the time required to:

- Research
- Analyze
- Write/compile
- Review
- Ask/answer additional questions, if needed
- Publish or deliver final product.

Timing is often related to the type of search requirement: *ad hoc* or standing. *Ad hoc* requirements address specific problems or issues and are generally relatively narrow, requiring less research time. Researchers usually have to sprint when they answer *ad hoc* requirements. Standing requirements fulfill more generalized needs and often take significantly longer – sometimes months or even years. Researching a standing requirement requires the stamina and timing of a cross-country runner. Standing requirements are usually broader – in some cases much broader than *ad hoc* ones. Standing requests may require near-continuous research and reporting.

Generally two search strategies are available; the choice is situation-dependent. The strategies are variously referred to as the "Hunter" or "Focused" strategy and the "Gatherer" or "Broad" strategy.

Hunters seek specific information and adopt a focused strategy to go after specific pieces of information. Gatherers search widely. They pull information which will either be usable or eventually must be discarded. The "Hunter/Focused" strategies are usually applied to *ad hoc* requirements and "Gatherer/Broad" strategies often work better when dealing with standing requirements.

OSR researchers need to be familiar with both, and be aware that sometimes they will need to combine the strategies. Occasionally, when using a Gatherer or Broad research strategy it is necessary to concentrate on a particular aspect for a short period of time. In that case the "Hunter" or "Focused" strategy may be paired with the broader "Gatherer" collection strategy.

In the open source world, collection is sometimes accurately called acquisition, since researchers typically look for information which already exists somewhere. Their challenge is to find it.

The OSR researcher or research desk needs to choose between acquisition techniques. Choices in the digital age are either 1) information sources can push the information to a requestor, like an advertising circular mailed to a person or 2) researchers can pull the information that is already available, much like going to the library and pulling a specific book off the shelf.

Through dashboards and RSS feeds, researchers can have many products "pushed" to them but most research is "pulled."
- Push (by producers):
  - Deliver via message traffic, email, hard-copy, or briefing
  - Posts to web page or social networking forum
- Pull (by collectors):
  - Browse websites for finished products, knowledge bases, or data archives
  - Patrol wikis, blogs, and forums
- Set up automated RSS feeds or Alerts that will then push information.

Resource materials are as varied as the Internet itself. Some types are more appropriate to the particular research project than others. Deciding which material types are most likely to yield the information about your own or your client's needs is crucial. It often determines how effective the search will be.

Information resources may be a package of services, capabilities, and sites all jumbled together like a tipped-over grocery bag. The OSR researcher or research desk must look at that mixed-up mess and make sense of it. Researchers or the research desk consider how, and whether, different research resources should be brought into play. Some of these might include:

- Alert services
- Audio-visuals
- Blogs
- Books and magazines
- Chatrooms
- Corporate sites/materials
- Databases
- Directories
- Email
- Forums
- Games
- Government sites
- Gray material and ephemera
- Libraries
- Listserves/discussion lists
- Meta-search engines
- News media
- Non-Internet resources
- Observation
- RSS feeds
- Search engines
- Social media
- Subject matter experts

- The Dark Web
- The Hidden Web
- The Open Web
- Think tanks or subject matter experts
- Usenet groups
- Wikis
- Or something else (There are *always* other possibilities).

The challenge is to figure out where in the wide, wide information world you are most likely to find the information that you need. Myriad factors must be considered, even in the first step of the planning process.

Second Phase (Security Planning)

Protection is important! It is important for yourself, to whoever you are doing the work for, for your family and associates. Before you begin any project, take a book from the shelf, or tap on the keyboard, plan your security.

Practitioners who need to develop a security plan base their decisions on both the type – and level – of threat and the potential risk associated with their particular research work. A risk assessment is essential for every search plan. Based on the risk assessment you will develop an "OPSEC (operational security) Recipe." This is a plan based on the threats, requirements, and capabilities facing a practitioner at a given time. An "OPSEC Recipe" employs a selection of tactics, techniques, and procedures (TTPs) for risk mitigation. That recipe is linked to your available equipment, search methods, and the assigned work. The OPSEC recipe is continually reviewed and must be updated whenever conditions change during collection.

Every SOP needs to include at least a basic security plan, an outline based on a risk assessment that identifies potential threats to routine research. Having a second security plan, one based on a heightened threat, is never a bad idea. To develop either of these plans you must assess the threat, the risk, your possible protections and your own vulnerabilities.

Understand the scope and public visibility of your online activities and digital fingerprint. Keep in mind that unless you use specialized services all of your Internet searches can be seen and linked to you by the system operator (sysop) of every Internet node your search request passes through. It can also be seen by the sysop at any site you are accessing. Not only can the search request be seen, the sysop can tell a great deal about you, your equipment, your location, and even your intent.

Adversarial sysops may prevent you from getting on their site again. They can counter-collect, using hacking tools to get back at you and your system, stealing information from your computer. The thievery might include bank account passwords and financial information, social security numbers, information on your clients, friends and relatives, etc. It happens!

Some security measures are basic. Good anti-virus, anti-malware, and firewall programs are essential for everyone who uses any part of the Internet. But that is insufficient for open source research. You also need to block or clear many cookies and remove any spyware – remember that dangerous cookies and spyware are found everywhere on the Internet. To provide a margin of safety in open source research you may need Virtual Machine ware that will mask your computer and its information against prying eyes. Non-attribution programs are often essential. Above all, you need to practice secure tradecraft.

Non-attribution programs and services mask your identity and location. Some are free, such as the Onion Router, and others are available at a nominal – or more than nominal – cost.

There are also sites that you can go to and they – rather than you – travel to a site and gather information for transmittal back to you.

The sysop at the site being visited sees the location and download information about the other site – not yours. You can use such sites, and some non-attribution techniques, to keep prying eyes away from your own research system:

- **Browsershots.com:** https://sourceforge.net/projects/browsershots/
- **BrowserShots.org:** http://browsershots.org/
- **PDFmyURL:** https://pdfmyurl.com/
- **Web2PDF:** http://www.web2pdfconvert.com.

Your security plan should explain how to mitigate risks, and what steps to take at:

- Friendly sites: Is there really a need to hide the search?
- Neutral sites: Need to hide the search in some cases?
- Adversarial sites: Need to hide searches in all cases?

But security requires more than just masking your identity, or even using a firewall, a good anti-virus program, and an anti-spyware program. One of the advanced security methodologies is a Virtual Machine.

This type of program creates an electronic computer within your physical computer. When a properly configured virtual machine (VM) program shuts down, everything related to your browsing session is wiped away. This includes any viruses, cookies, or counter-collection items that were installed in your electronic computer. Poof. Gone! An improperly configured machine can also wipe out all the material you were collecting, however. VM ware clearly has to be carefully set up.

Security is a major issue for researchers. Unless you are going to be doing the most mundane research that will never go beyond ninth-grade school papers using Wikipedia, you need to review security. Ignore this step and you are likely to be snared.

In fact, you should consider whether you need to go back and even reconfigure your research system to make yourself, and any clients, safer. More detailed information on security is found in Appendix D. OSR users should read that over and implement the lessons that apply to their particular research work before continuing on to the next chapter.

Third Phase (Selection of Research Tools)

The third phase is the time to select the research and retrieval tools you believe are most likely to achieve the best results. The tools you need depend on the categories of material you are likely to encounter. If you are doing a straight Web search, search engines may be the option. A standard browser search will suffice. But if you are more likely to find your information in PDFs – where expert material is often located – you may want to consider a specialized method of searching. If you think you are likely to find what you need in a video, programs to download and save in that format will be needed. If you are likely to be scraping some database you will need different tools, including database or spreadsheet software.

When using non-Internet search techniques, the important tools might include:
- Books and magazines
- Corporate materials
- Libraries
- Observation
- Subject matter experts
- Any of the other non-Internet resources listed earlier.

There are other key tools the OSR researcher or research desk needs when searching the Internet. All should be readied in advance of any search:
- Platform programs are the type of programs that will read and download material accessed on the Internet, such as PDFs, HTML and various video formats.

- Search string/keyword lists are used to help researchers prevent duplication in their efforts. These aid in identifying topics.
- Site lists are used to keep a record of where information was derived from. Site lists are also often used to find a starting point to guide the researcher or research desk to appropriate resources.
- Databases/file folders are used to save information for later review and use.

Platform reader programs are often, but not always, bundled on the computer at the time it was purchased. Not all the platform programs that a researcher or research desk needs come pre-loaded on their system, however. You may have to purchase or acquire others.

The researcher or research desk must identify and use keywords in search strings. This is an important, if basic, step. Once the search objective is defined, researchers often narrow down what they are looking for by developing precise keywords related to the subject or objective. Researchers who choose the right keywords move closer to their objective. Those who choose the wrong ones may very well get more frustration than information; they find themselves further away from accomplishing their goal.

Some resources that may be helpful in developing keyword lists or deciding on keywords include:
- **Google Correlate:** https://www.google.com/trends/correlate/
- **Keyword Discovery:** https://www.keyworddiscovery.com/
- **Keyword Shitter:** http://keywordshitter.com/
- **Keyword Tool:** https://keywordtool.io/
- **KWFinder:** https://kwfinder.com/
- **OneLook:** http://www.onelook.com/reverse-dictionary.shtml
- **SEOchat:** https://tools.seochat.com/tools/suggest-tool.

Brainstorm the key words and use available information resources that include:

- Thesaurus, either hard-copy or digital
- Dictionaries, either hard-copy or digital
- Text from returned web pages or similar resources that may include some related keywords
- The index of a good book on your subject.

Consider searching for the more-obscure and most-limiting terms first; this reduces the number of search engine responses but it filters the responses and increases the percentage of useful returns. For example, if you are only interested in the Russian Mafia's activities in Moscow, don't only type in "russian mafia" but also include "moscow" as a limiter in that search.

Remember that word order can affect the results. Searching "russian mafia moscow" will produce different results than "moscow russian mafia." Word order determines much. The first word in the search box often receives the most weight.

Articles – a, an, and the – are generally ignored by search engines or database search tools, so you generally don't include them in your search. These and other common terms are known as "stop words." The stop words vary from search engine to search engine so learning the stop words for the particular engines you use becomes important. If stop words are important in your search, put them – or any phrase they are associated with – in quotation marks.

Conduct most searches in lower case. Lower case searches usually find examples in both upper and lower case; often upper case searches will find only items in capital letters.

Always make certain the spelling is correct.

Particularly if the search involves anything outside the US borders, check for important words in a foreign language, or slang terms.

After a thorough keyword search in English, learn the keywords in the foreign language. They are likely to help you find additional materials. You can often determine these key word translations by putting the English language word into a machine translation tool and then searching on the foreign word that is returned. Check both singular and plural translations.

You may also want to use specialized regional search engines.

In some cases you may need to seek help from a person who knows the language and is familiar with slang terms and colloquialisms. For instance, suicide vest is a term that will get you English language sources. And when you translate it into some Arabic languages you will get translations of English language stories. Unless you know that the term used in some countries is actually "belt blaster" or "belt buster" you probably will miss valuable stories in local media.

Even words in the English language might not turn up what you want in English-speaking countries. American English is different in some ways from the English used in the British Isles or elsewhere in the Commonwealth. "Bonnet" and "hood" refer to the same part of a car, depending on where you are and what brand of English you are searching. Even when people use the same word, they may spell it differently. It's Color and Favorite on the west side of the water, Colour and Favourite across the pond. Same word, different spelling.

Anyone doing research in or about a foreign country may want to spoof their search engine location so that they appear to be in the country of interest or an adjacent area. Regional settings and foreign language keyboards are worth looking up on the Internet to determine how to make any needed changes in the search engine or browser. Browser location settings may also require changes. Services such as Google display different results to the same question depending upon where the query appears to originate. This setting not only determines the results you see, it also has security implications if system operators can determine your location. The Internet has detailed information on these issues as they apply to your particular computer system and browser.

Grammar matters! Type the search terms in their proper form and you are more likely to get results and/or suggestions that are helpful. That is, of course, unless you expect the item you are looking for to have been posted in slang or in some offbeat version of the language. Be aware of, and use, cultural and sub-cultural terms or slang in searches when that is appropriate. Example: How about "across the pond?"

Depending on what you are looking for and where, you may get more usable information on marijuana by typing "maryjane" or "420" than "cannabis." There are even regional variations within the same country. "Buggy" in the northern United States is a horse-drawn cart but southerners may use it to mean a shopping cart. To a computer user it may have a third meaning. "Rain" in England may be referred to as "cockney sprinkles," a "French welcome," or even "Dickensian mist."

Concepts do not always translate directly. Nor do all names.

Become familiar with, and use, a variety of browsers during research. In addition to being a good security and precautionary measure, different browsers offer different options and functions for research. Some of the more popular browsers are Firefox, Safari, Internet Explorer, Chrome, and Opera. Newer ones, like Brave and Vivaldi, develop a following over time. Know every browser that you use, its strengths, and the extensions you can apply to it that may be useful. Importantly, understand the quirks of the browser's operations. Choose the best browser systems for the particular work you are doing. Customize its features to make it more useful to you.

You may also want to change browsers from day to day or even search to search. Using different browsers is often a security issue – operators of the website visited do not have as many clues to connect one person to the collection activities when different browsers are being used – but changing browsers may also be a necessity for reasons totally unrelated to security. Often sites are built with a particular browser or set of browsers in mind. Occasionally a browser, for various reasons, may be wholly or partially incompatible with a site. Using a different browser may allow access to an otherwise unavailable site, or to the services that are on that site. Also, different browsers allow different selections of useful extensions and add-ons. Study, also, the security dangers associated with different browsers and extensions.

Browsers, even when they properly show any site, may react differently. One browser, when using a common paint and drag technique, may provide clean copy for databasing. In another browser, on the same site, a copy and paste technique may bring along portions of the site that are distracting and should be cut out before being put into a database. Some browsers, on some sites, will bring along working links; other browsers may not. Pictures that can be moved with a simple flick of the mouse from the web page to a database in one browser may have to be copied using a print screen command and then pasted into the database. In some cases it may not be possible to use a copy and paste technique and you will have to resort to other methods. No general transfer technique works on every site, with all browsers. You must be aware of how a particular browser system works on a particular site.

Know what specific security features each browser has and how to activate any security features that are available – features including privacy browsing, as little protection as that might be.

Become familiar with the primary functions and characteristics of the major browsers so that you can decide which ones to use, and when. For example, Firefox has a set of extensions that can be used for information exploitation, such as a plug-in that pulls metadata off photos. However, Firefox is also community driven and some of the people in that community may be hackers and/or counter-collectors. At the same time Firefox is open source and well-vetted. You have to weigh conflicting pros and cons when making decisions. While you don't want to become paranoid about browser use, you need to be aware of all potential problems or threats and then evaluate the likelihood you would be affected by any particular issue.

Different search engines use different algorithms to produce their results. Algorithms are about what the algorithm writer intended, not about what the researcher or research desk needs out of a search. There is often a large gap between the two.

Different search engines may collect different versions of the same pages in their database. Some search engines collect everything on a page; the algorithm for other search engines may limit the amount of a site they collect.

There are also different types of search engines that will cover specific subject areas and particular file types. Become familiar with the many different constellations of search engines. Use the search engine types that produces the best results for you.

Good search engine rules of thumb can lighten the work load and make searches more efficient:

- Put the most important search term first; some search engines look for that word first and then find subsequent words within the original set.
- The first word should be the most uncommon or obtuse search term when you want to limit the number of results returned. You can use this to filter your results to those that best apply to your needs.
- Search on the singular word form initially. Search engines will usually look for the plural forms of words when the

singular form is inputted, but some will not search for the singular form when the plural form is entered.

- Use lower case letters. Case sensitivity varies from search engine to search engine, but typically you only need to capitalize what normally is capitalized. Some search engines will pick up all forms of a word that is in lower case, but will not pick up lower case forms of the word if it is capitalized in the search string.
- Limit searches to the types of documents that are most likely to yield the results you want. An expert's paper on water poisoning is more likely to be found as a PDF document than as a web page, but also keep in mind that a web page or a media article may report on it or link to the expert's paper.
- Remember that most search engines allow you to search within searches. Going from the general to the specific in searches usually provides the most results at first. Getting more results, when they are the haystack and not the needles, is hardly a bargain. The more specific you get, the more rewarding and relevant the search is likely to be.
- Spelling is a common search error, but some search engines will fix it for you. Misspellings will obviously bring back different results. When you think that a search word may have been misspelled by the Web poster, try intentional misspellings in your search. Remember, too, that some words – particularly proper names or foreign words – may have multiple transliteration spellings. Someone may use the name of Jan, but in searching you may want to add in searches for Janice, Janet, and Jahn. Names in foreign languages often have a different spelling and may be in a different alphabet or writing system. Always conduct at least one search in the correct spelling, and with the proper keyboard of the area, when doing when doing foreign language searches.
- Most relevant results are usually near the top of the list that a search engine returns, but on many search engines the first

results are often paid-for positions. Those returns are seldom useful.

- First get the outline of your search, the outer edges as if it were a jigsaw puzzle. Then fill in the details as they are available.
- Set and adhere to time limits for doing the initial search.
- Consider searches of the Deep Web and Dark Web
- Don't limit yourself to putting a few words in a search box; learn and use special techniques such as "site:" searches.

Fourth Phase (Assign Research Roles)

The fourth step, important when more than a single researcher is involved, is to assign research roles. Teamwork is important if more than one person works on a project. Make certain everyone knows and carries out their particular roles. Assigning specific tasks often decreases redundancy.

Assign roles based on the qualifications and capabilities of the searchers. Give the hardest jobs to the best researchers. You could also split up the assigned roles by sub-topic and then have the team members coordinate after each person has conducted research.

Use an intranet to coordinate team members, or employ services like **Slack** at http://slack.com/ if that meets your security profile.

Set timelines will help keep team members on track.

Fifth Phase (Conduct Research)

The fifth step is to conduct the research. The proof of the technique is in the results of the actual search:

- Do the search of the most obvious sites, using the terms likely associated with the research question.
- Visit the safest sites first. If the information from safe sites satisfies the query there is no need to use any problematic resources.

- During the research, document both the keywords and the sources you used. You will need source information later and you should know where you found the information.
- Expect progress to be slow, even stuttering at times, no matter how well you have planned.

During the research phase save all the materials that you may want to reference later. Just because something is on the Web now does not mean it will be there on the following day, or even later this afternoon. It may be taken down or it may move. If you are going to an adversarial site – one that you or your client would not want the system operator to know you visited – it is essential to have a copy to refer to without returning to the live site. If the information is a text article, you may want to copy and paste the text into a Word document or a database. If the information is an entire website you may want to use offline browser software, copying the entire site in a few minutes or hours. Video sites require special copying programs. A variety of tools, and knowledge of how to get the most out of those tools, will be needed to meet the varied needs.

When appropriate and where allowed, collaborate with other research community members about your topic. For example, you may want to work with people you know, the people you feel confident about, using secure chat tools. Collaboration inevitably poses a trust issue and that issue must be resolved before making any contact or agreement. In some cases collaboration may prove impossible because of the sensitivity of the research or a client's instructions.

During the research you will want to routinely assess the information being collected to ensure that your effort is fully answering all the questions. When information gaps are identified they should be noted in both the documentation and in the final product.

Avoid "mission creep." During research it is all-too-common to find material that is perhaps interesting, but is slightly off track. In many cases there is a tendency to drift down that rabbit hole. Keep the original search foremost in mind. Avoid extraneous issues that seem to crop up – they can be true time wasters. When you find yourself in a rabbit hole, quit digging. Get out.

Even Sherlock Holmes, the great detective, understood the need to go back up any rabbit holes you have gone down. "I confess that I have been as blind as a mole, but it is better to learn wisdom late than never to learn it at all," he reportedly said in *The Man with the Twisted Lip.*

At the same time, whenever you are on a page that seemingly offers good information, follow the "look around rule." Balance the "mission creep" problem with the "look around rule," which says that any time you are on a site, look around for closely related material. There will often be links to similar material or other sites on the page you are viewing. They may be valuable. But always strive to strike a balance. This is a judgment call if there ever was one.

Avoid the "search without end." In some cases you could spend the rest of your life delving into various branches of a subject. The achievement is likely to be inverse to the time spent if you don't know when to quit. Remember, the information you need may not be on the Internet, may not be in a book, and may not be public. Always plan for, and stick to, cutoff times.

Learn basic searching patterns and choose the one safest for you in the particular work. After you have checked and utilized the safest sites and are ready to conduct research elsewhere on the Internet, you should consider what type of basic search pattern(s) you are going to use. There are multiple search patterns for conducting research. Some primary patterns are:
- Create a diversion to obscure the search

- Pearl chaining
- Brute force.

Creating a diversion: Intersperse real searching for information that is actually of value to you or your client with searches for innocuous information. This keeps outside "viewers" such as site operators from pinpointing the real purpose of your search. Search in varying orders and at different times. Be consistent with your inconsistency. Appear to have no particular interest in anything. Just wander. Eliminate any patterns in your searching. This type of search suggests that your visit to the site is random and that you are unfocused.

Since browsers often retain information on what was viewed and system operators are able to see this information, you should look up items that have nothing to do with your real interest, subject A. For instance on the first day you may want to conduct research early in the morning. You could look up information on subjects B, C, and D, then A. Change browsers and look up information on C, E, F, and A again. Wait three hours and look up G, A, and B. Work on other things for the rest of the day. The next day, search in the afternoon using a different browser and look up G, A, B, and D. Anyone watching your searches will be less suspicious.

This search pattern is optimal when using Virtual Machine software and you are coming from non-attributable accounts.

Site meters and other tracking services of a domain often log which browser and/or search engine was used to visit it. Because there are a myriad browser settings for everything from language to time zones on your browser, the system operator at a site can actually identify you individually each time you visit. It doesn't sound possible, but it is true. By utilizing multiple browsers, a variety of settings, and different search engines, your interest can be somewhat obscured when you must make multiple visits to the same site.

Pearl chaining or "dominos" is another search technique. You search for a key word or phrase, then using new leads from the results – other words or concepts – you move from one location on the site, or to other sites, until the question is answered or all the sources have been exhausted. Pearl chaining is simply following a thread from key words until you achieve the desired result. This type of search is often most helpful with academic-quality materials that include citations. The same concept applies to domains that provide referral links.

Brute Force is directly searching for an item of information. You put the terms you are looking for directly into the search box and click "go." Brute force searching is what most people do with search engines. This typically provides the least amount of security but searches at the fastest speed. The brute force technique uses many key words or phrases to search for a topic; it makes no effort to hide the purpose of the search or to follow a chain. Security can be improved by clicking on the cached copies that some search engines will display rather than on the actual link to the site. But remember that the cached copy was downloaded by the search engine some time ago. The cached copy may differ from what currently is on the site and in cases of long pages may not have picked up the entirety of the material.

The brute force method should be used primarily for research on topics and sites that pose no security or counter-collection risk.

In many instances a researcher or research desk may use some combination of these techniques. Whatever procedure you use, be aware of, and follow, the safe search hierarchy – safest sites first, adversarial sites last. Search on the safest sites first because the risk only grows as you move up the threat hierarchy.

Documentation Sub-phase

Make certain you can find each source again if you need to refer back to it. Web pages and addresses change or disappear. Proper documentation allows researchers to find sources again, or at least be certain of what they were. Bookmarks are no good when the page disappears, if there is a software or hardware failure on a researcher's computer, or when researchers have so many bookmarks they cannot find the one they need. There are also serious security problems posed by computer bookmarks if an adversary gains access to the researcher's system. Use bookmarks at your own peril.

Consider saving all usable researched resources into a database, word processor page, spreadsheet, knowledge management system or an offline browser. Copy and save relevant reference materials for:

- Collaboration with others
- Possible evidentiary use
- Identification of intelligence gaps
- Refresher work when analyzing material and writing reports.

Once information is retrieved and researchers have integrated the information into whatever they choose for an appropriate digital or analog database, they prepare for all the remaining phases of the production process (evaluation, analysis, interpretation and integration).

Sources must always be clearly identified when databasing the information – where the information came from, who collected it, and when it was collected, along with all information relating to the reliability of the information. During the databasing process, consider identifying information gaps and how those might be filled.

When finished, saved material should consist of:
- The text and any pictures, audios, or film clips
- Web location/URL
- Publisher, author, or poster identity
- Collector's identity

- Date and time collected, and where known – when posted.

Where can such information to be saved be found? In many cases:
- Web location: In URL
- Publisher: May be found in collected text or the URL
- Author: May be found in collected text, if identified
- Date posted: May be found in collected text
- Date of collection: May be found in collected text or entered by hand.

Remember: All saved information, no matter where saved, must be properly tagged for use of analysts or others who need it. It must be relocatable. Think chain of custody! For long-term projects it is imperative to save search results to easily-searchable databases or spreadsheets such as Access, Excel, or their clones. Spreadsheets work well for those projects that are not text-heavy. For shorter-term projects saving the material to word processing files, or saving the online files to a computer folder, may be sufficient.

Saving to a database or spreadsheet is usually simple and fast. Divide the computer screen into halves. One part displays the web page in use and the other half of the screen is a database or other file which will be used to hold the information. For those who have two screens, put the web page to be copied on one screen and the place to save it on the second screen.

Download the article to your computer and paint (select) it. Then drag and drop, or copy and paste, the text or the picture into the location where you will save it. The drag and drop method is often quickest, but sometimes that will not work and the copy and paste technique must be used.

On the relatively-rare occasions where neither of these methods work you can always save the page to your computer or do a screen capture (usually control/print screen keys held down together, and then paste the captured material into the database or word processor file). Screen capture only copies what is on the screen so several, or even many, captures may have to be pasted together. (Screen captures are usually pictures so they cannot be word-searched like a text download. This is a major problem with screen captures.)

An alternative is to do a "view>source" of the page text and copy that. When using this viewing-the-source method there is always a great deal of "spaghetti code" that may need to be cut out since the capture includes all the code that determines how a page will look. (In a few instances, particularly when viewing a page set up by an adversary, it makes sense to download the source code of a page and go through it line by line because source material may contain hidden information that can be useful. This can become a matter of due diligence.) Saving the source data will include only text, so pictures and other important portions will be lost. However, pictures and audio-visuals can be saved by finding the URL in the source data, going to that location, and doing a "save."

You can always use many word processing programs in place of a database, but remember that searching a large word processing file when you need information from it later can be daunting. When you use a word processor storage method, remember to save the file after each article is moved into the word processor. Otherwise you will lose all unsaved material if you inadvertently close the file without saving. Another option is to use an offline browser.

Some items do not fit into databases. Extremely long web pages, PDF files, and audio-visual files are among the web items that may not go into your database or word processor file. Save these with an offline browser to a project library file folder on your computer, but in the database or the word processor file mark down the name of the saved file, the location where it is stored, and some key words about the file so you can find it later. Choose words that will jog your memory about what is found in the file. As your project library file folder fills, the items can be saved in separate sub-folders by subject, date, or any other scheme you devise (subject is quite common). To make it easier to find saved items on your computer, develop a consistent naming format. Consistency in file organization and naming, starting at the beginning, will help you find what you need when you need it.

A knowledge management system or an analytics program such as Hunch.ly functions in much the same way as a database, often with the added efficiencies of a publishing program. It provides help in collecting, analyzing, and organizing the material. It also aids in the production of a completed OSR report. Knowledge management and similar analytics systems are seldom intuitive. There is a decided learning curve to them. They differ somewhat in the way they work and their elements, but they offer the most comprehensive answer to the collection, analysis and production problems in OSR. They include:

- **ClueMaker ($$$$):** https://cluemaker.com/
- **Hunch.ly ($$$$):** https://hunch.ly/
- **IBM i2 Analyst's Notebook ($$$$):** https://www.ibm.com/us-en/marketplace/visual-analysis-environment
- **Palantir ($$$$):** https://www.palantir.com/palantir-gotham/.

Revision Sub-phase

During research the collected results must be constantly assessed and the search parameters revised. Pivot when and where necessary. If the initial search does not produce the required information alter the research plan.

- Add keywords or change the order if you are not in the ballpark.
- If you are in the ballpark, most search engines allow you to search within current results to further narrow the search.
- Use advanced search features of search engines and Boolean search techniques to look at formats you may not have considered, including PDFs or video files.
- Use advanced techniques such as "site:" searches.

- Reconsider where the information might have been stashed and what methods you need to get to it.
- If your plan is still not fruitful, consider whether a visit to the library would be helpful. There is often a great deal more information available on some subjects in fiber-based media – like books and magazines – than there is in digital format. While this situation is gradually improving, the materials available in libraries may be more extensive and more reliable than some material found on the Internet. But they may not be as current.

As an example of rearranged keywords consider this example. Keywords on the initial pass might be:
- Nigeria rebel force
- Nigeria insurgent
- Nigeria terrorist
- Nigeria rebel groups
- MEND Nigeria
- Okah Nigeria
- oil Nigeria
- kidnap Nigeria
- hostage Nigeria.

On the second pass the researcher or research desk might use:
- rebel force Nigeria
- insurgent Nigeria
- terrorist Nigeria
- Movement for the Emancipation of the Niger Delta
- Bakassi Movement for Self Determination
- Niger Delta People's Volunteer Force
- explosion Nigeria
- Niger Delta vigilante.

Continued Research Sub-Phase

Inevitably there will be other roadblocks to overcome as the project unspools. Never consider any problem insuperable.

You may find references to an article that seems like it would be a useful resource, but when you click on the link a screen orders "Enter Login and Password." And you have neither! This is not a site you have access to. How do you work around this?

Do a secondary search for the title. If the article is interesting to you, there is a good chance that it was interesting to someone else and has been published or posted elsewhere. Do a secondary search; cut and paste the title into your search engine and place quotation marks around it. Often you'll be able to find the article somewhere else online. It may have been published by another site, newspaper, or saved on someone's personal website. If that doesn't work, try querying online databases.

Expensive databases that you don't subscribe to are often available through many public or college libraries. In some cases you may even be able to access the library's databases from your office or home. Enrolling in a course at a community college can give you full library access online to databases, journals, and sometimes even expensive resources such as LexisNexis. This is a good way to save money. It is preferable to buying individual database access in order to query the many 'closed' pay-wall sites on the Web that have journals, dissertations, and data-driven research.

If you don't already have a library card – get one. Use larger libraries where possible. Established community, college, and university libraries are more likely to link to premium databases such as LexisNexis, the ones that collect and store a king's ransom of information and articles.

At the same time be cognizant of specialist libraries that concentrate their collections on your specific area of interest. Try to obtain access to those special library sites.

Librarians anywhere are usually helpful and try to get you the information you need. But remember they are there to help you – not to do your work. Treat them with respect. Ask for their help only when you have exhausted your own knowledge and resources.

If you have difficulty in ferreting out the article online or in a library, think outside the box. Try to find the author instead. If it is permitted by the rules you work under, send the author an email and request a copy.

The bottom line is that you should not give up trying to find good material you deem worthwhile until you've exhausted every option. If you look hard enough, 95 percent of the time you will successfully locate the information you need.

In this phase of the OSR process mentally review your progress in identifying the objective, identifying key words, and selecting the appropriate search tools and resources. Documented data should be captured in a database, a notebook, or a digital text document that you keep available. Remember:

- Conduct the initial search.
- Document, document, document everything you find.
- Assess the information.
- Revise the strategy.
- Continue the research as needed.

Sixth Phase (Analyze Collected Material)

Step Six is to review the collected information, both to assure the accuracy of what you have and to determine what you might be missing. Missing information may require additional searches, going back to Step 5.

Unless both the information and the sources that you provide are vetted and validated, the client has no way of knowing whether to rely on them. (The outlines of the vetting phase are dealt with here. There will be further development of the *minutiae* of this critical step later.)

Evaluate both the information and the site you got it from. Reliability of the site may be considered important but that is not a guarantee of the information's validity. Good sources can provide bad information and bad sources occasionally give out good information. Evaluate carefully because:

- Few – make that no – safeguards exist to ensure Internet information is accurate.
- Anyone can publish anything on the Web.
- It is often hard to determine a Web page's authorship.
- Even if a page is signed, author qualifications are usually missing.
- Sponsorship is seldom indicated.

Collected material should match the customer's requirements. Any analysis or interpretation of the collected materials in order to extract the information matching the client's needs should be done carefully. There are a variety of elements in the analysis. One common list used in the research world calls for collected materials to be analyzed for:

- Accuracy (consistency with other materials, validation, sources.)
- Authority/Qualifications (Do the authors really know what they are talking about?)
- Currency (Is it timely or dated?)
- Objectivity (Is it from advocacy groups, are there balanced viewpoints? Link analysis and any claims to speak for groups may provide evidence.)

- Relevancy (Particularly applies to the Internet since not all Web pages containing the key words are relevant to the subject.)
- Coverage (Does it completely cover the subject?)
- Appearance (Does it appear to be professional and business-like or is it clearly an amateur effort?).

Seventh Phase (Draft and Finalize Product)

The seventh step is to draft and finalize the product. After vetting and validating your sources and creating a draft product, when time permits, it is wise to send that draft to people who are knowledgeable about the subject for their review.

Sherlock Holmes was a believer in the value of running things by others. "At least I have a grip of the essential facts of the case. I shall enumerate them to you, for nothing clears up a case so much as stating it to another person" he said to Watson in the adventure titled *Silver Blaze.*

During the review process you should also submit any pertinent supplemental documents. The reviewer should re-check the draft product to ensure that it meets legal and security requirements and that the product fits the request. If your research response is tactical and time-sensitive, such as a quick email responding to a request for information, it is still wise to at least "carbon copy" (CC) someone who theoretically may have knowledge of the issue so they can comment. Provide all reviewers a feedback mechanism.

A production overview is needed since this is arguably the most important part of the information cycle after collection. Production is the point at which information is converted into an actionable format and undergoes final assessment prior to delivery to a customer. It completes the cycle in which you were tasked, you refined the requirement, collected or acquired information, tracked it, analyzed it, and converted it into a deliverable product to be acted upon. Now decisions will be made, actions will be taken, people will be positioned, policy will be formulated, etc.

At this point you may want to use the three Colin Powell Criteria in drafting the finished product. Powell's criteria are well-known but too-often forgotten:
- Tell me what you *know* - Facts
- Tell me what you *don't know* - Gaps
- Tell me what you *think* - Analyst judgment or assessment.

Finally, protect yourself and your work. If applicable, ensure the finished product includes a "Fair Use" statement and that it complies with any specific legal guidance. Consult your attorney or legal counsel to draft a Fair Use statement appropriate to your needs.

***

Project:
In the SOP techniques section outline the strategies – broad, narrow, or mixed – that you will use and under what circumstances you will use them.

Project:
Using the information in this chapter, and in Appendices F and G, list the resources you would generally use to conduct searches. Create a separate list of resources you would use if forced to do time-limited "quick and dirty" searches.

Project:
Using the information in this chapter, and in Appendices F and G, create a basic format to build from when doing research, recognizing that you can add or subtract items as needed.

Project:
In the SOP technologies section list the tools, programs – including anti-virus and anti-malware programs – and procedures you plan to use to promote security for you and those around you.

Project:
In the SOP's planning section, outline the phases you plan to follow in carrying out research.

Project:
In the SOP technology and techniques sections make generalized initial lists of possible resources to exploit and the techniques to use. As you develop your skills, add to or alter these lists.

Project:
In the SOP planning section develop a rough timing outline you can use, including left and right limits for various phases of your typical research. As you develop your skills, add to or alter this outline.

Project:
In the people section of your SOP write down whether/how many people you anticipate will work on any project. If more than one person will be working on a project, detail how you plan to assign roles and provide team direction and cohesion.

Project:
In the SOP's digital library section detail how you plan to consistently name your downloaded material in order to be able to quickly and easily access it later.

8. Search Engines, Web Directories, and Other Search Options

Search Engines are tools. For many people these are not only basic Internet tools, they are the only search tools they know how to use. Some know little – or nothing – beyond putting a word or two in the search box and waiting for an answer microseconds later. Their Web capabilities start and end with that search box.

Search professionals use many more tools and techniques, of course, but search engines are as indispensable for professional researchers as they are to any sixth grader doing homework. Squeezing every drop of information out of basic tools like search engines is both a requirement and a challenge.

Search engines, as important as they may be, are not the whole of OSR. Let's be clear. They are no more essential to your information search than dozens of other techniques and tools. Still, knowing how, why, and when to use search engines is important. So is learning how to structure search engine queries.

Search engines sit in a central, almost unique, position in popular research. They allow people to search text – and some other formats – across billions of web pages. To some who don't know better they are sum total of OSR. Because of their ubiquity and ease of use, nearly everyone who gets on the Web uses one search engine or another.

But search engines are not intuitive. They cannot and do not think for themselves. They cannot think for you either. They only answer your query based on 1) the precision of your question, 2) the information contained in the search engine's database, and 3) the algorithms programmed into that search engine.

Search engines, when used thoughtfully, may provide answers to some head-scratching questions. For instance searches for standardized words and phrases such as "business confidential," "FOUO" (For Official Use Only), or "distribution prohibited" may reveal the contents of sensitive documents.

Search engines often collect, but do not offer easy ways to look for, the particular type of information researchers need. OSR operators learn how to prompt – some say "trick" – a search engine into giving up information it may not even realize it has available.

On the other hand a search engine may spew out pages of information that is useless to your search needs because of the way it has been programmed. The problem of the researcher may be how to get to the needle hidden somewhere in the haystack.

Moreover, search engines have absolutely no way to validate the information they collect. When a site that the search engine collects from insists the sky is cerise that search engine may tell you the sky is cerise.

And search engines are as dangerous as they can be fallible.

Search Engines Expose You to Dangers

System and site operators have had decades to develop ways to spy on their users. Many of the spy tactics are based on the way most users employ their search engines. Many search engines are free because their operators make money off your searches, hooking you up with advertisements that are based on things like your own search terms or your location.

Basic security measures are a must whenever you use any search engine. This is something that is largely overlooked by users, even when the dangers are understood.

Avoid clicking on the URL that a search engine serves up. Entering a site that way provides snoopy system operators with too much information about you. Instead, either type or copy and paste the URL provided by the search engine into your browser. That single simple step helps limit the information that a webmaster receives about you. It dramatically improves your security.

For all but the most routine searches try to mask or change your IP address. Changing browsers each time you use a site, as well as changing the time zone and the language, also help thwart snoopy webmasters.

When you are going to any site, remember that the more sensitive the information it contains – and the more you need the information from that site – the more likely it is that the webmaster or sysop is monitoring the users.

Heavily used websites are more difficult for sysops to monitor effectively and the chances of detection on those is more limited, but those that have light traffic are easily watched. Where possible try to hide in the crowd, to be a needle in the haystack. At the very least try to sign on a site at the time of day when you feel the traffic is peaking.

No matter what time you sign on to a website, if you have any reason to consider the site and its sysop to be antagonistic to you or your client, avoid using the on-site search box. On-site searches are quite noticeable. It is easy for the webmaster to see every search term you use and all of your activities. When searching the site of a possible antagonist it is always wise to search from outside the website by using the "site:" advanced search method taught later in this chapter.

Learn the ins and outs of every search engine you use. Employ the complexities built into each one to maximize your search effort but also to improve security while you minimize your search time.

Because of the complexity of search engines, researchers keep up to date on advances, changes, and differences in search engines by using the information from sites such as:

- **Search Engine Land:** https://searchengineland.com/
- **Search Engine Watch:** http://www.searchenginewatch.com

The Search Engine Watch website provides current information on many aspects, including alliances – search engines that draw from the same information database but present somewhat different results because they use different algorithms when displaying their information.

OSR professionals follow these specialized sites in order to learn the details they need to know about search engines and keep up with the almost-daily changes that occur throughout this ever-changing resource.

And changes are coming all the time. As Web traffic on mobile phones has swamped traffic from computers, some Internet leaders have adopted a "mobile-first" response. Already there are plans to develop different search engines for mobile phones and computers. Sites and content that are not mobile-friendly will likely suffer a penalty under an upcoming search regime.

Basic Searches

At the most basic level there are two key ways of directly searching the Web:

- Search engines
- Web directories.

These are often confused, but there is a major difference. Knowing that difference, and capitalizing on it, may help you discover the answers you seek. In addition to these two there are some techniques and expedients that, when used with, or in place of, search engines may provide doors, even if back doors, to the important information that is otherwise elusive.

Search Engines

Search Engines are tools that allow anyone to search millions of web pages or Internet sites.

Typically search engine "hits" are displayed as a title link that can be clicked in order to go to the particular page located somewhere in the information universe. The link is often followed by a posting of the site/page URL and a brief description of what is on the page. With some search engines there may be additional help, sometimes hidden in a drop-down menu, such as a link to a databased copy of the web page that was collected earlier.

Search engines have three main parts. To use them effectively it is important to understand how the parts work, what each does and – crucially – what they will not do.

Search engines are electro-mechanical marvels that send "spiders" to scour the Internet. Spiders do not operate in real time. Spiders travel from a search engine to an Internet site, then send back information to the search engine's database about the pages they visit.

The search engine will eventually display the databased information to the search engine user, in some ranked order, based on whatever secret algorithm the engine uses. Human input to search engine results is nil except for writing the algorithms and determining the search patterns that govern the spiders' actions.

A search engine's "spider," also called a "robot" or "crawler," visits sites and locates information – but it goes only where and when it is allowed to go. The spider has no goal other than grabbing as much information as its own rules and the wishes of a website's operator allow. Some spiders collect every word on a site, others have a word limit; in such cases some material in lengthy pages may not be collected or indexed. That means that in any foreshortened site visits the spider, the search engine, and eventually you may miss important information because the spider never collected any information from part of the page.

After the spider sends back information from the visited site to the search engine, the material is placed in the engine's database. The spider then uses any links within a site to travel to other pages or sites where it continues its ceaseless work. Spiders work behind the scenes. The search engine user never sees them and, in fact, never has any way to know that they even exist or understand what they do.

A key part of the search engine, the index, is a database that stores the information that the spider found and returned. When a user's query comes in to the search engine the index algorithm software sifts through the data stored in the index. The index, using those unseen algorithms, matches the query with the information in the database and sends whatever information it decides matches the query out to the search engine user.

Before sending the information to the user, a third part of the search engine performs another job that is also hidden from users. The statistical interface assigns relative weight to each search term. Factors the statistical interface may consider include:

- Frequency of the term's occurrence on the webpage
- Rarity in the database
- Filter Bubbles (personalization algorithms in some engines auto-filter out some results and indirectly sanitize the search engine's return of any opposing viewpoints)
- Whether the search term is found in the URL
- Location of the search term on the page, proximity to the top often being advantageous
- A myriad of other factors that the public is never allowed to know.

Be aware that many search engines now use a popularity algorithm to determine the order of their returns rather than the "most-mentioned in text" figures. This scheme means that the most useful sites may be ignored or downgraded because the returns are skewed toward the most popular sites. Because of this skewing it is wise to go at least three pages, or about 75 items deep, into the returns when conducting searches.

Search engines can only send a user the information that is stored in their index databases. If the index information is old, incomplete, or if the spider missed some site that actually had valuable information the query will not be properly or completely answered.

The rarity, or prevalence, of the search term in the engine's database means that researchers have to excel at selecting keywords.

Researchers also need to understand that they are actually searching a search engine's database. They are neither searching the entire Web nor are they searching in real time. They are searching what the search engine Web crawler or spider found at some time in the past – hopefully the recent past, but still the past.

Search engine lists are valuable resources. While some important ones are listed below, make yourself aware of any site that has collected the URLs to multiple search engines. Using a search engine list affords the researcher or research desk a wider choice among these important search tools. Lists include:

- **Arnold International Search Engine List:** http://www.arnoldit.com/lists/searchlist.html
- **International Search Engines:** https://www.brightedge.com/blog/international-search-engines/
- **Search Engine Colossus:** http://www.searchenginecolossus.com/

- **Search Engine Guide/Directory:**
  http://www.searchengineguide.com/searchengines.html
- **Search Engine Links:**
  http://www.searchenginelinks.co.uk/
- **Wikipedia List of Search Engines:**
  https://en.wikipedia.org/wiki/List_of_search_engines.

Wikipedia's list provides a good deal of background information that could be useful when choosing among various search engines.

The world of search engines is as large as the planet; finding the best one(s) for your particular project is a challenge. As you go through any list, note those search engines that track in languages other than English, and in pictures, or by things other than text. Some leaders in the field include:

- **Advangle (Google and Bing):** http://advangle.com/
- **AOL:** https://www.aol.ca/?r=www.aol.com
- **Archie (FTP):** http://archie.icm.edu.pl/archie_eng.html
- **Ask:** https://www.ask.com/
- **Bing:** http://www.bing.com
- **Bing vs Google:** http://bvsg.org/
- **Censys (Hosts, servers and networks):** https://censys.io/
- **Dogpile (Web, pictures and video):**
  http://www.dogpile.com/
- **DotHop (Web, pictures and video):**
  http://dothop.com/home
- **DuckDuckGo (Does not track user):**
  http://www.DuckDuckGo.com
- **Ecosia (Bing-powered eco-friendly):**
  https://www.ecosia.org/
- **Entire Web:** http://www.entireweb.com
- **Exalead:** http://www.exalead.com/search/
- **Filemare (FTP search):** https://filemare.com/
- **GenerateIt (Source code):** https://www.generateit.net/seo-tools/source-viewer/

- **Gigablast (Also a directory):** http://www.Gigablast.com
- **Google:** http://www.google.com
- **Google Advanced Search:** https://www.google.com/advanced_search
- **Google Newspaper Archive (Historical papers):** https://news.google.com/newspapers
- **Google Patents:** http://google.com/advanced_patent_search
- **Google Scholar:** https://scholar.google.com/
- **Hidden Wiki (Tor URLs and Directories):** http://thehiddenwiki.org/
- **Infospace:** http://infospace.com/
- **Instya (Multiple search engines and sites):** http://www.instya.com/#/web
- **iSeek (Education):** http://iseek.com/iseek/home.page
- **iZito:** http://www.izito.com/
- **KeywordTool (Keyword search box aid):** https://keywordtool.io/
- **Lycos:** http://www.lycos.com
- **Mamont (FTP search engine):** http://www.mmnt.ru/int/
- **Mention Alerts (Brand checking, $$$$):** https://mention.com/en/
- **MetaCrawler:** http://metacrawler.com/
- **Million Short (Remove top referrals):** https://millionshort.com/
- **Mozbot:** http://www.mozbot.com
- **Napalm (FTP Indexer):** http://www.searchftps.net/
- **NerdyData (Technology source code):** https://nerdydata.com/search
- **Newspaper Archive (Genealogy and news records search):** https://newspaperarchive.com/
- **Not Evil (Tor search, access from The Onion Router):** https://hss3uro2hsxfogfq.onion.to/
- **Oscobo:** https://oscobo.co.uk/
- **Podcastsearchengine:** http://www.podcasts.com/

- **PublicWWW (Source code search engine):**
  https://publicwww.com/
- **Quora:** https://www.quora.com/
- **Search.com (Metasearch):** http://www.search.com/
- **Search Both: (Google and Yahoo from various locations):** http://us.searchboth.net/
- **Searx:** https://searx.me/
- **Shodan (Internet of Things):** https://www.shodan.io/
- **Sputtr:** http://www.sputtr.com/
- **StartPage (Privacy aware):** https://www.startpage.com/
- **Teoma:** http://www.Teoma.com
- **That's Them:** https://thatsthem.com/
- **Full Wiki (Wikipedia search):**
  http://www.thefullwiki.org/
- **Tor2Web/Torch (Tor search):**
  https://xmh57jrzrnw6insl.onion.to/
- **US Newspaper Directory (Library of Congress):**
  http://chroniclingamerica.loc.gov/search/titles/
- **US Newspaper Directory (Library of Congress Chronicling America):** http://chroniclingamerica.loc.gov/
- **Virtual Search Engines (Jump site):**
  http://virtualfreesites.com/search.html
- **Wolfram Alpha (Semantic search engine):**
  http://www.wolframalpha.com
- **Yahoo!:** http://www.yahoo.com
- **Yahoo (Advanced):**
  https://search.yahoo.com/web/advanced
- **Yippy:** http://yippy.com/
- **YouGottheNews (US media):** http://yougotthenews.com/.

Search engine size matters. The larger the database of any general search engine the more likely it can provide the information you are looking for. To get a relative estimate of the effective size of a search engine, run separate searches using a few words important to your project on different engines. Compare the results. While that will not show you the actual size of the search engine database, by comparing the figures on your subject you can get a sense of the relative size – and hence probable utility for you – of the various engines. Those search engines that have cataloged the most key terms that apply to your project are more likely to provide the information you need.

As is true with every tool a researcher or research desk employs, the particular search engine, its limitations, and its best uses, must be clearly understood. Researchers who want optimal results need to learn the syntax and understand the capability limits and quirks of each search engine they use. It is not enough to know that pay-for-placement sites or the more popular web pages are often returned first regardless of whether they really have anything useful to you. OSR professionals dive into the weeds and understand search engine basics such as statistical interfaces, concept-based search mechanisms, and how link analysis is used to return and rank hits. These are among the many things that can affect information retrieval.

The *minutiae* of search engines is almost never-ending. For instance, stopwords are commonplace words that search engines ignore – stop paying attention to – in a search. Common stopwords vary from search engine to search engine but they typically are things such as: to, as, of, a, an, the, this, or that. Stopwords can change the result of a search so you should consider their presence when doing any search. To prevent the stopwords' effect on some websites, put suspect words in quotation marks or place a plus (+) sign in front of them, forcing the search engine to look for them. Checking the Internet for "stopwords" and your browser name is often a useful exercise.

In the same vein, words with the same spelling may have different meanings. That difference may alter the search results dramatically. Placing a minus sign in front of words or concepts you do not want included may exclude them from the results. If you are interested only in jaguar, the car, you could enter "jaguar –cat" in the search box.

Knowing any search engine's intricacies, and how to coax it to suit your particular needs, is important.

Professionals understand the search syntax employed by whatever search engine they are using; they don't simply assume. This is particularly important when using foreign search engines.

Search engines do not employ a common syntax. Many, but not all, understand that a phrase enclosed in quotation marks means you want to locate the exact phrase – not something close to it, but the exact words. While many search engines will exclude a word that has a minus sign (-word) in front of it, you cannot be certain unless you have checked the syntax of that particular search engine. Learn about and understand your search engine tools like mechanics know their wrench sets.

Because of the differences in search engine algorithms and the fact that different search engines may have collected different web pages, results invariably vary from one search engine to another.

Search engines are also the open mic of the Internet, picking up every mistake anyone ever made when posting information on a page. They know only what they find of a page, they cannot guess what someone intended or flag the fact that someone blundered and posted something they shouldn't have. One, or more, search engines may pick up information that was never intended to be public, or that was left up in some obscure corner of the Internet long after it should have been taken down. When you think through likely errors in the information smudge and search for those, including misspellings, you can find valuable information.

Keep in mind that many search engines track users and their interests. This may be good for some users but it is often a potential security issue for OSR operators.

Tracking programs and devices are endemic to search engines and the Internet – everyone tries to track everyone else. Well, almost everyone. Non-tracking engines help close that book.

Yes. Privacy-aware search engines, which do not track users or record their searches, do exist. They operate differently from each other and are different from the engines that are not sticklers for privacy. Privacy-aware search engines seldom provide as many links as some of the more popular search engines. As a result, you must balance security issues against search completeness when using privacy-aware search engines. Security conscious researchers often use privacy-aware search engines at the beginning of their investigations and switch to search engines which offer a larger database if they cannot find what they need in the initial sortie.

Privacy-aware search engines may:

- Remove referral information, so website managers do not learn your search queries
- Collect limited, or even no, information about you or your search
- Set no cookies unless users want special preferences to be remembered
- Offer the use of a proxy to provide anonymity when viewing search results.

Privacy-aware search engines are increasing in public popularity, particularly among those who want to avoid the filter bubble created by search engines that offer links and returns based upon what you clicked on previously. Such search customization can easily create or intensify confirmation bias.

Some privacy-aware search engines that claim they don't track include:

- **DuckDuck Go:** https://duckduckgo.com/
- **Gibiru:** https://www.gibiru.com/
- **Jive Search:** https://www.jivesearch.com/
- **Mojeek:** https://www.mojeek.com/
- **Oscobo:** https://www.oscobo.com/
- **Peekier:** https://peekier.com/
- **Qwant (European):** https://www.qwant.com/
- **SearX:** https://searx.me/
- **Startpage:** https://www.startpage.com/
- **Swisscows:** https://swisscows.com/
- **Yippy:** http://www.yippy.com/.

Search engines track many parts of the Internet.

Social media searches of all types are generally more difficult and aren't done by most general search engines. With the current public emphasis on social networking, it is important to know how to find, and use, search engines that specialize in the social media field. These often facilitate searches among several social networking sites such as Facebook and Twitter. Many are fee-based. Specialized searchers include:

- **Social-Searcher:** https://www.social-searcher.com/
- **Tagboard ($$$$):** https://www.tagboard.com

Other specialized search engines merely show a presence on social media. Some will simply see if a user name is being used, or if it is still available, on dozens of social media sites. What this type of site actually shows is where a particular "handle" is in use.

Once you know a user's "handle," you can use that information to see where else that handle is in use, a clue as to where the person, company or brand might be posting to other popular social media sites. The "handle" may be used consistently by a user for everything from sign-ons to postings elsewhere in social media.

The "handle" is as a matter of self-identity and consistency; its use on different social media may show that one person is on a number of sites. It is also possible that several people are using the same handle. The researcher has to figure that out. Further detailed research is always needed when searching with handles.

Name check sites that may reveal handles include:
- **Checkusernames:** https://checkusernames.com/
- **Knowem:** https://knowem.com/
- **Namecheck:** Namecheck.com/
- **Namecheckr:** https://www.namecheckr.com/
- **User Search:** https://www.usersearch.org/.

It may also be noted that many people carry the "handle" idea one step further and use the same password on multiple accounts with the same handle. That is as unsafe as it is common, however. And that can lead to major information leaks!

Check sites that show if someone has been pwnded, such as **Have I Been Pwned** https://haveibeenpwned.com/, to see if you or others have had their identities or passwords revealed. There are serious ethical questions about whether a pwned identity or password is actually open source and how such information, when found, can be used legally. Even when not used to research about others, periodic checks of sites like this to protect your privacy and the security of your research team are wise.

Creating a Search

Effective searches are usually multi-step processes. Most amateur searchers make a single attempt and they are done. Finished. Kaput! Research professionals know an effective search requires putting far more skin in the game.

The first few pages returned – following the paid placement results – are what the search engine algorithm says will likely be the most relevant and productive. They may be the most popular sites but that doesn't mean they have the most, or even any, usable information. It will depend on the search engine's algorithm. If these pages fall short, and they often do, it is time to regroup. Refine the search and try again by adding a keyword or two, or changing the word order. Many search engines look for the first word and then try to find any following search words within pages that contain the first word of the search order. When you are close, but are not quite there, many search engines will allow you to add terms and search within the current results to further narrow your query.

Be aware of, and use advanced search techniques that effectively trick the search engine into providing information that it hadn't planned on revealing, methods such as a "site:" search.

Always write down and save the search terms you use, noting whether they produce information or not. Keep a notebook, file, or list to show what worked and what did not. Save that list. It may be useful later. If you have to replicate the search you will know what worked best, and what didn't work at all.

Google Search

Since Google is often thought of as the preeminent search engine in the Western world, a closer look at its capabilities and resources can serve as an introduction to all search engines. That is not to say that Google's extensive search features will be found on all other search engines, or that other search engines don't have features and capabilities that Google lacks. Rather, Google merits understanding as an example of what you can do with search engines, and how you can do it. Your knowledge of the way Google works will be handy when evaluating and using other search engines.

Consider Google to be a baseline.

On Google, before doing anything, review the **privacy**, **terms**, and **search settings** at the extreme bottom right side of the home page.

Privacy issues are always important! Read the terms of service here, or on any site, carefully. Save them. They tell you what you can do, and what the site can do with your information, or even to you. The terms of service statement is equivalent to a contract. It is a non-negotiable contract, one that you will be held to.

Not every search engine is like Google. Some sites lack a readily apparent page that contains the contract information. To find it on those search sites, put in the name of the search engine and phrases such as "terms of use" or "terms of service."

Before doing any search, look up the term "Google" using the home page. When the home page with links comes up, thoroughly acquaint yourself with the various features at the top of the page such as news, maps, images, more, settings, and tools.

Choose your search settings carefully.

The settings you choose on any search engine affect your results and the ease with which you can get those results. Pay special attention to anything you see that has to do with your search history as this can often be used to identify you and your interests.

Also pay particular attention when you click the "settings" drop down menu. When you are going to do searches of foreign countries decide if you want to search in the language of the area. At the same time, in the "search settings" consider what region of the world you want to be searching from. Google provides different results depending on the area it thinks you are searching from. In most cases your chances of finding complete information are improved by searching from whatever region or country you are concentrating on.

Once you have set up your search settings return to Google's home page. There are options there (often called the splash or landing page) for "Google Search" and "I'm Feeling Lucky." The latter option simply takes the researcher to the first page on Google's hit parade. Researchers are not gamblers, nor are they likely to find any, much less all, the information they need on a single page. "I'm Feeling Lucky" is never an option for real researchers.

There are a number of search functions available. Expert researchers should know how – and when – to use each of them.

Image searches – there will be more detailed information in another chapter – are highly useful. Images often provide information that text alone doesn't, or even cannot. Images provide both a breadth of information and a granularity that text simply does not. To use **Image Search**, select the "images" tab at the top of the Google splash page or, alternatively, go to http://images.google.com.

There will be a camera in the search box on the images page. Enter the query word or words in the image search box, then click the "search" button. The results page will show thumbnails of the pictures the search engine holds; to see a larger version of the image, as well as the web page on which the image is actually located, click on the thumbnail image. The Google image often has attached metadata – information about the picture – that may be useful. There are many types of metadata and a high percentage of metadata are useful. Some examples of metadata on pictures include: time, date, device, settings, and location. Right clicking on the image allows you to select "view image information," which will provide some basic metadata. However, to really profit from metadata you will need other programs and processes, discussed in the chapter on pictures and multi-media. The Google process, however, provides an indication of how metadata works and what it is.

Most, if not all, of the pictures shown in any image search are protected by some level of copyright. Before a picture may be used for any purpose by a viewer it must either fall under the Fair Use copyright exception or the picture owner must grant permission to use the picture. (The authors of this book are not attorneys and cannot advise anyone on the legality of using any picture or other material from the Internet. Contact your legal advisor to resolve all questions.)

Google Groups: https://groups.google.com/ has been devised as a discussion area. It is a free service. Members of the discussion groups initiate new conversations or reply to posted comments. Google Groups offers a home page, hosted by Google. Members of any group can begin new discussions or participate in discussion of already-posted topics. Each group is given an email address to facilitate the communication. Members of Google Groups have the capability to search and read all public Google Groups content. There is also a fast-search capability, allowing quicker, easier access to discussions that have already ended. Google groups has assumed the role of stockpiling group postings of previous decades, when the similar Usenet groups were more popular.

Google News searches for, and gathers, stories from sites worldwide. While it supposedly scours several thousand news sites the stories that appear are generally from a small group of providers. It uses a proprietary – that translates to "unknown" – algorithm to collect and arrange the stories. The page is updated several times each hour; new articles appear and older ones disappear frequently. Clicking on the item takes the user to the site where the article appeared. The site also has an advanced search feature which can be accessed by clicking on the down arrow at the right of the search box. That advanced search feature also allows users to search for archived news items. The Google news site can be found at https://news.google.com.

Google Custom Search Engine: https://cse.google.com/cse/ allow the user to create a search engine that will only search specific pages, websites, or domains designated by the website creator. This feature can be highly useful when daily or ongoing searches are planned on specific sites. Since they automatically alert open source researchers to new information on selected websites they save time that would be spent in repeated manual searches of the same site.

Custom search engines (CSEs) allow the user create a search engine that will only look at those five – or five hundred – locations the user thinks are the most valuable. By limiting the sites searched the custom search engine eliminates the dross that is inevitable when the results of all the spider's meanderings are included in the results. The custom search engine shaves the offerings down to only those results that are found on sites you know are useful or valuable. Custom search engines, used properly, avoid "junk" from sites that may be questionable. They concentrate their efforts – and your time – on the web locations that you determine are the most valuable to your work.

CSEs can be created in a variety of languages. They may be crafted to look only at individual pages, certain parts of a site, or the entire domain. Carefully used, professional researchers can create custom search engines to increase their reach while eliminating or reducing unproductive search time.

Searching Aids

Google uses a variety of special operators – discussed at length later in this chapter – that make searches more effective. In searches, Google assumes the AND operator. Type two or more words in the search engine and it will return only pages that have all the terms, even without the special operator AND.

When OR is entered between search terms, always in capital letters, Google searches for any of the words.

When quotation marks ("_") are put around search terms, Google looks for the exact, and entire, quoted phrase.

The tilde (~) sign, put in front of a search term, is a wide-ranging operator on Google. It searches on the term itself and expands the search to synonyms Google has listed in its algorithm for the search term.

When Google returns the hits from its database, analysts use the "text excerpt" line to determine the probable relevance. It may help you decide whether the site will be useful to you without ever clicking on the link. Text from the site, with keywords highlighted, provides some evidence the page has the information you are seeking. Often there will be links to other, similar, materials. These can be either gold mines or rabbit holes.

Many researchers make it a rule to never click on the title line link. While it seems unlikely, the ultra-cautious feel that line may contain hidden code that can be used to misdirect you to another page. Instead of clicking on the underlined title, security-aware researchers who want to look at the page manually type in the URL they see into their browser.

There is often a drop-down menu attached to the search return, indicated by a down arrow. That drop-down menu allows you to go to the cached page or to pages like it. Consider writing into your SOP a rule about whether to habitually look at a cache or similar pages. They are saved at different times and may show differing things. Caches also allow you to visit a copy of the website held by the search engine rather than the page at the actual site. This has the advantage of keeping site administrators unaware of your interest and identity. It also reduces the possibility of getting a virus from a malware-infected page since search engines take extraordinary measures to keep their pages clean of anything harmful. Looking at the cached page, providing that page does not have any pictures on it, is generally quite safe. However, if there are pictures on the page the search engine probably does not have them in its database. In that case the search engine reaches out to the page itself to pick up the pictures. When it does so the system operator of the page may see your search query and be able to identify your interest. If anonymity is essential you will want to set up your browser so that it will not automatically reach out to another site without your permission.

Remember that different search engines visit a site at different times and may have different cache pages. You may consider looking at cache pages of different search engines, seeing if there are any differences in what was saved.

Remember, also, that Google and other sites use geolocation in determining the results they send. Search engines detect where you are coming from and alter the results they send you accordingly. A researcher or research desk in Paris may not get the same results as one in Poughkeepsie, even when the researcher or research desk inputs the same key words. Be aware of where the search engine thinks you are coming from; the search engine is aware of your stated location.

Google Advanced Search Options

Advanced search techniques are at the heart of some of the best research to be garnered through Google, or any search engine.

Advanced searches allow you to narrow your probe, and the results, to a manageable size. They are filters that allow you get the most pertinent answers. **Google's advanced search page** can be found at https://www.google.com/advanced_search. It can make searching more productive.

Advanced search pages like Google's essentially automate what are known as Boolean searches. This way the user doesn't have to navigate the more complex Boolean path. While Google's advanced search features are often considered a model, only a few other large search engines have similar, or as-effective, options.

One of the Google Advanced Search options is "language." The language setting returns only pages written in the language you choose from a drop-down index. This option is generally set to do a single search in a foreign language. When many searches will be done in a foreign language a Google "preference" setting found elsewhere on the site allows all searches to be done in the language that the user chooses. This setting is often reset by researchers who specialize in subjects that are always written in foreign languages.

If you are searching in a foreign language it makes sense to be searching from the area where the language is spoken. There are a couple of ways to do this with Google. To search for what you would see if you were searching from another location, you can cut off the last part of the search result from a US location and add "gl=(two-letter Internet country code)." To pretend you were searching from a location along the Seine you could change the address to https://www.google.com/search?q=normandie&gl=FR, for example. This search change should not alter your language preference setting, however. Another way would be to click on the "settings" link at the bottom of the Google splash page, go down to "Region Settings" section, and then click the "France" radio button. When you use this method you will also be offered the opportunity to change the search language to French.

Be aware: Foreign language searches require extra-special efforts.

Transliteration is a bear! Names of groups, companies, and the acronyms for them often differ in different languages. The group is Doctors Without Borders (DWB or MSF USA) in the US but it is known as Médecins Sans Frontières (MSF) in France. If you are dealing with organizations in a country other than your own, determine what the proper name is in the language of that other country. Use both the names and the acronyms for searches. Searching, particularly on foreign sites, produces better results when you use the local terminology. Search all the possible terms: English language, transliteration, and native language. When possible, use the national keyboard of the country and language in which you are searching. In countries that have two or more official languages – such as Canada – search in all pertinent languages, using the proper keyboard, terms, and terminology.

Google offers a limited number of time-frame options, options that may be useful when you feel certain the information you are looking for took place on, or around, particular dates. Because of the limited specificity of Google time-frame options many researchers choose other search engines with more robust time-frame selections when doing date searches. Even under the best of circumstances, "date" is relatively useless in Webpage searches on any engine because the word has no defined meaning; it means whatever the individual site developer decided.

Domain searches are not the most intuitive searches available on Goggle. Yet used under the right circumstances, and in the right way, they can be highly useful. Domains are a way of categorizing sites, keeping likes together.

Domain searches can be used to limit the search to specific websites, limiting the sources but drilling down to the sites more likely to have the information you want. If you are looking for information about a corporate meeting in Germany it is far more likely that German sites and German Internet domains will have more extensive coverage than will ones from Zimbabwe, Japan, or the United States. The user looks up the national domain code for all German sites and restricts the search to those sites. When you want to see only what a single site has available, carefully choose the domain you want to limit your searches to.

There has been a proliferation of top level domain names (TLDs) in recent years, and the list is growing. The original main domain groups – some listed below – and country-specific domain names have now been supplemented by a plethora of other names.

- .com - commercial

- .edu – education
- .gov – US government
- .info – information
- .int – international organizations
- .mil – US Department of Defense
- .net – networks
- .org – organizations.

There are now more than 1,500 TLDs as the complexity of TLD naming continues to grow. Knowledge of TLDs, and the details of the various naming conventions, is essential for serious researchers. As with most Internet-related issues, a quick Web search – in this case using the terms "TLD" or "Top Level Domain" – will bring up informative pages about them. Access a current TLD list through Wikipedia's page or other sites. Researchers often keep a list of top level domain names in their SOP book, updating and reviewing it every three to six months.

Besides its advanced searches, Google offers a number of topic-specific search areas that the researcher or research desk should become familiar with.

Google Books at https://books.google.com/ searches books that have been scanned into Google's databases. This is a controversial program since some authors object to making their work available for free through the Internet.

Google Scholar is a service that allows you to search for scholarly papers, a resource that is too often overlooked by most people. Scholarly papers about a subject usually are far more accurate and reliable than blog information will be, but make certain the scholar you want to cite is a recognized authority in the field. **Google Scholar**, useful when conducting expert searches, is at https://scholar.google.com.

Trends are often important to understanding current issues. While there are a number of ways of searching for information on trending subjects, the **Google Trends** webpage located at https://trends.google.com/trends is a useful place to start.

Google – like many search engines – has a variety of capabilities that are not readily apparent. Click on the icon of nine blocks on the upper right of the splash page to see some of them. Click through and examine each. Then go to the bottom of that pop-up and click "more" to see additional capabilities. Check all of these out and see if they are useful to you. Then go to the bottom of that pop-up and click on "even more" to round out the resources. Understand what each of the links and capabilities can do for your searches.

Learn the ins and outs of Google; the **Google Guide** site at http://www.googleguide.com/contents/ should be thoroughly and carefully reviewed by researchers who want to become proficient with the many capabilities and shortcuts of that search engine. **Simply Google,** another resource that makes life easier for researchers, is at http://www.usabilityviews.com/simply_google.htm

Experience, and only experience, dictates the best search engine, techniques, and key words to use in researching any particular subject.

Use a number of different search engines, both for the sake of security and because they differ in how they search and where they search. Some search topically; some use different statistical formulas. Even search engines using the same spiders or crawlers produce differing results because of their display algorithms. But always remember, no matter what search engine you use, no matter how extensively it sends out spiders, all search engines provide information on only a teeny, tiny fraction of the Web. And their data is never displayed to you in real time.

Other General Search Engines

Keep in mind that Google isn't the only answer! There are many general search engines. While Google is often considered the most popular search engine in the Western world, there are scores of others. To get an idea of your constellation of choices, see **Search Engine Colossus** at: http://www.searchenginecolossus.com/.

As important as it is to use multiple browsers for reasons of security and efficiency, it is also important to utilize more than one search engine for completeness. Develop a list of search engines you like to use; ones that work for your projects. When the term is obscure, or searches on one search engine fail to provide a satisfactory or complete answer, go down your list of preferred search engines.

Metasearch Engines

Metasearch engines are popular with some, particularly in the opening stages of a project. Metasearch engines allow users to query multiple search engines simultaneously. These aggregation engines package data from other search engines to create their own results based on what are – theoretically – the best results from several search engines.

In reality metasearch results are often a mile wide and an inch deep; that is, their searches are shallow. Users get a handful of top results from each site the metasearch engine checks.

Because of the differences among search engines in what they collect and how they collect that data, the result offered up by metasearch engines may not meet the user's intended search criteria. Spamdexing – manipulation of search engine indexes by a variety of means – is another problem with metasearch engines.

Since metasearch engines take a very limited number of results from any search engine site their results should never be considered comprehensive. However, metasearch engines often provide a possible introduction to a subject and, moreover, can be used early-on to develop key word lists.

Assume that Boolean search techniques – discussed shortly – will not work when doing metasearches. Because search engines do not have a standardized way of treating Boolean logic, the special techniques you might use effectively on a single search engine that you are familiar with are removed from metasearches.

Researchers also need to be aware of which search engines the metasearch engines draw from. When using metasearch engines it is obviously best to use ones drawing from engines you don't use routinely since that enhances the breadth of your online effort.

"Clustering" search engines are considered a subtype of metasearch tools, organizing what is otherwise unstructured data into folders, putting like with like. They give researchers a skeleton to work from.

Important metasearch-type tools include:
- **All in One:** https://all-io.net/
- **All the Internet (Firefox):** https://www.alltheinternet.com/
- **Carrot2: (Clustering):** http://search.carrot2.org/stable/search
- **DMOZ Metasearch List:** https://dmoztools.net/Computers/Internet/Searching/Metasearch/
- **Dogpile:** http://www.dogpile.com
- **eLocalFinder (Local services) :** http://www.elocalfinder.com/HSearch.aspx
- **Etools:** https://www.etools.ch/search.do
- **Excite: http://www.excite.com/**
- **InfoSpace:** http://www.info.co
- **Iseek (Clustering):** http://iseek.com/#/search/web

- **Izito:** https://www.izito.com/
- **MetaCrawler:** http://www.metacrawler.com
- **MetaGer (Privacy):** https://metager.de/en
- **Myallsearch:** https://www.myallsearch.com/
- **SearX:** https://searx.me/
- **ZapMeta:** http://www.zapmeta.com/.

Megasearch sounds much like metasearch, but they are significantly different types of engines. Megasearch engines are sites where several different search engines can be accessed from a single site, but where each search must be conducted independently. Major megasearch sites include:

- **Search-22:** http://www.search-22.com/
- **Searchezee:** http://www.searchezee.com/.

Weblog Search Engines may be necessary when doing some types of research. A weblog, or "blog", is often a personal journal on the Web. Many are indeed highly personal, like a diary, and sometimes they contain the same type of information that can be either enlightening or damaging. The meaning of "Weblog" has been expanded to describe almost any type of site that is primarily opinion-oriented or allows commentary. Visitors to blogs are often able to comment on postings, and comment on comments to postings. Such blogs run the gamut of subjects; they offer opinions that vary from highly thoughtful to way-out. Some blogs have extensive readership and are influential. Most blogs are of interest largely to a close circle of family, friends – and enemies. Weblog-type search engines include **Tumblr:** https://www.tumblr.com/.

Search engines come in many different "flavors," specializing in different things. There are specific search methods for videos, pictures, and people. Regional and specialty search areas may also have dedicated search engines.

Some sites – such as Facebook, LinkedIn, and YouTube – often function surprisingly well as specialized search engines although that is not what they were designed to do. Use whatever search tool best fits, fits at all, or can be made to fit.

People and Entity Searches

People and the organizations they are associated with are common – in many cases the most common – type of searches. These are always important.

As an initial step, try to grab a handful of information. These six things, when ascertained and used in further searches, will usually lead to more-detailed information about any person who becomes a search subject:

- Name
- Physical address
- Birthdate/age
- Phone number
- Email address
- "Handle" on the Web.

Governments – national and local – often collect this type of information. Much if it is publicly available through such sites as **Black Book Online** at https://www.blackbookonline.info/ or local governmental agencies.

Many researchers use a variety of commercial "people search engines" to verify information they already have, or to add new information about a subject. They can be used to expand and deepen understanding or develop in-depth profiles.

Usually commercial people searches are conducted by a "best match" algorithm rather than an "exact match" formula. That has positive and negative consequences: You are likely to get a wide range of possibilities but if the people are indeed on whatever list of possibilities the engine provides you will need to dig deeper, much deeper, to find the exact person you are searching for.

While many people may have the same, or similar, names it is extremely unusual for people to have the same email or physical address, or the same phone number. If you know any of these they can be used as filters for your search, limiting the results to the individuals you are researching.

Background-checking sites have been developed extensively by the search industry. Aggregation search engines of this type are common, combining publicly available data from a variety of sources. Particularly in the US there has been a move to concatenate the materials available in many public or government records and make that data available to information seekers. Some sites are free; most cost money, terming themselves "premium." Usually even premium sites provide some information for free, luring users in. For the most part the "premium" information on commercial people search engines is seldom worth the cost. You can often compile the same information by checking several free sites because each one may offer slightly different information. On some sites the premium information is actually contained in the downloaded free page but is not made visible to the user. By downloading and laboriously peering through the source code of the page you may find much more additional information that has been hidden.

The accuracy of the information in any given people search varies, but by using several different search engines – as well as some sites that are not considered search engines themselves but can be used in that way – it is possible to achieve accurate results.

For instance, sites with resumes provide extensive, if one-sided, looks at a person. Resume posters often provide scads of basic information about themselves, their history, their accomplishments and their capabilities. There will also usually be useful information like phone numbers, addresses, and other contact information. All of this may provide leads to even more information.

Sites such as LinkedIn may go even further. Their design allows users to look for people by the name their employer, whether at present or in the past. This can be useful for gaining knowledge about particular companies, organizations, and their activities. Searching by company can provide an information treasure trove.

Many dating websites provide a plethora of personal information. At a minimum the location generally will be accurate. And if the user is really keen on developing a serious relationship the other details will generally hold true. Since many dating and professional enhancement sites include photos, using reverse-image search is often helpful in searches about people.

Social media sites can hold a treasure trove of information about someone, including pictures and information about friends and family.

With the wide variety of people and entity engines available, as well as sites that can be used for those types of searches even if not intended for that, it is possible to develop a highly-accurate picture of individuals and organizations. For instance, sites that report political contributions will often have personal information, including employers. Government sites that show home ownership or licensing will also provide personal information. Useful sites in person searches include:

- **411:** https://www.411.com/
- **Addresses:** http://www.addresses.com
- **AddressSearch:** https://www.addresssearch.com/
- **Advanced Background Checks:**
  https://www.advancedbackgroundchecks.com/
- **Ashley Madison ($$$$, Sex-oriented):**
  https://www.ashleymadison.com/
- **Been Verified:** https://www.beenverified.com/
- **Black Book Online (Public records):**
  https://www.blackbookonline.info/
- **Canada411 (Canada):** http://www.canada411.ca/

- **Classmates (Schoolmates, annuals):**
  http://www.classmates.com/
- **Combin (Instagram):** https://www.combin.com/4k/
- **Cubib:** http://cubib.com/
- **CVGADGET:** https://cvgadget.com/
- **DeathIndexes (Genealogy):**
  https://www.deathindexes.com/
- **Ebsco ($$$$):** https://www.ebsco.com/
- **Eharmony (Dating):** https://www.eharmony.com/
- **Emailchecker (Email verification):**
  https://www.emailchecker.com/
- **Facebook:** http://www.Facebook.com
- **Facebook Search:**
  https://lookup-id.com/facebooksearch.html
- **FamilyTreeNow (Genealogy):**
  https://www.familytreenow.com/
- **FastPeopleSearch:** https://www.fastpeoplesearch.com/
- **Findmypast/Mocavo (Geneology):**
  https://www.findmypast.com/mocavo-info
- **Geosocialfootprint (Twitter presence):**
  http://geosocialfootprint.com/
- **Hi5 (Social interaction):** https://secure.hi5.com/
- **Houseparty (Social interaction):** https://houseparty.com/
- **Howmanyofme (Name popularity):**
  http://howmanyofme.com/search/
- **Hunter (Email addresses):** https://hunter.io/
- **Indeed (Resume):** https://www.indeed.com/
- **Infobel (Phones)** http://www.infobel.com/
- **Intelius ($$$$):** http://www.intelius.com
- **LexisNexis ($$$$):**
  https://www.lexisnexis.com/en-us/gateway.page
- **LinkedIn (Professional enhancement):**
  http://www.linkedin.com
- **Lullar:** http://com.lullar.com/

- **Match ($$$$, Dating):** https://www.match.com/cpx/en-us/match/IndexPage/
- **Meetup (Social Interaction):** https://www.meetup.com/
- **Mocavo (Family history):** https://www.findmypast.com/mocavo-info
- **MyLife:** http://mylife.com
- **Netbootcamp Facebook Search Tool:** netbootcamp.org/facebook.html
- **Nuwber:** https://nuwber.com/
- **OKCupid (Dating):** https://www.okcupid.com/
- **OpenSecrets (Political contributions):** https://www.opensecrets.org/donor-lookup
- **OurTime (Dating):** https://www.ourtime.com/
- **PeekYou: (User names etc.)** http://www.peekyou.com
- **People Finders:** http://www.peoplefinders.com
- **People Lookup:** http://www.peoplelookup.com
- **Phone Book of the World:** http://phonebookoftheworld.com/
- **Picodash (Instagram and Twitter):** https://www.picodash.com/
- **Plenty of Fish (Dating):** https://www.pof.com/
- **Political Money Line:** http://www.politicalmoneyline.com/
- **Prophet: (Recruiting information):** https://recruitingtools.com/
- **Radaris:** http://radaris.com/
- **Reunion:** http://www.reunion.com/
- **ReverseGenie (Reverse-search engine, email, phone):** http://www.reversegenie.com/
- **Ripoffreport (Bad business experience):** https://www.ripoffreport.com/
- **Rootsweb ($$$$, Genealogy):** http://home.rootsweb.ancestry.com/
- **SearchSystems (Public records):** http://publicrecords.searchsystems.net/

- **SkipTracer:** https://github.com/avinashbot/skiptracer
- **Snitch-name:** http://snitch.name/
- **Snoop Station:** http://snoopstation.com/index.html
- **Social Bearing (Twitter search):** https://socialbearing.com/
- **Spokeo:** http://www.Spokeo.com
- **Stalkscan (Facebook searcher):** https://stalkscan.com/
- **ThatsThem:** https://thatsthem.com/
- **The Ancestor Hunt (Jump page):** http://www.theancestorhunt.com/blog/where-to-find-high-school-and-college-yearbooks-online
- **Tinfoleak (Twitter searches):** https://tinfoleak.com/
- **TruePeopleSearch:** https://www.truepeoplesearch.com/
- **TruthFinder:** https://www.truthfinder.com/
- **Twitter Advanced Search:** twitter.com/search-advanced
- **USA People Search:** http://www.usa-people-search.com
- **US Search:** http://www.ussearch.com
- **VitalRec (Vital records):** http://vitalrec.com/
- **WebMii:** http://www.webmii.com
- **White Pages:** http://www.WhitePages.com
- **Yasni (Europe):** http://www.yasni.com/
- **YellowPages:** https://people.yellowpages.com
- **YoName (User names):** http://www.pearltrees.com/u/3739540-domain-default-page
- **Zaba Search:** http://www.zabasearch.com
- **Zoom Info ($$$$, B2B):** http://www.zoomInfo.com.

Key Video and Photo Engines

Videos are in a class by themselves. They have become increasingly important over the years. In many cases videos are replacing text. Even newspapers are using videos on their sites, often without posting any corresponding text article. Videos and photos are central to the search techniques of the Bellingcat collective. They deserve, and get, closer study later in the book. In the interim, be aware of some key video search engines.

- **Bing:** https://www.bing.com/videos/
- **DailyMotion:** http://www.dailymotion.com
- **Google:** https://www.google.com/videohp
- **Instagram:** https://www.instagram.com/
- **LiveLeak:** https://www.liveleak.com/
- **MetaCafe:** http://www.metacafe.com/
- **YouTube:** http://www.youtube.com.

Key Image Search Engines

- **AP Images ($$$$):** http://www.apimages.com/
- **Bing Images:**
  https://www.bing.com/images/
- **Canadian Press Images ($$$$):**
  http://www.cpimages.com/fotoweb/index.fwx
- **Deviant Art (Digital art):** https://www.deviantart.com/
- **Dreamstime (Stock photos):**
  http://www.Dreamstime.com
- **European Press Photo Agency ($$$$):**
  http://www.epa.eu/
- **Flickr:** https://www.flickr.com/
- **Flickr Geotagged:** https://www.flickr.com/map
- **Flickr Hive Mind (Flickr data mining):**
  http://flickrhivemind.net/
- **Fotosearch (Stock photos, $$$$):**
  http://www.Fotosearch.com
- **Getty Images (Stock photos, $$$$):**
  https://www.gettyimages.ca/
- **Google Images:** https://images.google.com/
- **Google Search by Image (Chrome Browser):**
  https://chrome.google.com/webstore/detail/search-by-image-by-google/dajedkncpodkggklbegccjpmnglmnflm?hl=en
- **idGettr (URL of photostream to get Flickr ID number):**
  https://www.webpagefx.com/tools/idgettr/

- **Inlite (Barcode reader):** https://online-barcode-reader.inliteresearch.com/
- **Instagram:** https://www.instagram.com/
- **iStockphoto ($$$$):** http://www.iStockphoto.com
- **JPEG Snoop:** https://www.impulseadventure.com/photo/jpeg-snoop.html
- **Karma Decay (Reddit reverse-image search):** http://karmadecay.com
- **Localizeus: (Geotagging):** https://loc.alize.us/
- **MyPicsMap (Geotagging with Flickr):** http://www.mypicsmap.com/
- **PA Images ($$$$):** https://www.paimages.co.uk/
- **Photobucket (Online hosting):** http://photobucket.com/
- **PicSearc:** http://www.picsearch.com/
- **Pictriev (Faces):** http://www.pictriev.com/
- **Pinterest:** https://www.pinterest.ca/
- **Reuters Pictures ($$$$):** https://pictures.reuters.com/
- **RootAbout (Reverse-image search):** http://rootabout.com/
- **Shutterstock ($$$$, Stock photos):** http://www.Shutterstock.com
- **SmugMug (Photosharing, $$$$):** https://www.smugmug.com/
- **Stalkture (Instagram viewer):** https://stalkture.com/
- **Tin Eye Reverse-image Search:** https://tineye.com/
- **Twitter Images:** https://twitter.com/search?f=images&q=test&src=typd
- **WolframImages/ImageIdentify (Reverse-image search):** https://www.imageidentify.com/
- **Yahoo Images:** https://images.search.yahoo.com/
- **Yandex Images:** https://yandex.com/images/.

Regional and Specialty Search Engines

Regional or subject-specialized search engines and sites concentrate their searches on specific parts of the globe or specialized subject areas. Searching these sources requires experience, and usually a good knowledge of the local language, terminology, history, and social order of an area – or extensive knowledge about a subject. Sites that may help when concentrating your focus on specialized areas include:

- **Alleba (Philippines):** http://www.alleba.com/
- **Arabo (Arabic language sites):** http://www.arabo.com/
- **Baidu (China):** https://www.baidu.com/
- **Board Reader (Message boards):** http://boardreader.com/
- **Creative Commons (Non-copyrighted materials):** https://search.creativecommons.org/
- **Daum (South Korea):** https://www.daum.net/
- **EDGAR (Electronic Data Gathering, Analysis and Retrieval system; US Securities):** https://www.sec.gov/edgar.shtml
- **Eniro (Sweden):** https://www.eniro.se/
- **Ezilon (World regions):** http://ezilon.com/
- **Goo (Japan):** https://www.goo.ne.jp/
- **Labeleb (Arabic language sites):** https://lableb.com/
- **Onet (Poland):** https://www.onet.pl/
- **Parseek (Iran):** http://www.parseek.com/
- **Sabdam (Multi-language):** http://sabdam.com/index.html
- **SAPO (Portugal):** https://www.sapo.pt/
- **Searchch (Switzerland):** https://www.search.ch/
- **Search Engine Colossus:** http://www.searchenginecolossus.com/
- **Search Engine Guide:** http://www.searchengineguide.com/pages/Regional/
- **Slideshare (Presentations and graphics):** https://www.slideshare.net/
- **So (China):** https://www.so.com/
- **Wiki (Community-written sites):** http://wiki.com/
- **Yamli (Arabic search engine, also uses Roman characters):** http://www.yamli.com
- **Yandex (Russia, FSU, and Europe):** https://yandex.com/.

Keyword Searches

Keywords are the way most people talk to their search engine. They enter a keyword – the subject they want to get information about – and up pops the information the search engine has. However, often there is too much junk data and too few hard facts. "Noise" is inevitably a problem. Keyword results often provide a deluge of information about something, but not the looked-for information.

Keyword searches can be improved by some basic tradecraft – advanced searches, Boolean logic, and advanced operators. In the hunt for information, data retrieval on a computer is often a trial-and-error process. To the greatest extent possible, researchers will employ logic in the information hunt – particularly the special logic that guides computer operations. **Keyword Tool** sometimes helps researchers to find "just the right word" at https://keywordtool.io/.

In all open source research, it is important to speak and understand your computer's language! By understanding and using the computer's rigid thought process you can construct filters that will get you to the needed information without being inundated by the Internet noise.

Filtering and the ability to construct search queries, whether for a search engine or in an on-site search box, are valuable skills that must be constantly honed. Speaking the computer's language is a talent that translates into success for the researcher.

No single formula exists to construct an always-effective computer query or search filter. Construct queries using your knowledge of the subject as well as your understanding of the computer, particular peculiarities of the search engine or directory, and the site's search capabilities. The advanced search features of sites, Boolean logic, and advanced operators are ways of talking to the computer – using keywords and special codes – so that the search engine knows more specifically what you want it to find. Using these features with your keywords produces search results that are more likely to answer your requirements, and in less time.

Advanced Search Pages

Some search engines, and even some individual sites, may have capabilities that will be named something like "advanced searching."

These internal system-specific advanced programs automatically create a query similar to what are known as Boolean searches through a fill-in-the-blank page. You never see the actual query in the computer's language, however – only blank spaces for you to fill in.

There appears to be some movement away from these site-specific searching aids, but they are highly useful when they are available, such as on **Google** at https://www.google.com/advanced_search or **Twitter** at https://twitter.com/search-advanced. When these are not available, the researcher or research desk often needs to know and use Boolean logic and some special tricks to get needed information.

Creating Your Own Search Queries

When constructing your own search queries, consider using either Boolean Logic Operators or Advanced Operators. They often speak the language that your computer understands.

As a first step in constructing search queries, identify the specific information you need.

In the second phase, identify those operators – the specific search codes – that are most likely to give you the best results.

Third, build the queries and test them against available data. When the data is retrieved, determine whether the result meets your search criteria. If it doesn't meet the criteria, refine the query and try again.

What Boolean Logic Is...

Boolean Logic is named after British mathematician George Boole who developed the concept long before computers existed. It is now a system of computer logic.

Boolean Logic make searches for data on search engines and other sites, including databases, more efficient. When it is used correctly it talks in the manner that computers understand, providing more accurate and specific results. Boolean Logic applies the concept of mathematic equations to computer query terms. Boolean Logic allows concepts to be organized into sets – and search engines are excellent at producing sets of information. Boolean operators such as AND, OR, and NOT help you construct a logical search.

Some computer programs allow more than one way to create a particular Boolean search. It is not unusual to have two different ways of creating a Boolean-type search on a site or database. Some Boolean searches are simple – a single word or symbol may be all that is needed – but others are complex techniques known as "nested searches" because multiple terms are enclosed within parenthesis marks ( ).

Boolean Logic Operators

Boolean Logic requires the use of "operators." A Boolean operator is a word or symbol that performs a particular function in the Boolean Logic language. Operators define the relationship between the key words or the concepts. Many operators are also known as "Google Hacks," even though some will not work on Google and they are not hacking in any sense of illegality. Others term them "Advanced Operators." They can also be called by what they really are: Work-arounds.

There are many ways to use Boolean Logic. Boolean Logic can be simple or convoluted. Testing the various operators on sites you commonly use, and marking down the usable operators for those sites in your SOP, is always a good idea. When used properly,

Boolean operators simultaneously cut search time while improving the results. The irony of Boolean Operators is that they provide better answers to queries by reducing the number of off-point results, thus eliminating the "noise" usually found in Internet searches.

Advanced operators are never hit and miss propositions. The use of advanced operators requires careful thought. You must understand why you are using a particular one in any particular search. Boolean searches should not be employed "for real" until you have developed a high comfort level with them and understand the Boolean rules of the particular search engine, database, or website.

Nested searches – Boolean queries that use the parenthesis – are generally ineffective on search engines. There is a high probability they will create problems with your search. Nested searches often produce useful results on databases, but only when correctly crafted.

Common Boolean Operators

Boolean searching symbols do not work on all sites or with all search engines, or databases.

Even when Boolean searching is available, the symbols or operators sometimes vary. The AND, OR, and NOT operators are standard. They are among those most often available to the researcher. The use of other operators is spottier, much spottier. While users have to learn about specific site usage as they go, the most common Boolean operators are:

- AND or the symbols (+) and (&) finds instances of two or more search terms in a single record or file.
- OR, or the (|), finds at least one of the search terms.
- NOT or (-) and (!) eliminates pages with terms that follow the NOT, minus sign, or the exclamation point.
- The question mark (?) replaces a single letter.

- The asterisk (*) replaces multiple characters.
- Quotation marks (" ") around typed words can be used to ferret out the exact wording.
- Proximity signs or NEAR finds terms within a specified number of words.
- Parenthesis ( ) are used in a nested search. They perform what is inside first. In the construct (((aaaa AND bbbb) AND cccc) AND zzzz) the a and b will be acted on initially, then the c will be done, followed by the z.

AND

AND, the plus symbol (+), or the ampersand (&) may be used to search for pages or records that contain at least a single occurrence of each of the key words. When the user's terms or concepts are combined using the AND operator, any retrieved record has all of the search terms somewhere. The AND operator does not require that the search terms appear on the page or document in the same order listed in the query. It simply returns a document because it contains all the search terms.

The AND is always written in capital letters.

The AND operator generally takes precedence over other operators. Search queries using the AND operator are usually conducted first, before any other operator. After the AND search, searches will be conducted using other operators.

AND is considered the universal default operator in US engines. When any two or more words put in the search box they are assumed to be linked by AND. The search engine automatically defaults to the AND operator even when that operator is not used.

The more concepts you link together with AND, the fewer pages or records you will retrieve because all of the words must appear in the pages retrieved.

In normal usage, term 1 AND term 2, term 1 + term 2, or term 1 &
term 2, will bring up files that contain occurrences of both term 1
and term 2. Example: car AND Ford.

OR

The OR operator, alternatively the pipe symbol (|), retrieves pages
or documents that contain any of the listed words. The OR is always
written in capital letters.

OR is among the most basic of the Boolean logic operators and is
widely used since it gives the analyst wide search results.

The OR operator increases the number of items returned since it
searches for and displays pages with any of the words included in
the query. Example: Moscow OR Leningrad.

Note: Some keyboards show the pipe symbol as a single vertical bar,
while others depict it as two smaller vertical bars stacked atop one
another.

NOT

The NOT operator excludes any search term following the word
NOT. Some systems use the minus symbol (-) or the exclamation
point symbol (!) in the same way.

NOT-type operators eliminate words from a search so that the result
is more focused. A NOT operator search should be carefully crafted
because it can inadvertently exclude valuable information.

Words that follow the NOT operator are excluded from the search
and will not be returned in the pages or documents.

The NOT is written in capital letters. Examples: dolls NOT fashion;
dolls -fashion

" " Exact Sequence of Terms

Quotation marks (" ") and occasionally parenthesis (( )) can be used to find an exact sequence of search terms. Typing Grand Canyon plane crashes in the search box will return a variety of results, stories about the Grand Canyon – and maybe Copper Canyon as well – in addition to a variety of aircraft accidents. "Grand Canyon plane crashes" will return only pages that include those words, written in that order. The displayed material is also likely to provide additional key words.

Search terms placed between quotation marks return only documents that exactly match the search terms. Example: "to be or not to be".

? Single Character Wildcard

The Single Character Wildcard is often either a question mark (?) or the underscore (_). The single character wildcard is often used to help find words of differing spellings in a query.

Single character operators can be used in a search query to locate words where a single character may be different. The single character wildcard may be placed at any point in the search term. Example: A search using gr?y will locate instances of both gray and grey.

* Multiple Character Wildcard

The Multi-Character Wildcard is the asterisk (*) or sometimes the percent symbol (%). A multiple character wildcard can be used in a search query to find multiple unknown letters in the search term.

The asterisk or percent character can be placed anywhere within the search term to stand for more than one letter. This logical operator is useful in locating words that have different prefixes, suffixes, or spellings, as well as phrases where you may not remember one of the words.

Examples: national* should bring up nationalism, nationalist etc. "Fourscore and * years ago" will bring up the correct number of years.

? Fuzzy Operator

Question mark (fuzzy operator) (?) is often used to expand queries to include words with similar but not exact spelling. When the fuzzy operator is available it must be placed at the beginning of the word.

This operator is useful when you are unsure of the exact spelling. Example: ?Abdul returns Abdul and Abdel. The equal sign (=) can be sometimes be used in much the same way, checking for alternate spellings. Example: Osama=Usama

! Phonics Operator

An exclamation point (!), or the pound sign (#), in front of a word is sometimes used to look for words that sound alike but may have different spellings in the pages. The phonics operator, when and where it is available, searches for words that sound similar to the words in your search term. These are often names and other proper nouns. Example: !Mohammed returns Mohammed, Mohhamed, etc.

~ Stem Operator

The operator tilde (~) or dollar symbol ($) placed before the word finds variations of search terms based on the word's stem. A properly-done stem search, when it is available on a site, will retrieve examples of the search term's root and variations of the root search term. Variations are often found in the prefix or the suffix of the search term.

The symbol is often used to check for words derived from the stem, regardless of the conjugation or tense. Example: ~hide should bring up pages with hiding, hide, hidden.

in Social Media Search

The hashtag is a word with the pound symbol, #, put directly in front of it. Searching with hashtags – the hashtags are "tagged on" to the posted material – pulls postings from some social media platforms. Example: #worldseries.

, Word Frequency

Commas (,) are occasionally used in multiple-word searches to look at the frequency with which the words appear. This search is rarely available, but when it is it assigns the highest scores to pages where the words appear most often. Pages containing all the words are also weighted so that they are shown among the highest results. Example: car, Ford, Fairlane

< Word Weight

Less than (<) is the threshold operator used at some sites to eliminate documents that do not "weigh" enough (i.e., the word or terms are not used often enough in the message). This is another rare operator. Example: (Fairlane <4) & Ford query will select all documents that have a score of at least four for Fairlane and contain the word Ford.

NEAR or w/x Proximity Operator

Proximity operators "NEAR" or (w/x) search for two terms that are located a short distance from each other. One proximity operator is a "w," followed by a slash, followed by a number showing the maximum number of words that one search item should be away from another. For example: Search term w/7 search term will locate instances where the search terms are within seven words of each other.

A variation is the "NEAR" proximity search, such as "representative NEAR smith." Some search engines have their own unbendable algorithm for what it considers to be near; that distance cannot be set by the user.

Any pages or documents containing both search terms that appear within the specified proximity will be displayed.

Many researchers find the proximity operator to be among the most useful Boolean tools. Unfortunately it is not widely permitted and when it is, it requires finesse and experience to use properly.

( ) Nesting or Grouped Keyword Operator

Nesting, or mixing the Boolean operators, is a way to combine several search statements into one comprehensive search. The order in which the operations (such as AND, OR, NOT) are processed can vary between systems. Searches within parentheses are usually performed first and operations proceed from left to right. Nesting is a complex activity that requires specialized study. It is a quick way to get into very deep trouble. Grouped keywords become extremely complex. Proficiency with this operator format requires extensive practice and additional information from the Internet or fiber-based resources such as books. This is not an operator to be used lightly – ever.

Advanced Search Boxes

Some search engines have effectively duplicated Boolean searches with advanced search pages that take away many of the difficulties of Boolean searches, replacing them with simple text entry boxes. Typical of these pages is the **Google** advanced search page at https://www.google.com/advanced_search.

It effectively automates the Boolean process on the website.

Look at the first set of boxes on the advanced search page. The "all these words" box mimics the AND command. The box for "this exact word or phrase" duplicates what happens when you put quote marks around a phrase or sentence. "Any of these words" is the equivalent of the "OR" command while "none of these words" works like a Boolean minus sign. "Numbers ranging from to" is far easier than the Boolean version.

The search page then allows you to narrow the search by language, region, or last update. The "site or domain" box limits the results in much the same way that the "site:" command – covered later in this chapter – does. "Terms appearing" encompasses other Boolean-type commands – it specifies the location on the page where you really want to search for the terms. "Safe Search" has a number of options that can be explored to limit the results if you choose to do so, but these often inhibit complete research. This should seldom be turned on. The "file type" is an important command. Some file types – PDFs, spreadsheets, PowerPoints – are more likely to be used in postings by professionals and experts. Resumes, for instance, are likely to be found as PDFs while presentations would likely be found in slide show PowerPoint formats. Searches for your subject in those formats are likely to produce results that carry more credibility. And "usage rights," which doesn't have a Boolean counterpart, may impact how or even whether you may use the information you ferret out.

The Google Advanced Search Page also has links that allow you to find pages that are similar to, or link to, a URL. You can search pages you have visited, use Boolean-type operators in the search box, and customize your search settings.

Yahoo has its own version of an advanced search page. The page has many of the same features as Google. It can be found at https://search.yahoo.com/web/advanced.

Bing once had a special advanced search page, but removed it. You can still do some Boolean-type searches from Bing, however, if you want to use advanced searching techniques Bing has instructions for advanced searches at http://help.bing.microsoft.com/#apex/18/en-us/10002/0.

Whatever search engines you plan to use will likely allow some form of advanced or Boolean search. There is an excellent chance that information about using advanced search techniques on that search engine is located somewhere on the site, or elsewhere on the Web. Go to the search engine of your choice and see if there is a link to an advanced search page. If no such page is readily visible, go to your search engine and enter "advanced search" following the name of the search engine you want to use.

Remember that each search engine differs on whether and how it allows advanced searches and which of the Boolean operators it allows. The information contained here – especially as that data relates to the operators used – is generalized about a wide variety of search engines and sites. You have to see which types of searches any search engine(s) you use allow(s), and what specific operators are accepted. These need to be entered in your SOP along with other information about that specific engine.

Search Engine Shortcuts

Search engine shortcuts are sometimes called "hacks," but they are not hacking. They are also called advanced operators or filters, and in this sense, they qualify for the name. Shortcuts often serve the same purpose as Boolean Logic but are sometimes easier to use.

Search engine shortcuts allow a researcher or research desk to use the built-in capabilities of search engines. They are not obvious but they can improve searching ease while helping you achieve better results. Shortcuts or advanced operators are not available on all search engines. Where they are available, they don't all work the same way.

Lists of the shortcuts or advanced operators are available online. The lists are updated at irregular intervals so they should be downloaded and checked for changes regularly.

The best-known advanced operator information is found at:
    Google: http://www.GoogleGuide.com
    Yahoo: http://www.seobook.com/archives/000212.shtml

While Google and Yahoo are among the best known engines to offer advanced search operator capability, others do as well. Remember: All search engines do not necessarily use the same operators; some reject them all. Help pages of sites often provide information on any search operators that work on their system. Additional information on search operators for specific search engines often can be found by typing "advanced operators" and the name of preferred search engine in the search engine box.

Like many things on the Internet and in OSR there is no "one way" that shortcuts work all the time. Each search site you use must be thoroughly understood. Search sites have distinct personalities, just like people. You may like, or abhor, the personality of different search engines and your decision on whether to use that engine will depend on your experiences with it.

Once you know how a site works you can test different operators. When you have determined what works and doesn't work on those sites, the useful operators should be included in your SOP.

Many, but not all, shortcut operators follow the key words you are using, in a format like this: Key word(s) operator name:term or query word. In most cases there should be no space after the colon. Both the operator and the term or query word abut the colon. The operator serves as a preparatory command and the colon triggers the execution command. When search engines see a space after the colon, they may end the operation and move on to the next listed command.

Advanced operators can often be stacked, one after another, to obtain highly selective filtering results quickly.

Shortcut or advanced operator commands, such as "site" and "link" are often among the most useful research tools. If you learn how and when to use this family of filter tools, if you carefully consider how they can be employed in your research project, you will grab the lead in the research race. They will do much of the heavy lifting for you.

Several shortcut operators, or filters, are widely used on search engines.

Site is often considered the most useful of the filters. It is the Swiss Army knife of OSR. The site filter restricts the search to a single website or top-level domain such as com or gov. When used creatively, the site filter may be what saves the day. For example, not every website has a search box to seek out specific key words. "Site:" is a filter that can probe an entire website for any occurrences of your key word as efficiently as an on-site search box. When search engine results are not available on a site, or seem skimpy, this is the recommended fallback.

This filter is useful to get results by using either the actual domain name or the domain type. It is also highly useful in searching a site without going to the site itself and starting the search from the splash page. When used that way "site:" becomes an important security workaround. "Site:" searches can also be used to restrict the search to individual directories within a site when the directory is identified in the URL as part of the site name.

The "site:country code" is useful in many foreign searches because it shows only sites registered in a specific country.

To use it, put in the key words and follow with site:xxx where xxx is the domain type, URL, or the domain name/directory you want to restrict the search to. Note that there is no space between the site and the domain name or URL.

Filetype is useful when you are looking for information in a certain sort of file. The information contained in some types of files is often more accurate and useful than textual information found elsewhere on the Web. For that reason many researchers routinely restrict their searches to key filetypes. Often PDFs, spreadsheets, and databases are created by the knowledgeable or subject matter experts. Spreadsheets will often hold financial information, for instance. Presentations are often in PDF files and may be associated with advanced knowledge on a subject. Databases contain extensive information but are often somewhat difficult to ferret out.

To use this advanced operator, enter the key words and follow with filetype:xxx where xxx is the designation of the filetype. Some users have had good results on some search engines by using ext: rather than filetype:. Again, note that there is no space between the filetype: or ext: and the type of file.

File types can be important to search for, even when you don't have advanced filetype searches available on your search engine. In that case use the extension abbreviation for the type of file as a key word, such as:

- Configuration files (.txt or .rft)
- Databases (often .mdb or .db)
- Diagrams and pictures (.vsd, .jpg, or .gif)
- Excel (.xls)
- Papers and documents (.doc, .pdf, or .sdw)
- Presentations (.ppt or .odp)
- Rich Text Format (.rtf)
- Spreadsheets (.xls, .ods, or .sdc)
- Text (.txt or .ans)
- Word (.doc or .docx)
- WordPerfect (.wp).

Keep in mind that similar programs of different providers – word processing programs of different providers, for instance – use different extensions. Even the same developer may have several different extensions for the same type of file – doc and docx for example. All applicable extensions should be searched when doing this type of inquiry.

The **Fagan File Finder** at http://www.faganfinder.com/filetype/ may prove useful in the filetype search.

Terms and words which suggest a desire to keep information close to the vest – words or phrases such as "confidential," "sensitive," or "business restricted" – are often used in conjunction with filetype searches for presentations, spreadsheets, databases, and reports that are intended for use by select or limited audiences.

Link is useful because people with similar interests may link to a page they like. That expands the search from a page, but only to those sites that have links to that page, in essence a page of similar interest. The link: operator differs in that there are no key words in this search. The operator is simple: link:url you want to check.

Numbers Range is useful for restricting the search to a range of numbers. This is most often useful when you are interested in material about certain years, but it may be used for other number ranges as well. In this case enter the search term(s) and the years of concern. There is no colon. The search looks like xxx 2018..2020. Two dots separate the numbers of the years.

Inurl can be used to find files that contain the key word in the URL, which generally indicates the file is largely about the key word subject. Since different types of files, such as FTPs, may contain the type or service designator, this shortcut operator may also be used to find stored material in parts of the Internet that are seldom visited by most users. The search looks like inurl:xxx.

Other important shortcut operators that are often of use include:
- intext:xxx terms must appear in text, often in the summary of an article
- define:xxx displays a definition

- info:url displays data about the page
- related:url show pages that relate to a URL

Directories

Web directories are created and filled out by humans. They don't use spiders.

There are fewer directories that deal with general subjects than there used to be. On the other hand, there are probably more directories that are business oriented.

Subject directories are much smaller than search engine databases. Good subject matter directories, produced by specialists in their field, may be useful but the directory quality depends largely on the expertise of those who made or contributed to the directory and the way they crafted their own search for information.

For the most part, Web researchers seldom stray far from search engines or go to subject directories.

But where they exist, and to the extent they are managed by knowledgeable sysops, directories can provide high-quality results. They are seldom bleeding edge in their contents; usually even the best are a little behind the latest advances in an area because knowledgeable contributors demand that new, leading edge, ideas prove themselves first.

To a certain extent, Web directories have been replaced in usage and reliability by Wikis, particularly by Wikipedia, and some social media sites, a Web 2.0 feature.

Directories are hierarchical structures. They offer information on sites in a topic-specific fashion, far different from search engines. They point to what are supposedly the best or most popular websites – repeat that, websites.

Directories deal with an entire subject areas. They do not drill down through the use of key words. Directories, unlike search engines, are usually about subject and consider the website as a whole, not any particular page or subject on a page. The inclusion of a site in a web directory is generally based on the site's overall content, not on keywords. Search engines list the pages they display based on key words rather than the overall subject. Directories usually list web sites by subject category and subcategory. Directories try to get their users into the neighborhood; it is up to the users to locate whatever digital house they want.

On the positive side, since Web directory entries are found, curated, and listed by humans rather than by spiders or web crawlers the information in them has had some preliminary vetting. Results found in good directories are often of higher-quality, but are more general, than the results found with search engines.

They always represent the interests of the directory's compilers; they show any disinterest of the compilers in a subject by the absence of important information.

Directories strive for targeted and relevant results rather than maximum returns. A directory entry may list websites ignored by search engines, but recent postings and new developments are often missing. Directories provide quick, overall, basic, information about subjects but they seldom drill down to particulars.

Directory creation and upkeep is labor-intensive. The Web grows at a rate that makes it all but impossible to keep up with any changes, additions, or site closures. While human-selected material in general directories may be superior to machine-selected links, many directory operators simply could not keep up with the pace of the expanding Web. Most large directories have closed, or like Gigablast they have also become search engines.

246

Major subject matter directories include:
- **Ask:** https://www.ask-directory.com/
- **Best of the Web:** https://botw.org/default.aspx
- **Directory:** http://www.gigablast.com/Top
- **Open Directory (Legacy site):** http://dmoztools.net/.

Subject directories have the potential to be true expertise sites, unlimited in depth and breadth. However, they also require increases in time and attention as the directory expands and becomes more useful. The better that general directories become, the more they require maintenance and upkeep.

Other types of directories may not be as labor intensive nor as difficult to maintain. Niche directories, particularly commercial directories, are easier to set up and operate. They cover a smaller subject area and sometimes rely on others to populate them. Often someone pays – whether that someone appears in the directory or uses the directory.

Directories may not have disappeared, but their content has changed dramatically. They often make economic and digital sense when they cover smaller areas, particularly commercial areas that can be easily monetized.

It is important to remember, too, that some directories allow web site operators to submit their site for consideration. A human then looks at the site and determines whether to include it in the directory. Some directories charge for inclusion. The presentation position may even be based on the amount paid, a factor to consider when evaluating any information gleaned from a directory site.

Assessing directory information requires wrestling with the identity and possible biases of those selecting the material, the availability of data on how – or whether – the directory information is reviewed and annotated, whether payments or arrangements may compromise objectivity, and whether the process for selection of materials and contributors is transparent.

Other assessment questions involve the subjectivity and rating of resources, the length of time between updates, the effect of time on the currency of the information, and any potential arbitrariness of links.

There are also niche directories, the latter focusing on specific areas, languages, or subjects. These topic-limited directories may be quite useful, but locating one for your particular needs is always a challenge. Nevertheless, if you do find one that fulfills your individual needs explore it thoroughly and mark its address in more than one place – bookmarking it is never enough if you experience a computer disaster.

Examples of the current generation of directories include:
- **01Web Directory (Business):** https://www.01webdirectory.com/
- **Alive:** http://www.alivedirectory.com/
- **Angie's List:** https://www.angieslist.com/
- **Aviva Directory:** https://www.avivadirectory.com/
- **Dirjournal:** https://www.dirjournal.com/
- **Finances Online:** https://financesonline.com/
- **G2crowd:** https://www.g2crowd.com/
- **Gimpsy:** https://www.gimpsy.com/
- **Jasmine Directory:** https://www.jasminedirectory.com/
- **List of Companies:** http://www.listofcompaniesin.com/
- **MagicYellow:** http://www.magicyellow.com/
- **Product Hunt:** https://www.producthunt.com/
- **Tuugo ($$$$):** http://www.tuugo.us/
- **Yalwa ($$$$):** https://www.yalwa.com/
- **Yellowbook:** http://www.yellowbook.com/.

RSS directories are similar to web directories. Instead of web sites, these list collections of RSS feeds.

Alternative Ways of Finding Information

There are additional ways of getting information. You need not limit yourself to search engines and directories. These include:

- Scouts/Personal Contacts
- Intelligent Agents/Search Alerts
- Personal Search Lists
- Aggregation Sites/Portals.

Personal Contacts/Scouts

Before long you may become aware of others who are searching for material that is somewhat similar, if not identical, to your own needs. Their interest may not be for the same reasons; often the reasons are dissimilar. The members of these communities may be nearly obsessive in their dedication to such things as cataloging aircraft flights, ships etc. Others post or maintain pages on subjects dear to their hearts and minds. To you they can become invaluable friends whose interest and knowledge are extensive and whose labor is free.

"Scouts," or "spotters" as some call them, often gather material for their own needs and reasons but also share it with others. The key to working with scouts is to locate people who are interested in the same subjects you are, people who are willing to share their findings, and importantly people you are also comfortable around and willing to share with.

They must be people you trust! Never pair up with anyone if you have the slightest concern about them, their reasons, or their research.

People who could become scouts for you are found through Internet forums, blogs, UseNet sites, web-based discussion groups, and mailing lists. Social media, selectively used, may be a good place to meet potential scouts. LinkedIn members and groups often are useful in any scout search. You can sometimes find these people by subscribing to newsgroups and signing up with email lists dealing with your subject. Scouts may upload a variety of material to newsgroups or they may distribute data through mailing lists.

Scouts can dramatically extend your information reach. Their human discretion in picking useful material assures a cerebral rather than mechanical approach to information gathering. Scouts search areas you may not have time to look at – even if you were aware of the existence of the sources that they search.

Sherlock Holmes had his own version of scouts – the street arabs and urchins of London, the Baker Street Irregulars – who he used as substitute eyes when he had to watch in many directions at the same time.

Invaluable as sources, the people who serve as scouts may also become friends whom you can query for information and rely on for feedback. In their own areas they are often as knowledgeable as the people on any experts list.

If there is any major drawback to the use of scouts it is that they are doing "their own thing." They are not employees; they are fellow researchers, following their subjects on their own time. You have to take what they are willing to give, and that means the bad along with good. Generally, from experience, what they have to give is very valuable. There is little that carefully selected scouts send that cannot be downloaded for possible later use. But the key there is the words "carefully selected." There are far too many people with axes to grind or would-be propagandists who post junk, loads of it. Using that kind of scout is never wise.

Like everything on the Internet, the postings of scouts have to be carefully considered and vetted,

In *ad hoc* searching, with its short-time fuses, the use of scouts is probably not feasible. That is because scouts have to be collected and watched over the long-term for them to be considered both reliable and useful. It takes time to develop mutual confidence. For *ad hoc* researching, along short timelines, scouts seldom enter the picture.

Intelligent Agents/Search Alerts

"Intelligent Agents" or "Search Alerts" are not people you will sit down in your kitchen to share stories or a cup of coffee; they are computer programs that search the Web on your instructions, looking for information based on key words you provide. Alerts are time- and energy-savers. They send you links to the stories that match your interest.

When you don't have to go looking for information, but have it piped automatically to you, you save many key strokes, much time, not to mention significant amounts of good humor. Alerts are, in effect, personal algorithm-guided continuous search engines. In years past there were more Alert providers than today. It is not outside the realm of reason that Alerts will eventually disappear. Meanwhile, they remain useful tools.

Alerts are considered as comprehensive as the search engines they are associated with, at best. While search engines cover only a fraction of what is actually available on the Web, the Alerts that engines and companies send can overwhelm any user who is incautious when setting one up. Common words, when used as search terms, can produce more trash than useful information. Keep in mind that unless you enter narrow, specific, search terms you may be overwhelmed by the results. Caution in word choice is always imperative when creating an Alert.

Key Search Alert systems today include:
- **Giga Alert:** http://www.gigaalert.com
- **Google Alerts:** https://www.google.com/alerts
- **Mention ($$$$):** https://mention.com/en/
- **MozPro ($$$$):** https://moz.com/tools/fresh-web-explorer

- **Talkwalker:** https://www.talkwalker.com/alerts.

While the set-up at various Alert sites is somewhat different, Google Alerts sites can be thought of as a useful example. The Google Alerts site allows you to choose:
- How often
- Sources
- Language
- Region
- How many results.

On Google's site, to avoid being overwhelmed, many people restrict the Alert delivery to once a day although users also have a choice of "as it happens" and "once a week." However, if the material is needed immediately or if you want to ramp up the number of articles you are receiving, ask for the information to be sent "as it happens."

Experience shows that it is best to ask for a "comprehensive" search rather than limit the intelligent agent to single categories such as news, blogs, web, video, books, and discussion groups. You have a choice of "all results" or whatever the algorithm decides are the "best results." It is best to have all results, from all sources, sent immediately and then you can pare the results to a more manageable size.

Google Alerts allows the use of some Boolean Operators in searches, eliminating a good many of the "false positives" you get with a straight word search. To learn more about the use of **Boolean Operatives** and how they work in Google and Google Alerts go to http://www.googleguide.com/crafting_queries.html.

When using Alerts, intelligent agents, or search engines, look carefully at the material that you find usable. See if there are words, combinations of words, or short phrases that you can plug into further searches – words, combinations of words, and phrases that would likely be found elsewhere about your subject. Create new Alerts using these terms.

A specific type of Alert are Page Change Alerts sent by website monitors. These sites are useful when you are watching specific Web pages for changes, additions or deletions. They continually recheck page(s) you list for any alterations. This type of overwatch is particularly valuable when you are doing a project that extends over weeks, months, or even years because it reduces the number of times – and the amount of time – spent on re-reviewing pages of potential value.

Periodic reviews of important sites for any updates is generally more useful than total reliance on any Alert system, but automatic Alerts are a useful back-up. Page change alert sites include:

- **Distill:** https://distill.io/
- **Follow That Page:** https://www.followthatpage.com/
- **Google Alerts:** https://www.google.com/alerts
- **Update Scanner (Firefox add on):** https://addons.mozilla.org/en-US/firefox/addon/update-scanner/
- **VisualPing:** https://visualping.io/
- **WatchThatPage:** http://www.watchthatpage.com/
- **Web Page Changes Providers Listing:** http://www.rba.co.uk/sources/monitor.htm
- **WebSite-Watcher ($$$$):** http://aignes.com/.

The **Google Custom Search Engine:** https://cse.google.com/cse/ can be used in much the same way as an Alert when properly configured to search one or more selected sites for any key words. It allows the user to limit the search to certain sites, homing in on changes about selected subjects at selected sites.

Avoid using any intelligent agent, custom search, or Alert with the expectation it will fill your information needs. These are not the first-string players in your information lineup. But they serve a definite role, like place kickers, and do provide the extra depth you need. They are particularly useful to have working for you as part of long-term projects since they pick up a drizzle of information – often news items – which you might otherwise miss.

All Alerts often help by identifying sites that have material on your subject of interest. Note any websites occurring often in the Alert results; you may want to add those sites to your personal URL list.

Personal Search Lists

Developing personal lists of useful go-to web sites is important, even vital, for the top-notch searcher. Many researchers rely heavily on comprehensive lists of their own making. These lists can run to dozens, or scores, of pages. Obviously, when you are going to do a daily search of key sites for the information that is pertinent to your work, you will need a shorter, select, list of the most important sites. Those are the sites you decide are most likely to have information that you and your sponsors need. Many researchers maintain both list types. They will use a select list of sites – perhaps 10 or less – for the most frequently used sites and scour the longer list occasionally in the most thorough searches. Page-change alerts or a Google Custom Search Engine may be effectively used in conjunction with personal search lists.

Aggregation Sites and Portals

Aggregation sites, or aggregators, such as the **Google News** site at http://news.google.com/, are often associated with news providers. They offer a variety of stories from different sources to get a quick overview of events. If you only have 15 minutes a day and your search subject seems likely to show up in a news site, it is worth including an appropriate aggregation site on your short list. If you are researching Hollywood personalities a daily check at an aggregation site may be useful; if you are researching the effect of rust on metal in the desert environment an aggregation site probably is not going to do much for you except keep you abreast of news about what is happening elsewhere around the world.

The most important factor in doing daily searches with site lists and aggregation sites is that you are in total control. You are making the decisions about what you see, and what you download.

Portals function as the Internet's multi-tool knives, they are like a Leatherman or a Swiss Army Knife. They have many functions, they provide a little bit for everyone – or almost so. But only occasionally are they useful for OSR work. Just like directories, portals have a limited utility for many serious searchers. Understand the limits and work within them.

***

Project:
Take the Google Search Engine education program, available at https://www.google.com/insidesearch/searcheducation/lessons.html. It has sections for advanced users as well as beginners.

Project:
To better understand how Boolean techniques cut the number of results while increasing the applicability of the results, go online and:
- Try searching for "apples and oranges."
- Try searching for tomato AND apple; note the size returned.
- Try searching for tomato OR apple, note the size returned.
- Try searching for link:reuters.com.
- Try searching for tomato apple 2018..2019.

Project:
On the Web use the search terms "advanced searches," "Boolean logic," and "advanced operators" to find more about these techniques and how they may apply to your unique set of circumstances, search needs, equipment, and programs. Keep in mind that OSR is a system of systems. You must learn and use what works best with your particular system and suits your unique needs, then mark that down in your SOP.

Project:
Use the Google Guide and your own exploration of the Google site to determine what capabilities you believe you may want to use, and enter descriptions and directions to those capabilities in your SOP. Choose at least one other search engine, explore it in detail, and enter information on that resource in your SOP.

Project:
Decide upon, and list in your SOP, any directories you will try to use consistently.

Project:
Decide whether you will use Boolean Searches in your research, and if so which ones you believe will be most productive for your purposes.

Project:
Decide whether you will seek out and use scouts in your research. If so, write in your SOP where you expect to encounter them and what steps you plan on taking to recruit the help.

Project:
Decide whether you will use intelligent agents and Alerts in your research. If so, which ones should be employed and what key words can provide the best results for you. Enter the information in your SOP.

9. Gray Literature And Ephemera

Both Gray (often written as Grey) Literature and Ephemera are challenging. They are as tricky to find and gather. Gray literature and ephemera are often physical items rather than digital files.

Ephemera and gray literature can be ignored, but only at peril to any research project. "How dangerous it always is to reason from insufficient data," Sherlock Holmes mused in *The Adventure of the Speckled Band.* That musing could well apply to gray literature and ephemera.

Gray literature may be, but is not always, literary in nature. It is any type of material produced outside of normal publishing, distribution, or acquisition channels. It can be found by specialized means or by direct local access, such as the "freebies" that are given away at conventions. Gray literature cuts across every scientific, political, socio-economic, legal, business, religious, and governmental discipline. Almost any area of human interest can produce gray literature. It is found at all levels of government, within academia, and in business and industry. It may appear in any format or be made of any material.

Gray literature resources include, but are not limited to, research reports, technical reports, economic reports, trip reports, working papers, discussion papers, unofficial government documents, conference proceedings, preprints, research reports, translations, studies, dissertations and theses, reports of telephone calls or meetings, trade literature, market surveys, or newsletters. Even clothing, jewelry and trinkets are shoehorned into this category. Distribution is generally limited to small, local audiences and the material is usually distributed on a one-time basis.

Ephemera may be – but is not always – a subset of gray literature. Ephemera is material that is intended for one-time or time-limited use. Business cards, fliers, leaflets, paraphernalia, and posters are examples. While libraries seldom collect either gray literature or ephemera, historical societies and museums may collect examples of gray literature and ephemera that relate to their theme subject or their area of specialization.

Although many pieces of ephemera also qualify as gray literature a piece of gray literature may not be ephemera. Sometimes it is hard to decide what category to place items in, but the categorization of things is far less important than the value of the information that they provide.

Ephemera and gray literature are valuable to collect, especially if they are current and are relevant to your research subject.

When developing a history or time line, older examples of gray literature and ephemera may become invaluable.

Since ephemera and gray literature often deal with interests and topics that are not mainstream they often fill in information blank spots and knowledge holes. Importantly, the wording and terms used in gray literature and ephemera may also help researchers narrow their focus and improve searches.

Intelligence agencies, in particular, find the collection of gray literature and ephemera useful, but these off-beat OSR fields are also highly useful to researchers doing competition research.

Gray literature seldom is available commercially. Generally the producers of gray literature make little or no effort to disseminate or popularize their product beyond its intended initial audience. For those reasons it is a challenge to locate and obtain gray literature items.

Most pieces of gray literature and ephemera remain unindexed, unpublished, or both. Short print runs, limited distribution, their appearance in a variety of formats, and the fact that they often have a limited time of availability make collection of gray literature and ephemera difficult.

Many pieces of gray literature and ephemera are fiber-based. When digital examples are available online they are often located on the "hidden web" and are thus difficult to search out. Examples may be found by looking through the offerings of agencies, groups, or institutions who are likely to produce this type of material. Useful items are often produced by:

- Nonprofit organizations
- Academic researchers
- Governments
- Corporations
- Individuals
- Commercial organizations
- Formal associations
- Societies and clubs.

Sometimes hints of gray literature and ephemera can be found in reference lists and bibliographies, or through directories.

Gray literature is difficult to find, but may be available through resources such as **GreyNet** at http://greynet.org/ or **GreyGuide** at http://greyguide.isti.cnr.it/. Sometimes, particularly with regard to publications, gray literature can be searched out by thinking of the items in terms of journal or directory searches.

Researchers devoted to a single subject, or a subject that is collected over a long period, often develop a personal library of gray literature and ephemera. Magazines, books, and many other publications are now available online. Examples that OSR specialists often seek include:

- Trade publications of various kinds

- Smaller journals
- Books
- Specialty reports.

While even current examples of gray literature and ephemera are often difficult to find on the Web or elsewhere, older reports and other examples probably have not been digitized or brought online. They likely never will be. That suggests that if you have a use for gray literature you should start collecting immediately and continue searching on a regular basis.

While you seldom will see gray literature and ephemera in a library you will find bags of it at trade shows and conventions. That is the best, and sometimes the only, place to collect either of these. When study of a particular subject is considered a long-term project, many researchers attend selected conventions and trade shows just to gather potential material – dubbed "loot" – by the armload.

Conventions and similar gatherings are venues for the collection of usable ephemera and gray literature. They also have the potential for face-to-face meetings with scores of like-minded people, many of whom are decision-makers. Overheard discussions at these get-togethers may yield valuable information. Networking opportunities are what you make of them. Demonstrations, discussions and classes are often on the schedule, allowing you to improve your knowledge and abilities in some areas. Attend those activities that will affect your work, or those activities where your work will have an effect on others.

Prepare for trade shows and similar gatherings. Learn who plans to attend. Look carefully at the agenda and decide in advance what events or classes you might want to attend. Pay close attention to timing or scheduling issues such as openings and endings. Make certain you get addresses and contact information from any "new best friends." This includes LinkedIn, Twitter, and Facebook addresses, or "handles." After the event many researchers ask conference or convention attendees to create a post-event summary report, then use those individual summaries to create a report detailing who was there, what was discovered, analyzing the event, and soliciting any recommendations.

The veracity of the information in any gray literature and ephemera is sometimes difficult to determine. It is often slanted toward some position or organization since much ephemera and gray literature is sales-oriented. Bibliographic information may be elusive and hard to locate in gray literature material. It often lacks crucial information needed for analysis and interpretation including:

- Author
- Publisher
- Publication date.

Gray literature and ephemera are good reminders that the Internet is not the whole of OSR. Non-Internet resources can make significant contributions. It is proof, again, of the need to be capable of thinking outside the box and avoiding cookie cutter collection methods, while also understanding there is also value in the box and its contents!

***

Project:
Search the terms Gray (Grey) Literature, Ephemera, and White Paper with your search engine; check websites which deal with these forms of material. In your SOP write whether you will routinely plan to search for gray literature and ephemera on your subject, and if so where and how.

10. The Deep Web and Dark Web

Deep Web

Exploration and exploitation of the Deep Web, that part of the Web not captured or reported by search engines, is moving ahead apace.

Just as the Web of today bears little resemblance to the Web of the early 1990s, the Deep Web will likely become shallower within a few more years. Projects are continuing to better tap this information resource. The success of those efforts is likely, but never guaranteed.

At the moment though, Deep Web content can be difficult to access.

Deep Web content can be highly useful to researchers. Much of it is produced by academics and specialists.

The Deep Web is rich in documents, data, and statistics.

The Deep Web, Hidden Web, or Invisible Web as it is alternatively known, also contains significant amounts of proprietary documents and information.

Much of the Deep Web is really public or semi-public information, information put up so that it can be shared, at least shared with a limited number of people. Billions of pages on the Hidden Web fall into more than half a dozen major categories of content that search engines cannot easily access, locate or save. For instance, material in sites that have paywalls, or sites that require users to enter a password for entry, are unsearchable by spiders. Spiders may be able to access the splash page of a site but they cannot fill in a search box, pay a fee, or provide the password.

Pages that remain dark in the Deep Web and do not become part of the Open Web include:

- Dynamic pages, such as plane schedules or stock pages that change rapidly or often and are not considered worthy of saving
- Streamed pages
- Pages whose content is denied by robots.txt files, robot meta-tags, firewalls, paywalls, or sign-in requirements
- Multi-media sites that cannot be properly explored
- Orphan content (No links are available)
- Archives
- Databases.

Navigating the Deep Web is challenging. It requires intelligent searching. To use the Deep Web efficiently you often have to know exactly what website you want to explore and then how to reach inside and search directly.

Deep Web searches are far different from the portion served up by search engines. Deep Web searches are inevitably hands-on efforts – once you know how to get to the site. While access to the Deep Web does not require a hacker's talents it does need special knowledge and capabilities.

Sometimes site operators do not want certain material or their pages to be accessed by search engines. System operators may put a notice on their site – assuming that it will be visited by a search engine spider – saying that certain pages or even the entire site are off-limits and are not to be searched. "Robots.txt" files or robots tags forbid admittance to search engines. Thus the contents which site operators want excluded may remain unknown to search engines, and to you, even after a spider has visited.

To see if robots are allowed to roam freely on a site or are prohibited from some areas, type "robots.txt" after the site's home address (with a concluding forward slash [/]) and hit the enter key or click next. If any folders or pages at the site are denied to a search engine's robots those locations should be listed. When folders on such a list look like they may contain denied information that appears promising, type in the name of the denied page or folder after the main URL of the site and the forward slash; then hit "enter." That often makes the information in the denied page visible.

Some site operators use a robots meta-tag on individual pages to exclude search engines. Again, the spider may or may not follow the meta-tag's orders. But if they do honor this "keep out" tag it is always wise to personally review any site that looks like it might be useful, even if a key word search does not show any results for that site. Google, for instance, sometimes gives an indication that a denied Web page exists, even if the page has a robots.txt or robots tag that is supposed to prohibit the engine from going there. A visit to these unindexed pages may be useful even if there is no summary of what they contain on the search engine results listing. Detailed information on how robotstxt files are set up and used is available at http://www.robotstxt.org.

Occasionally website system operators put up a page, or pages, that are unlinked anywhere, either on or off the site. The site operators give the URL of these uber-private pages to the people they want to see the information, but no others. Since spiders collect information by following links, a page or any subdomain pages that are unlinked will never be visited by a spider. There is no way that a search engine – or that search engine's user – will ever know the unlinked page exists, even when a spider visits the parent site. Only people who are given the exact URL will know the page is there and understand how to access it.

It is not as likely as in the past, but it is sometimes possible to see entire directories and discover unlinked pages by chopping off sections of URL addresses from the tail end until the home page address is reached. An unlinked page address may show up in a directory that is displayed through this archaic process.

Search engines, even if they are able to enter a Deep Web site, don't know how to effectively handle many graphics files, nor can spiders readily deal with databases such as Oracle, DB2, or SQL. In fact, material which is written in many formats other than html, or the alternative called htm, are not readily searchable by spiders. When the format of a site isn't searchable its information doesn't end up in a search engine's database. And if it isn't in the database no search engine user will give you useful information. A search engine, on occasion, may be able to reach and report on a database's front page, but since the spider cannot enter a search term or password it is stymied and can go no further.

It's not necessarily true that databases are totally unknown to search engines. Sometimes a search engine will spit out the name of a site where Deep Web material is located but it is generally safer to assume that looking for information in databases will require special techniques and pre-knowledge.

Academic sites are often useful places to gather meaningful information and may be lumped with the Deep Web or Ephemera sites for special attention.

Some present-day search engines, directories, and websites that are available on the Open Web are striving, collectively, to trace the outlines of the Deep Web. They may be helpful in locating hidden resources, sites or databases:

- **Academia:** https://www.academia.edu/
- **Academic Torrents:** http://academictorrents.com/
- **Answers:** http://www.answers.com
- **Archive Grid (Archive locations):** https://researchworks.oclc.org/archivegrid/
- **Archives Portal Europe:** http://www.archivesportaleurope.net/
- **Best of the Web:** https://botw.org/
- **Beyond Citation:** https://www.beyondcitation.org/

- **Bibliotheca Alexanderina (Internet Archive Backup):** http://www.bibalex.org/
- **Bielefeld Academic Search:** https://www.base-search.net/Search/Advanced
- **Brightplanet:** http://www.brightplanet.com/
- **Center for Research Libraries:** http://www.crl.edu/
- **CiteseerX (Digital world):** http://citeseerx.ist.psu.edu/
- **Cornell University Library arxiv (Science):** https://arxiv.org/
- **CrossRef (Metadata):** https://search.crossref.org/
- **DeepDyve ($$$$, Online library of scholarly research):** https://www.deepdyve.com/
- **Deep Web Research Article and Links:** http://www.deepwebresearch.com
- **DeepWeb Tech (Science, $$$$):** https://www.deepwebtech.com/
- **Digital Library Online Books Page (Database of more than 25,000 English works free, online):** http://digital.library.upenn.edu/books/search.html
- **DirectSearch:** http://directsearch.net/
- **Encyclopædia Britannica:** http://www.britannica.com/
- **GoBackinTime (Chrome add-on):** https://chrome.google.com/webstore/detail/go-back-in-time/hgdahcpipmgehmaaankiglanlgljlakj?hl=en-US
- **Google Scholar:** https://scholar.google.com/
- **GPO (US government documents):** https://www.gpo.gov/fdsys/search/home.action
- **GPO's Catalog of US Government Publications (Database of federal publications):** http://catalog.gpo.gov/
- **Highly Cited Researchers:** https://clarivate.com/hcr/
- **HighWire Press (Catalog of content, from over 900 different journals):** http://highwire.org/lists/browse.dtl
- **InfoPlease:** http://www.infoplease.com/index.html
- **Ingenta Connect (Scholarly publications):** http://www.ingentaconnect.com/

- **Internet Archive/Wayback Machine:** http://www.archive.org/index.php
- **LexisNexis ($$$$):** https://www.lexisnexis.com/en-us/gateway.page
- **Martindale's:** http://www.martindalecenter.com/
- **National Library of Australia Trove:** https://trove.nla.gov.au/
- **National Archives of UK:** https://discovery.nationalarchives.gov.uk/
- **OAIster:** http://www.oclc.org/en/oaister.html
- **PQDT Open (Dissertations and Theses):** https://pqdtopen.proquest.com/search.html
- **Project Gutenberg (Online catalog of nearly 20,000 free online books):** http://www.gutenberg.org/wiki/Main_Page
- **Questia (Research papers, $$$$):** https://www.questia.com/hbr-welcome
- **Refseek: (Academic search engine):** https://www.refseek.com/
- **ScienceDirect (Peer-reviewed articles and journals):** http://www.sciencedirect.com/
- **Social Science Research Network:** https://www.ssrn.com/index.cfm/en/
- **USASearch:** https://webarchive.library.unt.edu/
- **US National Archives (Government documents):** https://www.archives.gov/research/alic/reference/govt-docs.html
- **US National Archives (Main page):** https://www.archives.gov/
- **Wiley Online Library:** http://onlinelibrary.wiley.com/
- **Worldcat (Catalogue of library and academic resources):** https://www.worldcat.org/
- **World Digital Library:** https://www.wdl.org/en/
- **WWW Virtual Library:** http://vlib.org

- **Zillman's Academic and Scholar Search Engines and Sources:** http://www.zillman.us/white-papers/scholar-search-engines/

Unfortunately, the Deep Web is often misunderstood and conflated with the Dark Web.

Dark Web

In the Dark Web – that part of the Web which sometimes caters to criminal activity and always to secrecy – many servers are set up so that they will accept only searches coming through special sites or systems. Dark Web sites often reject access requests coming from conventional browsers.

This is known as the "hidden services" portion of the Dark Web. The Dark Web, particularly the part that provides "hidden services" and is made up of "darknets," often serves ends which various governments consider either anti-social or are patently illegal. Even governments find it challenging to enter and exploit the Dark Web, but access may be useful under select circumstances.

There are several darknets. While services such as Tor, Freenet and I2P access the main darknets; there are also some smaller friend-to-friend darknets in the mix.

Tor Project at http://www.torproject.org is free software designed specifically to protect against government traffic analysis. It was originally developed by US agencies and later freed for public use in order to provide people with a safe way to avoid censorship by authoritarian rulers. Tor is one of the main ways to access the Dark Web. When properly set up and deftly used, Tor effectively hides all web identity information such as search history, communication activity, and traffic.

Tor and similar services, while good, have some imperfections. "What one man can invent another can discover," Sherlock Holmes said in *The Adventure of the Dancing Men* and that should be a warning to everyone conducting OSR. It is hard to be too wary on the Web.

While the few known vulnerabilities of Tor do not seem to make it outrageously insecure to non-nerds, they become significant to those whose freedom, and in some cases even lives, may – or do – depend on anonymity. None of the Tor vulnerabilities are determinative, but all are worrisome to those who understand how even the most minor types of glitches, collectively, can rip a deadly hole in security and allow identification of the user. Simple things can wreck anyone's secrecy efforts. For instance, when on Tor, even opening downloads while still using the browser can reveal a user's identity.

Tor gained fame as "The Onion Router Network" – hence TOR Network – because it layers everything like an onion. Peeling away one layer only brings up another layer, beneath which are more layers. Tor is an open distributed network. A user's connection to any site is bounced around among relays operated by volunteers worldwide.

In a simplified explanation, as information packets are passed through the Internet using Tor they are encrypted. Each time the Tor message passes a node the encryption is stripped off to reveal only the next node to be used. System operators at any given node see only where it last came from, and where it is going next – not the original user and not the destination site. At no point in the pathway are the identities of the recipient and the requestor available at the same time. There is no linkage between the two.

Some professional researchers who need heavy security when they use programs such as Tor like to test and make certain where they will emerge.

There are programs, such as **IP2location** (\$\$\$\$): https://www.ip2location.com/, that help skittish users determine if they are using a location they feel comfortable about.

The Tor Browser is available for PCs and computers using the Windows, Linux, and Mac operating systems. Tor's security can be enhanced with The Amnesic Incognito Live System (TAILS). A properly-configured Tails operating system, which extends the utility of the Tor browser, brings users closer to absolute anonymity.

Tails: https://tails.boum.org/index.en.html is a freeware system that is designed to improve security and leave no trace of your activity unless you explicitly ask for less security.

Tails is a Swiss Army knife for protection. Designed specifically for use with Tor, it is a self-contained operating system based on Linux that works from a DVD or a USB thumb drive. When using Tails you completely bypass your computer's normal operating system. When you close a Tails session your normal operating system resumes and the computer has "amnesia" about what you did, when and where. Setting up Tails, as is true with all good security systems, will often try your computer abilities and probably your patience. There is a lot under the hood when installing this, or similar programs. Detailed instructions are available on the Internet; it is wise to download and print out the set-up before starting installation in order to closely follow the complex process.

An advantage of Tails is that you can carry it on a thumb drive and plug it into any public computer or unsecured system, yet have a high level of confidence that you are not being tracked.

Tails allows you to save items or documents to an external hard disk or thumb drive, but it is configured so that it completely bypasses your computer's hard drive.

All parts of Tails are preconfigured for security. One of the program's greatest assets is that if any application attempts to connect to the Internet directly – something you may not always be aware of – the connection will be automatically blocked. Tails also sports an array of cryptographic tools, including the **HTTPS Everywhere** extension of the Electronic Frontier Foundation https://www.eff.org. File deletion and disk cleaning extensions provide further security.

Some Dark Net search capability involving the onion browser is available at sites such as:

- **Exonerator (Reports whether an address was a Tor relay):** https://exonerator.torproject.org/
- **Hidden Wiki (Tor URLs and Directories**): http://thehiddenwiki.org/
- **Not Evil (Tor search, access from The Onion Router):** http://hss3uro2hsxfogfq.onion/
- **OnionShare (File sharing over Tor):** https://onionshare.org.
- **Tor2Web/Torch (Tor search):** http://xmh57jrzrnw6insl.onion/.

Non-Tor programs that can aid security and anonymous or protected browsing include:

- freepto (Linux)
- Ipredia OS
- WhoNix
- Jondo Live CD (Linux)
- Freenet
- Lightweight Portable Security.

***

Project:
Open the SOP file. List any Deep Web sites you plan to use.

Project:
If you do not plan to use any Deep Web sites, explain why.

Project:
Open the SOP file. Indicate whether you will use the Dark Web. If you decide to do so, find and copy relevant portions of the Wikipedia articles on the Deep Web and Tor, I2P or Freenet to your SOP.

Project:
Decide whether you want to download and test Tor and Tails, I2P, Freenet, or similar programs to reach the Dark Net. If so, show in your SOP what and when you want to add any of these to your capabilities.

Project:
Go to a major website such as nytimes.com and follow the directions for finding robots.txt files and accessing the material in them. Type "robots.txt" file after the site's home page URL (with a concluding forward slash [/]). Strike the enter key or click "next." If folders at the site are denied to robots, those will be listed. Choose any of the folders on such a list that look like they may contain promising information, type in the name of the folder after the main URL and hit the enter key. That usually makes the information in the denied page visible.

Project:
If you plan on using the robots.txt search expedient in the future, go to the techniques section of your SOP document and write down the instructions on how to use this technique. Also explain under what circumstances you plan to check sites for robots.txt files.

11. Webscraping and Offline Browsing

Webscraping

Webscraping is a challenge; make no mistake. Many consider it the Everest of OSR, a pinnacle that even challenges climbers in the profession.

Webscraping involves the collection of unindexed or unstructured data, or big data, and giving it the structure needed for detailed analysis and interpretation. Webscraping is usually the collection precursor to detailed analysis of the scraped material.

Observation and data are always useful and can provide meaningful information, but Webscraping and the subsequent analysis can become key knowledge.

Large amounts of proprietary information are posted on the Web, often on the Hidden Web, to make it easier for selected people to work with the data. Much of this data is not protected by firewalls; the vastness of the Internet and its complexity are often seen as the shields for these data troves. In its raw form the proprietary information has no obvious meaning and the people who put it online for their own convenience sake think the meaningless of the raw data, along with some minimal security measures, make it unattractive and safe from intruders.

Not smart! There are always people who will look for, download, analyze the data to extract information, and ferret out its hidden meaning.

Webscraping transfers online data into a local program where it can be carefully, and safely, analyzed. It eliminates the need to get and manually enter reams of information into a database or spreadsheet program for analysis. It nearly always requires familiarity with, and ability to do, some programming in Perl, Python, or some other computer languages.

Databases and spreadsheets share some characteristics, but are significantly different. Many – some say the majority of – databases are often relational, linking two or more two types of information together to improve flexibility. Another type, flat databases, store all information in a single file.

Database information is stored in sections called "records," which may consist of several "fields." Fields hold a single information type. Databases often, but not always, are built using structured query language (SQL).

Spreadsheets differ. Their information is presented in tabular form, in columns and rows. It is often, but not always, largely numeric.

In many cases the data available for scraping consists of economic, political, historical, personnel, governmental, or corporate information.

Data suitable for scraping may cover many subjects but it is seldom within easy reach. Even non-proprietary information is not generally easily available to the average Internet user. Nor is it unusual for owners of information to either inadvertently or intentionally try to close off access to whatever data they put on the web. Information owners seldom make it easy to snare or analyze usable data.

Site managers are understandably picky about who gets to use their information. After all, you are often taking a site's content with the intention of using it in ways that are outside the direct control of the site's system operator. System operators get nervous at the very thought of that. They throw up roadblocks where and when that is possible.

Site managers may employ barriers such as Flash, Javascript, or CAPTCHA roadblocks to prevent their site from being scraped. Storing the data in PDF files or in other formats makes it difficult to download and analyze.

Analysis and interpretation may be impossible when large data sets are not in a database-readable form. For this reason, much of a collector's effort may be spent developing and using workarounds that make the scraped contents coherent and readable.

Webscraping – it may also be called data extraction, collecting, or catching – is hardly an OSR beginner's business. Many well-trained open source researchers and collectors have never done it; many may never collect this way. Webscraping capability is generally considered to be at the far end of OSR talents.

The techniques used in any webscrape are unique to the particular webscraper, the target of the collecting effort, and the complexity and size of the data set. Webscraping searches are inevitably tailored to the particular data set. Every webscraping session, and every workaround, is unique. Cookie cutter scrapes do not exist.

Differences in format, data types and ways that data is handled on a site require scrapers to be on-the-fly problem-solvers

Webscraping uses special "crawling" engines to collect the data sets. Often these sets are large and take much time – forget about the effort – to download.

While a primary reason to do webscraping is to a make analysis easier, there are other ones. Not the least of those other reasons is that the data might be taken down or altered – particularly if the parties who put the data up know that you are interested in their information. Put another way, it's safest to have your own copy of the original data set, a copy that you can analyze in different ways at your own pace, also a copy that serves as proof.

Scraping tools are software, or computer code, that automatically extract data from web sites, spreadsheets, or databases. They perform automatic "cut and pastes" of information from the storage medium into the scraper's database or spreadsheet file for later analysis.

While scraping uses automated programs to do the actual work, it is often sensible to make the effort look – at least to the managers of the site being scraped – as if a human being is visiting the site and checking the pages. The closer to making the scraper traffic appear to be human activity the less likely you are to encounter objections or problems from a site owner. Human-guided traffic usually subjects a site to minimal stresses. It is not as likely to bring down the site, or damage information on the site, something which is always potentially a problem with aggressive scraping.

Thinking through the scrape is essential.

Plan what you need to download, and when to do it. Follow through on that plan. Scrape during off-hours, at times when the site isn't likely to be most active. Avoid setting patterns. Stagger the hours so you don't come online at the same time each day. Do not make parallel information requests; do them sequentially and space them out so there is an interval – it doesn't have to be long – between your information downloads.

Importantly, think about what you actually will use and need. Avoid snaring material "just because it's there." Save downloaded material on your computer or on a hang-on drive so that it can be reused. Avoid reinventing the wheel on downloads.

Effective and efficient use of particular scraping tools, databases, and spreadsheets is beyond the scope of this book, but much more information is available on the Internet, in libraries, and in bookstores.

The actual webscraping is only the first, but arguably most vital, part of the process. The scraped material must be analyzed for whatever results the collector hopes to achieve. Never do analysis on the original file; always analyze a clone of the original. Keep the actual downloaded material pristine.

Webscraping has five discrete stages:

- **Acquire** is the first – perhaps most important – step since everything that comes after that point relies upon the data being acquired. While it is possible in some cases to gather data for analysis by creating surveys or similar methods, webscraping is usually a more efficient way to gather data. Webscraping is often time-intensive and requires deft planning to discover where the data needed for the project is stored, and how it can be snared for download or "scraping."

- **Extract** is the next step. The information is changed from whatever format it was stored in by the original collector and converted so that it can be queried and analyzed in a database system. Many original collectors store data in formats that are difficult to work with, such as PDFs, to prevent effective use of the information by others.

- **Clean** is the stage at which data sets are "normalized" and prepared for analysis. Data inconsistencies in names and numbering, or formats, may prove problematic. Files or parts of files may be corrupted and must be corrected or removed. For many researchers this is the most exasperating part of the process, a time when information holes may have to be patched by the combination of datasets, removal of duplicate information, and making certain that all parts of the dataset are using similar values. The cleaning stage is granular and requires a review from many angles.

- **Analyze** is the stage of determining the meaning – hidden or obvious – of the data. It is the "questioning" of the data to find answers. This is the reason for all the other work.

- **Report** is the final stage. The data are not useful unless they are presented in a way that makes them understandable and useable.

Tools and Programs

Webscraping can be done with a variety of tools. Almost all require payment but some vendors offer limited "tests" of the tools. A few tools are relatively simple to use; most are far more complex. To get data from some websites, scraping is only possible by using custom-coded tools. Choosing the right tool for the job is among the first of the challenges facing would-be collectors.

For those who have never done webscraping, and relatively few computer users have, it's best to learn by initially using simple extraction tools and simple databases. Outwit Hub is considered a useful basic program for many newcomers to the field. Beginners can work up to more complex tools. Tools and programs needed at various parts of the process include:

- **Chrome webscraping extension:**
  https://chrome.google.com/webstore/detail/web-scraper/jnhgnonknehpejjnehehllkliplmbmhn
- **Docudesk:** http://www.docudesk.com/
- **DownloadStar (Firefox extension):**
  http://addons.mozilla.org/en-us/firefox/addon/download-star
- **DownThemAll (Download manager):**
  http://www.downthemall.net/
- **Google Webscraper (Free Chrome extension):**
  https://chrome.google.com/webstore/detail/scraper/mbigbapnjcgaffohmbkdlecaccepngjd
- **Google Sheets:** https://www.google.com/sheets/about/
- **Import.io:** https://www.import.io/
- **Outwit Hub (Free):**
  https://www.outwit.com/products/hub/
- **ScrapeBox ($$$$):** http://www.scrapebox.com
- **Scrapy (Open source, collaborative):** https://scrapy.org.

Scraping services – vendors that do the job for you – come at a price but they eliminate the frustrations and the learning curve that are required to achieve personal webscraping competence. Scraping services or vendors can be found by entering those terms in a search engine. They include:

- **Connotate ($$$$):** http://www.connotate.com/
- **DataHut ($$$$):** http://datahut.co/
- **DiffBot ($$$$):** https:/www.diffbot.com/
- **Mozenda ($$$$):** http://www.mozenda.com/
- **Scraping Hub ($$$$):** https://scrapinghub.com/.

A Convoluted Process...

Take things one baby-step at a time. This is especially important with webscraping, which is convoluted. Always take time to strategize when doing webscraping. Arguably webscrapers are required, more often than other researchers, to think carefully. Carefully! At every step.

Determine where the needed information is likely to be held, who is holding it, and whether it is likely to be posted online or held internally. Internal data sources may be impossible to access legally. They may be databases, emails, wikis, files or blogs that are not online, that are behind firewalls, or are effectively inaccessible. But any accessible online data sources are, for the most part, legally available.

Some information resources, often dubbed primary sources or authoritative ones, may be the originators of data. Secondary, or supplemental, sources may hold part of what you need and can sometimes be used to augment information garnered from primary sources. Usually the most authoritative sources are cleanest, though they are not necessarily the easiest to use.

Once you have identified what information you need and where to get it, you need to determine the quality of data. Not all data is high-quality. Poor quality information leads almost inevitably to poor results. The "garbage in, garbage out" (GIGO) rule is proven by webscrapes.

Test small data samples from the resources that you plan to use. Use data extraction services or your own capabilities to gather samples of the information. The planned source may have export capabilities, which is good (and fortuitous), or you may have to copy and paste the sample from the data source.

Assess the test data and determine whether the collected information will be useful for your needs. At the same time try to determine the reliability of the data. Just because someone has put something in a database or collected it does not prove it has high reliability. You need to consider both the reliability of the underlying data itself, and the reliability of the extraction process. Any process that misses data or miscues it will lead to unreliable results. GIGO!

Once the quality and reliability of the data have been determined it is time to create an automated data extraction process – the actual webscraping process – or hire a vendor to gather the information for you.

Webscraping is a complex process. Start by identifying the overall workflow, Develop granularity from there. Look carefully at the project to determine what parts of it can be automated, either by your own tools or through a vendor. Then determine which tools, processes, vendors, and people will ultimately be involved, and at what stage.

Develop, to the extent possible, your quality assurance process in advance. Things do go wrong. Try to identify probable glitches, the ways to determine when these might occur, and the steps to take when the inevitable happens.

Buy or build the software and the capabilities needed; hire or assign the personnel or vendors. Make certain they are all integrated seamlessly into the process. Set up communications channels with all of the people involved and fix the final destination of the scraped data.

Then test, under both normal conditions and heavy loads, your process before deploying it.

Scrape!

Whenever scraping, take an early look at the result you are getting to see if it actually matches what you want to collect and would be useful for analysis. Before you invest the time in analysis, make certain the data download will actually provide the information you expect. Early integrity checks of the downloaded data can warn of potential problems before you start using the information in earnest. Count the fields, sum some columns, and test the techniques you expect to use with the data.

Once downloaded, or scraped, save the original material in a safe place. Never touch that original except to make a clone, or several work copies. Always do all analysis off the copy! Keep the actual downloaded material pristine.

Let's repeat that. Always, always work off a copy! Never touch the original except to copy it. It is far too easy to corrupt the working file during analysis. In fact consider it unusual if the working file is not corrupted or made unusable at least once.

When manipulating scraped material, maintain a detailed log of everything you do. If something goes awry during the process, and it often will, you will know what you did correctly up to the point where the file was corrupted. You will also know what you did that the system didn't like.

When you are working cooperatively, version control is more than important; it is crucial. Version control becomes essential in the collaborative environment.

As with all Internet-related subjects, the Web can provide answers to most questions. There are tutorials about almost any subject involving computers on the Web, including webscraping and the tools you are using. YouTube often has instructive videos on most programs – including programs used to scrape data.

Webscraping can pose legal questions that should be discussed with your attorney. Some sites, in their terms of service or through a robots.txt notice that few people read, prohibit the practice. That has the potential to cause expensive legal problems for the would-be data collector.

Keep in mind that your webscraping can also cause problems for the site being scraped. This may bring unwelcome civic attention to your efforts. Problems, ranging from slowing response time to potentially damaging the programs or data sets, are possible. Many collectors of large datasets work at times – usually in late night or early morning off-hours – when the website is less likely, or unlikely, to be active. Paced consistency in scraping is often a better option than speed.

Offline Browsing

Offline browsing shares one similarity to Webscraping – you are gathering file cabinets of information for later review and analysis. Offline browsers capture and save web pages or whole sites rather than data sets.

An older technique, offline browsing got its name because once the page or site is downloaded to the researcher's computer all further work or reviews can be done offline, on the researcher's system. There is no need to go back to the site and no likelihood the website operator will know what the researcher is doing with the downloaded material.

Offline browsing can save time, fulmination, and frustration.

It is not unusual to grope your way around complex or disorganized sites. An offline browser allows you to travel through the site when it is most convenient for you, in a way that denies the site operator any knowledge of your interest or activities. The offline browser process also allows you to keep a permanent record of the site and the material on that site at a given time and date.

Using an offline browser is sometimes called mirroring or website extracting. That is an apt description. Offline browser software usually will download or "mirror" web pages, email groups, or newsgroup posts in their entirety and store them on your computer. Obviously, many site managers don't appreciate this and some have become adept at preventing offline browsers from snagging their pages. Even if it doesn't work every time, trying an offline browser on any major site in your search plan is wise.

There are good security reasons to use an offline browser.

"Dwell time," the amount of time spent on a page is often important to security. To a watching system operator an unusual amount of time spent on a page – and that can be as little as about a minute on some sites – suggests that you are someone other than the usual user.

Offline browsers allow you to:
- Get on.
- Automatically copy a site and its links.
- Get off.
- Review and analyze the material leisurely, without the site administrator knowing what you are doing or where you are

concentrating your research efforts. It also allows you to keep a permanent record of the site and its material.

Website mirroring can be used to download an entire website or portions of one. Many information shops parse through the copy, paying particular attention to page source code, which may include information not be visible on the web page presented to viewers.

Key mirroring sites include:
- **GNU Wget (Command line controlled):** http://www.gnu.org/software/wget/
- **HTTrack Website Copier:** https://www.httrack.com/
- **SurfOffline ($$$$):** http://www.surfoffline.com/
- **Web Data Extractor**: http://www.webextractor.com/download.htm
- **WebsiteExtractor ($$$$):** http://www.esalesbiz.com/extra/
- **Website Ripper Copier ($$$$):** http://www.tensons.com/products/websiterippercopier/

***

Project:
In your SOP confirm whether you will likely have a need for Webscraping, and if so what tools and educational materials such as manuals and programs you will likely need for the work. Plan a learning trial and experimental run-through to become familiar with the process if you intend to add this to your repertoire of talents.

Project:
In your SOP confirm whether you are likely to use offline browsing. If so, find and select one or more programs. Use them at least once to learn the basics. Write any directions to using the programs in your SOP.

12. News Media Systems

The US, British, and other governments spend tens of millions of dollars each year to sweep up tidbits of news on web sites, or to buy magazine and newspaper subscriptions. They download television programs. There have to be reasons – tens of millions of them.

Estimates from friend and foe alike suggest that up to 80 percent of intelligence needs can be satisfied from openly-available resources, many of them media sources.

The world's media may be considered, collectively, to be the planet's largest – if loosely linked – spy system. Add to that libraries and book stores. These, when lumped together, are larger than all the world's professional spy agencies.

Media of all kinds remain one of the largest sources of Open Source information. They may air or publish their news on an up-to-the-minute, daily, weekly, monthly, or periodic basis. Occasionally they create a one-off or special.

Media may cater to specialized audiences or to a general interest readership and viewership.

Intelligence agencies are dedicated to collecting everything but only doling out their data in sips to select people. Most public media are dedicated to collecting widely and blasting out their product to anyone who will listen in firehose streams. Drinking from those firehoses, as well as the other rivers of knowledge that crisscross the information landscape, can lead to the critical thinking so necessary today.

Many in the free-world media are dedicated to making every shred of information – including as much interesting proprietary and secret information as they can gather – available to everyone.

Sir Arthur Conan Doyle had his most famous character, Sherlock Holmes, suggest a verity, the truth of which continues to this day. "The Press, Watson, is a most valuable institution, if you only know how to use it," Holmes lectured his partner in criminology in *The Adventure of the Six Napoleons*.

Effective use of the mass media is an important part of modern OSR. The utility of news media to the individual researcher or research desk depends almost entirely on what is being researched. Anyone doing extensive investigation of rust inhibitors might find very little need to use the mass media information. However, a specific medium or two that specialize in rust issues – yes, there are such niche media, called "trades" – would probably provide much useful information to a researcher looking into corrosion.

Open Source researchers have to get specific individual parts of this vast pseudo-intelligence gathering organization working for them and their projects, just as Holmes suggested. That requires looking at the news media from the 30,000 foot level, understanding how it generally works, and then using that understanding to pan for the golden nuggets buried amidst the vast pile of data and otherwise-useless information that the media puts out each day.

For the Open Source specialist, news media are important for:
- Near-real-time reports of events that may affect you or your client's operations
- Leads the media may provide regarding the issuance of reports, studies, and other material that would otherwise be overlooked .
- Archived media material that may be useful in compiling reports and studies.

Media Types

Media are broken down into three general types:
- Digital
- Electronic
- Print, or fiber-based.

Traditional media such as radio, print, and television are now available online. There are thousands of media sources available in dozens of languages. Independent/alternative news sources are increasingly available.

There is also an ongoing hybridization in the publishing industry – the distinct types are morphing into multi-channel forms. Newspapers and magazines produce digital copies of their publications. They use sound and videos in much the same way as electronic media. Television channels and radio stations have websites. Digital resources produce fiber-based materials or visuals.

The existence of the three categories remains important despite the ongoing merging of the forms. Open source researchers must be aware that while strict format lines of the past are disappearing (or may have already disappeared) they must be prepared to collect all types and forms of information. OSR operators in any medium must now be prepared to snag a wide variety of formats using scanners and other technology, including Web resources that may not be immediately apparent. For instance, radio feeds of police, citizen's band, ham, aviation, rail, marine, and other bands are put on the Internet at sites such as:
- **Broadcastify:** https://www.broadcastify.com/listen/
- **WebSDR:** http://websdr.org/.

This is an entire sub-field in itself, one that can be carefully developed by Open Source researchers. The Open Source Center of the US government OSINT operation has sections that are devoted solely to radio and television transmissions.

Researchers can find helpful information about specific electronic wavelengths and sites that need monitoring, as well as other essential details on the Internet.

Useful websites include:

- **FCC:** https://www.fcc.gov/
- **RadioReference:** http://www.radioreference.com/
- **Radio Tracking Forums:** https://forums.radioreference.com/.

Radio stations around the world can provide immediate information in case of disasters. Researchers may use them to provide general information about events in a given area. Tens of thousands of broadcasts on commercial stations can be accessed over the Internet at sites such as:

- **Radioline:** http://www.radioline.co/world-radios-podcasts
- **RadioNet:** https://www.radio.net/
- **TuneIn:** https://tunein.com/radio/World-c57954/
- **WorldRadioMap:** http://worldradiomap.com/
- **Worldwide Radio (Chrome extension):** https://chrome.google.com/webstore/detail/worldwide-radio/ofncbjjbfchlegacifnndkkbdoaedcof.
- **Worldwide Radio (Firefox extension):** http://addons.mozilla.org/en-us/firefox/addon/worldwide-radio.

Digital Media

Digital news media are often considered the main object of OSR research. They and social media are growing in importance. The digital media are often near-real-time, and many appear to be less-controlled. However, more and more countries – and individuals – are attempting to manipulate these mass media, often with some success. Individual sites and even the entire Web may be banned or closed down in some areas or countries by governments. Information may be excised in an effort to bring digital media to heel. The Internet has increased popular accessibility of media. It has also upped the prevalence of fakery in news while prompting continued efforts aimed at tighter control by powerful people.

Periodicals are now widely available in digital formats on the Internet. In those digital formats many publications now feature videos and sound bites that cannot be included in their fiber-based products.

Not many years ago, intelligence agencies detailed people to collect the daily and weekly newspapers or magazines overseas, then send them by diplomatic pouch to an analysis center. Today much of that same material is gathered over the Web. Moreover, the collected information is more current – it may be only a few hours or at most a day stale.

Outside of the intelligence world, a wide variety of periodicals cover many of the more mundane subjects that businesses, students, and the general public are interested in. The move toward Web 2.0 and beyond, as well as the trend toward "citizen journalism," blogging, and criticism, make these part of an ever-expanding field that must be factored into information searches.

There is also a small but growing online community, exemplified by the Bellingcat information collective, which uses digital media to improve justice and security in the world.

Electronic Media

Radio and television are generally considered the main electronic media, although multi-media on disk or tape can be shoehorned into this category.

In some countries electronic media are controlled to greater or lesser degrees by the government, in which case their output has to be viewed as an extension of the government and that government's policy. That can be useful for tracking changes, or impending changes, in activity and policy. (See Paul Linebarger's seminal book, *Psychological Warfare*, particularly his section on Propaganda Intelligence.) Because electronic distribution is generally cheaper than print media and is now easier for users in many areas to access, the monitoring and analysis of both electronic media and digital media in financially distressed nations or areas of low literacy may provide more useful information than the monitoring of fiber-based media.

In the United States and some other Westernized nations, many electronic media only have enough time to skim, restricting themselves to what they consider the most important information in their broadcasts. Time constraints challenge reporters in the electronic media, but good electronic journalists can and do compete head-to-head with practitioners using other formats.

Print Media

Some of the original printed media were books. Books remain a valuable resource for selected subjects. Books, if they are good ones, generally reflect the state of knowledge about a given subject at least six months or more prior to the date of publication.

Books should never be discounted, but even with new publishing techniques that can cut publication times to mere days, books should be considered of little use when examining the current state of affairs about dynamic issues.

Books are extremely useful for pinning down historical background and unchanging facts, however.

Sherlock Holmes valued books and the knowledge they contain. He used such a book, one containing unchanging facts, in solving *The Adventure of the Lion's Mane* noting: "There is a great garret in my little house which is stuffed with books. It was into this that I plunged and rummaged for an hour. At the end of that time I emerged with a little chocolate and silver volume. Eagerly I turned up the chapter of which I had a dim remembrance. Yes, it was indeed a far-fetched and unlikely proposition, and yet I could not rest until I had made sure if it might, indeed, be so." Those dimly-remembered words that jumped off the printed page enabled him to solve the problem.

Book sites are important resources for researchers. Some sites offer free portions, or even complete books.

- **Abe Books ($$$$ Used and new):** https://www.abebooks.com/
- **Amazon Books ($$$$):** https://www.amazon.com/
- **Barnes & Noble ($$$$):** https://www.barnesandnoble.com/
- **Google Books ($$$$):** https://books.google.com/
- **Project Gutenberg:** https://www.gutenberg.org/.

Where possible, on book sites search inside digital publications for helpful information. Some sites allow searches for authors, titles or ISBN numbers, or the use of advanced search options such as inauthor, inpublisher, and intitle.

Periodicals – newsletters, magazines, newspapers and the like – offer more currency. Periodicals may be broadly focused, as a weekly news magazine, or more tightly focused, as a newsletter on the oil industry in the northern Gulf of Mexico.

Newspapers of Record are a useful information source since, of all media, they often provide the timeliest comprehensive record of major, and sometimes even minor, events. Newspapers of Record provide the most probable place for "one-stop shopping" about ongoing events in any area. They are generally useful for obtaining information about governmental actions and are helpful when following some activities, even in a closed media society. In the latter case their messages have to be very carefully vetted for the propaganda underlying the message.

Newspapers of Record are known by a number of different terms worldwide, such as "journal of record" and *"presse de reference."* The characteristics of Newspapers of Record vary. The term is somewhat squishy; it is not formally defined. There are two general types of Newspapers of Record:

- Professionally produced publications that record all major events and some minor ones in a particular area
- Publicly available papers authorized or maintained by a government to publish public or legal notices. This type may also be called an "official paper."

Among the well-recognized newspapers of record are:
- Argentina *La Nación*
- Belgium *De*
- Canada *The Globe and Mail*
- Canada *La Presse*
- Chile *El Mercurio* Santiago
- France *Le Monde* Paris
- France *Le Figaro*
- Germany *Frankfurter Allgemeine Zeitung*
- Hungary *Népszabadság* Budapest
- India *The Times of India*
- Ireland *The Irish Times*
- Italy *Corriere della Sera*
- Peru *El Peruano*
- Portugal *Diário de Notícias*
- Serbia *Politika*
- Netherlands *NRC Handelsblad*
- Peru *El Peruano*
- Portugal *Diário de Notícias*
- Serbia *Politika*
- Spain *El País*
- Switzerland *Neue Zürcher Zeitung*
- United Kingdom *The Times*
- United Kingdom *The Daily Telegraph*

- United States *The New York Times*.

Trade publications are another highly-useful sub-type of periodicals. They are most useful when the information search covers a distinct subject area. They are often magazines, papers, or online versions of newspapers and magazines that deal with specific trades, fields, or professions.

"Trades," as these publications are colloquially called, provide the detailed information that is important to the people who work in a particular field. They may be of little or no interest to the public as a whole, however. Some "trades" are free to people who express an interest in them. Advertisers who want to get their message to professionals and participants in the particular field are often the financial engines of "trades."

Trade publications report on the select field in detail. Someone who likes movies might read a consumer publications like *Entertainment Weekly* because of their coverage of movie and television stars. But someone working in the movie industry will probably scour trades such as *Variety* and *The Hollywood Reporter* – publications that closely cover the *minutiae* of Hollywood happenings.

Trades provide more granular information than consumer publications would. Trade reporters are often considered subject-matter experts in their fields.

The Media World is Wide

Using media of any kind requires careful thought and intelligent selection of the best sites and sources. It is important to find and use those that will be most valuable to the researcher. Fortunately online media lists include thousands of sites.

Search for newspapers, magazines, or stations in the area of the investigation and use these – or the media in larger cities nearby –

to keep abreast of what people are talking about locally. To locate local media, type terms like "media lists" into your search engine.

Some useful media lists and maps include:
- **Abyznewslinks:** http://www.abyznewslinks.com/
- **Actualidad:** http://actualidad.com/
- **BeelineTV:** http://www.garywlee.com/tv.html
- **FreeTV:** http://www.freeetv.com/
- **Magatopia:** http://www.magatopia.com
- **Newspapermap:** https://newspapermap.com
- **Newspapers.com ($$$$):** http://newspapers.com/
- **Online Newspapers:** http://www.onlinenewspapers.com/
- **Radiolocator:** http://radio-locator.com/
- **RadioStation World:** http://www.radiostationworld.com
- **Radiotower:** http://www.radiotower.com/
- **World Newspapers:** http://www.world-newspapers.com.

Useful media, depending upon the subject and geographical area you are researching, might include:
- **Aeroflight Aircraft Magazine Guides**
  http://www.aeroflight.co.uk/media/mags/worldmags.htm
- **Aircraft Magazines List**
  http://www.aircraftinformation.info/magazines.htm
- **Al Arabiya**: http://english.alarabiya.net/
- **ANSA (English language)**:
  http://www.ansa.it/english/index.html
- **Arab News**: http://www.arabnews.com/
- **Asharq Al-Awsat: https://aawsat.com/english**
- **Asian Age:** http://www.asianage.com/
- **Aviation Magazines:** http://www.world-newspapers.com/aviation.html
- **Channel 4 News (UK):** http://www.channel4.com/news/
- **Christian Science Monitor:** http://www.csmonitor.com/

- **Clarín (Argentina, Spanish language):**
  http://www.clarin.com/
- **Corriere della Sera (Italy, Italian language):**
  http://www.corriere.it/
- **Corriere della Sera (Italy, English language):**
  http://www.corriere.it/english/
- **Daily Star (Lebanon):** http://www.dailystar.com.lb/
- **Dawn (Pakistan):** http://www.dawn.com/
- **De Standaard (Belgium):** http://www.standaard.be
- **Diário de Notícias (Portugal, Portuguese language):**
  http://www.dn.pt/
- **Egypt Independent:** http://www.egyptindependent.com/
- **El Mercurio (Chile, Spanish language):**
  http://www.emol.com
- **El Mundo (Spain, Spanish language):**
  http://www.elmundo.es/
- **El Peruano (Peru, Spanish language):**
  http://www.elperuano.com.pe/edicion/
- **El País (Spain, Spanish language):**
  http://elpais.com/elpais/portada_america.html
- **European Media Monitor:**
  http://emm.newsbrief.eu/NewsBrief/clusteredition/en/latest
  .html
- **Express Tribune (Pakistan):** http://tribune.com.pk/
- **Frankfurter Allgemeine Zeitung (Germany, German language):** http://www.faz.net
- **Financial Times (UK):** https://www.ft.com/
- **Globo.com (Brazil, Portuguese):** http://g1.globo.com/
- **Google News:** http://news.google.com/
- **Guardian (UK):** http://www.guardian.co.uk
- **Haaretz (Israel):** http://www.haaretz.com/
- **La Nacion (Argentina, Spanish language):**
  http://www.lanacion.com.ar/
- **La Presse (Canada, French Language):**
  http://www.lapresse.ca

- **Los Angeles Times.com:** http://www.latimes.com/
- **Le Figaro (France, French language):** http://www.lefigaro.fr
- **Le Monde (France, French language):** http://www.lemonde.fr/
- **McClatchy DC Bureau:** http://www.mcclatchydc.com/
- **National Public Radio:** http://www.npr.org/
- **NBC:** http://www.nbcnews.com/
- **NDTV (India):** http://www.ndtv.com/
- **Népszabadság (Hungary, Hungarian language):** http://www.nol.hu/index.html?ref=sso
- **Neue Zürcher Zeitung (Switzerland, German language):** http://www.nzz.ch
- **News18 (India):** http://www.news18.com/
- **NewsNow (UK):** http://www.newsnow.co.uk
- **NRC Handelsblad (Netherlands Dutch language):** http://www.nrc.nl
- **Globo (Brazil):** http://oglobo.globo.com/
- **Politika (Serbia, Serbian language):** http://www.politika.rs
- **PressReader (Magazines):** https://www.pressreader.com/
- **ProPublica:** http:www.propublica.org/
- **PubliCola:** http://www.seattlemet.com/news-and-profiles/publicola
- **Rayogram/News:** http://www.rayogram.com/news
- **Real Clear World:** http://www.realclearworld.com/
- **Reuters:** http://www.reuters.com/
- **Rue89:** http://www.rue89.com/
- **Russia Today (RT):** http://rt.com/
- **Spiegel Online (English):** http://www.spiegel.de/international/
- **Sydney Morning Herald:** http://www.smh.com.au/
- **Tehelka (India):** http://www.tehelka.com/
- **The Associated Press:** https://apnews.com/
- **The Daily Telegraph (UK):** http://www.telegraph.co.uk

- **The Globe and Mail (Canada):** http://www.theglobeandmail.com/
- **The Irish Times (Ireland):** http://www.irishtimes.com
- **The Local (Berlin):** http://www.thelocal.de/
- **The Mail and Guardian (South Africa):** https://www.mg.co.za/
- **The National (UAE):** http://www.thenational.ae/
- **The New York Times:** https://www.nytimes.com/
- **The News (Pakistan):** https://www.thenews.com.pk/index.html
- **The Relief Web-Thomson Reuters:** https://reliefweb.int/
- **The Seattle Times:** https://seattletimes.com/html/home/index.html
- **The Telegraph:** (United Kingdom) https://www.telegraph.co.uk/
- **The Times (UK):** https://www.thetimes.co.uk/
- **The Times of India (India):** https://timesofindia.indiatimes.com/
- **The Wall Street Journal:** https://www.wsj.com
- **The Wires: A.P.:** https://www.nytimes.com/section/aponline/news
- **The Wires: Reuters:** https://www.nytimes.com/section/reuters
- **Today's Front Pages:** http://www.newseum.org/todaysfrontpages/
- **Topix (Entertainment):** http://www.topix.com
- **UT San Diego:** http://www.sandiegouniontribune.com/
- **Voice of America:** https://www.voanews.com/
- **Voice of San Diego:** http://www.voiceofsandiego.org/
- **Washington Post:** https://www.washingtonpost.com/
- **ZDF Heute (Germany):** http://www.heute.de/.

Country- and region-specific sites are helpful to some information searchers. These are among the news sites you may find essential in your research.

- **Al Bawaba:** https://www.albawaba.com/
- **Al Jazeera:** http://www.aljazeera.com/
- **All Africa:** http://allafrica.com/
- **Arab News:** http://www.arabnews.com/
- **Asia News Network**: http://www.asianews.network/
- **Asia Times:** http://www.atimes.com/
- **BBC:** http://www.bbc.com/
- **Beijing Review:** http://www.bjreview.com.cn/
- **China View:**
  http://www.xinhuanet.com/english/world.htm
- **Bangkok Post:**
  https://www.bangkokpost.com/?mode=homepage
- **Channel News Asia:** http://www.channelnewsasia.com/
- **Daily Star Bangladesh:** http://www.thedailystar.net/
- **Daily Times Pakistan:** http://www.dailytimes.com.pk
- **Deutsch Welle:** http://www.dw.com/
- **EFE News:** https://www.efe.com/efe/english/4
- **El Khabar (Algeria):** http://www.elkhabar.com/
- **Expatica (Belgium, France, Germany, Netherlands, Spain):** http://www.expatica.com/
- **France 24 AFP:** http://www.france24.com/
- **Interfax (Russian language):** http://www.interfax.ru
- **IRNA:** http://www.irna.ir/en/
- **Japan Times:** https://www.japantimes.co.jp
- **Japan Today:** https://japantoday.com/
- **KCNA (North Korea):**
  https://www.northkoreatech.org/the-north-korean-website-list/korean-central-news-agency/
- **Korea Times:**
  http://www.koreatimes.co.kr/www2/index.asp
- **Kurdish media:** http://www.kurdmedia.com/
- **Mideast: Khaleej Times:** https://www.khaleejtimes.com/

- **Middle East Online:** http://www.middle-east-online.com/english
- **New Kerala:** http://www.newkerala.com/world-news.php
- **Newscom.au:** http://www.news.com.au/
- **Outlook India**: https://www.outlookindia.com/
- **Pakistan – Dawn:** https://www.dawn.com/
- **Pakistan – Frontier Post:** http://www.thefrontierpost.com/
- **Pravda:** http://www.pravdareport.com/
- **Scotsman:** http://www.scotsman.com/news
- **Sputnik News (Russia):** https://sputniknews.com/
- **Xinhua:** http://www.xinhuanet.com/english/.

Avoid publications that have adopted, or are adopting a new trend in journalism. Some media have moved from fact-based reporting to opinion-based journalism. Long pieces, heavy with hard fact, are giving way to "chunked" news on some sites. Current reports are often short items containing limited facts. The feeling in some journalistic circles is that people will not stay with "long" pieces. Info-tainment is now developing as the alternative to traditional journalism. Should that trend continue, it may have a significant impact on media's role in OSR.

Media Information and Resources
Mainstream news media often process, massage, and provide a tremendous amount of information. But reporters almost always have more information available than is presented by their medium. Time and space limit media reports; no reporter ever has unlimited amounts of either. Something or some things must be left out of stories because of time and space restrictions. That means media cannot really carry "the full story."

More-complete pictures can often be obtained by looking at the variety of media which may have covered the same event, person, or situation. Information contained in competing media reports can

301

be compared for agreement, disagreement, and completeness. That often provides a more accurate picture of any situation.

Understanding a news provider, and how that provider operates, is as important as the content that the medium provides. The content of periodicals, radio, television and digital resources generally is developed and produced by, or through, one of six channels:

- Local reporters
- Correspondents and news bureaus
- Handouts and press releases
- Wire services
- Specialist reporters
- Letters to the editor and other reader-generated materials.

Local reporters cover events and people in their geographical area. They provide local news reports for a newspaper, television, or other media outlet.

Whenever a researcher or research desk wants to acquire information about events happening in a local area it is best to go directly to a periodical or other media resource in the locale. Detailed information on a factory opening and its staff is more likely to be found in a local paper or television station's report than in a network newscast or the *International Times*.

When performing media information searches, always think locally.

If there is more than one medium in the area, researchers search out the same subject as seen through the lenses of multiple media. There is often a difference in the selection of facts, the way the facts are presented, and in some cases there may appear to be a difference in the actual "facts" themselves when the reports of different media are compared and contrasted.

Correspondents and news bureaus cover areas and subjects outside of the area where the news medium is printed, broadcast, or distributed. Large publications and major electronic media have correspondents or bureaus in their national or regional capital. Few – and the number is constantly getting fewer – newspapers and magazines have correspondents or bureaus outside their own country. Major television networks seem to be better equipped in this regard, making the collection of network multi-media reports – and transcriptions of that material – an area of serious consideration for researchers who specialize in international studies.

Correspondents and news bureaus of different media often select or emphasize different sets of facts within a story. They sometimes opt to cover different stories during their workday. Correspondents and news bureaus often provide alternative views of the stories covered by wire services, sometimes writing about different aspects of the same events or situation.

In the United States large newspapers that use many correspondents and news bureaus include:

- **New York Times:** http://www.nytimes.com/
- **Washington Post:** http://www.washingtonpost.com/
- **Los Angeles Times:** http://www.latimes.com.

The major television networks often make more extensive use of international correspondents in their coverage than other media.

Wire services provide the bulk of the non-local news text for most publications. A wire service story will usually appear much the same in Bahrain as it does in Boston. There may be editing or shortening of the piece that changes the length. Wire service news stories are usually written so that they can be chopped to fit the available space by removing paragraphs, often starting from the bottom. But the paragraphs of the same wire service story appearing in different publications should be essentially the same.

As with all reporting, the selection of facts in the stories depends on both the writers and editors. While stories from the same wire service will be much the same no matter where they are printed, stories from different wire services about the same people, event, or subject will often differ in the selection of facts, the weight given to various issues, and the overall importance of the story to local readers. By tapping into aggregation sites that use different wire services and sources you can sometimes eliminate the need to search a variety of newspapers to obtain comparison information.

Keep in mind, particularly with wire service stories, how the two source rule applies: Something is not deemed accurate unless there are at least two independent sources.

Wire services make that tricky. Two, or even ten, publications may report something as fact but stories actually comes from a single source – they were all written by the same reporter and distributed by the same wire service. All facts contained in wire service stories from the same service are considered single-sourced, no matter how many publications carry the story.

Major international wire services include Reuters, the Associated Press, United Press International, Agence France Presse, and DPA. Regional wire services such as Bernama (Malaysia), IANS (India), AAP (Australia), and Antara (Indonesia) offer comprehensive local, regional, and even world-wide coverage. Moreover they provide different perspectives on the news. Networks play a similar role among the electronic media.

With wire services it is important to keep in mind that there are:
- News cycles
- Different "wires" within the services.

In simplest terms, a news cycle means that generally a story will be put on the wire and sent to subscribing media for either a daily cycle, morning cycle, or an evening cycle. Thus the same stories, or updates of those stories, may sometimes appear on some wires two or more times a day. Some media subscribe to more than one cycle, but not all do so. With many news sites the rule is "the law of ephemera – collect it now or never."

Wire services usually have more than one "wire." For instance there may be an A Wire for the most crucial news, a B Wire for less important information. There may be regional wires, a sports wire, a financial wire, feature wire etc. Generally the readers, listeners, and viewers have no idea if the news service has different wires, or which wires any publication or medium subscribes to. Just because you see a particular wire service is used by a medium that does not mean that the editors of that publication or station see, much less use, all of that wire service's output. Searching different publications that use the same wire service give a collector a better chance of seeing more of any wire service's output.

To some extent the news cycles on many media – particularly those that self-generate news such as online media, large newspapers and networks – have been replaced by the rolling deadline. In the rolling deadline a story is posted as soon as it can be written or produced. It may be updated as new facts emerge or it may never be changed. Some version of a story – often not the original one – remains active for as long as there is any apparent reader, listener, or viewer interest. In the heyday of newspapers an article might have been published in all editions over a single day. Now stories may remain viable and visible for days or even weeks somewhere on the website of a news medium. Stories can now remain on a site as long as readers show an interest.

Handouts and press releases reflect the views of the organization or agency that wrote or issued them. Responsible media may use many handouts, but they generally rewrite the text of the "news releases." When they do so they often rewrite without much – if any – fact checking. For that reason it may be difficult to determine how accurate the "facts" presented in the rewritten material are.

Moreover readers never know that a news story originated from a press release.

Specialist reporters have a news or media "beat" that covers specific subject areas. The reporter may become a specialist in oil, military affairs, politics, yachting, crime, or any of 10,000 subjects. Specialists work for individual newspapers, wire services, or niche publications that serve defined audiences. Reporters for newsletters or other specialty publications usually function as specialists. Unlike "general assignment reporters" at large publications, specialist reporters may become subject-matter experts within their fields.

Reader-generated materials and letters to the editor are assuming a more important role than in the past. They sometimes show public attitudes – at least the attitudes of the subscribers and the publisher – almost as well as polls. This resource may be valuable in gauging the views and interests of the public in an area. When doing propaganda analysis or public attitude analysis as outlined in Paul Linebarger's book, *Psychological Warfare*, these – along with media roundups – are key sources.

Article and Story Types
As important as the information source is, it is almost as crucial to categorize the type of report. There are several types of articles or stories:
- News, aka hard news
- Features, aka soft news
- Editorials and essays
  - Columns
  - Editorials
  - Reader submissions.

It is important to understand what is supposed to be found in each.

Hard News stories emphasize facts. Their stated purpose is to inform. These stories often follow what is known as the Inverted Pyramid structure, with the most important facts appearing at the top of story. Less important facts are revealed as the reader goes down in the story. This helps the editors "cut from the bottom" to shorten an article because, at least in theory, the least important points are being cut out and the more important parts remain at the top of the story.

Investigative reports are a form of hard news story but may not be written in the Inverted Pyramid style.

Hard news stories are crafted by trained journalists, but often the writers are not experts in the subject matter.

Features exhibit a more personal writing style. They are written by trained reporters who may, or may not, be subject matter experts but they often have done extensive research. Some journalists have developed a reputation in this field. Reporters writing in this *genre* may pair facts with interpretations to both inform and explain.

Features are often termed "soft news" stories.

Columns are often written in personal styles and are done by staff members or syndicated authors. Their purpose may be to advise, entertain, analyze, interpret, and/or comment.

Editorials are written in an essay format by a medium's staff with the implied blessing of management. They present the opinions of the medium's editorial board in order to persuade, comment, or provoke thought. Some publications attempt to balance their own opinions with opposing views, often placed on a facing page, called the op-ed page.

Reader submissions and letters from readers are just that. They are letters, comments, or essays submitted by members of the public and selected by the editors. They usually express opinions or provide commentary. Sometimes these unofficial points-of-view provide an insight into what people really think.

Non-articles

Non-article items have an important role. They impact the effect of the stories or the publication.

Images include photographs, visuals, charts, and/or illustrations produced by camera operators, photographers, artists, or journalists. They may stand alone or supplement an article.

Their stated purpose is to inform or explain, but they can also be used to generate a subtle or overt emotional response. An all-too-common example of this is choosing a picture of a happy-looking official to illustrate a positive article – even if the picture was taken at a different time – or illustrating a negative piece with a scowling photo. Flattering or unflattering expressions are commonly used to convey subtle bias. Pictures may be worthless – they are certainly not worth a thousand words – in the days of Photoshopping.

Comics and Editorial Cartoons are informal drawings or artwork produced by staff or syndicated artists. They are used either for entertainment value, or as commentary.

Advertisements are usually brief and descriptive text, often with artwork, and are displayed informally. They are produced by the medium's professional staff or by the advertisers themselves with the intention to persuade, promote, or inform readers, listeners, and viewers about goods, services, or ideas. Ads often provide much of the financial wherewithal of media outlets.

Headlines are brief descriptive text intended to attract readers to an article, provide basic knowledge, and serve as an overview of the story.

Headlines help the viewer or reader select the articles that interest them and get to the most important facts quickly. They are also designed to move people into the text of a story. They are important in news articles but are increasingly impactful in video news feeds and in messaging applications. Headlines are usually created by an editor, not the story's writer. They may also function as "teasers."

Picture cutlines are brief explanations of photos and illustrations. A picture may be worth a thousand words but in most cases the pictures still require at least a few words of explanation. Cutlines are the work of an editor.

Placement of a story is important. Prominence is given to what the editors or producers designate as the most important articles. The story placement may vary with regional/topical specialization of the medium and can be a deliberate attempt to either highlight or "bury" news. Placement is determined by editors.

In general, newspapers give top stories placement on the front page or the first pages of each section. Placement "above the fold" is considered better than on the bottom half of any page. In radio and television the most important stories are usually "played" first, but they may be held as "teasers" and reported out toward the end of a newscast. Whether a story makes the news may be as significant as the story itself.

The leading paragraph of a story – called the lede – is designed to entice you to read the rest of article. Selection of facts in the lede, and all material in any story, is based on what the reporter or editor believes is important, not what is important for your purposes. The details or essential elements of information that you are looking for may be found anywhere in the article or story – even buried in the last sentence. The subject matter of the article may not be important for your purposes yet the story may contain valuable information. In fact, some peripheral information used as background may be more useful or even better researched and vetted than the article's specific subject matter. Information that appears tangential to a journalist could be the most useful to you. Read or view any story completely. Some potentially valuable information for your purposes is probably not in the headline, opening, or first paragraph, irrespective of the fact that newspapers and journalists assert that is where the most important information is.

A story's "angle" on the topic may itself be the important information. News wire services sell basic news to many news providers, often of different editorial outlooks, so they generally try to play stories "down the middle." Public affairs representatives, on the other hand, provide information from governments, NGOs, and private companies. They have a "viewpoint" they want to get across.

Competing reporters may witness the same event but choose different "angles" and select different fact sets to appeal to their medium's target audience and the medium's management. It is almost a certainty that any supplemental information in a story will differ in stories on the same subject, or about the same event, when it is reported by different media.

What isn't reported may be more important than what is said. The bottom line is to seek multiple reports in order to verify and confirm or deny factual information. Reliance on single-source reporting is dangerous. Even when reported out by conscientious journalists many stories will be considered incomplete or inaccurate to the thinking of some readers.

Article Accuracy

Article accuracy changes over time and often for reasons that have little or nothing to do with bias. Initial reports are often incomplete or incorrect, particularly as media race each other to "break" a story. Competitive media may feed off one another, even when their information is incorrect. However, rivals are often quick to challenge or point out any inaccuracies in a competitor's version. Accuracy generally improves over hours, days, and weeks when the facts sort themselves out. But accuracy of remembered events can diminish over months or years as memories fade.

Ideals that many take for granted are culturally and individually subjective. Truth, decency, professionalism, privacy, and objectivity may not be viewed the same in different locations or by all media. Truth and accuracy are commodities, as are lies and alternative facts. Both are salable, the price depending on the needs and desires of the buyer.

Some media are dumpster fires of misinformation. Others may be less crass, but may still be economical with the truth. The researcher must know and avoid them.

People often report what they believe or want to believe, not necessarily what is provably true. News consumers often patronize sources that align with their own beliefs. As a result "hard news" may not be equally accurate in different media and cultures. Interpretation and argumentation may be standard practice with some media.

Not all journalists are created equal. Less-developed regions may have fewer highly-qualified journalists; journalists in some areas may be less educated or not as proficient in the official language. Mores – customs, practices, conventions – often determine what journalists may see and report.

There are often unseen and unknowable right and left limits of reporting. Sexual issues may be off limits in some cultures; pictures of dead bodies may be effectively banned in other areas. The social rules of the society impact all reporting.

Mass media reports are information; how much reliance should be placed on any report from a particular source is always a question.

While information from the reports of trained professionals in the independent media is usually more reliable than from the man on the street, information derived even from seemingly unbiased media may still be wrong or skewed. Decisions made on the basis of wrong or skewed information have a high probability of eventually proving to be bad decisions.

Media accuracy may be affected by factors such as time constraints, media ownership demands, available funding, culture, and social mores, as well as the availability and choice of information sources. Information accuracy is also affected by things such as omission, commission, story selection, placement, source selection, spin, and labeling.

It is important to determine the confidence level of all information, Media are often the biggest influencers for any population. The influence may be subtle or overt.

Media usually cater to their audience. One audience may want to know what is happening in the world, whether or not it meets their own personal desires. Other audiences want to see only news that excites them, that fits snuggly into their world view. A medium's audience is often a determining factor of information accuracy. When the medium's audience shows that they only want to hear a certain viewpoint, irrespective of factuality, that medium's "news" becomes entertainment and a "feel good" experience.

The source of any piece of information can color the point of view. A story about new medical equipment will be seen differently by a doctor, a patient whose life depends upon the treatment, and people who never had a sick day in their life. Culture and geography have an effect. Stories about blizzard survival or avalanches probably have more limited appeal in Arizona than in Alaska. Media focus may also be affected by race, religion, and partisanship. An information medium's ownership, or source of income, may also affect the focus, *The New York Times* and the *New York Daily*

News both serve New York readers, but they differ as much in their coverage as they do their readership. A medium which ignores the interests of the people it serves has a short shelf life. Readers and advertisers often effectively but clandestinely control what will be covered, will be written about extensively, or will be left uncovered.

A medium's survival usually depends on profits and profits depend on sales – whether selling the concept of flicking on the TV for the 10 o'clock news or reading the morning sports page. Somebody has to be willing to foot the bill. Money and influence are always present, even when unseen, in media reports.

Media Control

All media are controlled in some way. Who or what exercises that control, and how heavy-handed or light-to-the-touch those control levers are, is important for the researcher or research desk to know. There are three major types of control:

- State controlled, organization-dependent
- Semi-controlled
- "Independent" media.

The category that a medium falls into will likely affect the level of reliability and the amount of trust any researcher or research desk places in the information received from that media source.

Controlled Media

These media, controlled by political, religious, or organizational leaders, can be of any type – print, digital, electronic or mixed. While censorship mechanisms exercise control before data dissemination and thus produce only what that leadership wants, these media are useful resources in some cases. Their only interests lie in doing the will of, and supporting, some governmental or non-governmental organization or operation. Despotic regimes will always control media in this fashion. North Korean and Russian media fall into this category. Researchers do not look for unbiased information at such sites; they are looking for what the sponsoring groups are saying or what their followers are being told to do, think, or believe. In some cases these may be the most important media to follow. They are certainly among the most baffling to interpret.

The more centrally controlled a nation, organization, or region is, the more important it becomes to understand the messages found on these controlled sites. Decipher the meanings of information products produced by controlled media by employing Propaganda Analysis (PROPANAL) methods found in Paul Linebarger's seminal book, *Psychological Warfare,* and other propaganda interpretation manuals.

Controlled Media analysis makes several key assumptions. Among these are the belief that the number of important information sources is manageable and that it is possible to obtain effective knowledge of each source. Other assumptions are that monitoring is a useful methodology, and that the formula for public communications is "one to many." Controlled media will never accept, much less encourage, backtalk, or alternative views.

In analyzing controlled media there is usually a hierarchy of "authority." That hierarchy does not imply believability, but rather it suggests what can be called "a reliability of intention."
- Top leader
- Known pseudonym of top leader
- Known advisor to top leader
- Top leader says he always reads this column or watches this show
- Person associated with a major party
- Regular contributor to major medium
- Person associated with minor or fringe party
- Contributor with track record of poor analysis.

Heads of state are an authoritative source simply because they are the head of state. Similarly, editorials or publications within a controlled-media country fall along a spectrum of more or less authoritative. Learn the media environment of your research area but remember that the placement in any spectrum may be inexact.

Commentator ranking also occurs along a spectrum. By definition, commentators in a controlled media environment are considered to be authoritative sources simply by virtue of their position.

The truth of what someone says may be less important than the impact of what is said, who is saying it, or what the target audience is (refer back to Lasswell's formula for evaluating communications in Chapter 2).

Semi-controlled Media

These, too, can be any type of media. Less authoritarian and even democratic regimes may use this type of control. While controlling entities may not actively censor the news before publication, they often use a variety of means – including control of the newsprint supply or the airwaves – to pressure media managers into some type of self-censorship.

Independent Media

Despite the term, these media – whether they are fiber-based, digital, electronic, or mixed – are still subject to the will of someone or something. But they usually give their staff greater latitude in selecting the stories covered and in the way reporters craft their stories. These media have the ability to be more "balanced" in their selection of facts and stories. Diffuse control comes through such channels as ownership, political persuasion, and public or economic pressure regarding content. The particular public that any medium, especially a commercial medium, serves will materially affect the reporting. A commercial medium's success is often gauged by the number and position of consumers, whether readers, listeners, or viewers. "Independent" media are highly subject to the pressures from corporate ownership, interest groups, and advertisers – and they face competition from the Internet.

Coverage Issues

Many news sources can be exploited by wily researchers. The news media are among of the larger venues for conducting open source research. Their information may be correct, or it can be misleading. Research professionals need to understand some basic facts about how news is gathered, produced, and disseminated in order to properly interpret news sources.

Among media people there is a saying that "all news is local." The most valuable news is often the information that is closest to home, the news that directly affects readers, viewers, and listeners. Because of this fact, researchers will usually get their best results from those news sources that serve specific publics and groups, whether they are geographically- or subject-based.

There are many types of media – radio, television, digital, mixed, and print. Print media can serve as the archetype of media in most discussions. Understanding how newspapers work allows you to extend that knowledge to television, radio, and other media.

The actual objectives of information providers vary. Analysts need to be somewhat cynical and assume that:

- Governments want to provide as few embarrassing facts as they can get away with, and as much information that will please people as possible.
- Politicians and NGOs want people to support them.
- Advertisers want people to buy their product (whether anyone reads their ad is irrelevant).
- Producers and editors want you to watch their program or buy their paper (whether you believe them or read them or not) and want advertisers to know who watches, listens, or reads.

- Writers and reporters want you to watch or read their specific articles and then want you to look for more of them (whether or not you are actually informed).

All of them want to give you only the amounts and types of information they need to achieve their own objectives, and often no more. Purposeful communication is structured communication.

Every information source may have some type of bias, slant, or agenda. It is the open source analyst's responsibility to understand where any source stands on a spectrum.

Media Report Vetting

The quality of reporting and vetting of sources varies significantly across the media spectrum. Qualifications of news producers may vary widely. Different cultures often have different journalistic standards and traditions so it becomes important to understand the culture to which any medium belongs.

Among the vital questions are: Whose news medium is it? Financial interests and the personal agenda of the owner, producer, editor, and individual reporter enter the picture. With so many players the situation quickly becomes convoluted. When evaluating media it is important to know who might benefit and who might be harmed by a report or the manner in which the report is presented. It is essential to know the qualifications of the writers or editors. Do the people have or need any special topical or regional expertise?

Analysts try to understand the motivation of the medium's owners and that of all the people involved in reporting out a particular story, as well as the implications that those motivations might have.

What are other sources saying about this same topic? That question overtly helps the analyst make a judgement about reliability. The two-source rule keeps many journalists out of trouble.

A more subtle issue is the cultural factors that affect the writing and reporting. Cultural assumptions, taboos, and tradition may impact the way information is presented or perceived.

A difficult question for the analyst is what information is assumed, or is deliberately left out – and what other sources might have more information. There is always the question of what information can be gleaned from any source.

Providers of news vary.

Governments and agencies often produce hand-outs by professional public affairs officers or even by propaganda agencies. Accuracy varies, largely depending upon the transparency of the government or organization. Propaganda pieces may be designed to mislead or misinform, or they may simply be aimed at persuading.

NGO publicity offices generally have a high degree of expertise. A persuasion agenda, overt or subtle, is often present.

Internet news blogs tend to be independent, but many also prove to be highly opinionated or biased. Their subject matter expertise and reliability standards vary greatly. In general, non-professionals in any field are not high-scorers.

Some news providers are motivated by reasons other than profit. When you are browsing any open source for information, remember who the media sources are. You know government sources will play the Information Operations role and possibly use propaganda to help their cause. This is a consideration you might want to take into account when looking at your information. When you see material from an NGO it may be based on an agenda or have some ulterior motive. The bottom line is to keep a clear picture in your mind about what you are looking at and who the information actually comes from.

News wire services and news networks are sometimes the most factual. They need to sell their information to multiple customers who have differing outlooks. But because their product goes to a variety of outlets, many of which have little or no interest in the particular subject, wire service coverage may be less extensive and provide fewer details. In any event, news service and network reports are still only as good as the sources that the reporters use.

News media outlets may be either commercial, not-for-profit, or government-run. They may have an agenda or multiple agendas, depending on the variety of views held and promoted by the individual journalist, editor, management, or advertisers. One or more of those people may deliberately exclude or exaggerate information or carefully incorporate opinion as fact. Subject matter expertise may vary greatly.

Always think about the audience the author is trying to reach. It is important to understand who or what the intended audience is and what the information provider is trying to tell them. Sometimes knowing about the audience is more important than analyzing the material itself. Audience targeting may fluff up the stories or headlines. Lasswell's outline becomes a major consideration in any evaluation of media. Consider, always: Who is the intended audience?

All news providers target specific audiences. The audience or the readership determines:
- Topics addressed
- Depth of coverage
- Style of writing
- Documentation of sources
- Level of writing
- Ideology.

Commercial bias is not unusual. The drive to draw readers, listeners or viewers to the medium's advertisers can lead to sensationalism or self-censorship of unpopular subjects.

Expediency bias crops up when competition between outlets and individual reporters favors the publication or airing of information that can be obtained quickly and easily. The immediate need for copy, sound, or visuals may suppress information-vetting or careful story selection by a news medium.

Personal bias creeps in, or sometimes rushes in, when individual reporters see events or facts through the lenses of their own beliefs. Personal bias can unintentionally, sometimes intentionally, skew the selection of facts.

There are eight types of media bias.
- Omission
- Commission
- Story selection
- Placement
- Word choice
- Spin
- Selection of sources
- Labeling.

Omission must be considered the most frequent issue faced by media. Even in a small village, hundreds of different interactions take place each day. Most are not considered newsworthy. And even things that are part of a newsworthy event may not be covered. When a reporter on a major newspaper writes about a city council meeting not every item on the agenda will receive coverage. A story that is 10-column inches in length, or takes up 90 seconds of air time, may be considered quite adequate to cover a meeting that lasted four or five hours. Decisions are made, in all media coverage, about what things must be left out because they are uninteresting or are deemed relatively inconsequential.

Commission involves everything from word choices to subject choices, and every choice may affect the way something is seen by the news user. The choices of fact or assumptions of the journalist – including unintentional errors – may skew the viewpoint.

Story selection and Placement is a matter of both judgement and placement. Whether a story will be used at all, how much of the meeting or event will be covered, and where it will be included in the lineup if it is used, affect the way a story is perceived. In newspapers a story that falls "below the fold" – meaning on the bottom half of the newspaper page – suggests the story is considered less important than one "above the fold." A story in the first section of a newspaper on page A2 is generally judged as more important, or more interesting to readers, than one on page A19. Since there is a drop-off in readership as the reader moves deeper into a paper, placement of a story subtly but effectively suggests its importance level. The lead story in a broadcast, likewise, might be considered to have more gravitas than one positioned two minutes before sign-off. The first quarter hour of each half-hour segment, including newscasts, is the broadcast equivalent to "above the fold." That is when stations are rated; "Getting them over the 15" is the measure of success. Lead stories often go first in television news. Top stories will be concentrated in that segment to keep viewers tuned in, and ratings up. Enterprise stories, special projects, or "think pieces" usually are aired just prior to the 15 minute break, so that is also a critical time. The general rule is that if the viewer stays engaged for the first fifteen minutes they will remain there for the last quarter hour.

Perception of importance affects whether an issue is even brought up, and if it is, where it will be "played."

Spin may be obvious or subtle. How something is presented affects the impression. Spin presents facts in a way that differs significantly from the way most people would see them had the information been presented honestly. The difference of only a word or two can lead readers, listeners, or viewers to far different understandings about events. Unless an analyst can compare two or more sources there are few ways to determine if spin is a problem that must be accounted for in a given situation.

Word choice is often associated with spin. It may be intentional – commission – or unintentional. "Said," "intoned," and "screamed" all have different impacts on the news recipient. All may be correct in their usage at the time. But they do have an impact. Word choices are worth analyzing. Words may be manipulated – for good or for bad – to suggest a feeling, response, or opinion that is not obvious to the reader, listener, or viewer. In many cases of spin, the key words of a sentence are manipulated to inject subtle editorial commentary.

Occasionally word choices are mandated by a stylebook. In some media reports everybody is assured of even-handed treatment by a requirement that all second references will be handled in the same way. Thus serial killer "Mr." Jones gets the same treatment as "Mr." Smith who saved three people by rushing into a burning building.

Selection of sources affects stories. There are knowledgeable ones; not all sources are good ones, however. The difference between a good source and a questionable one may affect a reader or viewer's opinion. Many media insist on "balance" and when a "pro" view is expressed a "con" may be required in a story. Selection of sources sometimes focuses on believability. However, the description by an astronaut of the moon disappearing behind the curve of the earth should not require a rebuttal argument from the head of the local flat-earth society.

Sometimes labels are applied by tagging a subject or participant in a story with membership in a group or organization. Favorable or unfavorable labels can then be expanded to other group members through that label. Not all labeling is biased or wrong, but labeling is often a subtle form of bias that can be easily overlooked by the casual reader. Labels tend to emphasize one part of a person over the other aspects of that person.

Bias can be an occasional problem in individual reports or it can be endemic and pervasive within some particular media. Fringe publications and resources abound.

Many media have reputations for truth-telling while others are known to be economical with the truth. Some online sites now give an approximate idea of media bias that prevails among some specific publications and media resources. Such sites include:
- **Media Bias Chart:** https://www.adfontesmedia.com/
- **Zimdars List:** https://docs.google.com/document/u/1/d/10eA5-mCZLSS4MQY5QGb5ewC3VAL6pLkT53V_81ZyitM/mobilebasic.

Fact Checking Media Reports

In the United States and other Western countries there are fact checkers, watchdogs, and tools that can be used to review important stories appearing in the media. In most cases they will not be useful to researchers but occasionally they may cover stories that are important to you or your client. Believability sites, or digital forensics sites as they are sometimes known, are information watchdogs. They include:
- **Adfontes Media:** https://www.adfontesmedia.com/
- **AFP Fact Check:** https://factcheck.afp.com/
- **AP Fact Check:** https://www.apnews.com/
- **CrossCheck:** https://firstdraftnews.org/project/crosscheck/
- **Digital Sherlocks (Atlantic Council):** https://www.digitalsherlocks.org/about

323

- **EUDISINFORMATIONREVIEW:**
  https://euvsdisinfo.eu/
- **FactCheck:** https://www.factcheck.org/fake-news
- **Fairness and Accuracy in Reporting:** http://www.fair.org
- **Fight the Fake:** https://www.france24.com/en/fight-the-fake
- **Full Fact (UK):** https://fullfact.org/
- **Global Fact-checking Sites:** https://reporterslab.org/fact-checking/
- **Hoax-Slayer: (Social media, email):** https://www.hoax-slayer.com/
- **Hoaxy:** https://hoaxy.iuni.iu.edu/
- **Lead Stories:** https://hoax-alert.leadstories.com/
- **Media Bias/Factcheck:** https://mediabiasfactcheck.com/
- **New York Times Fact-checking:**
  https://www.nytimes.com/spotlight/fact-checks
- **Politifact:** https://www.politifact.com/truth-o-meter/
- **Polygraph:** https://www.polygraph.info/
- **ReviewMeta (Product reviews):** https://reviewmeta.com/
- **Snopes:** https://www.snopes.com/
- **TruthorFiction:** http://www.truthorfiction.com
- **Verification Junkie (Analysis tools):**
  http://verificationjunkie.com/
- **Washington Post Fact Checker:**
  https://www.washingtonpost.com/news/fact-checker/

***

Project:
Open the SOP to the news section. Determine whether or how you plan to use news media in your work, and which types of media are most likely to be use to you.

Project:
In the SOP's news section list the top media sources you will use. If you plan to use none, provide your reasoning.

Project:
In the analysis section of the SOP determine all criteria you plan to use when evaluating media reports.

13. Citizen Journalism – The Newest Medium

"Citizen Journalism" – also called "participatory journalism," "grassroots media," or "people's media" – is a recent phenomenon. It is a field created and driven by advances in technology. Citizen journalism allows anyone anywhere in the world to reach out to everyone else in the world with their message, all at little expense.

Much of it is arguably not journalism at all, but is more accurately characterized as "my two cents" and "spread the word." On the other hand, there are people and groups – like the Bellingcat collective – who exhibit levels of talent and expertise that equal or exceed the abilities of both those in the traditional media and even national intelligence agencies.

Professional journalists go through years of training with a rigid curriculum. Through their contacts they have access to a wide variety of people, resources, and facts.

Citizen journalists, by definition, have no such access nor have they undergone the extensive training and preparation.

Good intentions cannot substitute for the wide variety of sources or rigorous training. No one wants a barber or hairdresser to display a pair of scissors as their only credentials before they begin to cut your hair. Investment counselors should have some *bona fides* besides knowing how to read a stock ticker. You want the pilot on your flight to have thousands of hours in the left seat of a plane, not time on the control stick of a computer flying game.

Citizen journalism is too often a contradiction in terms. But as imperfect as it may be, it is here to stay.

Citizen journalists often lack professional training. Their amateur musings are not constrained by traditional journalism's rules, but their efforts are sometimes cited by traditional journalists because of their ubiquity and, in some cases, their utility.

Even traditional journalism has succumbed to the "citizen journalism" presentation style with dozens of people who weren't on the scene "commenting" about, or adding an opinion to, news stories that were reported out by the professionals who actually were there.

Citizen journalism is as much, or more, part of New Media as it is part of journalism. Citizen journalists can create flashmobs, groups of people who show up at a site when called together by someone on a social media site. Citizen journalists are responsible for the "Arab Spring" and the "Occupy Movement."

Citizen journalists may also provide first reports. In disasters they may be "on the scene" and reporting long before their professional cousins ever get on the road. Citizen journalists may be eyes and ears where and when trained journalists are not present.

Citizen journalists can be, and are, everywhere so they often capture local activities and then they distribute their information widely, even internationally. Only after citizen journalists have pronounced the "first word" about some calamitous event do trained reporters arrive at the scene. It is no longer unusual to see that some major news stories, such as terror attacks or disasters, are covered initially by citizen journalists through tweets and social media.

Because citizen journalists often deal with areas that traditional ones do not, they can be a useful information resource – yet like most things in OSR the utility of any particular resource depends on the researcher's needs.

Citizen journalists operate primarily on the Internet in blogs and on Twitter-type sites; but personal broadcasts, mailing lists, newsletters and other media may be used to "get the word out."

Objectivity is always a question about any resource, but particularly so in citizen journalism. These "reporters" see things through their own eyes and speak with their own mouth. The quality of the writing and other communications skills vary. Poor communication skills of some citizen journalists lead to false impressions or misunderstandings. But reliable citizen journalists, those working on sites such as Bellingcat.com, can do much good.

Communities of reliable citizen journalists can be useful when their work aligns with your information needs. Like all OSR resources, the products of citizen journalists must be carefully examined and their work vetted.

***

Project:
In the SOP write a paragraph explaining how, or whether, you plan to use citizen journalists and, if you intend to do so, where you will access their products.

14. Tradecraft of Knowledge

Modern information collectors, no matter who or where they are, rely on tradecraft, both on and off the Internet. Tradecraft helps meet the many challenges facing both individual researchers and information shops. Information voyages require an understanding of tradecraft to navigate the shoals and sandbars of the Internet.

Save, Save, Save...

Backup and save what you are doing – probably on every half hour or hour. Autosave and automatic backup on computers are wonderful and should be used, but never rely on them. Save what you are doing to least two locations – one site on the computer and one off the computer, such as a thumb drive.

Losing hours – even days – of work because of some computer glitch and having no way of retrieving the work will make anyone cry. A "save" to a couple of locations takes seconds, seconds that can save hours or even weeks of work.

Command Line

Knowledge of the "command line" is essential for advanced OSR work. Yes, the average Windows user gets along quite well without knowing how to use the command line. But average users seldom do efficient and effective research.

Ant failure to familiarize yourself with the command line can lead to information impotence.

Command line operations are now an advanced method that may even be required in some research activities such as Webscraping. Before the age of Windows the command line was the only way to use personal computers. The command like is the stick shift of OSR, overtaken by new techniques but still critical in some cases.

Windows usually requires a mouse or touch pad to move around the screen, select sites or programs, and initiate the many operations. The command line is an older way of using a computer, typing in commands at screen prompts. This method is a holdover from the MS-DOS (Microsoft Disk Operating System).

Windows still has a command prompt feature, allowing users who understand the process to simulate the MS-DOS process. Some even refer the Windows command line version as the "DOS prompt" although, on Windows, users are not actually using the DOS system. A similar method in Apple computers is termed "terminal commands."

In Windows the command line prompt can be reached from the Apps Screen, the Main Screen, or the Start Menu depending on the program version. To use the system valid commands, as well as optional parameters, must be typed into the command prompt.

Many useful commands can be initiated from the prompt. The method may be used for running programs, to start scripts or batch files, begin administrative actions, or solve a variety of computer issues. Some OSR programs, apps, and resources only operate from the command line. Users who don't know, or learn how to use, the command line are behind from the start in OSR operations.

As with everything on a computer, the commands must be typed exactly. Misspellings or improper syntax vitiate everything. The computer cannot recognize or correct mistakes of an operator.

Good information about use of the command line can be found on the Internet, and in books.

Hidden Elements and Metadata

There are those who maintain that OSR is all about "documents." If you include "documentation" within that meaning it becomes a persuasive argument. Open Source Research is about searching for information, but more importantly information that documents and proves the information that is collected.

Often the documentation you need is contained – sometimes apparent, often hidden – in the documents that an OSR operator uncovers,

Documents, and the sites they are on, contain hidden – and widely unknown – elements that can often be exploited by knowledgeable researchers. Those hidden elements may relate to accounts, material that was removed, the computer, or server. Or there may be highly-personal information. While such "secret" elements can often be removed, even people who know how to do so seldom follow through. Hidden data may include a wide variety of information such as:

- Metadata
- Various document versions
- Hidden text, objects, slides, rows, columns or worksheets
- Comments
- Tracked changes
- Document reviewers' identities
- Routing information
- Presentation notes
- Server or computer information
- Custom XML Data.

Researchers who know the details of how a program or piece of technology works, and the hidden elements that such programs bring to light, have the ability and knowledge to exploit those secretive elements.

FOCA, found at https://www.elevenpaths.com/es/labstools/foca-2/, stands for Fingerprinting Organizations with Collected Archives. It helps a researcher unlock many types of documents and find the hidden elements that aid in analysis of Web pages, word processing and PDF files. FOCA also makes metadata visible. It can be considered the black light of the OSR field, making thing stand out when they are otherwise seemingly invisible.

Too many online users ignore metadata. Sure, it's widely collected by Internet providers and professionals but it can't be all that important, can it?

Officially, metadata classifies material: It is this, but not this and was produced by this person, not that person. Metadata is often called "information about information." That's the techie version; another version that puts a completely different light on metadata is "information about somebody and their computer activity."

Metadata may be created during collection – such as the date that something was downloaded – or it may be hidden within whatever was collected.

Metadata can be powerful. It narrows and identifies; it is often a peek over the transom, showing how something was produced or by whom. Metadata can simplify analysis and interpretation. While it is not always important, it can be. To squeeze the most information out of any document or site it is crucial to look for and carefully study all the available metadata.

Metadata is often attached to online and digital materials including pictures, word processing files, and web pages. Metadata types will differ, depending on the file type. Metadata on a word processing file may tell who wrote the item and when, the file size, who approved it, and a good deal more background. The background information – metadata – on a picture may tell when and where the picture was taken, what kind of camera was used, or who owns the publication rights. On web pages metatags may provide key words and a description of the material. And the metadata found on any file type often provide dates and times.

Metadata is usually hidden inside a file; it often has to be ferreted out. The metadata search procedure varies from file type to file type, and depends on the particular program you are using on your computer. Researchers can use the Internet to learn the specific procedures to search for common types of metadata files.

While the research community generally accepts that metadata is fair game for discovery and use, some still; argue against that contention. Although governments and their minions say that metadata doesn't matter and collecting it is not intrusive, others say it can be too revealing when the pieces are put together.

A basic view of the metadata of a document or picture may be as simple as right-clicking on the object and then a click on the "properties." While some basic metadata is often available this way there are tools that may provide additional information, including the identity of the creator and other facts that can be effectively used by researchers.

Common metadata information includes formats, dates, processes or equipment used, and update information.

Webpages often contain many pieces of metadata. The metadata in web pages, including meta tags such as <description> and <keywords>, are worth examining. In fact, a truly-complete search requires a researcher or research desk to examine the source code of some web pages to see if there are useful tidbits of knowledge there that are hidden when looking at the page as it shows on the screen.

For webpages, the so-called Robots.txt file serves as a major meta-tag. This meta-tag on a site tells the search engine spider what not to look at, index, follow, or archive about the page. "Go on, there's nothing to see here," is another way of thinking about that tag. Researchers can't know whether there really is nothing of value on the page until they look. But there is always a question why the system operator doesn't want other people to look at the page and its contents.

No law mandates that a search engine's spider must follow the orders of the Robot.txt file. Many spiders do; some do not. However, that doesn't mean the information in the forbidden pages is unavailable to knowledgeable searchers. There are ways around a Robots.txt file, but you have to know the prohibition exists before you can start looking for what system operators forbid you to see. The way to find and defeat a robots.txt file is covered in Chapter 10.

There are other hidden things on a web page and some tags are meant to direct, or keep out, search engines.

Tags of all kinds are usually invisible to the Web user but they help guide search engines – and researchers – to the subjects they seek. They also assist in identifying a page's content. Located at the start of an html document – in the <head> section – meta tags describe what the website operator says are the important parts of the page contents. Expert researchers use meta tags to hone their searches, homing in on needed material.

For the researcher, a handful of Web tags provide the most value. To view the meta tags, right click on the page and, from a drop-down menu select "view page source." The meta tags will often be found on the first parts of the page; they will be denoted by the opener, <tag name> and the closer, </tag name>.

Search engines often use the **Title Tag** to fill in the search result that users get. It is what the site owner titled the page – in theory what the page is about. Page owners writing about rust who wanted to make information about that subject less accessible the page developer could use a Title Tag such as "kitchen knives" and that might throw off the search. When the Title Tag is unclear, if the words of the page title do not accurately describe the contents, or if the tags lack context, search engines have no way of knowing.

The **Description Tag** is often used by search engines to fill in the descriptive part of the search result – in a few words it expands the title and may serve as the snippet beneath the title when the search result is displayed.

The **Robots Tag** serves the same role as a Robots.txt message – saying to the search engine "you're not allowed to go there." While a robots.txt notice puts an entire site or sections of the site off limits, the Robots meta tag forbids the indexing of a particular page or following any links on that page. The **No Follow Tag** is used to dissuade search engines from following links on the page – links that may be internal or situated elsewhere on the Web. Since following links is a very important part of the OSR process it is important to know when there is a link on the page that the system operator wants to keep secret.

Alt text is a meta tag used in image optimization. Images have become increasingly important over the years but a search engine text file has no way to display those audio-visuals. This meta tag shows that there are images on the page and describes them. It is a textual supplement to a picture or other video content.

Metadata is a complex subject, one that too few professional researchers pay sufficient attention to. While it seems to many to be a niche area, the study of this subject separates true professionals from amateurs.

An **Understanding Metadata Primer** pdf can be found at https://groups.niso.org/apps/group_public/download.php/17446/Un derstanding%20Metadata. **A Complete Guide to Meta Tags** is available at https://searchenginewatch.com/2016/10/05/complete-guide-to-meta-tags-in-seo/.

Tools that will read a variety of metadata types include:
- **ExifTool:** https://www.sno.phy.queensu.ca/~phil/exiftool/
- **GetMetadata:** https://www.get-metadata.com/.

Another type of hidden data is subdomains. These are parts of the domain, sectioned off from the main domain name. The subdomain generally has its name listed before the actual domain name and is separated by a period as in subdomain.domain.com.

Subdomains are one of the ways site managers organize their pages.

They are often used to create testing versions of a website, private pages, online e-commerce stores, and sites for mobile use (the latter may be designated by an "m." before the domain name).

Discovery of subdomains can be difficult, but this is an integral part of an effective and complete information search. The search for, and exploitation of, subdomains is usually a "techie" project as many subdomain search engines are written in python computer language. Users planning subdomain searches must have more than a passing familiarity with use of the command line. The search can be made through sites and services such as:
- **Amass:** https://github.com/OWASP/Amass
- **Knock:** https://github.com/guelfoweb/knock
- **SubBrute:** https://github.com/TheRook/subbrute
- **Sublist3r:** https://github.com/aboul3la/Sublist3r
- **SurfaceBrowser:** https://securitytrails.com/.

Source Code

There is a lot to a web page that few users ever see. Information may be there, hidden in the source code that never displays on the visible page.

To call any research complete, the source code of key pages should be searched – a taxing and often-enervating job. Not only does the researcher or research desk have to know html – how a web page is constructed – but most of today's web pages are made up of "spaghetti code," long lines of text and tags that have to be reviewed and their purpose understood.

Looking at source code is comparable to panning for gold: Virtually all of what you see is as valuable as sand and gravel but occasionally there is a useful nugget of information. Source code examination may reveal information not visible on the page presented to the public. While the displayed page may be barren of information, the source code may include email addresses, phone numbers, or some other content that will otherwise go unseen.

Source code is easier to view in some browsers than in others. In Firefox the Alt key brings up the menu bar. On the bar select "Tools," then "Web Developer" and then click "Page Source" on the menu. For other browsers use the Internet and look up the name of the browser with a query such as "source code on (browser name)." To view the source code when you have no other way do so, go to the **GenerateIt** site at https://www.generateit.net/seo-tools/source-viewer/ and enter the URL of the page you want to examine. Copy the source code text that is displayed and paste it in a word processing page; then go through it line by line.

Some pages contain externally linked CSS files. Such pages will not actually have the file, but the file will be linked and the page will have a path to get to the external file. You may have to use the Internet to learn how to follow CSS links.

Reviewing a page's source code is usually boring, but like panning for gold it may eventually pay off. Resources of help in reviewing Source Code include:

- **NerdyData (Technology source code):**
  https://nerdydata.com/search
- **The Silver Searcher (Source code search engine):**
  https://github.com/ggreer/the_silver_searcher.

Freedom of Information and Sunshine Laws

Governments write, collect, and archive scads of information and documents. The general rule in the US is that these records belong to the public, not to the officials, functionaries, or the people who drafted the records. In some cases just going to a public agency and asking nicely – remember, there is almost always a person involved in getting the information – will get you the information or the records. But you cannot count on a smile, "please," and nice words.

The US federal Freedom of Information Act (FOIA) applies to "records" of most federal agencies under the aegis of the President. The courts and Congress are exempt. At the state level there are similar public records laws, sometimes termed "sunshine laws" or "open records acts." The details of these state and municipal laws vary widely and involve different procedures, but they allow access to official records that can be invaluable.

Journalists in the United States rely heavily on the FOIA and similar public records laws. Because of the complexity of these laws the FOIA open record techniques are used primarily by reporters and lawyers. But if the information is available under the FOIA or public records acts anyone, not only reporters, can demand it. Knowing the proper verbiage and the techniques to demand documents – and how to outwit the bureaucrats trying to outwit the records requesters – becomes important.

Entire books are written on the subject; there are a number of online resources that explain how to frame an FOIA demand and what to expect. (Expect little if you don't follow up.) Anyone in the information business, not just reporters, needs to have at least a passing acquaintance with the FOIA and state open records procedures.

In general, federal FOIA requests must be in writing and follow the regulations of the particular agency. The law says the request must "reasonably describe" the record or records, an argument that is frequently used by some reluctant agencies to deny access. Having exact titles, locations, and dates is helpful.

Because sunshine laws are written in such a way that they exempt information from disclosure when government employees might not be able to locate the documents, knowledgeable researchers often go into great detail about the records needed and even suggest physical locations and/or systems where the documents might be located.

The law applies only to documents that already exist. An agency cannot be required to compile or create documents in order to fulfill a request.

Hope for, but never expect, quick results. Normally a federal agency is given 20 business days (or 10 calendar days for an expedited request) to either provide the information or explain why it is withholding the data. However, there is an "unusual circumstances" exception that some agencies seem inclined to use on a more or less permanent basis. Expect all requests to take longer than the statutory time limit. An acknowledgment by the agency that they have received your request does not qualify as fulfillment under the law, though some will try to use this excuse for not meeting the specified time limit.

To speed up the process some information professionals request expedited processing, but not everyone or every request is entitled to that. Researchers who are going to call for federal expedited processing must be familiar with the conditions under which it can be claimed; a detailed statement about those conditions will be required.

Federal agencies are allowed to charge "reasonable" fees for direct costs such as searching and copying the record, although reductions and waivers can be requested by researchers. It is always wise to indicate the amount you're willing to pay as part of your request letter, then ask the agency to contact you if the search and copying fees exceed that amount.

Federal law doesn't require a press pass to get the reduced fees that are available to reporters. The federal definition of news media is wide enough that many information seekers can use it to cut their costs. In some cases researchers who gather information of interest to some part of the public and use their skills to turn the material into a work that is distributed to an audience may be considered part of the "news media." That claim can reduce the costs. There is also a "public interest" fee waiver available.

When submitting any FOIA request it is essential to know and understand the rules, often arcane, of the particular agency you are querying. Different agencies require different submission methods, but when using whatever method is required be certain to clearly label your communication as an FOIA request. Make certain there is no question about what it is.

It is quite possible, even probable, that the agency will claim some exemption, in which case you will have to do further investigation to see if the exemption claim is valid. Some are; many are not.

Obsessive secrecy is common among bureaucracies. Claims of exemptions run the gamut. The agency may claim the information is classified. The agency may say the information or document is exempt because of internal personnel rules or practices, or is exempted by some statute. It is not unheard of for an agency to claim there is a trade or commercial secret involved or that some attorney or deliberation privilege is involved. Claims of exemption because of personal privacy are not uncommon. Some agency personnel are experts at twisting the language of legal exemption beyond all reason or recognition. Always check, and if appropriate challenge, any exemption claim. Exemption claims are often tortured readings, or even misstatements, of the law

Getting a document may only be the first step. Sometimes the document is so heavily redacted – parts are blacked out – that it is impossible to make sense of, or even read coherently.

Expect, and prepare, to have to submit an administrative appeal regarding what you were, or were not, provided. Save every scrap of information related to the FOIA request, including envelopes. Make certain the appeal is filed within agency timelines and falls within the reasons allowed to contest the initial decision. State and local open records process may be even more convoluted than the federal one.

There are detailed resources and guides available on the Internet to help researchers understand the rules and how to submit a properly formatted request and appeal. Some of them are at **Reporters Committee for Freedom of the Press,** under the Legal Resources menu, at https://www.rcfp.org/.

The FOIA Request Generator aids users in creating their FOIA demands at http://www.refp.org/foi_letter/generate.php.

Dataleak Sites
While OSR tries to catch publicly available information that is insufficiently protected or mistakenly made public, there is part of the information universe devoted to "outing" anything that others would like to keep secret. These Dataleak Sites are often clandestine for at least part of their activities. Some open source advocates may, in fact, believe that all "information should be free"

and feel that nothing should be secret. Other people insist some Dataleak sites are associated with groups or organizations – possibly even foreign intelligence agencies – whose intentions are to make someone look bad or to force someone to reveal sources and methods.

Open Source investigators – usually those dealing with issues at the national and international level – may want to explore such sites to see whether and how they may fit into their search plan and if they should be routinely searched as part of the SOP. Workers for, or employees at, some government agencies will be legally prohibited from even accessing such sites, however, and researchers should determine if they fall under the exclusion rules before going to any Dataleak sites.

These sites include:
- **Al Jazeera Investigations (Arabic region):** https://www.aljazeera.com/investigations/
- **BalkanLeaks:** https://balkanleaks.eu/
- **Cryptome:** https://cryptome.org/
- **GlobalLeaks (Whistleblower software):** https://www.globaleaks.org/
- **Wikileaks:** https://wikileaks.org/.

Backlinks
Backlinks is the term used to describe the links that other sites make to the page that a user is viewing. Backlinks may be described as a vote of confidence. They can be one indicator of how much trust to place in a site's information – the quality of the backlinks sites is always worth looking into when evaluating authoritativeness.

"Birds of a feather flock together" is a useful phrase to consider when looking at backlinks. If the backlinks are from good sites they are very, very good but when the backlinks go to questionable sites you may want to mark your potential resource as "horrid."

Search engines often use the number of backlinks as a factor in ranking a site but seldom evaluate the quality of the linking site.

Small SEO Tools has a free backlinks checker tool that is available at https://smallseotools.com/backlink-checker/ and there are many for-pay sites, as well.

Who Is and IP Lookups...

Tracking a website owner or operator, whether an individual or an entity, is often a starting point in verification. Identifying the people or organizations who run a site may prove to be important. WhoIs lookup sites were more instructive a few years ago but still remain useful.

Using WhoIs sites effectively today is more challenging. Now many site-sellers provide users – for a price, for a price – with a level of privacy that approaches anonymity. Such site sellers effectively refuse to divulge the ownership information without a court order, thwarting any effort to determine who owns or operates a site. Still, many site owners won't pay their site-sellers the price for the privacy so WhoIs lookups remain useful regarding those sites.

WhoIs sites take the URL you enter and search domain name registries and registrar tables. The information they return can be used for a variety of purposes.

A variation is reverse DNI sites. These will get you the domain name and some information on a site if you have the IP address – sets of numbers from 0 to 255 that are separated by periods. You may be able to use this information to determine the name of the Internet service provider assigned to a particular IP address.

Enter the address of the website into a site like IP Lookup which determines the IP address and shows information such as the host, location, and other WhoIs data regarding the address, or addresses, entered. A number of sites claim to provide a plethora of data, including meta information, hosting data, and site age. BuiltWith is somewhat different in that it reveals what was used to build a site. Occasionally that can be useful information.

- **BuiltWith:** https://builtwith.com/
- **DomainTools ($$$$):** https://www.domaintools.com/
- **ICANN:** https://whois.icann.org/en
- **IP2Location:** https://www.ip2location.com/
- **IPAdress (Tracing):** https://www.ip-adress.com/ip-address/lookup
- **IP Fingerprints (Location):** ipfingerprints.com
- **IPLookup:** http://ip-lookup.net/domain.php
- **Lookupserver:** http://lookupserver.com/dns
- **Riherds (Reverse DNI lookup):** http://remote.12dt.com/
- **Robtex:** https://www.robtex.com/
- **SiteDossier:** http://www.sitedossier.com/
- **URLSCAN:** https://whois.icann.org/en
- **Whoisology**: https://whoisology.com/
- **WhoisRequest**: http://whoisrequest.com/
- **XL-WhoIs:** https://le-tools.com/XL-Whois.html.

Sam Spade is a downloadable utility freeware package that does IP lookups and many other chores for OSR researchers. Access it at http://www.majorgeeks.com/files/details/sam_spade.html.

Cookie Management

Cookies are small text programs that are downloaded onto the devices that access the Internet. They remember, and may later transmit, something about you – sometimes on behalf of the site you visit and sometimes on behalf of a company or agency that wants to know details about you and your interests. Cookies may be designed to tell system operators about the device, or about the browsing habits of the device user. They are also used as a recognition method so the website's operator can identify users. They may allow you to return to the site repeatedly without logging in or otherwise serve your needs and interests. They may also track your activities. In short, cookies may be good for you; they may also be dangerous to your research work.

There are different cookie "flavors," although any particular cookie may fall into more than one category.

First-party cookies come from a server or a domain managed by the website publisher. Third-party cookies come from a server or domain other than the website's publisher; this third party processes the collected information and often sells or uses it for its own purposes. Third party cookies can be used to develop an extensive profile of you, your searches, and your techniques. When cookies are installed from a server or domain managed by the website publisher, but the information collected is managed by a third-party, they are not classed as first-party cookies.

Cookies are also classed by the length of time they remain active on the user's computer.

Session cookies sweep up and store data when the user accesses a website. They are usually used to store the information needed to provide whatever service is requested by the user and are active only for that occasion.

Persistent cookies are stored on the device of the user. They can be accessed and managed over whatever period of time the cookie developer decides. The time can be short or the cookie could remain active indefinitely.

There are a number of different roles for cookies. Technical cookies allow the web user to use the site effectively. These cookies focus on the technological needs of the site.

Personalization cookies allow users to access the service, personalizing it by matching the display to the requirements of the user's device.

Analytics cookies allow website operators to track and analyze the behavior of the users.

Advertising cookies control the advertising space that a publisher has included.

Behavioral advertising cookies store and utilize information about the user's activity by monitoring browsing habits and developing a profile based on those habits.

Cookies on your system are neither good nor bad; it is how others use them that determine that. Because they can be used to obtain, store, and use information about an investigator's or a researcher's online activity it is usually best to limit the number and types of cookies on your equipment. However, particularly with technical cookies, doing so might make a site totally or partially unusable. Cookie issues could best be resolved at the time they arise. A major factor in any decision about cookies is whether the researcher or research desk believes the system operator who has access to your cookie information will use them in, or against, your interests. Unfortunately you will seldom know if or when they are being installed on your system.

It is generally a wise practice for researchers to restrict or monitor cookie placement when on a site – and then clean cookies from the system after getting off, but before going to another site. That is also a pain. Few do it, but it should be considered as part of security measures when accessing sites that might be hostile.

It is definitely a good idea to prevent third-party tracking cookies from being installed on your computer or to eliminate them if they do slip through.

Some services will disrupt tracking cookies:
- **Ghostery:** https://www.ghostery.com/
- **NoScript:** https://noscript.net/
- **Privacy Badger:** https://privacy-badger.en.softonic.com/
- **UBlockOrigin:** https://ublock.org/.

The **Privacy Badger** of the Electronic Freedom Foundation at https://privacy-badger.en.softonic.com/ can help solve many cookie problems.

Kicked Off the Page...

"You have used up your free access" – the message makes it clear you cannot see the article or access the information you wanted. And the snippet you glimpsed briefly looked like it might be the exact information you needed!

There are several ways to approach the problem and get the article out of the cookie jar. The article may been denied to you because you have used up your permitted accesses for the month or whatever period of time the site set.

That time period was based on a "cookie" that the site set, sight unseen, in your browser system when you accessed the site before. So.... Use a different browser! Put the URL you previously clicked on into a new browser and see if that brings up what you want.

A second way of handling this situation is to stay on the browser that has the cookie, look on the Internet for instructions such as "how do I remove the cookies from my browser." Follow the instructions and remove the particular cookie set by the site, then try accessing the article again. Most information professionals believe it is best to remove only the one cookie that applies to the site, not all the cookies on your machine. Some other cookies are useful to you and you would need to restock your helpful cookie jar.

If those don't work, try using the Incognito window in Firefox or similar so-called anonymization services found in other browsers.

Some pages, particularly on commercial sites, will appear on the screen briefly, only to be covered within seconds by a form that tells you to subscribe, whitelist the site, turn off your ad blocker, or do something else you don't want to do. But you really, really, want to see what the site has just hidden.

You can dutifully follow orders, of course. For those who don't necessarily want to obey orders from site managers as their first alternative, try saving the page to your desktop. Go back to where you first encountered the URL of the page and click on it again. Quickly, *before* the message that says you cannot look at that page unless you pay or do X or Y, save that page. Quickly, in this case, is usually a matter of split seconds so you must be prepared to do a fast "save." After speedily saving the page, minimize the covered-over online page, and open the copy you have saved to your computer. Often the page you wanted to read will be saved and shown rather than the form that covered the material you originally wanted to look at.

A variation on this is quickly – again the technique requires speed and attention – do a "select all" on the drop down menu, then a "copy." The text should now be in your computer. You only have to figure out a way to display it. The easiest: open an empty text or word processor file and paste the text in it. Inelegant, perhaps, but it works.

In many cases you probably know the title or headline. Copy it into your browser, with quotation marks around it, and hit the "enter" key. There is a chance someone reposted it elsewhere on the Internet and a search engine may have picked up that repost.

If you can see who the author is, search online for that person. If you can locate an email address, write the person and tell him or her how much you would like to read the article but cannot access it. It often helps to explain why you want to read the piece that they obviously researched so well. Many writers will respond with a copy of the article or requested information.

There are several ways to collect material off pages the system operator doesn't want you to see. You just have to decide what works best, and quickest, in the particular situation.

Failing Links and Dead Pages

A somewhat similar situation is a failed link, called Web Rot by some. When a Web page appears to have disappeared into the ether but the site remains, don't give up. Go to the site's homepage and use any on-site search engine to look for key words. It is all-too-common that page addresses will change but the actual text or page remains somewhere on the site. Or try a search inputting the title, headline, or author into the site's search engine.

If there is no on-site search engine at the location you are searching use the "site:" command to, limit the search to that site and enter a key word or title: site:urlofsite "key word(s) or title."

To access pages from the past, a primary means is **The Wayback Machine**, below. Its search engine can resurrect useful sites and pages that have been taken down, changed, or disappeared. This site has many uses but one is to use it when looking at locations that may have minutes of meetings and similar periodic postings.

To a much more limited extent the cache page results on a search engine may show what a website looked like when a spider indexed it previously.

Also check the wide variety of archives online; it may already be there:
- **Archive-It:** http://www.archive-it.org
- **Archive.is:** http://www.archive.is

- **ArchiveTeam (Archiving projects):**
  https://www.archiveteam.org/index.php?title=Main_Page
- **Arquivo.pt(Portuguese archive):**
  http://www.arquivo.pt
- **Icelandic Web Archive:** http://www.vefsafn.is
- **Library of Congress Web Archives:**
  https://www.loc.gov/programs/web-archiving/archived-web-sites/
- **Perma.cc (Limited to Harvard affiliates):**
  https://library.harvard.edu/services-tools/permacc
- **UK Web Archive:** https://www.webarchive.org.uk/
- **Czech Republic Web Archive:** http://www.webarchiv.cz
- **TheWayBackMachine:** http://www.archive.org
- **Webrecorder:** http://www.webrecorder.io.

Another option that provides several ways to find, view, and download archive sites is use of the **Firefox Archive Add-on** at https://addons.mozilla.org/en-US/firefox/addon/view-page-archive.

This gives you options to find, view, and download archive pages from sites such as:
- Archive.is
- Baidu Snapshot
- Bing Cache
- Exalead Cache
- Gigablast Cache
- Google Cache
- Megalodon
- Memento Time Travel
- Naver Cache
- Qihoo 360 Search Snapshot
- Sogou Snapshot
- Wayback Machine
- WebCite
- Yandex Cache.

To stay ahead of failing links, develop a habit of saving any of the information that you may need later when you first find it. Download all potentially-useful material to your own project library immediately, whenever you come across it. Snare anything and everything that you judge useful. Do it at the outset of your investigation. It may disappear today or tomorrow; in fact, expect it to disappear before you need to return to it.

Programs and addons that make downloading easier and faster include:

- **Down Them All:** https://www.downthemall.net/
- **Resurrect Pages**:
  https://addons.mozilla.org/en-US/firefox/addon/resurrect-pages.

Promises Unkept

Some unscrupulous site managers – eager to drive traffic to their location – will try to trick Web search engines to steer you there even though they have nothing for you. A few do it to try to get you to click on links that will download malware to your computer or that will pay them money.

Some of the more common tricks of the trade include adding false keywords to meta-tags – for instance the names of popular stars on pages that have nothing to do with entertainment.

Then there is the "hidden text" scam, where words of the same color as the background are placed in the page text. Search engine spiders don't detect color; they just pick up the text words. Similar is the "tiny text" scam, words written so small that they may appear to the viewer as a straight line, if they can be seen at all.

Of course, the difference between your search and the page contents may not be due to a greedy system operator. The page may have been updated and changed but the search engine spider may not have returned yet to document that change.

Restrictions on Identifying Information Sources

For those researchers able to go beyond simply observing, for those who can ask questions of others and get answers, there is a potential difficulty in identifying information sources. Whether the contact is in person, by phone, through email, or over a social media account, both you and the person you are talking to need to understand the rules and establish them at the start of any conversation.

Unfortunately, while "off the record" or "on background" are terms of art with specific meanings there is enough confusion that – unless both sides explain to each other what they understand by them – misunderstandings are almost inevitable.

When no rules are set down – and any must be agreed to in advance, not as an afterthought – anything said is "on the record." Everything can usually be used as long as the quotes are accurate and the statement is consistent with what the interviewee said.

"Off the record" or "on background" may be rules laid down at the start of an interview by either side. Normally the person asking the questions wants everything to be "on the record," but either party may ask – or demand – that something is "off the record" or "on background" so long as that condition is made clear before the statement at issue is made.

Whenever there are restrictions, both sides must clearly understand what that means and how much is restricted. If both parties agree that part of any discussion is "off the record" or "on background" both parties have to be clear about what part is which.

"On the record" means that whatever is said or done may be directly attributed to someone by name, title, organization, or in any other personally identifiable way. Unless something else is agreed to – in advance – everything is considered "on the record."

"Off the record" means that what a person says can't be attributed to that person – not under any circumstance, not in any way, period, end of discussion.

An "off the record" discussion is often a comment "for your ears only." It is designed to help questioners to the extent that they now know what information they need to be looking for – but should be seeking in some other place, with some other person. The rule with "off the record" backgrounding is that the information must be obtained from another source and attributed only to that source if it to be used.

"Off the record" discussions have potential drawbacks. There are several reasons people may speak "off the record." Some sources may want to provide context. Some are whistleblowers. Others may want to gain the upper hand in internal politics or succeed in infighting over policy or personnel issues. At times "off the record" is used to "float trial balloons" and gauge a reaction before an official announcements is made. When the only person who knows something – and knows no other person has that information – tells an interviewer something "off the record," the technique can be used cynically to prevent information from being used at all

It is possible, but extremely rare, for a public speaker to demand that an audience adhere to an "off the record" rule. That seldom works out well.

"Speaking on background" allows use of the information on whatever terms are agreed to by the source. Usually this prohibits attribution by name, organization or any other identifier. "Industry sources" or "company officials" is often the way speaking on background is denoted. In some cases "speaking on background" information will be unsourced, as in a statement such as "according to anonymous sources."

There is another term called "deep background." That means different things to different people. Some consider it equivalent to "off the record" while others see it as another way of saying "speaking on background." Since that phrase is dark-brown muddy at best, the meaning should be clarified before any conversation continues.

Public speakers may use a version of "speaking on background" known as the Chatham House Rule. When the Chatham House Rule is invoked by any speaker, the event (including academic debates, educational lectures, news conferences, political rallies, and public government meetings) is altered in character. The source becomes a confidential one.

The Chatham House Rule provides anonymity to speakers. It is intended to aid open discussion. There is no set penalty for breaking the Chatham House rule, but generally rule-breakers will be ostracized or refused admittance to any subsequent talks of the sponsoring organization. The rule is: "When a meeting, or part thereof, is held under the Chatham House Rule, participants are free to use the information received, but neither the identity nor the affiliation of the speaker(s), nor that of any other participant, may be revealed."

Created in 1927, the rule was refined in 1992 and 2002. As constituted, it is designed to prevent tying any individual, either directly or indirectly, to anything said. It does not, however, prohibit distribution of information about what was said.

There is a similar case in which an object, such as a small sculpture, may be placed in front of the speaker and as long as comments are made "behind the..." sculpture they are unattributable to a person, or by a time or place.

A somewhat distant "relative" of these is the "embargo." Usually used in the news business, embargoes are an agreement between the reporter or media and a news source to withhold publication of the information until some set time and/or date. Embargoes give publications the time to explore the information and evaluate its importance, but they often provide the source the ability to release the same information to several publications simultaneously so that no news provider is favored, nor do any feel left out.

In OSR the researcher's word is binding, whether on embargos or in other aspects. In *The Valley of Fear* Sherlock Holmes set an example of how important it is for researchers to remain true to their word. Chided for not investigating a person whose identity he had agreed not to look into, the detective explained his inaction simply: "Because I always keep faith."

Marketing Resources

Marketing tools often include such things as biographies, press releases, contact information, and identification about personnel, job openings, mission statements, webinars, financial information, white papers, speeches, newsletters, executive presentations, reports, and announcements. Never overlook the possibilities of searching out and using marketing materials whenever you are researching people or organizations. You can use these tools as jump-off points to search other sites, particularly those on social media.

Facial Recognition

Facial recognition uses faces as data. The concept remains unproven – in fact it is known to be failure-prone under many circumstances and instances. And it remains unregulated; users can employ it for any reason or purpose.

At present facial recognition should be considered a lead to be explored, a "maybe" that is worth following up.

Facial recognition combines cameras and AI algorithms to scan the faces of people in crowds, photos, or videos and then match the digital codes of their facial patterns to those in a database of people whose identities are already known. Facial recognition is one of the biometric identification systems that can remotely identify people by name without their consent, or even knowledge. Paired with the now-ubiquitous surveillance cameras, facial recognition systems allow identification and tracking of any individual in a camera's field. Recently systems have even been programmed to reportedly detect the emotions displayed by the subjects.

Powerful facial recognition software is on the cusp of becoming available to the general public at reasonable prices. There are no restrictions on how it may be used in the circumstances. Everyone, including OSR researchers, are denied any control over whether or how their face is linked to their identity in databases, and how pictures can be shared. There are no opt-out rights. Facial recognition can be, and is, carried out without anyone's permission. Anyone can be photographed anywhere, and if a picture appears on social media the users of facial recognition software can often identify that person. Once identified, open sources can be used to fill in other details.

Widely available to governments, the systems are now deployed worldwide.

National governments have been using various systems for years, trying to spot terrorists, suspects, and others deemed security threats.

The facial recognition capability has now drifted down to local governments and security contractors, making it possible to track and locate people suspected of criminal activity, to identify protestors, or to locate missing people.

Commercial providers also have carved out a role in allowing people to enter a protected area, or even to sign on to a computer system. It is being used to speed up loading of planes and there is no doubt additional uses will be carved out in the near term. Non-governmental uses are being developed even now, but there is – as yet – no widespread use of facial recognition by commercial or civilian users, or researchers.

Searching for the term "facial recognition" on the Internet, or at **Facefirst** (\$\$\$\$): https://wwwfacefirst.com, may provide additional information.

Systems currently in use are improving in sensitivity and accuracy, although the glitches that remain in correctly identifying some racial and gender groups, as well as close relatives, have proven difficult to resolve. Angle-related problems will probably be resolved sooner rather than later but they remain significant difficulties to accuracy.

Translations and Language Use

There are many languages in the world. People who write or speak about your subject often do so in languages other than yours.

Widely-used Web languages include:

- English
- Chinese
- Spanish
- Japanese
- Portuguese
- German
- Arabic
- French
- Russian.

Never limit yourself to your own lingo. Search in the language of the group, organization, or individual you are following. But you can be assured that good searches are generally harder to conduct in a foreign language than in the researcher's native language.

In social media, particularly, but even on news sites, you need to be aware of any of the alternative or non-standard terms, sub-cultural language, or slang that may be commonly used in the area. Localized language or the private *patois* that is common to a profession or group may be misleading, if not un-understandable.

Often you will need to type words in the writing system of the language. The Roman alphabet does not always suffice. For those occasions the **Google Input** tools which can be found at https://www.google.com/inputtools/ may provide the needed keyboard.

To make your research easier, and the result more accurate, when searching in a foreign language develop a list – cheat sheet if you will – of key foreign words, phrases, and symbols. Those are aids that will probably provide good results. Start your list with the words and commands you are likely to see on foreign language search engines or on sites written in that language. Alternatively, or in conjunction with any words list, use image searches to see pages with pictures that appear closest to your needs.

Every language is complex. Just as there are different words for the same thing in English, most languages have multiple words or shadings of meaning for the same concept. Sherlock Holmes, in *The Adventure of the Three Garridebs,* solved a problem by noticing the subtle spelling and language differences that were found in an advertisement and commenting, "Yes, it was bad English but good American."

Different spellings of the same word will have a significant effect on search engine results. Sometimes words which are spelled differently sound similar. And sometimes a word spelled the same way may have two different meanings and even two different pronunciations. Since many languages – and this applies particularly to concepts – don't translate cleanly, it may be difficult to get to the true meaning of a passage.

When you find what appears to be useful information you have to tease meanings, and they may be subtle differences of meaning, from the collected information. The options are:

- Human translations
- Mechanical translations.

Language barriers create the same problems as an unbreakable code – you don't know what the other person is saying, even when that knowledge may be critical. For that reason humans – linguists, interpreters, and translators – can be key support resources for researchers.

There is a difference among the three. Interpreters change spoken language from one tongue to another; translators work with written materials. Linguists work with both spoken language and written materials.

Linguists – or good translators and interpreters – may be helpful in dealing with cultural nuances, slang, and dialects. Keep in mind that when searching for information about a subject in a foreign country or a foreign language you need to search for the word(s) people actually use in their speech – which may not be a simple translation of an English language word.

The gold standard of OSR is, and will continue to be accuracy in everything. Translations require accuracy. Human translations are considered superior to machine ones. Yet even if a researcher has a qualified humans available they can be easily overwhelmed by the amount of work. While some would argue for a full and complete translation of everything, human limitations often make that impractical.

To mitigate the problem researchers have developed four formats or levels of translation. The open source researcher has to choose among them when using human resources. Going from the easiest and fastest, they are:

- Gisting
- Summary
- Extract
- Full translation.

Gisting is designed to show the general meaning of a piece. It is a look-see. Gisting translations are often used to determine whether there is enough information, of high-enough quality, to forward the item on for a more accurate and complete translation.

Summary translation requires the reading of the entire text, and the summarization of the main thrusts. It falls short of an exact translation. No one would suggest it is accurate enough to put quote marks around.

The Extract is a precise translation of part(s) of a document, text, or resource. Extracts often result when Gisting or a Summary reveals the importance of parts of a document that also contains there is information that may be of limited value.

Full Translations are what the words imply – a complete rendering of the document or verbiage. Full translations are time- and labor-intensive, but they may be necessary for complete understanding. Technical reports and position papers are among the document types that usually require a full translation.

While it is always best if the researcher speaks the language like a native – and thinks in that language like a native – or uses a human translator, there are mechanical workarounds when the best isn't available. Linguists always are at a premium, but they are especially scarce when you need one *tout d'suite*. Because of that, there has been a serious move within and outside the open source community to use machine translations on Web materials.

Many consider mechanical translations to be second string solutions but they can be immensely helpful. There are machine language translations of scores of languages, from Afrikaans and Hawaiian to Yiddish and Zulu.

Mechanical translators may have problems sensing – and properly rendering – things like shades of meaning, idiomatic or slang speech, uncommon words, metaphorical allusions, or informal expressions. But machine language translations may be the only thing available. Make the most of whatever you have and try to reduce the chances for errors.

Use machine translations for topic identification and as an aid in determining whether some passage should be reviewed and revised by a human translator. Generally it is possible to get decent – that is not to say absolutely accurate – translations from a good mechanical translator. Machine translations can usually be used as indicators that something is probably worth a human review. Never use machine translations alone for information that is critical to your work; they should never be considered reliable. Machine translations can provide the "gist" of text, but "gisting" is at best an approximation.

Translation programs can also be used to locate Web information about your subject that are written in foreign languages, pages you might not normally see. First type the English language word you want to search for into the translation system and ask it translate the word into to the language you want. When the word is translated, copy and paste it from the translation page into the regular search page. That will usually bring up pages written in the foreign language. Then use translation programs to translate those pages into English. Check the probability of accuracy by translating from the English language version back to the foreign language and compare the texts. They usually won't be exact duplicates, of course, but if the final version doesn't look close, the translation may be questionable. Remember, too, that some wording – in any language – simply does not translate well.

If you are doing extensive work in a foreign language it is important to choose the correct type of translation engine. When you are going to use machine translators extensively, understand that there are differences in how translation programs work. Dig down. Details matter. Make certain you use the best type of translation engine for the language and your topic.

- **Dictionary-based:** Translates words without correlation to context
- **Example-based:** Translates by analogy
- **Interlingual:** Rules-based translation
- **Statistical:** Uses bilingual corpora.

Babelfish, Systran, and Google Translate are among the most popular translation programs. Some information professionals use two or more translation programs and compare the results. Others use Google Translate for the body text, but when words don't come back correctly those words can be isolated and dumped into Systran. The options are many, and all the options are yours. Popular translation engines include:

- **Babelfish:** http://babelfish.com/
- **Bing/Microsoft Translate:** https://www.bing.com/translator
- **Foreignword.com**: http://foreignword.com/
- **Google Input Tools (Typing in a foreign language):** https://www.google.com/inputtools/try/
- **Google Translate:** https://translate.google.com/
- **Google Translate Add-on:** https://addons.mozilla.org/ en-US/firefox/addon/to-google-translate
- **Online Translate:** http://www.online-translator.com/
- **PROMPT- Online:** http://translation2.paralink.com/
- **Systran:** http://www.systransoft.com/
- **Word2Word:** http://www.word2word.com/.

Generally you either paste the text you want translated into a window of the translation program, click a button and read the result – or you click somewhere and the entire page will be translated.

This year machine translations are better than last year, and that was better than the year previous. Overall, most online translations have above 90 percent accuracy but they vary from language to language and site to site. While significant room for improvement remains, searches made in the language of the area rather than English, as well as use of the correct script, generally improves the result.

Although machine translations should always be considered inexact and in need of human verification, one workaround to be better-assured of mechanical results is to triangulate. Do translations on three separate machine language translation engines, matching up the wording and meaning to find the common denominators among them while discarding the outliers.

Those who use mechanical means for translations of important documents, or any technical papers, should always make certain the output is reviewed by at least one qualified human translator. If important documents or technical papers were originally translated by a human they should be reviewed by a second qualified person. When the outcome of the research depends on what was actually said or written, accuracy is vital. In translations, as with many other things in OSR, "two is one and one is none."

Deception, bias, and incompetence are of particular concern in any translations made during research. Even people doing a translation can intentionally or unintentionally add, delete, modify, or otherwise filter the information. Local hires may not have been fully vetted to determine their ability level or things in their background that may make them prone to deception or bias. Be aware of the potential for deception, bias, and/or incompetence in all translations.

If you suspect deception, bias, or just incompetence, test the accuracy of any translation by giving the same material to one or two additional linguists and compare the results. At a minimum you will know how far to trust the translations you are getting.

Emojis

Emojis – those little expressive symbols that have become popular in messages – are a means of communication. They should never be ignored or forgotten. Modern information professionals need to be aware of emojis whenever they are used, and of their appearance – which may vary depending on the platform they appear on. There are over 2,500 official emojis, which provides a great deal of opportunity to use them to convey a wide variety of thoughts and messages. Besides the official batch there are many additional unofficial ones.

Simple emojis can be used to communicate complex ideas. For example, they have reportedly been used in the past for selling drugs – one type of leaf symbol meaning "marijuana" and a dollar sign symbol meaning "for sale." Crystal meth might be noted as a gemstone; injectable drugs, including heroin, could be shown by a syringe.

Emojis can be used in many ways. As a code, one symbol stands for a word or even a concept completely different from the picture. Emojis can also be used as a cipher, using the symbols to replace an alphabet or other writing system.

The **CodeEmoji** site at https://codemoji.org/#/encrypt does a good job of explaining cipher encryption with emojis. When used in these ways the messages require decoding – they may be simple cipher, or complex enough to require the use of codebreakers. That is beyond this book. Nonetheless, when sent in the open, and even if they require decoding, emojis are fair game for open source work and should be treated as any page or a message needing translation.

Researchers must be aware, whenever and wherever encountering an emoji, and particularly many in a series, that information is being conveyed even when the message may not be apparent to the uninitiated. A useful guide to the **official emojis** is found at https://emojipedia.org.

Audio-to-Text Transcription

Transcription tools make it possible to turn audio materials into a written transcript. The development of audio-to-text conversion tools saves time as well as frustration. Things often go better – not to mention faster – when you can search the transcript.

- **Otter (Meeting/interview transcription):**
  https://otter.ai/login
- **Temi: (Meeting/interview transcription, $$$$):**
  https://www.temi.com/.

More than two dozen transcription tools are outlined at the **Tow-Knight Center for Entrepreneurial Journalism**, which can be found at https://medium.com/journalism-innovation/the-best-new-ways-to-transcribe-c4c342abf172.

Truncating URLs...

Learn to truncate a website's URL, going back one forward slash (/) at a time until you reach the home page address. This will allow you to see whether you can look into any of the website's file folders. When you can, you never know what you will find. Sometimes, when trying to do a complete job, it is worth clicking every link on the home page – or on every page and then truncating each web address. This technique previously provided more information about a site and the material on it than it does now because site owners were not as careful then in their set-ups. Hpowever, it remains a worthwhile exercise whether you uncover any useful information or not. When you can say you truncated all of the URLs visible on a site it shows you have done due diligence, not a job that was just "good enough."

Databases

Databases are usually created and maintained by businesses, governments, experts, or at least by people who are knowledgeable in a particular field. They are high-value targets for any researcher. Databases are often found on scholarly sites, ones offering better-quality resources.

Databases organize information. They are almost invariably devoted to a specific subject. Search engines cannot and do not download or index database information – which is often massive. Even if search engines had the bandwidth to download and save the mountains of information in databases, they are often protected by firewalls or sign-ons that keep search engines out. Most search engines will find and record the existence of databases – they just cannot move through the front door since they can neither sign in nor enter a term in the search field.

You can often find databases related to your subject by adding "db" or "database" behind the general subject you are looking them up in your search. Or, when you get on a site that seems likely to have a database, type "database" or "db" into the site's search engine. This will often reveal the existence of any database. If one shows up in a site search, click on the link just as with any other search and proceed from there to use, or try to use, the database.

Some databases that may be useful to you, or might suggest the types of databases that are available to you, include:
- **American Religion Data Archive:** http://www.thearda.com/index.asp
- **Ancestry:** https://www.ancestry.com/
- **Britannica Online ($$$$):** https://www.britannica.com/
- **CountryWatch:** http://www.countrywatch.com/
- **DOD and Military Electronic Journals:** http://www.au.af.mil/au/aul/periodicals/dodelecj.htm
- **Dudley Knox Library Databases:** http://libguides.nps.edu/az.php

- **EBSCO ($$$$):** https://www.ebsco.com/
- **FirstGov:** https://www.usa.gov/
- **Georgetown University Library Dissertations:** https://guides.library.georgetown.edu/dissertations
- **Google Scholar:** https://scholar.google.com/
- **Government Databases (Louis J. Blume Library):** http://lib.stmarytx.edu/c.php?g=288016
- **Government Printing Office:** https://www.gpo.gov/fdsys/search/advanced/advsearchpage.action
- **Libraries on the Web:** http://www.lib-web.org/
- **Monash University Databases and Resources:** http://guides.lib.monash.edu/subject-databases
- **National Inventory of Dams:** https://catalog.data.gov/dataset/national-inventory-of-dams
- **ProQuest:** https://search.proquest.com/
- **Reference Desk:** http://www.earthstation9.com/index.html
- **Search Systems:** http://publicrecords.searchsystems.net/
- **The Academic Web Link Database Project:** http://cybermetrics.wlv.ac.uk/database/
- **The Educator's Reference Desk (Lesson plans):** https://eduref.org/
- **The Invisible Web:** http://www.invisible-web.net/
- **UNBISNET:** http://unbisnet.un.org/
- **University of Michigan Library (Maps and atlases):** https://www.lib.umich.edu/clark-library/collections/maps-atlases
- **US National Archives and Records Administration:** https://www.archives.gov/
- **World Basic Information Library:** http://military.wikia.com/wiki/World_Basic_Information_Library.

Plagiarism Searches

Plagiarism – appropriating someone else's work and publishing it as your own – has led to the downfall of many people. It is often associated with copyright violations. Plagiarism checks have also become common among instructors in higher education.

Checking published documents – particularly the theses of people holding higher educational degrees or the writings of politicians – is common among operators running a political opposition research program but is an oft-forgotten technique in many other OSR reviews. Computers have made this type of search far easier than it was once, while the ubiquity of materials on the Internet has made it easier to find and copy others' writings. Some sites will check to see if entire websites have been misappropriated. Resources available to the researcher include:

- **Copyscape ($$$$):** https://www.copyscape.com/
- **HelioBlast:** https://helioblast.heliotext.com/
- **Plagiarisma ($$$$):** http://plagiarisma.net/
- **PlagiarismSearch ($$$$):** https://plagiarismsearch.com/
- **Unicheck ($$$$):** https://unicheck.com/.

Dumpster Diving

Valuable Open Source information is literally thrown away every day, waiting to be collected by the thoughtful researcher. Dubbed "dumpster diving," or "trash picking," the wastebasket becomes a friend to researchers and a foe of anyone they are collecting on.

Few people outside the investigative community give much thought to what they are throwing away. Even organizations that try to recycle often do it for economic advantages – paper, metal and plastic may bring back money – or for social reasons. Too few do it for security.

Because it can be financially remunerative, many people who are looking for a cash turnaround rather than information are dumpster divers. Occasionally their efforts turn up in media reports when something that probably should not have been thrown away is found and becomes a news story. Protection against dumpster divers of any sort is a major security measure – one that is often overlooked.

How useful dumpster diving is can be readily seen by the fact that a highly-placed US intelligence official was convicted and sentenced to life in prison for working with Moscow operatives. He had thoughtlessly thrown away important evidence of his betrayal, not thinking it would end up on a prosecutor's desk. Expecting anything to be buried forever in a trash heap can be a major mistake.

In the United States the Supreme Court has said that, as a general rule, anything left in curbside trash cans is considered "abandoned" and is free for the taking. Municipal ordinances, often designed to assure recycling is economically viable, may make the trash the property of the local government. For that reason dumpster diving may be illegal in some locations, but where it is lawful it is one way to acquire critical information

Trash cans, dumpsters, recycling bins, and even members of the nightly cleaning crew can help researchers piece together inside information. Recycling containers are often sought out, not only because they don't contain old banana peels and coffee-impregnated paper cups, but because that is where people trash their notes, their drafts, and the information miscellany that can tell as much about an operation as an inside snitch. People may shred things, but too many rely on shredders that cut pages into thin strips that can be readily pasted back together instead of cutting paper into the rice-grain size slivers that make good ticker-tape parade snow. Cross-cut shredders that actually do the job are a good security investment in many situations. Some of the best shredders will even take care of CDs and credit cards. Hard drives and thumb drives require special erasure and disposal techniques.

While a single letter, paper, document, or even a slip of paper with a phone number may seem insignificant at first glance, when it is combined with other knowledge that one piece of trash may fill out the mosaic of crucial clues. Moreover, many things that can contain Personally Identifiable Information (PII), including Social Security numbers, make their way to the trash.

Dumpster diving – also called trash picking – is safest when people wear long sleeve shirts, jeans, heavy leather gloves, and leather boots because people do throw away sharp and dangerous items.

If you can do it to others, others can do it to you. Remember that. From a self-protection standpoint, keep in mind the fact that any trash containing sensitive information may be intercepted at many points – while the material is at your location, while in transit, or even at the dump or recycling facility. Open recycling bins and trash cans are never safe storage for sensitive material on the way to the dump or recycle site.

Threats posed by loose paperwork are almost too many and diverse to mention. Important items include:

- Attendance records
- Correspondence
- Coursework or information about training, marketing or sales
- Credit card information, including offers
- Customer or order information
- Delivery and deliverable information
- Development plans for future projects
- Digital media such as floppy or CD disks
- Emails
- Employment data
- Financial records of any type
- Insurance information
- Internal notes and memoranda
- Maintenance records

- Medical files or information
- Payroll Information
- Personal notes
- Price lists or invoices
- Reports
- Rosters or phone tree information
- Schedules
- Shipping or other labels
- Supplier data
- Travel information.

Internet of Things

The Internet of Things (IoT) promises – or perhaps the word is threatens – to open vast vistas of personal information. The IoT contains information loads that are far beyond what any government was capable of gathering only a few years ago.

This information grocery store is widely available to anyone who wants to shop in it and learns how to exploit it.

The IoT links devices and resources, giving them a communications pathway through the Internet. IoT devices collect, transmit, receive, and exchange data. Usually the data transmission and any IOT activity is unknown, unseen and unmoderated by humans. Are the IoT exchanges openly available information? That remains to be legally determined in many cases! But until, and unless, courts weigh in decisively expect that the area will be exploited.

Lines are continually being blurred; what only governments were once to be able to do, civilians can now do better. Linking the IoT and the ever-developing techniques of today and tomorrow promises to provide everyone the intelligence – read spying – capabilities which were available only to first-world governments in the past.

Today the IoT links things as diverse as buildings, security systems, defibrillators, televisions, automobiles, insulin pumps, digital assistants, and refrigerators. The number of items connected to the IoT, and their vulnerabilities to exploitation, has exploded.

The major problem with smart TVs, smart refrigerators, or other parts of the IoT is that they are often smarter than their owners.

A smart TV may well be spying on you – revealing what you watch and how long. Unknown to you the TV may well be linked to your computer and have stored, somewhere in its memory, every document or keystroke including user names, credit card information, and passwords. Your car may be leaking information about your speed, location, or upkeep record. Digital assistants are more than willing to help you buy anything from food to underwear. They can help you because they have collected databases of information about you, your daily contacts, your wants, and your needs.

The IoT sends all kinds of information about you, your habits, your environment, and your likes and dislikes, to servers that are located who knows where for who knows what purposes. That is the outgo; there is also the potential for incoming. Some parts of the IoT are interactive – that "other side" may be able to reach in and "correct" problems by turning off your heart monitor, your car's braking system, or changing the temperature inside your refrigerator.

You need to read – read for understanding – every privacy notice that pops up on any electrical device you buy. But knowing what a company says it will do with your information is not the same as how it, or hackers, can tinker with the underlying technology to affect you. Dealing with "smart anything" requires an understanding of what information you are sending, where, to whom, for what purpose, and who can share in that information. Security suggests you should know what others can do to, or through, the smart technology you are using. This usually turns out to be a black hole, an information blank. Even the creators of the technology may not know or understand how their particular piece of technology can or would be misused. Technology developers think in terms of use, not misuse.

But the fact is, with the IoT, areas that were previously open only to government interception have become available to many others, for all sorts of reasons, and all sorts of exploitation.

Civilian commercial information sites increasingly move into areas that once were the exclusive domains of government. Today's technologies enable anyone with even modest computer skills to do things that were once reserved for advanced nation states. Some of the newest techniques may be deemed illegal by some governments, but the capabilities are there and they can be exploited by anyone who is knowledgeable.

As more items in our daily environment are controlled by, or use, the Internet for communication, the amount of data they can provide to the information interloper grows. Legacy devices, produced at a time when manufacturers were more interested in getting a working product than in providing security for users, are of special concern. But even modern IoT products face the talents and techniques of a hacktivist army – some of whom would and could turn devices into a lethal weapon. The threat of information theft from the IoT, and the parallel possibility of using the capacities for many nefarious purposes, is significant. Of serious concern: In time IoT exploitation will be used for crimes, including murder.

The IoT has serious implications – both good and bad – for open source researchers. The collection of "smart devices," cars, planes, and buildings connected to, and controlled through, the Internet, grows apace. The exponential growth of linked devices is expected to balloon the size of the IoT to tens or hundreds of billions of connected items.

Security measures for many IoT devices is largely an afterthought. The unsecured information on IoT devices is readily available to researchers, hackers, cyber criminals, and operatives of unfriendly foreign powers. Users seldom know of the security threats that may be posed by any compromised IoT devices, whose systems may be interrogated and used for any number of purposes.

Patching IoT devices is often difficult or even impossible. Security verification – making certain that the orders being sent to or from the item through the IoT – is nil. Knowledgeable intruders can often do what they will with connected devices. Devices usually lack any useful forensics capability. IoT items may include:

- Entertainment devices such as toys, DVRs, TVs, and music systems
- Home automation items, such as controllers of EVAC, electricity, and lock systems
- Hubs and routers controlling a fleet of other IoT devices
- Medical devices such as drug dispensers and heart monitors
- Office equipment including printers and computer peripherals
- Security alarms and cameras
- Smart appliances such as stoves and refrigerators
- Transportation vehicles and systems, including cars, trains and aircraft
- Wearables such as watches, fitness trackers, and smart clothing.

Hackers can also use IoT devices for such mundane things as DDoS attacks and in Botnets, or accessing and controlling devices using well-worn default passwords and usernames. They can be used to burrow into private networks.

Users of IoT devices seldom know what data the item collects. How data is stored, whether it is encrypted, if there is third party access, and how long the information is retained are other questions that can seldom be answered by IoT users. Opt-out measures, even when available, are usually difficult and often will destroy the usability of the item.

In most cases the IoT should not be considered part of the open source information world. However, because of continuing lack of oversight by manufacturers, coders, and users of the IoT, this area continues to be wide-open for exploitation. Vulnerabilities promise to grow geometrically.

A major search engine that can be used to find IoT resources is **Shodan,** which can be explored at https://www.shodan.io/. An acronym for Sentient Hyper Optimized Data Access Network, Shodan collects data from computer ports making it useful for penetration testing. There is a limited-use free version as well as a for-pay product.

Other IoT sites of interest include:
- **Censys:** https://censys.io/
- **Thingful:** https://www.thingful.net/
- **Zoomeye:** https://www.zoomeye.org/.

Mobile Phones
Mobile phones have become a popular way of accessing the Internet and information. They can be used in the stead of computers for research, but screen size, keyboard size, and a dearth of special research programs – not a lack of computing power – make them last choices for most OSR professionals.

Security is another significant problem when using a cell for OSR. Phones are precise identifiers. A phone is tied to a unique number that can and does identify you in much the same way a Social Security number or home address will. Few people share cell phones or phone numbers, making a number almost as individual as DNA. You, or others, can be traced by the phone number and calls made on it. Phone numbers are included on all sorts of documents and postings. Once s researcher ties a phone number to a person that is gold.

Mobile security is imperative in theory, but scant in reality. Android phones are open source and are unvetted. The IPhone is safer, provided users are careful about the security settings. But safer is not the same thing as safe.

The upshot is that mobile phones, in particular, leak like colanders. This benefits researchers who are on the lookout for others who are using them. But savvy researchers generally stay away from them as a tool. Those who do use them make certain the phone's history is cleared and they take steps to make certain the phone will not show location. For some people using old-style burner phones that may be as simple as removing the battery when not in use, or for many newer phones as difficult at leaving it behind when trying to prevent anyone from tracing your activities and routes.

Phone messaging apps may – or may not – be highly vulnerable to intrusion by intelligence agencies, but they usually are of significant concern.

Private messages are always off limits for OS researchers; none-the-less one-way channels and two-way groups may be accessible for some researchers. Important phone apps include:
- **Telegram:** https://telegram.org/
- **WhatsApp:** https://www.whatsapp.com/.

The ubiquity of phones and cell phones and their reach is, overall, a positive for OSR. Everybody, it seems, has a phone, even grade-schoolers and some of the poorest people in the world. People who don't have running water in third-world countries will often still have a ringing phone.

People tend to break out their cell phones to record unusual, abnormal, or violent events of all types. People post commentary and visuals – still pictures and videos – to social media and photo-sharing sites, or sites such as YouTube. Cell phone users provide more material for researchers than would be available if computers were the only source of postings.

But the yin and yang of mobile phones poses problems for the researcher. Phone numbers are useful identifiers. Postings from phones can provide much good information, particularly in developing disasters. But some parts of the Internet are not computer-friendly. Researchers who want to check sites like Tinder, Snapchat, or YikYak cannot search those sites from their computer. Some portions of the electronic world can only be reached by cell phones. Researchers cannot live with them; they cannot live without them.

For open source researchers the answer to many of the problems is to set up and use one of the many cell phone emulators available for use on the Internet. Most are designed with the game-playing segment of the public in mind, but with some thought they can be used in place of an actual cell for OSR work. Emulators are seldom easy to set up and in many cases are complicated to use. But when you need one they can be a valuable piece of technology to have available. They include:

- **Android Studio:** https://developer.android.com/studio/
- **BigNox:** https://www https://bignox.com/
- **BlueStacks:** https://www.bluestacks.com/
- **Droid4x:** https://droid4x.en.uptodown.com/windows
- **Genymotion:** https://www.genymotion.com/#!/
- **KoPlayer:** http://www.koplayer.com/.
- **PrimeOS (Operating system):** https://primeos.in/.

Another use of the phone for open source researchers is checking phone numbers to confirm the name of the listed owner. This is not always an easy task and it is complicated when people on some sites will list their phone numbers in both numerals and text, as in

123 four five six 7890 or a similar version. They may do so in order to avoid commercial webscrapers who grab numbers and sell them to phone solicitors; they may also do it for reasons that are hardly altruistic or defensive.

Despite the problems of using phones and their numbers, there are online services that can provide information. For those who have a phone number that they want to link with a name, the **CallerIDTest** at https://www.calleridtest.com/ may be helpful.

Others may benefit by using the phone number lookup search boxes that can be found at **ThatsThem,** https://thatsthem.com/, the **TruePeopleSearch** site, https://www.truepeoplesearch.com/#, or the **411.com ($$$$)** site at https://www.411.com/. Many of the background check sites also offer some form of reverse-phone lookup.

***

Project:
In your SOP document write in the techniques section whether you see any possibility of using dumpster diving.

Project:
Whether or not you anticipate using dumpster diving, describe protective measures you will take against the tactic in the security section of your SOP.

Project:
In your SOP describe how or whether you will use a cell phone or emulator and any details about what defensive measures you will employ with phones.

Project:
In your SOP write whether you will explore and use the IoT, and if so indicate how you will learn more about it and access it.

Project:

If you have a need to search in foreign countries, in your SOP outline the techniques you will use to find information if that differs from the method you will use in your home country.

15. Videos, Pictures and Multi-media

Pictures are powerful. They have a significant impact. Pictures may be worth 1,000 words or $1,000. Maybe more, when they are the right ones, haven't been tampered with, and provide the information you need.

For most of history, people learned the things they needed to know in life exclusively through sight and sound, without any ability to read or write. Technology, over the last century and half, is restoring the old ways and degrading the role of reading and writing.

Visuals of all kinds can be as convincing as they are have become pervasive. They appear to be almost synonymous with truth and facts. Photographs and videos have long been touted as the ultimate proof of an event.

That is part of the reason for the ever-growing trend toward the use of all kinds of imaging: video clips, pictures, and multi-media. This is particularly true on Web 2.0 and social media sites. Today's information voyages seem incomplete without pictorial and aural encounters. In fact, the amount of Internet video and still pictures is overtaking, and in some views has already overtaken, text transmission.

It is no longer unusual to see that what previously would have been written text about a subject has now been completely replaced by visual or multi-media files. Even newspaper websites will offer videos alongside, and in some cases in place of, text.

Multi-media and video files are not only growing in popularity on the Web. They have increased the Web's utility but also problems for the researcher. Researchers who ignore or denigrate visual and multi-media resources increasingly fall behind the capability curve.

Photographs, videos, illustrations, and even sound clips – the latter are called actualities – provide context and meaning beyond the sterile textual descriptions of any event, location, person, or item. "Show me, don't tell me," has acquired a whole new meaning.

Multi-media and visuals often add the tone and details that are otherwise unavailable. Small facts are not necessarily insignificant. Some pictures may show identifying marks. Some visuals locate an object in relation to other things. Photographic evidence can also help track where people have been, what they have done, or what is happening at a location.

There is a vast amount of information – large and small – deducible from pictures, multi-media and overheads. These are the basis, along with geoint, for one of the two prongs of modern OSR.

While there is the possibility of using pictures, videos and multi-media for predictive analysis, some of the most useful techniques involve understanding activities that have already taken place. Pictures and videos often function well in documentation.

By using pictorial materials and other multi-media the open source researcher can prove that an event took place, when, where, and who was involved. From war crimes to civil actions, this prong of OSR is useful in providing evidence about actions and events.

Most people are acquainted with the documentary/textual world of online investigation, usually exemplified at the lowest level by putting a word or two into the question box of a search engine. But there is another branch that operates from a geo-centered, image-based, starting point. Location-based questions, or research that starts with a visual record such as a picture or video, take a different path and use a different approach than text-based research.

Bellingcat operators and other users of this evolving open source technique connect a visual of an event to other visuals and use these, along with geo-programs, to establish the time and location. They then employ social media and the plethora of other online resources to round out the story behind the picture.

Researchers using this approach look for buildings of the likely size, vegetation matches, or features that appear similar. They start with large objects that can be identified and move progressively to smaller ones. They narrow the search, "interrogating" photos and videos for all the details that these can reveal.

Clues are found not only in the "big picture" but also in the micro-detail. When viewing pictures or videos, these modern investigators catalog both massive clues such as rivers, mountains, or large buildings as well as the micro-details of objects or sites, such things as color stripes on buildings or even potholes in a road. Recurring patterns, such as one seen on the bottom portion of a largely-hidden fence, become the fingerprints that can confirm a location.

OSR investigators like Bellingcat's know, as did the great detective, that it is important not to overlook anything that could bear on the problem. Anything! "You never learn that the gravest issues may depend on the smallest things." Sherlock Holmes is quoted as saying in *The Adventure of the Creeping Man*.

The location-based searches conducted by Bellingcat, and others like them, use the "smallest things" in research. Some observable factors may be temporal details, ones such as weather, traffic, fuel prices etc. And there are more permanent ones such as building height or a river's path. Everything, from shadow analysis to reflections to advertising and gas prices, may prove to be useful information. Large and small, the visual clues – when put together – form a matrix of incontrovertible evidence.

Some describe the process as a magnifying glass search for details; others may say that they pull back to let the visual "talk to them." Either way, the use of visuals and video evidence is complex and occasionally the visual may be silent or an essential detail may be overlooked.

With any visual take what is available, whether you consider it detailed enough for your needs or not. Use any low quality visuals to look for pictures of better, higher resolution. "Pictures like this" or reverse-image searches may reveal better quality images.

When using photos in searches be aware of things that you don't know – perhaps cannot know. What is behind, on the side of, over, or what you cannot see because of some obstruction are often important. These are the unseen aspects of any scene that make visualizing and finding the actual location problematic.

Understand that distances are hard to estimate in photos; angles are often confusing. Perspective changes perception. It can easily confuse and delude. Perspective's trickery often makes pictures difficult to relate to each other. Always account for perspective.

Light and shadow can be deceptive. "Light spread" is the term of art for the problem of identifying or measuring shiny or light-colored objects in overhead shots, making them appear larger than they actually are. Shadows may obfuscate details, but occasionally they can usefully reveal outlines.

Scraps of visual information, pieces of evidence, can be brought together to achieve stuttering progress.

Searching for exact locations based on photos or videos is often a matter of elimination rather than selection. You make guesses, not all of which turn out to be correct, and sometimes you will be forced to backtrack.

In many searches, particularly photo and geo-searches, drawing a rough map of major features helps you orient yourself, reducing the possibilities to manageable size. That may reduce the researcher to one or two haystacks when searching for those golden needles.

Aerial photography is the precursor of many modern visual OSR techniques. An understanding of that field is useful. While it is important to always keep at least one direction in mind – most people use North – when examining photos taken outside for details, some people use a trick from aerial photography and find it easier to scour for any micro-details by aligning pictures so that shadows fall towards them.

Accessing and examining multi-media files may be relatively easy in comparison with the task of saving some multi-media to your computer. This often proves challenging at the outset. Whenever a researcher lacks the programs, prowess, and experience to save and use multi-media, that person quickly falls behind.

Multi-media – sometimes referred to as audio-visuals – can be of many different types:
- Audios
- Charts
- Graphs
- Illustrations
- Maps
- Photos
- Videos
- Webcamera (Webcam) feeds.

Photos
Finding pictures has been made easy – for anyone who knows what they are doing. Search engines such as Google have made the process relatively simple. Google has a picture search engine that is easily reached by clicking the "Images" link in the upper right hand corner of the splash page. When the photo search page comes up, enter the subject, type of picture, or the identity you are seeking.

The search engine displays pictures that meet Google's digital search algorithm.

Pictures of locations and often-named items are relatively easy to uncover. People, abstract concepts, and less common items are more of a hit-and-miss – or miss-and-hit – proposition.

Particularly with people who are on social media, the face you want may be buried far down among the photos presented or it may not be present at all. If you are searching for people, keep in mind that identifying which of the pictures is the person you are searching for can be a very tedious (sometimes impossible) process that involves eliminating pictures one by one. Click on a picture at some photo sites and that site will take you to the page where the photo originally appeared. This often helps in determining whether the picture is who or what it purports to be. It can also be a security hazard, giving sysops a heads-up about your interest.

Pictures or videos with people in them can sometimes be used to help answer questions of rank or position of influence, based on anything from the captions to the relative positions of people.

Be careful; be very careful with visuals such as pictures and videos.

Years ago a picture was worth a thousand words and was considered irrefutable evidence. That has changed because of "photoshopping" and "deepfake" videos where faces, images, voices, and sound tracks can be seamlessly changed and grafted. Places can be made to appear different. People can be shown engaging in questionable behavior or heard saying things they didn't even think.

Pictures and videos are no longer the incontrovertible evidence they once were, but rather they are just a starting place. From there the researcher has to go on the road to proving their provenance.

Suspect the authenticity of unnatural poses or motions in videos, or of any picture or video that contains no identifiable features.

Google is not alone in picture searches. Other sites, search engines, and directories also have photo libraries; some can be used in a similar manner to the Google photo search site.

- **CC Search (Creative Commons searches):** https://search.creativecommons.org/
- **Flickr:** https://www.flickr.com/
- **Google Search by Image (Chrome Browser):** https://chrome.google.com/webstore/detail/search-by-image-by-google/dajedkncpodkggklbegccjpmnglmnflm?hl=en
- **Photobucket:** http://photobucket.com/
- **PicSearch:** https://www.picsearch.com/image-gallery.html
- **Smugmug**: https://www.smugmug.com/
- **Yahoo Image Search:** https://images.search.yahoo.com/.

With reverse-image searching you can look for matching or similar pictures, often as easily as by dragging the one you already have to the search box or inputting a URL address. Reverse-image search engines will then try to match your photo, including the features of someone in a photo, to pictures that are stored in its database.

Reverse-image searching is also a useful method to determine if a picture of a person is indeed that person, or if the picture has been misappropriated by someone who created a false identity. Personal photos are often misappropriated – let's use the correct term, stolen – from the Web.

The fact that the Internet makes it easy to locate and download a picture of someone, while attaching a new name and *faux* identity to the photograph, makes it far too easy to use stolen pictures when creating fake identities. Reverse-image searching is useful when you have reasons to suspect the provenance of a picture, or even when you have no suspicions but just want proof the picture is legitimate.

Reverse-image searches can be used in other ways, some of which may not be apparent. For instance, pictures can be used to find sites and posts that – for whatever reason – never came up in a search engine's offerings. Sites and posted material you are unaware of may have a photo of a search subject under their own name or an alias, leading to more information that would otherwise be unavailable.

Reverse-images searches may also be useful in gathering a photo album of an event or situation, leading you to a site that may have other useful pictures or videos.

There is a lot more science than magic to the process of reverse-image searches. Internet pictures are not composed of brush strokes or swaths of painted colors and gray tones. They are saved in code, a collection of 1s and 0s. The search engine simply uses an algorithm to match one picture's code to another.

- **Bing Image Search:**
  https://www.bing.com/images/discover?FORM=ILPMFT
- **CamFinds App:** https://camfindapp.com/
- **Google General Image Search:**
  https://www.google.com/imghp
- **KarmaDecay (Reddit search):** http://karmadecay.com/
- **Reverse Image Search:** https://www.image-search.org/
- **Reverse-image Search:**
  https://www.reverse-image-search.com/
- **Tin Eye:** http://www.tineye.com
- **Yandex:** https://yandex.com/support/images/similar.html
- **Wolfram Image ID:** https://www.imageidentify.com/.

Reverse-image photo searches can be hindered and even defeated by any number of techniques. Anything that distorts or changes the digital code – those 1's and 0's – of a computerized picture will stymie effective photo searching. Perhaps the easiest way is by simply "flopping" or "mirroring" the photo, turning it around so the right becomes the left and vice versa. Changing between landscape and portrait formats, or resizing, may also inhibit identification in a reverse-image search, as will "zoom in" cropping that saves only part of a larger picture. Even using a color filter to change the tone of a picture may change the digital code of the file sufficiently to fool reverse-image search algorithms. So will adding some graphics, watermark logos, or voice-overs to alter the digital code.

Assuring the provenance of pictures is a specialized field unto itself. OSR professionals may do it through sites like:

- **Forensically (Photo analysis):** https://29a.ch/photo-forensics/#forensic-magnifier
- **FotoForensics (Photo analysis, jpg and png only):** http://fotoforensics.com/.

Knowledgeable help about photos and whether they have been altered is sometimes available through people on sites like **Reddit Pic Requests:** https://www.reddit.com/r/picrequests/, where photo enthusiasts and correction specialists congregate. The regulars to the site are often helpful to people who have questions about, or problems with, photos. Since many pictures are blurry, Reddit members are often willing to sharpen them, make visible some details that may be important when investigating with photos, or do other things with pictures that may help your research project.

Another resource, when dealing with blurred pictures that have that appear cottony or slightly out of focus is **SmartDeblur:** http://smartdeblur.net/download.html.

While videos still cannot be reverse-searched, thumbnail pictures that are used to promote or identify them can be. If it seems like a long shot, it's at least a shot. Actually, using the thumbnail is often more successful than it might seem at first glance. A reverse-image search on the major search engines, using either the picture itself or imputing the URL of the video thumbnail, can bring up multiple copies of the film clip.

Saving pictures is relatively easy. Virtually all computer set-ups provide that capability. But the "where" is another issue. When saving pictures or any visuals it is important to save them to a single location, using a naming convention that will allow their seamless and quick retrieval.

Meta-tags and Metadata

What most factory computer set-ups lack is an easy way of accessing photo metadata – the data about data. Pictures posted on the Internet often have metadata attached: information about the picture, such as how, where, and when it was taken.

Much of a picture's metadata information may be useless to the researcher, but in some cases the meta-tags will show where the photo was taken, and the date and time. Other information may sometimes be teased out of meta-tags – for instance information on the type of camera may be useful in linking a particular picture to an individual photographer. Flickr does not remove the metadata from pictures posted there. Other sites – such as Facebook – do. But even those that remove metadata from public viewing may retain the original posting. You never know what useful information may be extracted from a picture's meta-tag and metadata until you examine it.

Pictures, particularly those photos posted on social media sites that were taken with mobile phones or cameras that geo-position, will often be geotagged to show where and when they were taken. This can be crucial information when establishing the veracity of data, but since metadata can be spoofed further investigation is always wise. If pictures are not meta-tagged it is often worthwhile to use a reverse-image search and try to find one with metadata. Even if you fail you are no further behind after the abortive try – you didn't have some information before and you still do not have it. Failed searches are considered a wash.

Always try to locate files with the geo-tagged location and the time the picture was taken or uploaded. Mainstream media photos usually are never geotagged so looking for metadata information on news media photos is generally useless.

When checking for geotags you should view the original picture, not a thumbnail, to extract that metadata. This is not always easy or as straightforward as it would seem. Metadata extraction is an entire field of specialization.

There are a number of resources to expose geotags:
- **Camera Summary (EXIF data in jpgs):** https://camerasummary.com/
- **EXIF (Jeffrey's Image Metadata Viewer):** http://exif.regex.info/exif.cgi
- **EXIF-search ($$$$):** https://www.exif-search.com/
- **Find EXIF:** http://www.findexif.com/
- **Metagoofil:** http://www.edge-security.com/metagoofil.php.

Audio-Visuals and Multi-media

Increasingly the Web is moving away from text and toward multi-media.

Many people no longer write about something; they present the subject in a video or in audio format. Some newspapers are even showing audio-visuals on their websites without displaying any text about the same subject, an impossibility, unthought-of only a few years ago.

Today people take and upload videos to the Internet for no apparent reason other than they can. People shoot videos out the windshield as they drive to work or home, videos that may be useful in geolocation. There are social media and dashcam videos, footage from plane or ship spotters, or even video shots taken by people with obsessive personalities. Increasingly the information professionals have to view multi-media as well as text in order to obtain a comprehensive, or even useful, information picture.

Soon, prognosticators say, 80 percent of all online traffic stream will be video-related. Good video searching capabilities, effective video search engines, and download capability are musts for the up-to-date researcher or research desk.

OSR, because it is a system of systems, challenges users to master many programs and technologies. Two programs are indispensable when dealing with multi-media. "Winrar" will open most such files. **Winrar,** at https://www.rarlab.com/download.htm, has a useful trial version. It unpacks like a zip file. To play the wide variety of multi-media files many researchers use the **VLC media player** available at http://www.videolan.org.

Key Video Engines and Resources

- **360 Daily:** http://www.360daily.com/
- **AOL Videos:** https://www.aol.com/video/
- **Bing:** https://www.bing.com/videos/explore?FORM=RECMVI
- **Crowdtangle (Facebook):** https://www.crowdtangle.com/videosearch
- **DailyMotion:** http;// www.dailymotion.com
- **EarthCam:** https://www.earthcam.com/
- **Facebook Livemap:** https://www.facebook.com/watch/
- **Facebook Video:** https://www.facebook.com/pg/facebook/videos/
- **Geosearch Tool:** http://youtube.github.io/geo-search-tool/search.html
- **Google Videos:** https://www.google.com/videohp
- **Instagram:** https://www.instagram.com/
- **Internet Archive:** https://archive.org/details/opensource_movies
- **LiveLeak:** https://www.liveleak.com/
- **MetaCafe:** http://www.metacafe.com/
- **Metatube:** https://www.metatube.com/
- **StartpageImages:** https://www.startpage.com/

- **Veoh:** https://www.veoh.com/
- **Voxalead:** http://voxalead.labs.exalead.com/
- **Vimeo**: https://vimeo.com
- **Yahoo Video Search**: https://video.search.yahoo.com/
- **YouTube:** http://www.youtube.com
- **YouTube Enhancer (Add-on):**
  https://www.mrfdev.com/enhancer-for-youtube
- **YouTube Search Tool:** https://youtube.github.io/geo-search-tool/search.html.

Google and YouTube are considered by many to be among the video leaders, sites where you can find and download almost anything.

Some evidence suggests Google is the better search engine for those seeking something specific in the video, whether it involves fact-checking, how-to, or other informational needs. Video length does not seem to be a factor in Google video searches, but many feel the video quality enters into the Google algorithm.

YouTube appears to be more entertainment oriented, seems to favor longer videos in its searches, and is less focused on quality and sharpness in its rankings. YouTube's "how-to" libraries should never be overlooked by the online researcher.

Many newspapers have websites. Previously their fiber-based format precluded their printed products from using audio-visuals. Now they are rapidly adding videos to their online repertoire. In some cases their video stories are not backed up by text-based versions of the video contents. Their videos may stand alone; if you do not search their videos, or lack the capability of downloading media videos, you are potentially missing a major resource.

Television may have started the latest iteration of the video communication method, but TV users were left to the whims of station executives who decided what to show and when. The

Internet changed that and many online users can now watch the things when they want, in any order that suits their fancy, and pass over the visuals about subjects in which they are uninterested.

Things have changed, but the more they change the more they remain the same. Vision has long been humans' favored way of gaining knowledge. Vision and sound as communication methods came long before the written word. People talked long before they wrote, and what people saw or heard was what people have talked about through the millennia. Writing was invented to memorialize and codify what was seen, heard, or known, but throughout history the vast majority of people had no ability, and often even less need, to understand or use the written word.

Historically, humans have learned visually and aurally. The human learning processes have been largely based on vision and hearing. With a new-found ability to communicate through audio-visuals as easily, if not more easily, than with writing there is every reason to believe videos may well become the preferred method of communication, a method that challenges if it doesn't supersede the written word.

Every cellphone, with its ability to take, save, and upload audio-visuals, threatens the written word as the pre-eminent means of modern communication.

Social media has widely adopted both videos and photos. Literally, billions of them. There are no apparent reasons that the exponential growth will not continue. Social media such as YouTube are part of the change in information processing we are experiencing.

As hundreds of millions of video surveillance cameras photograph the world, and more millions of cell phone cameras click away, the amount of multi-media potentially available is impressive. While much of the results remains locked up and is still not available to information professionals, what is now publicly accessible is often useful. Many photos and videos are shared publicly, often left in storage on photo-sharing sites. Popular sites that are heavily into photo and video sharing are:

- **Flickr:** https://www.flickr.com
- **Google:** https://www.google.com.ua/imghp?hl=en&tab=wi
- **Instagram:** https://www.instagram.com/
- **Photobucket:** http://photobucket.com/
- **YouTube:** https://www.youtube.com/.

Other sites may be of use when working with videos. These include Daily Motion, Forevid, Mega Video, and Veoh, where videos are a mainstay. Many other sites post, or help with, videos as well.

It's generally no problem to look at multi-media files. Just as text files that answer your information questions should be saved, helpful multi-media files also should be safely tucked away on your computer.

Today, saving them is often problematic. Relatively few computers come equipped to automatically save the varied types of multi-media materials that its file systems will open. Special programs are often needed when saving multi-media. Many of the programs are available only at a price. All work a little differently. Their use should be explored but the differences need to be understood by the researcher or research desk before being deployed.

Some allow you to choose the format in which the video will be downloaded, or the resolution. Many information professionals try to maintain consistency in their download formats, but files that might be used in court or administrative procedures should always be downloaded and saved in their original format – if that is known. When it is unknown it is best to download and save the video in every format and size available.

The tools, programs, extensions – and ways – to save videos (and some audio files as well) include:

- **4KVideo Downloader (YouTube):** https://www.4kdownload.com/
- **Archive/Community:** https://archive.org/details/opensource_movies
- **Deturl (Download YouTube and others):** http://deturl.com/www.youtube.com/watch?v=uqnqLrakxY
- **Downface (Facebook download):** http://www.downfacebook.com/
- **Download Helper:** https://www.downloadhelper.net/
- **DownloadStar (Firefox extension):** http://addons.mozilla.org/en-us/firefox/addon/download-star
- **Downsub (File downloads):** http://downsub.com/
- **DownThemAll:** https://www.downthemall.net/
- **FastestTube (YouTube Browser extension):** http://kwizzu.com/
- **FVD Suite (Internet Explorer):** http://download.cnet.com/FVD-Suite-IE-Plugin/3000-12512_4-10822981.html
- **KeepVid ($$$$ for Windows downloads):** http://keepvid.com/
- **Magic Downloader:** https://magicdownloader.com/
- **Movavi ($$$$):** https://www.movavi.com/
- **Replay Capture Suite ($$$$):** https://applian.com/replay-capture-suite/
- **SaveFrom.net (Browser extension):** http://en.savefrom.net/
- **SnagIt ($$$$):** https://www.techsmith.com/screen-capture.html
- **TubeMate (Android):** http://m.tubemate.net/
- **Video Download Helper (Browser extension):** https://addons.mozilla.org/en-US/firefox/addon/video-downloadhelper
- **YouTube5: (Browser extension):** http://www.verticalforest.com/youtube5-extension/

- **YouTube Data Viewer (Metadata, Amnesty Internationsl):** https://citizenevidence.amnestyusa.org/
- **YouTube (Video restriction):** http://polsy.org.uk/stuff/ytrestrict.cgi?ytid=vg7wh_zf2X0
- **YTD Video Downloader:** http://download.cnet.com/YTD-Video-Downloader/3000-2071_4-10647340.html.

Livestreaming videos, sent and received in real time, may not be searchable. Unless captured in the minute, some of it sinks into the ether. Currency is the watchword when dealing with livestreaming sites. However such sites have their place in OSR, particularly with developing incidents. Sites and services to become acquainted with include:

- **Bambuser ($$$$):** https://bambuser.com/
- **Livestream ($$$$):** https://livestream.com/
- **Periscope:** https://www.pscp.tv/
- **Snapchat:** https://www.snapchat.com/.
- **Watson-IBM ($$$$):** https://video.ibm.com/
- **YouNow:** https://www.younow.com/.

Deepfakes

Photoshopping, airbrushing, and Deepfake videos have devalued pictures, and now videos, to the point that many aren't worth a plug nickel as proof. Although still photos were devalued as proof of anything in the Photoshop era, videos seemed to be authentic beyond question. Until about 2017.

Deepfakes have given a new and ominous meaning to the phrase "Who you gonna believe, me or your lyin' eyes." Deepfakes prove you simply cannot believe everything you see.

Deepfakes – those ultra-realistic fake videos generated by artificial intelligence software that purport to show a person doing something they haven't done or perhaps even saying something they haven't said in a language they don't speak – are a relatively recent Web innovation.

Deepfakes are not dubbing; they are the manufacture of a new film clip that recreates sights and sounds. They provide "photographic evidence" of something having been said or done – when nothing was said or done.

Software that effectively clones voices can be, and has been, paired with Deepfake video to create a virtual – although totally false – soundtrack that matches a visual presentation. Done skillfully, such a forged video can even be produced in a language that the person in the video neither speaks nor understands, literally putting words in people's mouths. Skill, processing power, patience, and time are the key elements in the creation of believable Deepfakes.

In the first years of these deceptively realistic computer-generated videos, they gained traction largely as fake porn. They were used to humiliate or harass women, but they have now evolved to the point of being weaponized against celebrities, politicians – or anybody for any purpose. Their development greatly adds to the effectiveness of propaganda, misinformation, and political or social sabotage. Most of the uses found thus far for Deepfakes are far from positive. Deepfakes have been largely produced by the mischief-prone and can negatively affect jobs, reputation, personal relationships, and ultimately even a person's mental health.

For the most part, Deepfakes have been face-swaps, putting an identifiable face on another body. But the technology can be used to alter any part of a video, changing one document into another in one example.

Deepfake creation tools are readily available and are often free. Some can be found in Google's artificial-intelligence library.

The Deepfake creation process is time consuming but it is no longer complicated. It is not a matter of simply grafting a face on a body, but of creating and using a variety of different facial positions to simulate the movements of a human face. Until 2019 the major problem was collecting enough photographs that would allow a sophisticated computer to draw people in successive frames. It required several hundred still photos or a single target video to develop a good Deepfake video. When the photo collection was large enough, or a video of the target was available, the program would find and match facial expressions, seamlessly replacing and adjusting them about five dozen times a second. New developments now allow passable Deepfakes to be created using a single still photo.

Essentially the algorithm that produces a Deepfake uses an existing picture and treats that visual as if parts of it are distorted. It uses the "correction" pictures or frames, morphing them in, "fixing" the supposedly-distorted video. The Deepfake algorithm makes frame-by-frame "corrections," a process that takes both time and heavy computing power.

Deepfakes are increasingly challenging to detect.

While Deepfake videos range widely in their overall quality, the technology and the capabilities at the high end are improving rapidly. Poor Deepfakes are generally easy to spot. Well-done ones – not so much. Although experts can generally find some glitch or anomaly, average users find it difficult to identify decent Deepfakes.

As a result, open source researchers now need to be aware that any video could be a fake.

A growing community of Deepfake artists on discussion boards and chat rooms is producing many how-to documents, offering advice and selling their services to those lacking the needed qualifications, computing power, and talents. The going price for producing some Deepfakes is reportedly as low as $20.

The best defense against Deepfakes starts with keeping an open mind. Avoid jumping to any conclusions – especially the conclusion that what you see is reality. Then consider the source; questionable or unknown sources increase the likelihood the video is a Deepfake. See if the clip appears elsewhere or is vouched for by a reliable source. If it does come from a good source that reduces, but cannot eliminate, the possibility it is a Deepfake. The lack of a second, reliable, source is suggestive the clip may be a Deepfake. Likewise, if the clip shows or suggests something that is "unbelievable" on its face, the clip probably isn't legitimate.

At present, the creation process is convoluted enough and fraught with so many quirky problems that most Deepfake videos are short. The longer a Deepfake video runs the more problems are likely to undercut its claim to veracity. Faces that don't seem "quite right" or are "weird" are often major giveaways. A waxy look, features that don't quite line up, and anomalies around the face are other indications the video might be a Deepfake.

Watch the mouth. Teeth and tongue may not be accurately shown by some Deepfakes. In much the same way as lip readers match changes of lip and mouth positions to the verbiage, video footage that doesn't track correctly with the sound, or bad lip synching, is a tip-off. The lack of an audio track where one is to be expected is also suggestive of a Deepfake. And a voice that doesn't sound quite like the person being portrayed may also be a clue.

Deepfake faces may flicker, particularly if the creation program wasn't run long enough or the computer was not powerful enough to properly remove and replace all the features on each frame shown in the original video. Watch carefully at the edges of the face; that is where anomalies are most likely to be apparent.

Body matches are problematic to make perfectly. Any differences in weight, height, or body marks such as tattoos or moles may be a giveaway. If the body doesn't match, the likelihood is great that the video is a Deepfake.

When OSR practitioners have questions, they often slow the video speed. Anomalies often show more starkly at slower speeds.

Deepfakes are not the only problem with videos, though they are a concern. Simple things – like editing in repeated frames to make Hitler "dance" at the surrender of France – illustrate how long video fakements have been around. Simply slowing the frame rate can simulate drunkenness. Speeding up, slowing down, or multiplying parts of the frame display can also affect the visual effect.

Webcams

There are millions of Webcams in operation but finding the ones you need, the ones that will provide the information you or your sponsor require, is usually – at best – a chore.

Webcams pose a variety of security issues that should be considered before any search. Webcam directories and search engines are sometimes targeted by spammers and hackers who place their own sites at the top of the list, even though they don't belong there. Webcam sites may be designed to lure users in, and then use redirection or malware insertion techniques. Researchers are wise to use heavy duty security software on both the browser and computer when searching for Webcams; it is important to be ultra-cautious when clicking links to anything but the most mundane travel sites.

Some Webcams show certain popular scenes or business locations – and these are usually the ones listed in Webcam directories. Some Webcam live feeds – those that are not listed on the specialized directories – often result from people misconfiguring their cameras. People will buy a device to allow them to keep an eye on something – a building entrance, a baby's room, a commercial area

– but do not set up the online feed properly. These misconfigured cameras may sometimes be found by using the same methods and sites used for gaining information on the Internet of Things (IoT). A potential resource to find the misconfigured equipment is **Shodan** at https://www.shodan.io/. Some Webcam sites include:

- **Airport Webcams:** http://airportwebcams.net/
- **CAMSCAPE:** http://www.camscape.com/
- **EarthCam:** http://www.earthcam.com/
- **Fisgonia:** http://www.fisgonia.com/
- **Insecam (Security cameras):** http://www.insecam.org/
- **Leonard's Cam World:** http://www.leonardsworlds.com/camera.html
- **Lookr:** https://www.lookr.com/
- **OpenStreetCam:** https://openstreetcam.org/map/
- **Opentopia:** http://www.opentopia.com/
- **Pictimo:** https://www.pictimo.com/
- **Reolink (Unsecured camera list):** https://reolink.com/unsecured-ip-camera-list/
- **Web Cam Directories**: http://www.leonardsworlds.com/webcam_directories/webcam_directories.htm
- **Webcam Network Project:** http://www.the-webcam-network.com/
- **WebCams SkiWillie:** http://skiwillie.com/cams.htm
- **WebCams Travel:** https://www.webcams.travel/
- **Worldcam.eu**: https://worldcam.eu/
- **World Webcams:** http://world-webcams.nsspot.net/.

Multi-media Tools

Multi-media exploitation sometimes requires a variety of special tools. Some tools used to create and edit audio-visuals include:

- **FilmicPro (App enhances iPhone video):** http://www.filmicpro.com/
- **Photo Mechanic ($$$$):** http://www.camerabits.com/.

Satellites and Overheads

Satellite imagery – often called "overheads" – has been a favorite of researchers, both government and civilian, for decades. Satellite photography was formerly the exclusive province of First World governments. No longer. Government overheads have gotten clearer and more detailed, but even the commercially available overheads offered today get better all the time. Highly usable overheads are available for free on the Internet now, or from private providers for a fee.

Imaging satellites are not spy satellites. Their overheads are used for everything from crop measurement to urban planning – and always for national defense and security purposes.

Overheads have definite limits. They can show a car but can't give you a clue where the driver intends to go or what the passenger is saying. Overheads provide an incomplete picture. But correctly used and properly interpreted, they are invaluable when trying to plot or triangulate where an event took place. Good overheads are error-free maps, but no map is considered a real-time depiction.

Commercial satellites – particularly those associated with European-based providers – now provide excellent resolution. Overheads vary in resolution in part because of government restrictions in some areas. The current product has such high definition capabilities that some countries force commercial vendors to reduce the quality and resolution of imagery that they provide. How enforceable that will be worldwide remains a question.

Assume the best overheads available to open source researchers may be detailed enough that you can see a newspaper on the ground but you will not be able to read the headline. Still, even at the Google Earth resolutions, overheads are useful for many research needs.

As accurate as overheads have gotten, what is now available on some commercial and public sites is not always completely trustworthy. Images of important governmental offices and sites, and likely terrorist targets in some countries, have been "fuzzed" or even wiped out and replaced with what appears to be empty terrain. Like Soviet-era maps, there is an inherent unreliability in some online overheads, particularly those showing military and government sites, or war zones. For that reason it is wise to use several different sites and overhead providers. The images one provider fuzzes out or replaces, complying with a government's orders, may be left just as the camera saw and shot it when you access sites that are not under that government's control.

Satellites photograph in different bands of light. They even use radar and lidar (light employed in much the same way as radar, measuring distances accurately) to see through clouds or for other purposes. Everything from geology and moisture to vegetation and natural color shades may be shown in satellite photography.

Overheads get better all the time. Work is underway to develop algorithms that will automatically classify objects, buildings, and uses based on their appearance in overheads – now a frustrating and time-consuming effort that must still be done by humans.

Any extensive use of satellite photography will push OSR operators toward developing wide-ranging knowledge about available satellites and their capabilities, including what satellites take pictures in what bands and what the best uses are for each.

Sites such as the **Sentinel Hub** at https://www.sentinel-hub.com/ provide a basic introduction to the various bands. The products are based on overheads from a number of different satellites.

Other help may be available from members of the coterie of satellite aficionados that has grown up online. Like plane watchers and ship watchers they can provide useful help to open source researchers.

***

Project:
Open your SOP file. Research the types of programs needed to save multi-media and overheads. Indicate the sites or programs you plan to use, and why.

16. GEO Searches

Maps and mapping are breaking out all over.

Maps have been providing two-dimensional "here-to-there" (or "there-to-here") information for thousands of years. In the past, maps were limited to a few lines, squiggles, some labels, a little bit of text, and perhaps a few numbers showing distances, heights or depths. Even the best maps were essentially "flat earth" depictions.

Fiber maps serve a purpose but are seriously limited in how much information they contain.

Fiber maps are not reality – they are "drawn" and thus discard some facts and much reality in favor of some other selected set of information.

Fiber maps still exist; they remain useful, even with all their limitations. But modern geo-information goes far beyond the two-dimensional paper map, moving into three dimensions and even a fourth dimension (adding changes over time).

Cartographic literacy has become increasingly important as a new generation struggles to discern what is, and what isn't, a fact as shown on a map.

Cartography and geography have morphed into the Geographic Information System (GIS), an ever-expanding field that answers the questions of "what" and even "when" as well as the "where?"

Mapmakers use digital mapping, geo-mapping, to effectively attach a book of data to the limited information previously available on a map. Maps always organized information but today the range of information available through modern mapping – geo-mapping – has become an information ecosystem.

Digital mapping is an information-intensive evolution that is really a revolution.

Geospatial information systems allow a better understanding of the physical, social, and other environments associated with a "place." Geographical information systems often provide topographic, aeronautical, hydrographic, cultural, and social data or other types of information that improve understanding.

Knowledge of geosystems is important for every researcher, but for some it is vital. Geospatial information is at the center of a highly-effective method of research, developed to a fine point by the Bellingcat organization. That system, further described in the next chapter, uses pictures or visuals to establish the what, when, how, and place (where). But whether a researcher uses the Bellingcat model, or relies more heavily on other traditional techniques, an understanding of basic geosystem use is vital in any open source research today.

Mapping Basics

Every map is made up of points, lines and polygons – these are the basics of maps. Points may be a city or an address in that city; lines may be highways or borders; polygons may be buildings or outlines of voting areas.

It is wise to think of any map as a document.

That document may be two-dimensional, single-themed, printed, or drawn within four corners, as in a gas station road map.

On the other hand, many modern maps are digital multi-dimensional documents replete with extensive text, many pop-ups, pictures, and even attached databases. In fact, modern computer mapping programs are based on material contained in a database which "draws" the base map and the other useful "layers."

Maps of all types have three things in common:
- Scale or distances
- Projection
- Symbols.

Any of this trio, along with a fourth – outright fudging – can lead to map misinformation.

Maps portray many things incorrectly – in fact every map distorts at least one of four things: shapes, sizes, distances, and directions. No map can get everything correct.

Accuracy in distances and area sizes are usually the essential considerations of map users so map makers often correct for those first.

The basic problem with maps – and the partial solution to the problem – is found in a single word: projection. A map's projection converts part of the earth's sphere onto a flat surface; the result is literally a squaring of the circle. What are represented as straight lines on a map are actually arcs – whether they be tiny ones or large ones..

To use any map effectively the researcher or research desk has to understand map projections and the special terms that are used by each mapping program. Without an understanding of mapping terminology, and the projections used, the charted information can be wildly incorrect.

Projection, as basic as it may be, is only one example of mapping problems.

Scale and symbology are other important factors in using any map effectively. But positioning is the central factor.

Latitude and longitude on maps should pinpoint locations. But perturbations in the earth and mapping programs make the exactness of any location questionable. The earth is neither flat nor perfectly smooth. Even with the best mapping techniques, the locations of sites or buildings may be off by a few feet or even more. Geocoding can never be considered inches-accurate.

In short, the effective use of maps – particularly digital mapping programs – requires more than a passing knowledge of the field. Knowing how to refold a roadmap is never enough.

Common modern mapping programs include ARCGis, ArcView, Google Earth Pro, Mapitude, MapInfo and the European MAPS.

Geo-information Sources

- Land and property records (cadastre) are basic to most developed societies. These ownership records and parcel data often are essential elements of information in any open source research. Those records are often part of many geosearches. This is information that is generally available at government offices or at the businesses which specialize in providing such information – usually at a price. Cadastre are often text records; they may be either digital or fiber-based.

Besides cadastral records, the range of open geo-sources is wide and varied. Important geo-information sources include:
- Paper maps, atlases, magazines, and periodicals
- Social media
- Brochures and gray literature
- Databases
- Photos (still imagery), videos, and webcam imagery (motion imagery)
- Commercial imagery
- Dissertations

- Digital resources (Internet and non-Internet).

Paper maps covering a large area must distort at least some features; distortions may be minimized by good digital mapping that simulates three dimensions but distortions are endemic in fiber maps.

Modern digital maps – often referred to as KML or KMZ files – improvements. They are information-rich products. Today, in the digital mapping world, it is possible to link large amounts of data to a map. Overlays and popups provide reams of data that could never before be displayed within the four corners of a paper map.

Modern mapping is about an area and potentially everything (and everyone) in that area. It can include everything from the chemical make-up of the earth below to the stars that can be seen above. Modern mapping is both visual and visualizing, integrating data of any kind with a specific location in order to make sense of a subject.

Today's digital map is not necessarily limited to questions about travel to or from some place; it's also about what's there, was there, or will be there. It may be about cities on land, vegetation in the landscape, patterns of life, and even the contours of the dry seabed on Mars, the craters of the moon, or any part of the universe. Maps extend beyond the earth.

Dynamic terrain visualizations – often called fly-throughs – are a major part of the geo-data world today.

Researchers need to look at the possibility that geo-searches and spatial analysis might provide useful information about subjects seemingly unrelated to maps. Many discover this a hard concept to get their head around.

It is as difficult to understand the possibilities of geospatial research as it is to properly fold a roadmap; neither is intuitive. Location logic is non-traditional.

Working with digital maps and images forces the researcher or research desk to be constantly aware of what they are doing. The resolution – measurement of the smallest discernable detail – varies and must be known and understood. Load time on computers may be long for large, detailed, files. Many mapping programs date their work because the images shown are not in real time. Coordinates that provide the location within several feet are sometimes available. Measuring distance and even areas on some digital maps may be simplified by internal programs that do the calculations. However, calculations may be in feet and inches or in the metric system, therefore requiring conversion.

Concepts often cannot be mapped effectively but anything that is located somewhere always has geospatial possibilities. If there is any geographical element, geospatial research can be brought into play.

In the modern age many consider geospatial research to have a special language all its own; like any foreign language it must be studied, learned, spoken, and practiced.

Digital maps are often layered, containing stacks of information that can be turned on or off with a mouse click. They may be a map mashup, providing users with information from several sources. All maps, including digital ones, are not real-time displays but a very few, such as traffic maps, may contain current depictions of an ever-changing situation.

There is a tendency among beginning users to leave all the layers of digital maps showing, because they provide so much information. That may be too much information. Most information professionals select only the map layers that are likely to answer their needs. Too many layers may confuse the picture.

Paper maps, on the other hand, are a single layer thick; what you see is what you've got. That may not be enough.

Paper maps have a fixed scale; in digital mapping zooming in for granularity and zooming out for "the big picture" are common so scales often vary widely in the same geo-document.

Pop-ups of information about features shown on the geo-document are common in digital maps. A digital map can often be likened to a database. Sometimes the information in that database is shown symbolically by colors or symbols; at other times pop-ups, when clicked or moused-over on a digital map, provide information that no paper map can.

Basemaps are the layer that provides the location context for digital maps. They are the simple "where" structure used to build up from, like a building's foundation. Other layers of data are constructed or "stacked" atop the basemap to provide granular information on one or more location-related subjects. Those operational layers may show anything that the mapmaker wants to illustrate, from fishing holes to city planning features. Common layers of digital maps may include:

- Governmental boundaries
- Buildings and property lines (cadastral data)
- Roads
- Terrain features and elevations
- Land uses
- Parks and open spaces
- Climatology
- Vegetation
- Utilities
- Businesses
- Transportation features

- Demographic, population, employment or political data
- Disease or health information
- Street level imagery
- Satellite or overhead imagery.

Mapping tools meet the challenge of providing quick and shareable information to improve geographical literacy.

Not every researcher or research desk needs to access the full range of geo-sites available, but most operators require a minimum geo-capability. Atlases, map collections, mapping sites, and postal zone lookups are among the generally used geo-sites.

Mapping Programs

Google sites are much-used for geographical information in the Western world. Mapping sites and online programs often offer researchers a wide choice of capabilities and views.

Google Earth is widely used in the West. It has far more features and capabilities than Google Maps. Google Earth Pro has numerous capabilities, including adding and subtracting information layers, displays of decades of historical imagery, or measurement of distance, perimeters, and area. The "pro" program originally came with a price tag, however now **Google Earth,** found at https://www.google.com/earth/download/gep/agree.html, is free. Easily-overlooked features on the site are the geographic coordinates of the selected site, shown at the bottom of the display, and the historical imagery (clock) in the set of icons at the top of the display. It often helps to see how an area built up or changed over the years. Clicking on the clock brings up a slider bar that will allow users to go back in time. While the historical imagery is one of the most used of the icons, mapping users usually become familiar with all of the capabilities allowed by the various icons.

Other programs, such as **ArcGIS** at https://www.esri.com/en-us/arcgis/trial, are more costly but can be tested or used in a free trial.

The capabilities of the various geo-programs are extensive, but vary with the particular program.

Ground level "street views" and rotation arrows on some mapping sites allow users to digitally "walk the neighborhood."

Map motion imagery may be collected at one frame per second or faster – fast enough to show movement – but it is often shown at no less than 30 frames per second. The display frame rate of motion imagery is generally similar to television, 24 to 60 frames per second.

Some programs, including Google Earth, offer 3D buildings and line-of-sight features that allow realistic views of what can be seen and what the area actually looks like. Tilting and the addition of variable horizons allow users to see an area in ways that no flat map can ever show.

Most digital mapping programs start from a distant view and allow users to incrementally move closer to a selected location by clicking with a mouse.

The mapping constellation is large and includes line maps, detailed maps, aerial/satellite photos, and hybrid types that include information such as street names, identities of buildings, and business locations. Key map-related sites include:
- **AD Contour Maps:** http://field.hypermart.net/
- **Acme Mapper:** http://mapper.acme.com/
- **All The Worlds Maps:**
  http://www.embassyworld.com/maps/maps.html
- **ArcGIS Explorer:** http://www.esri.com/arcgis/about-arcgis

- **ArcGIS Pro ($$$$):** http://www.esri.com/en/arcgis/products/arcgis-pro/overview
- **Baidu Maps:** https://map.baidu.com
- **BB Bike (Map comparison):**
- **Bing Maps:** https://www.bing.com/maps
- **CIA World Fact Book:** https://www.cia.gov/library/publications/the-world-factbook/
- **Crime Mapping and Analysis News:** https://crimemapping.info/
- **CrimeReports (Crime Maps):** https://www.crimereports.com/
- **CTRLQ (Address lookup on Google Maps):** https://ctrlq.org/maps/address/
- **David Rumsey Historical Map Collection:** http://www.davidrumsey.com/
- **Directions Magazine:** https://www.directionsmag.com
- **Dominoc925 (Military coordinates, location):** https://dominoc925-pages.appspot.com/mapplets/cs_mgrs.html
- **Dual Maps (Mashup):** https://www.mapchannels.com/DualMaps.aspx
- **Eaton Blackout and Power Outage Tracker (US):** http://powerquality.eaton.com/blackouttracker/default.asp
- **ESRI GIS Mapping Software:** https://www.esri.com/en-us/home
- **Falling Rain (Gazetteer):** http://www.fallingrain.com/world/index.html
- **Findlatitudeandlongitude:** https://www.findlatitudeandlongitude.com/
- **Flickr Maps:** https://www.flickr.com/map
- **Follow Your World (Imagery update notifications for Google sites):** https://followyourworld.appspot.com

- **Freeality.com Maps and Driving Directions:** http://www.freeality.com/maps.htm
- **GeoNames (Gazeteeer):** http://www.geonames.org/
- **GeoSpatial World Magazine (Mapping information):** https://www.geospatialworld.net/
- **GIS Bing.com/Maps:** https://www.bing.com/maps?FORM=Z9LH2
- **GIS in the Earth Sciences & Map Library (No longer maintained):** http://www.lib.berkeley.edu/EART/gis.html
- **GISPortal:** http://www.gisportal.com
- **Global Incident Map:** http://www.globalincidentmap.com/
- **Google Earth:** https://www.google.com/earth/
- **Google Follow your World: (Map change alert):** https://followyourworld.appspot.com/
- **Google Maps:** https://www.google.com/maps/
- **GPSVisualizer (Geocode):** https://www.gpsvisualizer.com/
- **GRASS (Open source GIS download):** https://grass.osgeo.org/download/software/ms-windows/
- **Here (Location platform, $$$$):** https://www.here.com/
- **Historic Aerials ($$$$):** https://www.historicaerials.com/
- **ICC Live Piracy Map:** https://www.icc-ccs.org/piracy-reporting-centre/live-piracy-map
- **Inspire (European geospatial data sets):** http://inspire-geoportal.ec.europa.eu/
- **Kakaomap (Korean):** https://map.kakao.com/
- **Latitude (Location conversion):** https://latitude.to
- **Latlong (Coordinate finder):** https://www.latlong.net/
- **Latitude/Longitude Distance Calculation:** http://jan.ucc.nau.edu/~cvm/latlongdist.html
- **LeMonde Diplomatique-Cartographie:** http://www.monde-diplomatique.fr/cartes/
- **Library of Congress Maps:** https://loc.gov/maps/collections/

- **Mapillary (Imagery, $$$$):** https://www.mapillary.com/
- **MapLandia Gazetteer:** http://www.maplandia.com/
- **Maps Mania (Google Earth mashups):** http://googlemapsmania.blogspot.com/
- **Mappy (Europe):** https://mappy.com/
- **MapQuest Complete List of Maps:** https://www.mapquest.com/
- **Maps of China:** http://www.maps-of-china.com/index.shtml
- **MarineTraffic.com (Shipping map):** http://www.marinetraffic.com/
- **MashedWorld:** http://www.mashedworld.com/
- **Maxar/DigitalGlobe (Commercial imagery):** https://www.digitalglobe.com/products/satellite-imagery
- **N2YO (Real-time Satellite tracking):** http://www.n2yo.com
- **National Geographic Maps:** http://www.nationalgeographic.com/maps/
- **Newspaper Map:** http://newspapermap.com/
- **NGA-GEOnet Names Server:** http://geonames.nga.mil/gns/html/
- **NGA Github (Map tools):** https://github.com/ngageoint
- **NIJ Mapping for Public Safety:** https://www.nij.gov/topics/technology/maps/pages/welcome.aspx
- **OpenStreetMap:** https://www.openstreetmap.org/
- **Perry-Castañeda Library Map Collection:** https://legacy.lib.utexas.edu/maps/
- **Perry-Castañeda Library Map Collection – Maps on Other Sites:** https://legacy.lib.utexas.edu/maps/map_sites/map_sites.html
- **Quick Maps:** https://theodora.com/maps/abc_world_maps.html
- **ReliefWeb:** http://www.reliefweb.int/mapc/

- **Routeview:** http://routeview.org/VirtualRide/
- **Site Atlas:** http://www.sitesatlas.com/
- **SpotCrime (Crime Maps):** https://www.spotcrime.info/
- **SunriseSunset:** http://sunrisesunset.com/
- **Terraserver ($$$$, Satellite and aerial photos):** http://www.terraserver.com/
- **The Internet Map (Visual display of websites by country affiliation):** http://internet-map.net
- **The National Map: (USGS Topographic information):** https://nationalmap.gov/
- **ThoughtCo (Indice):** https://www.thoughtco.com/geography-4133035
- **Topozone (USGS topo maps):** https://www.topozone.com/
- **United Nations Geospatial Information:** http://www.un.org/Depts/Cartographic/english/htmain.htm
- **United Nations Map Library:** http://research.un.org/en/maps
- **Universal Postal Union (International Zipcodes):** http://www.upu.int/en/the-upu/member-countries.html
- **USGS:** https://earthexplorer.usgs.gov/
- **Ushahidi ($$$$, Crowd-sourced crisis maps):** https://www.ushahidi.com/
- **USPostal Zip Code Lookup:** https://tools.usps.com/go/ZipLookupAction_input
- **ViaMichelin:** https://www.viamichelin.com/
- **Wigle (Wi-Fi networks):** https://wigle.net/
- **Windows Live Local:** https://www.bing.com/maps/
- **World Aeronautical Database:** http://worldaerodata.com
- **World Atlas:** http://www.worldatlas.com/
- **Yandex Maps: (Russian site):** https://yandex.com/maps/
- **ZoomEarth:** https://zoom.earth/.

***

Project:

In your SOP's Geosearch section indicate whether you will use geographic sites, and if so, how you plan on using them.

Project:

List in the SOP the URLs of geographic sites you will use in any research and your other endeavors.

Project

If you plan to use Google Earth Pro, list in your SOP the various resources and capabilities that you might want to utilize in your searches and what icon they are associated with on the bar at the top of the display.

17. Location-based Searching

Internet users are well-acquainted with the documentary and textual world of investigation. It is exemplified, at the lowest level, by putting a word or two into the search engine's question box. But another branch of Open Source Research is founded on geo-centered, image-based, techniques.

Location-based research, which usually starts from a visual record such as a picture or video, approaches OSR differently from the search box technique. The search box technique comes straight from the OSINT field of intelligence agencies. Bellingcat's method, instead, borrows its techniques and tactics from the intelligence world's field of Geo-intelligence (GEOINT) and the GEOINT subfield called Image Intelligence (IMINT).

Location-based research is so different that it requires a chapter of its own. While it supplements rather than replaces other traditional open source research techniques, it is often – and successfully – used as the primary search method. The location-based reactive process yields information over time as well as in space. Proven power lies in this challenging process.

In recent times one name has stood out in the use of this technique – the Bellingcat collective. Bellingcat-associated researchers have crowd-sourced their work and presented their evidence against a variety of powerful governments and national militaries, proving the viability of their techniques against some of the toughest targets on the planet.

One of their several strengths lies in their collaboration, combining their individual personal expertise and dogged persistence with the formidable abilities of many others. Their ever-expanding body of work affirms the power of non-linear thinking, thinking outside the box of conventional OSR techniques that has been so common in the past.

While Bellingcat's location-based method can occasionally be skewed toward predictive ends, it is generally reactive in nature. Location-based research methods are most effective when they are rearward looking. Reactive research is highly effective in gathering evidence and "proving" past events.

More like police than intelligence agents, users of this method deal largely with what has happened rather than what will happen. They are, unquestionably, the Sherlock Holmeses of OSR.

Location-based searching can be no less frustrating than other types of OSR, but the practitioners have proved trial and error becomes trial and success as the researchers first match up large details about locations and finally the small ones – literally down to cracks and dents.

Location-based searching often begins with the "what." The "what" is the one known factor – it is whatever event is shown in the video or the visual being scrutinized.

When starting any location-based search, think "place" first. Search planning, as described earlier, has to be altered somewhat in order to meet the requirements of location-based searches.

Location – the Where

The realtor's mantra, "location, location, location" can easily be repurposed for map-based techniques. All research requires verification at some stage. But early – even immediate – verification of the location is essential in the Bellingcat method. Location is key.

The visual research method is based on the assumption that some event – whatever is shown in a picture or video – took place at a particular time and that you can somehow geo-locate that event. Where and when did the event displayed in the source visual – either the video or photo – take place? That is the central question.

Location-based research matches clues seen in the visual source, things that are visible in a picture or video being investigated, to similar elements shown in other reference visuals. Matching the identifiable features visible in the source pictorials to similar things shown in the reference material proves legitimacy and accuracy. Moreover it may provide important context.

With location-based research, establishing the "where" and "when" is essential during the very earliest phases. The proof of time and location, and the linkage of the two – this is what happened at a particular site at a particular time – is referred to as "temporal location." It undergirds the method.

Every place, every square foot of water, land, or ice on earth can be given some type of address. Events can be geo-located accurately; they must be pinpointed for this technique to work.

Geo-locations are usually expressed in one of two major formats, either as decimals or by their coordinates. Other geolocation formats exist, particularly in the military, but for the most part researchers employ one of these two types: decimals or coordinates.

Cartographers generally divide the world into halves – above the equator or below the equator and east or west of the prime meridian, which passes through the Greenwich observatory in England.

Cartographers write coordinates (latitude and longitude) in the DMS system (degrees, minutes, seconds either east, west, north or south of the lines) or, alternatively, as decimal degrees.

Latitude is, by common usage and agreement, the first number; the second figure is longitude.

Geographic coordinates are often expressed in the DMS (degrees, minutes, seconds) system. The US Capitol is listed at Latitude: 38° (degrees) 53' (minutes) 23.28" (seconds) N and Longitude: 77° (degrees) 00' (minutes) 32.3316" (seconds) W. In decimal notation the US Capitol would be at Latitude: 38.889800, Longitude: 77.008981, give or take a few numerals depending on what part of the building you are measuring from.

Conversion of latitude and longitude between the DSM and decimal systems is problematic for most people but is made easier by the **Federal Communications Commission converter tool** found at https://www.fcc.gov/media/radio/dms-decimal.

Expect the final digits in any geographic coordinate to differ slightly in any geospatial rendering since the measurement may be made from different points of the same site.

Details

The substance of location-based research relies on identifying the details shown in the source visual so that they can be matched against details, both large and small, that appear in other visuals of the same location.

With all location-based searching a secondary mantra to "location, location, location" has to be "details, details, details."

Details, details, details – these all matter, as Sherlock Holmes explained to Watson in *The Boscombe Valley Mystery*. "You know my method. It is founded on the observation of trifles." The importance of even the tiniest details was reinforced in *The Man with the Twisted Lip.* "It is of course, a trifle, but there is nothing so important as trifles," Sherlock Holmes is reputed to have said.

As Holmes would have agreed, matching the trifling details of source visuals to the details shown in reference materials requires care and persistence in first identifying as many features as possible in the source material. Linking visible details in the source material to the matching details in reference materials is central to location-based research.

Source visuals that are short on discernable details may make this method difficult. When the source picture or video lacks details; when the source could have been taken "anywhere" at "any time" this method has hit a wall.

Tricks of the trade are many in location-based research.

In some cases photo stitching, with what is often called panorama software, may help in determining location because the "big picture" may better display those details that can be matched. Photo stitching combines several images that have overlapping fields of view, in effect creating a picture that would have been taken with a wide-angle lens, a picture that provides many more clues. Photo stitching requires careful attention in order to prevent misalignment. Many software companies provide useful demo versions. Software is available from:

- **AutoStitch ($$$$):** http://matthewalunbrown.com/autostitch/autostitch.html
- **EasyPano Panoweaver: ($$$$)** http://www.easypano.com/panorama-software.html
- **Hugin:** http://hugin.sourceforge.net/
- **Photostitcher ($$$$):** https://www.photostitcher.com/.

Location-based research also commonly uses other methods and techniques that are seldom found in text-based investigations.

Overlays of multiple images taken from videos can improve some pictures that are fuzzy. This, again, is one of those techniques that requires a researcher to learn specialized methods, use special tools, or call for help from specialists. Reddit members are often willing to sharpen fuzzy photos and bring up some otherwise-invisible details. Reddit's **Pic Requests,** found at https://www.reddit.com/r/picrequests/, may provide people who are willing to help. A do-it-yourself answer to blurry pictures is **SmartDeblur:** http://smartdeblur.net/download.html.

In overhead photos, particularly those of metro areas, the types of roof tops may be used for finding a location. Some researchers will create a lettered chart – a, b, c, d, etc. – of different roof types, noting what they are looking for as if it were a "word" made up of the letters on the chart. That way entire streets of houses can be searched by looking at a sequence of roofs as if they were the "word."

In some countries government buildings are built to a common floor plan and design, something that may help with geolocation of some official structures.

Searchers use many clues and helpful work-arounds when trying to pinpoint exact locations. The **Open Street Map** site found at https://www.openstreetmap.org/ is often useful in locating roads and streets worldwide.

Geolocation tools such as **Creepy:** https://creepy.en.softonic.com/ are often used to locate people and their activities. Like many tools, it requires some effort to learn how to use it effectively, but Internet instruction – with this and other tools – can get OSR practitioners over the hump.

Tagged items, those shown on editable maps such as **Wikimapia** http://wikimapia.org/ can be helpful in identifying large targets.

Billboards that are visible in any source picture may literally be a big help when trying to pinpoint a location. Since the billboard company wants to sell advertising it often lists the location of its wares, and that list can be used in pinpointing a location where a billboard or "hoarding" is visible.

Videos often have to be watched repeatedly when doing detailed OSR work. Particularly when working with videos, frames fly by so fast that it may be physically impossible to see the details. Blink and you miss it. For that reason it is important to use stop-action on the screen. Some video players give the researcher that capability. The **VLC media player** at http://www.videolan.org is one that allows you do this. It reads almost all media formats. When you pause the video on the VLC player you can then use the arrow keys to move, frame by frame, examining a scene and extracting the detail that is always essential in geolocation.

Many users find the "playback" and "video" sections of the VLC player to be most important. They use the controls there to zoom in or out, to crop, or to take needed snapshots.

As with all programs, sites, or resources, the more you know what something will do, and how to get that program to do what you want, the better your results will be. Choosing what programs you will use when conducting OSC is important, but knowing how to wring the most out of your choice is imperative.

Geotagging is Helpful

Sometimes a visual is already geotagged to show the location where the picture was taken, providing a shortcut to proving location. When accurate geotag information is available it is a real time-saver since it usually shows exactly where the scene was recorded.

Finding geo-tags is one of the dark arts of OSR. Sometimes portions of a site must be turned on to access geotags or – as in YouTube special searches looking at dashcams – extra steps are needed. Researchers also need to be aware that geotags can be spoofed and occasionally are fudged.

While many sites have visuals, on some of sites – particularly social media sites – the search for geotagged visual material is seldom fruitful. Although geotags may be removed at some Internet locations they are usually left on visuals that are posted at:

- **Google Earth:** https://www.google.com/earth/
- **Echosec ($$$$):** https://www.echosec.net/
- **VK:** https://vk.com/
- **Yandex Maps:** https://yandex.com/maps/
- **YouTube:** https://www.youtube.com/.

Some searchers, if they have an idea of the approximate location, find the VK site especially useful. They click photos>photos sent; enter the proper coordinates in the "near coordinates" space, remove the space between the coordinates, then click "enter." The site displays pictures listed near the location.

Street-level imagery is an important resource in location-based searches. Since many visuals are taken from about eye level and depict the scene on the ground, street level imagery can often be used to discern details and verify the "where." In cities, street level imagery is found on many mapping sites.

Not all mapping sites cover the entire world and even those that do may find their visuals outdated with no chance to fix them. Calamities such as war, flooding, or other catastrophic events can drastically and quickly alter some street views.

Mapping sites are set up differently so open source researchers must be knowledgeable in the working details of the sites they plan on using. Important street level sites include:

- **Bing Streetside (API):** https://www.bing.com/maps/
- **Google Street View:** https://mapstreetview.com/,
  aka **ShowMyStreetView** https://showmystreet.com/
- **MapJack:** http://www.mapjack.com/

- **Yandex Panorama:** https://yandex.com/maps/.

Another potential source of street level shots are dash cam videos which many people take and post, often without discernable reason, on sites such as YouTube.

Overheads

Overheads – aerial or satellite imagery – are also used effectively in location searches. But the researcher is faced with the problem of interpolating an image shown on the source document, usually taken at or near ground level, with a picture taken from far above. This is a knack that many researchers find difficult to acquire. Views from an overhead angle often skew perception. Matching ground level pictures to overhead imagery is an acquired skill. Researchers need to mentally change angles of view and understand how things which may be hidden from sight on the source material, or are otherwise not visible, may show up on the overheads and alter the scene.

Clarifying any patterns that are visible and discerning the common elements are central to this method. Drawing a rough map, diagram, or picture of the observed details – large and small – is often a helpful way to remind yourself of the various elements you have to match up when searching. It is often easier to find similar structures and surface layouts when you have fixed in your mind what you are looking for by drawing a preliminary sketch.

The type of overhead may factor into the identification process. Verticals are taken from straight above; obliques are angled shots. Each type presents unique problems of translating the image seen in an overhead and matching it to the source image. You can easily see the problem by taking an overhead of a local neighborhood or business district and matching it against a street view of the same blocks.

Sites providing many overheads include:
- **Bing Maps:** https://www.bing.com/maps/
- **European Space Imaging ($$$$):** https://www.euspaceimaging.com/
- **Google Earth** https://www.google.com/earth/
- **Google Earth Pro:** https://www.google.com/earth/versions/#download-pro
- **Terraserver ($$$$):** https://www.terraserver.com
- **Yandex Maps:** https://yandex.com/maps/.

Rivers and lakes are usually considered easiest to model when they show up in your source material. If water features are not present, roads and large structures are other easily-identifiable features that are apparent in many overhead pictures taken from airplanes or satellites.

Planet, at http://planet.com, is considered a small satellite by many but it catches the "big stuff." When looking for large details in an area – things like markets, stadiums, road systems and stores – **Wikimpia** at http://www.wikimapia.org helps searchers to sort out many of the "big things" and find "possibles" for further research. It also allows the quick trashing of the non-starters.

Important characteristics to look for when searching include:
- Shape
- Size
- Texture
- Tone or color.

Time – The "When"
Placing events at a location is the essential starting point for this process, but equally as important, and often more problematic, is charting the "when" factor. Locking in the time when the event occurred and linking it with the place through temporal location is

essential. Once you know "where" you have to know the "when." The "when" has to be established as closely as possible, though the hour or even the exact date may not be at issue.

Metadata on the visual is a go-to method, the first option for many researchers. It provides good evidence but not incontrovertible truth. For instance, while metadata can be spoofed it seldom is. But the metadata shown on a visual may be the upload time (and upload location) rather than time and location where the picture was captured. Skepticism is helpful.

Visuals uploaded from cellphones are more likely to have accurate metadata than any that are uploaded from cameras since phones are generally in contact with a base that syncs time continually. Cameras are turned off and on. They have no contact with a base that synchronizes time. Whenever researchers are using metadata as a time source they need to be aware of the possibility it is inaccurate and try to confirm the time by other means. But at least it is a start.

In terms of time, even temporary details may provide helpful clues in the search: signs with gas prices or phone numbers, the color of leaves on a tree – or a leafless forest, datable repair work on a road, signs of rain or snow. These are observables that can help establish some rough time elements, not the hour or the minute perhaps but a ballpark estimate of the day, month, or season.

The **WolframAlpha** search and computational engine found at https://www.wolframalpha.com/ can often be used to check a wide variety of offbeat things about a location, such things as weather, to help establish the timeframe.

Pictures that were taken outside in the daylight may be useful indicators of time when they are thought of like sundials. The length and direction of shadows – anything from people to poles – can be successfully used to tell the time. Internet sites such as

Suncalc http://www.suncalc.org are invaluable resources when used for these calculations.

When using Suncalc determine, through maps, overheads or other means, the orientation of the picture – north is the common alignment that must be determined. Then enter the probable or known location and probable date in Suncalc. Match the direction of the Suncalc shadow line to the north-aligned picture and read the resulting time.

In most cases you will be using ground-level, or slightly elevated, pictures for any calculations rather than satellite snaps or overheads. The shadows may be long or short – longer in the morning or evening and shorter at mid-day. In satellite photos, which are routinely taken as close as possible to noon, the time when shadows are short enough that they do not obscure important details, determining anything by shadows can be problematic.

The **Mooncalc** site at https://www.mooncalc.org/ may be useful for some nighttime pictures where the moon is visible.

After finding the "where" and "when" researchers can start looking for answers to other key questions. Answers to the "where" and "when" may lead to those other important elements, the "who" and "how." The "what" has been proven by the picture or video; the answer to "why" may remain elusive in this type of search. Motives are usually difficult, if not impossible, to pin down.

Identify the Posters

When everything of potential value has been extracted from the visual itself it is time to use those clues to search for information about the visual, including identities of people.

Particularly with the location-based process it is important to try to identify both the poster of the material being probed and the original poster of pictures or other materials. They may not be the same. To the extent possible it is important to find the original poster because these people are often witnesses. Their testimony and reasons for posting can prove important.

Moreover, in most cases the original poster usually has the best version of the visual in terms of sharpness and scale. Repostings are not going to be better than the original.

The goldmine is that first poster, if he or she can be identified. Metadata – if it has not been stripped off – and searches of whatever social media are popular in the area where the picture, video, or material originated may help to identify the originator.

Researchers who find, and are allowed to communicate with, the originator or author of important material might ask for an original, clean, copy of the picture or video but when they do so they will have to have it sent by means that don't alter the original, strip data, or compress the file. Direct email is often the preferred choice.

"Social discovery" is usually a requisite in location-based research.

Who are the people in a video or picture and how are they linked to the items or scenes shown? That is a question which must be answered. Social media, which allows a look into the lives of people and their thoughts, may be a good source for information about the visual or any people shown there.

There is a tendency to look to large, popular, sites such as YouTube or Facebook for photographic evidence linked to the original visual. And often it can be found there. But never neglect people in small, hyper-local groups who may also turn out to be the ones who will provide the visual evidence you need. Posters at "shop and swap" sites or the members of tight-knit community, social, or ideological groups often use smaller online resources and messaging apps. These are the modern back fences where people talk things over with their neighbors.

On hyper-local groups people are usually oblivious as to how their postings, pictures, videos and locally shared things might be used by researchers or even seen by the larger world. As a result they usually are more forthcoming and less guarded in their postings.

Reposts from such neighborhood sites may move a video or picture from a narrow audience to world-wide distribution, but the genesis may be hyper-local. Think small as well as large.

Reposts can be deceptive or misleading, as in a picture of an event from years-gone-by that is posted to show what is claimed to be a current event. Some people may post old pictures for "illustrative" purposes." On the other hand, "jokesters" and outright liars abound on the Internet; both are capable of offering up deliberately false and misleading information.

Captions can be used to alter reality; the picture may be real enough but words can suggest it shows something significantly different.

Remember: whether original posts or reposts, whether posted on a site for millions to see or on a "neighborhood" across-the-fence site, people do not always tell the truth.

To locate original posters, those researchers who are allowed to ask questions may use crowdsourcing or those social media sites which cater to people asking questions of the Internet community. In some cases sites like **Quora** at https://www.quora.com/ and **Curious Cat** at https://curiouscat.me/curiouscat may be used for crowdsourcing inquiries. However, be cognizant that any public inquiries about the matter being probed may also tip off people that you don't want to know about your interest in them and their affairs.

Use all available resources and work-arounds to verify the origin of any Internet materials. **InVID** at https://www.invid-project.eu/ is a resource that can help determine the origin of pictures and videos. Amnesty International has posted a **YouTube Data Viewer** at https://citizenevidence.org/2014/07/01/youtube-dataviewer/. A tool that may be useful to researchers is **Twitter's video search** found at https://twitter.com/vsearchengine?lang=en. There are also a variety of reverse image search engines, some of which use a camera symbol to show where to click for reverse searches, listed in Chapter 15, Videos, Pictures and Multi-media. **The Search by Image** app at https://play.google.com/store/apps/details?id=com.palmteam.images earch&hl=en_US may also be useful.

Jeffrey's Metadata Viewer at http://exif.regex.info/exif.cgi is helpful when using metadata to verify the origin of a video or picture.

Remember that creativity counts in OSR! Thinking outside the box, using a jig-saw puzzle mental outlook rather than a cookie cutter approach, is a must in every type of research.

Overheads are often useful in determining progress on construction sites, even at sites where builders try to be secretive.

Knowledge gained through overheads can often be supplemented by textual information such as advertisements looking for workers or announcing public bids on work, material and supplies. Social media posters and workers may unintentionally tell their friends and family "what's there" at sites they are visiting or are being built nearby.

Outlines and locations of even secret sites may be inadvertently revealed by such things as exercise devices that post starting points, ending locations, or the "outline" routes of runs made by people assigned to them.

Transportation Tracking

Bellingcat community members often need to track vehicles – ships, planes, trains, cars, and trucks. Vehicles of all kinds are generally registered by governments and often can be identified. Some online vehicle listings are governmental or commercial enterprises and others are catalogs put together by a small community of hobbyists and enthusiasts. Useful transport tracking sites include:

- **AirNav Radar Box (Aircraft location)**: https://www.radarbox24.com/
- **Cruise Mapper (Vessel location)**: https://www.cruisemapper.com/
- **Exact Earth Ship Monitoring ($$$$$)**: https://www.exactearth.com/
- **FleetMon (Vessel location)**: https://www.fleetmon.com/
- **Flight Aware (Aircraft location)**: https://flightaware.com/live/
- **Flight Radar 24 (Aircraft location)**: https://www.flightradar24.com
- **Flight Stats**: https://www.flightstats.com/v2/
- **Flight View**: https://www.flightview.com/flighttracker/
- **Marine Traffic: (Vessel location)**: https://www.marinetraffic.com/
- **MaritimeIHS ($$$$)**: https://maritime.ihs.com/
- **Megayacht Global (Yacht location)**: https://megayachtglobal.blogspot.com/p/yacht-tracking.html
- **Military Flights**: http://mt-milcom.blogspot.com/
- **My Ship Tracking (Vessel location)**: https://www.myshiptracking.com/
- **North American Rail Tools: (Railways)**: https://asm.transitdocs.com/
- **PlaneFinder (Aircraft location)**: https://planefinder.net/
- **PlaneMapper: (Aircraft location)**: https://www.planemapper.com/

- **Radio Tracking Forums:**
  https://forums.radioreference.com/
- **Railroads:** http://www.railroaddata.com/
- **Ship AIS (UK ship plotters):** http://www.shipais.com
- **ShipFinder (Vessel location):** https://shipfinder.co
- **ShipSpotting:** http://www.shipspotting.com/
- **Superyachts (Superyachts):**
  https://www.superyachts.com/directory/completed_yachts.
  htm
- **Track-Trace: (Plane cargo and aircraft):**
  https://www.track-trace.com/aircargo
- **Track-Trace: (Shipping containers and cargo):**
  https://www.track-trace.com/container
- **Vessel Finder (Ship location):**
  https://www.vesselfinder.com/
- **World Aircraft Database (Aircraft type and owner):**
  https://www.planemapper.com/aircrafts.
- **Yacht Finder:**
  http://megayachtglobal.blogspot.com/p/yacht-
  tracking.html.

When transportation tracker sites display a path, keep in mind that courses between locations are generally straight lines or line segments. When planes or ships are used for surveillance, searches often follow a track that is either circular or looks like a tractor's boustropedonic path across a wheat field, a back and forth pattern that covers the entire area.

Subgroups can be created about any field, such as transportation, and are useful ways of organizing URL listings. Here is what a maritime and piracy section of the transportation field might look like:

- **Global Incident Map:**
  http://www.globalincidentmap.com/

- **International Chamber of Commerce:** https://www.icc-ccs.org/index.php/piracy-reporting-centre/live-piracy-report
- **International Maritime Organization:** http://www.imo.org/en/MediaCentre/resources/Pages/Piracy-and-armed-robbery-against-ships.aspx
- **MARAD:** https://www.marad.dot.gov/environment-and-safety/office-of-security/msci/advisory/
- **Office of Naval Intelligence (Piracy analysis and warning, worldwide threat to shipping):** https://www.oni.navy.mil/News/Weekly-Piracy-Reports/.

Inevitably researchers find that they need specialized sections of their SOP if they are doing location searching. For instance, fires from forests set ablaze to the conflagrations that burn through war zones are often useful points of interest in searches. Useful fire tracking sites include:

- **Earth Observatory:** https://earthobservatory.nasa.gov/global-maps/MOD14A1_M_FIRE
- **Fires:** https://fires.ru/.

Another US government site that may be useful in disaster coverage is the **USGS Earthquake Site** that is found at http://earthquake.usgs.gov.

***

Project:
Consider whether you will use location-based searching in your work and include the answer in your SOP.

Project:
Determine whether you will create special sections in your SOP that will include websites that are especially useful in doing location-based searches.

Project:
If you are going to use a Geosearch capability, download **Google Earth Pro** at https://www.google.com/earth/download/gep/agree.html and use it to locate the mythical home of Sherlock Holmes and Watson at 221B Baker Street in London, then convert that location using the **FCC Converter** tool at https://www.fcc.gov/media/radio/dms-decimal.

Project:
If you are going to employ location-based searching, download to your SOP the Bellingcat Online Investigation Toolkit located at: https://docs.google.com/document/d/1BfLPJpRtyq4RFtHJoNpvWQj mGnyVkfE2HYolCKOGguA/edit

Project:
If you are going to use location-based research in your work determine your precise home "address" on the planet and put it in your SOP by as many notation methods as you plan on using.

18. Web 2.0 and Social Media

When you are building a structure, or remodeling one, you think in terms of the newest ideas, not blueprints from the 1900s. OSR is constantly growing and changing. There is no question that even more changes are coming in the Open Source world. Some are already on the doorstep, affecting both text-based and location-based searches.

The miracle that was the Web in 1990s still exists. Web 1.0 is alive and well. But a new wing has been added to the older structure, Web 2.0

Forward-thinking leaders in the information community utilize all of the Web – whether Web 1.0 or Web 2.0 and social media – in their work.

There Is a Difference

Traditional online media are considered Web 1.0. In its early days, when the Web relied on publishers sending out their wares to users, it was pretty much a one-way street. Now, with Web 2.0, the traffic runs in both directions.

Web 1.0 content is created by individuals; the content of 2.0 often has multiple authors.

The content on Web 2.0 is often dynamic and interactive, differing dramatically from the traditional, and static, online media in Web 1.0. Web 2.0 is often referred to as New or Emerging Media – the "New" stressing the newest means or technologies for moving digital information.

Web 1.0 is essentially about reading; Web 2.0 is often about writing and speaking.

Web 1.0 deals in home pages; Web 2.0 is about things like blogs and social media sites.

Where Web 1.0 is about information producers sending out the materials they create, Web 2.0 is about collaboration and sharing by communities of interest.

Web 1.0 is largely about consumption. Web 2.0 refers to the collaborative Internet – where the Internet user both a produces and consumes content. Web 2.0 employs a greater variety of interactive and collaborative Internet technologies. Using Web 2.0 effectively requires knowledge and mastery of many more techniques and systems than Web 1.0 does.

Web 2.0 allows for the concatenation of information from different sources, and even different types of sources to assist in interaction, collaboration, and information sharing. The social media parts of Web 2.0, including YouTube, Wikipedia, and Facebook, can all be searched as part of the information intelligence process.

Sometimes social media sites serve several different roles – they may be a social connection, a messaging center, and a gateway to a plethora of other sites. Because they have multiple roles social media can provide the otherwise-elusive context that is valuable to both location-based and traditional researchers.

Many claim the innovations and inventions of Web 2.0 have ushered in an era of instantaneous information, surpassing the methodology of Web 1.0. Web 2.0 is often talked up like it is a minor miracle.

The reality is that Web 2.0 and social media are actually only a logical progression, with intermediate steps along the way. Always important, but sometimes overvalued by those who focus all their attention in this area. Research on Web 2.0 and social media are not the be-all of OSR. They are only an adjunct, an important one in many cases, to the many other methods of open source research.

Changes in Information Flow

Web 2.0 is changing some patterns of information flow. Many consider 1.0 to be one-to-many, scripted, or formal, using only a handful of media types: press, print, radio, TV, personal or static business websites. The volume of material in Web 1.0 is manageable; the messages of the 1.0 sources are mediated by site owners. The identity and agenda of the senders are generally known, and many of the sites are often considered highly reliable.

Web 2.0, as a contrast, offers many-to-many or many-to-one types of communications. The communications are generally conversational in their tone. A variety of media types are found in 2.0; the sheer volume of the 2.0 output is challenging. Everyone chips in their two cents, even when their input isn't worth a single penny, even when they don't know what they are talking about. Messages and materials found in in Web 2.0 are raw and uncontrolled. Often the identity and agenda of Web 2.0 senders is unknown or at least unclear. For good reasons the reliability of 2.0 material is often considered suspect.

Social media are a subset of Web 2.0 – a very important subset. In social media both the creator and the user of content know the nature of their communication will be interactive. Social media posts are often comments on the observations of others, forwarded comments, or forwarded posts.

Information in social media is usually enabled so that it can cross various platforms and devices – computers, phones, tablets etc.

Social media communications can occur in real time or they can be asynchronous, communicated over different periods of time.

Social media communication is likely to be multi-directional.

For many social media users the resource is less about information and more about interaction. Social media is often about community and a poster's place in that community. For open source researchers, social media opens a new information pathway, a door to information that would otherwise be difficult to obtain – the snapshot of an individual's interaction with others, a picture of feelings, opinions, anxieties and emotions that supplements and outlines the hard facts that may be collected elsewhere in the information forest. Social media often provide an insight into motives and motivations that other information resources cannot.

Importantly, social media can easily be used to transmit falsehoods, thus making analysis and interpretation more crucial. Assessment is decidedly more difficult.

As a general rule, social media sites exert no editorial control – people can and do post anything, from crazy to sublime. Assessing credibility and the reliability of social media sources is usually baffling because key information about the post or poster is often unknown or unknowable. Moreover, social media are often the Internet's version of the open microphone, providing information that the posters, or their friends, may later wish they had not revealed. On some hyper-local sites users may lack any awareness that what they think or say may be seen outside of their own network. Posters believe they are communicating with friends or the like-minded – such is the underlying psychology of social media.

Most people think of social media as a personal communications method but it can also be a staple of business, big business, medium chains, and even mom-and-pop stores. Social media are widely used by businesses for their advertising, marketing, and branding efforts. For that reason, businesses use social mention sites such as **Social Searcher** found at https://www.social-searcher.com/social-mention/

or similar sites, such as **Mention**, at https://mention.com/en/social-media-monitoring-tools/, to keep tabs on who is referencing them and why. This type of site can often be used to track both people and organizations using, or on, the many types of social media sites.

Creators of 2.0 material do not have to put much skin in the game when it comes to technology and costs. Entry is fast and seems nearly free, but many social media sites monetize customers. Users become the product – their data points are sold to anyone with the dollars, pounds, rubles or francs.

Like all research resources, there are things that social media answers better than other investigative resources. When and why should OSR operators monitor social media closely? If used correctly, social media can help:

- Track people, their projects, their work, and their activities
- Monitor an ongoing crisis, event, or development
- Gauge or sample sentiment or intentions
- Help determine the reach of particular messages online
- Give insight into a group or provide knowledge about an organization's structure, finance, and capabilities.

Social media are an ever-evolving method of spreading information rapidly. Capitalizing on the inherent human need for self-expression, the growth of citizen journalism, and the ubiquity of shareable media content, social media have shifted the culture of communication.

Because so many people use some social media sites, names may not be useful in searching. Even Email addresses – because people may have several – are not the always the unique identifier needed by many site operators. Handles – the online name of a user – are far more useful.

Some social media sites assign unique identification numbers to their users and tie all communications from a particular user to that number. Researchers know that finding the identification number of a person or entity on sites such as Twitter or Facebook is a first, and important, step in research. When you find this unique number you can discover many things about the individual, group, or entity and burrow into many places you are otherwise excluded. Finding the unique identifier for a particular site – "how to" information on the Internet may be helpful – is sometimes changeable, not always easy, but the effort is often worthwhile when you are looking behind the curtain in social media.

Facebook and some other searches can be made easier by finding the unique identification number of posters through sites such as **WhoPostedWhat** at https://whopostedwhat.com/.

Social media is considered new. But venues similar to social media have been around for decades and more. In a long-past day the "agony columns" of newspapers were somewhat equivalent to social media. And they proved equally useful then. Sherlock Holmes found these precursors of today's social media sites valuable, telling Watson in *The Adventure of the Noble Bachelor,* "I read nothing except the criminal news and the agony column. The latter is always instructive." Social media of any type remain as instructive in the early 21st century as in the late 19th century.

Social media, more than ever, serve as the "rumor central" of today's world. Some of the claims researchers uncover when using social media can only be classed as preposterous. But even that may show what is commonly thought or believed in a particular community.

And social media is really all about community. Many online communities tend to be localized or limited to one topic area such as hobbies, interests, or work. Search engines often avoid cataloging such social communities because public interest is limited or the audience is too small.

Just as there are untold numbers of cities, towns, hamlets and communities across the globe, the Internet has an almost-numberless amount of social media communities. For that reason the study of social media are all-too-likely to become a deep bog unless the OSR operator uses them correctly, wading through with a map to find the hidden treasure you need.

Researchers have to avoid being buried under the haystacks of useless information that some in social media want to fling at you. But properly used, social media can be valuable.

Social media can offer a relatively-unvarnished look at a person or the people you are researching. Social media are especially useful in locating linkages between two or more people or organizations. Social media also promise to reveal someone's influence or relative importance within groups, networks, or organizations. These are the kinds of information that social media can give a researcher.

Much of the promise in social media for researchers centers on social network analysis (SNA). SNA is an interpretation of human relationships, mapping and measuring the interactions and the information flows between people, groups, URLs, computers, and similar or related entities. "Bots" and sockpuppets, creatures of false identity, are already proven to have serious impact in social media; their influence must be considered during the SNA process.

Understanding social media networks and their participants requires the analyst to determine where the influencers, the nodes, are in the network and how they relate to other nodes. SNA provides insight into the make-up, leadership, and structure of any social media network.

The Who, What, When, Where, Why, and How of someone's life and activity are often important to understand. Many of the answers to questions about people can be found amid social media posts, or through SNA.

People say different things on different social media sites. Their sense of privacy and personal safety differs from site to site. What they feel free to say on one site may not be kosher for another site. People are inconsistent, they will often reveal different aspects of themselves on different sites. It is important to check all sites where a person is likely to post to in order to get a complete picture of that individual.

Social media are considered important around the globe and are gaining in their importance. The cell phone is behind much of this. Today's cell phone provides users with a tool to easily post on, and utilize, social media. Most people, including many in the Third World, have cell phones capable of taking pictures, capturing video, and accessing the Web. People around the world, even in less-chance areas of the globe, now have the ability to immediately post text, sound, imagery, and footage to social media platforms. They make themselves heard in ways like never before. The result is that there has been an explosion of shared text and "raw and uncut" footage, a boon that is readily available to those individuals and organizations who choose to access phone-produced social media.

Material posted from cells tends to be more unguarded than other information and hence is often highly revealing.

While the modern cell phone, with its computer-like features, can be used for research it lacks many of the programs and the ease of use of a computer. In fact, most people use their cell to increase their presence on the Web and expand their personal universe rather than do serious research with the phone.

Whether you research using a cell phone or not, researchers need to understand things such as security, hashtags, likes, retweets, and key words, as well as all the *minutiae* of cell use. Cells are major contributors to the social media set of the Internet; their role and limitations must be both understood and appreciated.

450

Social media are sometimes referred to as enablers of people power, but that power is often undirected – more like a bomb explosion than the carefully timed and limited explosions that take place in a gasoline engine.

The social media phenomenon is growing and, like the expansion of the universe, its growth appears unbounded. The future of social media, at the start of the 21st Century, appears positive. It appears it will continue to grow in both importance and size. Video and audio promise to predominate in the future; text will likely assume less importance if the present direction continues.

Cell phone technology will undoubtedly evolve. Delivery systems are undergoing change, even now. Mobile phones, not computers, are already seen by many as the main entryway to the evolving world of social media.

In fact, some social media sites have no direct way to access them through a computer. They rely totally on cell phones, which have no way of storing any material found. For that reason it may be necessary – it is always wise – for researchers to have an Android cell phone emulator available on their computer and in their tool kits.

Web 2.0 Types

New media come in a variety of "flavors" or types. They can be used for, and in, many things. The list is almost as wide as the scale of human activities. The precise flavor must be chosen to match the OSR operator's tastes and needs. Major categories include:
- Knowledge-sharing types are an overarching group that may include blogs, microblogs, social networking sites and wikis.
  - Blogs allow the diffusion of information and opinions. Many look similar to Web 1.0 pages with the exception that they allow people to comment on, and discuss, the posted information.

- o Micro-blogs are popular and despite the terminology are really closer to social networking sites than to blogs. Twitter is an example.
- o Wikis allow the public to write, edit, and change the content in an informational system. Wikipedia is preeminent in the West.
- o Social networking sites allow people to connect, personally interact, and comment. These sites allow "friends" to get close to someone's mindset. Facebook is an example. But keep in mind that Facebook, like other social media sites may serve any of several roles – a social media connection, a messaging center and a gateway to other sites.

- Business networking sites promote commercial and/or professional connections and interactions. Popular ones include LinkedIn.
- Life-sharing sites are often big on social convergence, crowdsourcing, and photos/videos. YouTube and Flicker are examples.
- Community building sites allow for local collaboration.
- Photo-sharing and video sites such YouTube promote visual sharing.
- Virtual worlds or virtual communities simulate other life environments in the digital space.

Blogs and Podcasts

Blogs may be a funny-sounding word. It started as a contraction for "weblog," which was originally seen as a personal online journal. The term has been expanded to include almost anything in the xml format or RSS sites. Blogging, perhaps more than anything else, has transformed the Internet into a personal publishing tool.

The subjects of blogs are as wide as the universe. Blogs cover every aspect of human experience or interest. Researchers find that watching blogs can be useful, providing they are carefully chosen and properly monitored. Blogs usually fall into one of four major categories: opinion, personal, corporate, and professional interests. All can be useful in OSR, depending on the information sought.

Blogs are considered part of the Web 2.0 and the social media world since most allow comments on the blogger's post and may even invite open discussions. Posts are presented in reverse chronological order. The most recent postings on a blog appear at the top of the page; previous posts move down.

Blogs provide a way for people to publicly post and boast about their activities. They can share opinions with friends or the world at large. Blogs may look like traditional websites and many appear to be Web 1.0 sites with the addition of commentary capabilities. In addition to text, blogs often include audio clips, photos, artwork, or videos. Bloggers sometimes link to other websites and blogs – particularly to those sites that agree with their opinions or provide specialized knowledge about their fields of interest.

Because most blogs are uncensored, the material in them tends to be wide open. Things get blurted out in blogs that can be eye-opening, and in some cases even problematic for the posters. Opinions and pictures that come back to haunt, proprietary information that shouldn't be out there, and data that can be exploited, may creep into blogs.

Blogs tend to be discussion-oriented but the text itself may be factual or opinionated. Blogs often revolve around a single, or handful, of subjects. For that reason the community that congregates around a blog often posts other information about the same or similar issues. Many bloggers provide links to other sites, reports, research, news articles, or statistics about their specific subject areas. Those links can be invaluable in filling out a complete picture of any subject.

At the same time, because bloggers often hyperlink to resources that support their views and claims, blog comments and "facts" that are not factual often go viral. Incorrect information may be speedily spread across many sites that share common interests or views. Misinformation, mistakes, errors, and outright lies quickly become "conventional wisdom" or "common knowledge" in the blogosphere, the world of blogs.

Blogs often contain retrospective information, making them a useful source when creating timelines or histories.

Blogs maintained by subject matter experts (SMEs), or those sites that attract SMEs, may become a valuable information resource for anyone researching a topical area. When the interest focus is narrow blogs may be a better – and often are a more current – source of information on a particular subject than mainstream resources.

Blog searches using RSS feeds may be made easier when using programs such as **RSS OWL** at http://www.rssowl.org/.

Social media, and blogging in particular, has changed open source research. Open source researchers must be able to do more things, and display more talents, than ever before. Knowledge of blogging is one of those things.

Citizen journalism presses professional information seekers in new ways. It may be no coincidence that the rise of citizen journalism – much of it blogging – comes at the same time that trust in traditional news reports and the mainstream media is falling. Creation of fake news and disinformation, whether it is done for click payments or other reasons, rests squarely on social media and blogging sites.

The choice of blog sites is crucial to limiting the exposure to fact-free environments or to people who are economical with the truth. Anyone who chooses good sites has a smaller chance of getting burned by information mongers. Choose bad blogs and get bogged down with bad information.

The fake news and mendacity problem is particularly acute on Web 2.0 and social media sites because people send material from places they pick it up – and many are indiscriminate when it comes to where they get their information.

But a good choice in blogs can be a researcher's salvation.

Blogs may reveal the identity and thinking of the influence agents or the thought leaders in a subject area. More generally, blogs reveal atmospherics, sentiments, and areas of interest. Blogs where many expert or qualified users post often are obviously more useful than those that offer new material once every three months.

Usually blogs have a feedback mechanism to allow comments. They also want others to "follow" the blog and get updates on newly-posted material. Blogs often include some means to allow the site manager to let followers know when there are new postings.

Like any specialty area, there is a specialized vocabulary that has grown up around blogs, such as linklog, trackback, and blogroll. The main terms and their meanings are searchable on the Web.

There are search engines specializing in blog searches, such as **BlogSearchEngine** at http://www.blogsearchengine.org/.

RSS Readers are useful to aggregate any of the web feeds that become staples, feeding your information appetite. Among the popular applications are:
- **Bloglovin':** https://www.bloglovin.com/
- **Feeder:** https://feeder.co/
- **Feedly:** https://feedly.com/
- **Feedreader:** https://feedreader.com/
- **Inoreader:** https://www.inoreader.com/
- **NewsBlur:** https://www.newsblur.com/
- **TheOldReader:** https://www.inoreader.com/.

Podcasts are often thought of as the aural versions of a blog and are usually free. They share some of the same characteristics of blogs. Podcasts are worth searching out, and listening to, if they deal with any area you are researching or are interested in.

Search engines specializing in podcasts include **Podcasts.com** at http://www.podcasts.com/. Special media players or applications are usually required in order to listen to podcasts. Enhanced or visual podcasts include a visual display or images that simultaneously display with the commentary.

Micro-blogs

Micro-blogs, such as Twitter, limit the size of messages. They are not as full-featured as a regular blog but their stripped-down style makes them highly popular. No one has to have deep thoughts, or a good writing style, to describe what they are doing at the moment, where they are going, what they are eating, or why they detest someone or something.

Micro-blogging – the Twitter technique – is often about personal activities or opinions. Twitter and other microblogs really fall more into the social network category than they do under blogging. While they theoretically can be used in the same way as a blog, they are most suited to lifestreaming and opinions since they tend to scream "me, me, me." For that reason they are often pathways to someone's thinking and actions. They are particularly useful in following the "public musing" of people, or their activities.

Micro-blogs often serve as the Marathon runner of the Information Age, bringing the first blush of big news and unfolding events to the world. Twitter and other micro-blogs may provide the first and the fastest information available when disasters or significant events develop anywhere in the world. Twitter-type messages become particularly important during developing events or when looking for real-time information about fast-unfolding situations. At the same time, accessing the correct micro-blogs and finding the people who are near enough to the situation or events to be useful is challenging.

Geotagging can help. Titter geotags messages in two ways – self-reporting and GPS. Reliance on self-reporting is fraught from the outset; people can claim to be anywhere in the world when they are actually neighbors in the apartment above. GPS reporting is generally accurate as far as location is concerned, but not all Tweets are geotagged by their senders. Always look askance at the accuracy of micro-blog locations, but try to find people who are close to any major event.

Twitter has some geospatial operators that may be of help when trying to find people at, or close, to events. "Near" can be used as a search operator in Twitter's search bar as in near:Canada; to get feeds near a specific city use the city's name before that of the country, as in near:Calgary, Canada. Another search operator that can be piggybacked to provide greater reliability is the "within" a specified radius search. Either kilometers or miles can be specified in the radius of the search; there is a space between the "near" section and the "within" parameter. That search would look like near:Calgary within10mi. "Geocoded" – not the same thing as latitude and longitude – searches might look like geocode:52.1974563599,-113.2345123291,20km stampede. Put the desired distance after the location. When using a key word, add a space and the word after the geocode and radius.

Social Networks or Forums

Social networks are the new town square or kitchen table. Every part of the world has social networks where people meet to digitally discuss everything from what they had for breakfast to matters of international importance. In the United States, and indeed for much of the Western world, Facebook and Twitter are among the leading social networks, but there are many throughout the world. Social networks cover a wide range of practices and interests. They may focus on a common language or shared identities such as gender, profession, religion, race, or nationality. They may be single-subject or have many sub-forums and subcategories. In any event the exploration of social communities is an essential part of many information voyages.

Social communities differ; they provide different pathways to interact online. Social networks serve personal, academic, business and other purposes. Some of these online communities share some similarities to blogs. For those researchers restricted to passive observation only, the social network world still provides an abundance of data that could be harvested without directly engaging with a source. But for some US government researchers who are tightly controlled, direct access to much of the social network world may be off-limits.

Facebook has a reputation for intrusiveness, tracking your activity not only when you are on their site but gathering information about you, your interests, and your searches wherever you go. For many open source researchers who use Facebook heavily, one of the most important security measures is to thwart the tracking. To stymie Facebook's busybody tendencies, or at least reduce their effectiveness, the **Facebook Container** add-on found at https://addons.mozilla.org/en-US/firefox/addon/facebook-container isolates your Facebook identity and makes it harder it harder for the site to track visits to any other websites with third-party cookies.

Photos on social media sites, particularly social communities, are often difficult to download. You cannot just click-and-save in some cases.

The ease of downloading depends somewhat on the particular browser but for the stubborn cases there is generally a way to snag the picture. Often it involves viewing the page source and finding the actual location of the picture – it probably isn't on the page itself. Once you know where the picture is actually located you can use the listed URL, go to the place, and download the picture from there.

Social forums include:

- **Digg:** http://digg.com/
- **Mix (Formerly StumbleUpon):** http://www.stumbleupon.com/
- **Nextdoor:** https://nextdoor.com/
- **Reddit:** https://reddit.com
- **Xanga:** http://xanga.com/.

Professional Networks

Professional networks are designed to showcase members' abilities and tie those people with others who have like capabilities, backgrounds, and interests. Sites such as LinkedIn offer professionals a way to exhibit their abilities and digitally meet others with similar skills or interests.

These networks are also learning venues; places where new developments in any field are likely to be discussed. Professional networking sites can serve as a WhosWho of any particular field and are potentially a rich information mine.

Collectors have to carefully explore any professional network site, master its various tools, and learn the techniques to employ it effectively.

Academic experts can often be located by incorporating a trio of elements into the search terms at professional networks. The subject you are interested in is an obvious element. The domain – whether a specific site or a domain type such as edu – may be less obvious. Least obvious to many is the professional identification term such as "professor," "consultant," or "expert."

Professional social networks include LinkedIn and Plaxo.

Social Networking Search Tools

These tools are useful in identifying people using social networks and finding their postings.

- **SocialMention:** https://www.social-searcher.com/social-mention/
- **SocialSearcher:** https://www.social-searcher.com/
- **Whos Talkin:** http://www.whostalkin.com/.

When you identify one useful social media profile, including any "handle" or Internet name, you will often discover the same person uses that same name, or a very similar name, consistently in everything from sign-ons to postings elsewhere in social media. This is often more a matter of self-identity and consistency than it is of laziness. Consistency like this is a blessing to those doing research as it often helps identify the same person on different media.

Social Bookmarking

Bookmarking on Web 1.0 is a way of returning to useful web pages or sites. Individuals often bookmark pages by adding the page link to a "favorites" location on their web browser. That type of basic bookmarking listing is unique to the particular computer. It usually cannot be shared with any others who have similar interests.

Social bookmarking in Web 2.0 allows the sharing of bookmarks. These often are searchable by key words – subjects – as well as the name of the bookmarker.

Social bookmarking in Web 2.0 are a way to peer into someone's interests, concerns, knowledge fields, and cohorts.

Social bookmarking of topics of interest can be used to locate relevant social media information, a task that traditional search engines are not optimized to do. The speed at which information changes on social media means that a different approach is needed; a search engine spider that returns to search once a week or even once a day doesn't fill the bill. Social bookmarking employs search engines that are optimized to gather social media content using algorithms that prioritize recent content.

Generally the user selects a social bookmarking site, adds a button for that site to the browser, and begins bookmarking pages. Important social bookmarking sites include:

- **BibSonomy (Science-oriented):** http://www.bibsonomy.org/
- **BizSugar (Business):** http://www.bizsugar.com/
- **Delicious:** http://del.icio.us.

Video and Multi-media
The Internet uses words like "exploding" to describe the upward trajectory of video. Social media sites such as YouTube are part of that.

Video is increasingly part of the Internet experience. Any failure to search out and snare video materials leaves the tardy collectors in the dust. There may be no better way to get ahead of the online curve than to develop bleeding-edge abilities in this burgeoning area. (For more detailed information on Videos, Pictures and Multi-media see Chapter 15.)

Wikis
Wikis are essentially crowd-sourced online encyclopedias. Their subject focus may be narrow, or it may be as broad as the universe. In theory, and often in practice, subject matter experts contribute their knowledge to wikis, making these useful research tools.

Wikis may be private or public. Numerically, most are private and membership – the right to edit, add, or subtract to the storehouse of knowledge – is usually restricted to those in a specific group or community. Editing and any additions to wikis are usually made in real time; changes are posted immediately. However, in some cases the proposed changes are moderated and are not posted until they have been reviewed.

Wikipedia, at http://www.wikipedia.org, covers virtually every subject under the sun, the moon, and the universe. It is probably the best known of all wikis.

Wikis are highly-useful reference works, but their information must be evaluated for any inaccuracies. Although not everyone in the crowd that sources a site like Wikipedia knows or posts correct information, wikis are often a useful place to begin.

Besides Wikipedia there are many other wikis – sites that provide information and expertise that are crowd-sourced by users.

Wikipedia is an especially useful resource for the researcher or research desk when the question involves the resources, sites, programs, techniques, and computer equipment used in any online research. Wikipedia should be among the first go-to places when online research problems or computer questions arise. Many information professionals bookmark the site on their computers.

Researchers seldom stumble across wikis by chance. Ones that fit the user's needs must often be searched out. The **Lifewire** site at https://www.lifewire.com/wiki-list-by-category-3486723 offers an online directory of wikis.

Virtual Worlds

Virtual worlds tend to follow different patterns. The Massive Multi-player Online Games (MMPOG) such as the World of Warcraft may be among the best-known of the virtual worlds. However, persistent virtual world communities such as Second Life replicate real-world activities. Some virtual worlds are designed to be educational.

Community members in virtual worlds often communicate through avatars, a two- or three-dimensional representation of the person. Avatars can often be personalized but they may be inconsistent with details of the person they represent. Avatars are usually unreliable indicators of age, gender, and background.

Millions of people play virtual world games. Most are somewhere between their teens and age 35. Many players are male, but studies suggest about 40 percent of virtual world participants are female.

Virtual worlds are generally accessed for their entertainment value and as a place to socialize. But they can also become platforms for ideology, views, and even training in a variety of fields.

A feature of some virtual worlds is that virtual items, fake money, or commodities can be exchanged for real cash. Significant difficult-to-trace monetary exchanges are thus possible through virtual worlds.

Virtual worlds often provide some highly-secure communication channels. For those reasons some governments and agencies have concerns about their use for nefarious purposes.

Social Media Research Planning

Social media are often an information storage locker of people's lives, a closet just waiting for someone to rummage through. They are where private information is spewed out in a fountain of facts. Physical locations, family members, relationships, interests, hobbies, travel, employment, education, beliefs, friends – and sometimes enemies – are rolled out for savvy searchers to see. Negative information is usually not apparent on a person's pages, but it may lurk in the pages and postings of friends and associates. Posts of associates are valuable.

But any peek inside the information storehouse should be well-planned. Planning social media research requires operators to "put yourself in their shoes." Understand how the people you intend to research communicate among themselves. What language, what medium, what information that you want is likely to found be on Web 2.0? These are important to think about.

Important planning considerations include:

- Who, what, why, when, where and how of the potential post
- Location of those generating information about an event
- Language and cultural influences
- Who has access to that social medium
- Most popular sites for the geographic or economic area
- Sites change; plan the research every time
- Social media platforms lose popularity or close down, new ones develop
- Few things ever really disappear from the Internet but older items may be extremely difficult to locate.

Search structures on many of the leading social media change often and are convoluted. Knowing how to construct the search query is important. Often the best search queries are constructed outside the site's structure rather than in the search box. While the search details may change, the Internet – particularly the Web – is often a good source of information about constructing the most effective social media searches.

Social media of some type may exist in closed societies, but those communications are generally shut off from public view. Still, social media sites of expatriates who maintain contacts with people in their home country may provide useful information and give effective, if second-person, access to the activities taking place within the closed society. Sometimes such useful sites proliferate in countries which border a closed country or have some financial interest in the closed society. In-country relatives or business connections may communicate with people across borders. These secondary sources may be useful substitutes when direct contact is impossible.

Social Media Monitoring

Monitoring social media is challenging. One process created by open source experts is often adopted as a starting point and then adapted to the researcher's particular needs, experience, and tools. Your own process will be refined constantly as your talents and the landscape of the social media evolve.

The process used when tracking a "breaking news" event on social media sends the collector initially to locations like Twitter and Facebook, then to major media, followed by a foray on YouTube and other photo sites to see if there are video feeds or pictures. Social media dashboards or aggregators may show whether any discussions are taking place. Blogs may provide additional information as people sit down or begin to write longer pieces about the situation and offer opinions or make requests. After a thorough initial fly-through of these resources the search pattern is repeated as often as needed – wash, rinse, repeat.

Always use the safest social media sites and sources first as many of the important questions may be answered there. Problematic sites may not have to be used much, if they are used at all.

Situational awareness is among the most important uses of social media posts during cataclysmic events. Posts describing the scene locally or information provided by intervenors can be concatenated to paint a "big picture" of the situation. Such posts make the directing of resources to the most critical areas easier, much like a pointillist artwork can reflect a scene in tiny dots. On the other hand, the lack of information out of certain areas may indicate super-criticality because all lines of communication have been cut.

While social media can provide some speedy proto-results in unfolding stories, that information is largely uncorroborated and unvetted. The complete picture only develops over time, like the film from a camera. The time to develop a more complete picture may be shortened when major media or officials arrive on the scene, but accurate results are seldom immediate with social media.

Excitement, fear, failure to register what is actually happening, or a lack of understanding about important elements .can make some initial social media reports less-than-valuable. The first posters of information are usually non-professionals, doing the job as they understand it, reporting what they see through the lens of their own experiences. First reports, even those filed by professional reporters, are often incomplete and inaccurate when everything shakes out. First reports from social media are no different. If anything they are less reliable. Inaccuracy and mis-emphasis is always a danger with all first reports.

Citizen journalists are not trained professionals. Their posts must be considered as baseline information to improve upon rather than a final product. Amateurs may do a fine job under stressful situations; many do. But the quality and accuracy of these reports vary.

Social media, as offered through Web 2.0, provide average people a voice. It is the voice of immediacy and concern; the fact that an issue is raised by the public on social media may indicate the level of interest in the outcome. People seldom take time to talk about a horse race they don't have a pony in, or a bet on.

Changes in the volume or velocity of Internet social media posts are important to note. Such changes may indicate shifts in attitude that could be important. An uptick in the number of posts about a subject or the speed at which the posts are coming suggests a heightened interest or concern about the subject. It suggests the "urgency of now." When the volume or velocity drops precipitously, people may be losing interest or moving their attention to another subject.

Changes in tone may be important to note. Stridency, inflammatory commentary, or calls to action may suggest changes in outlook and portend further events.

Dashboards/Trend Monitoring

Dashboards can be used to monitor, gather, filter, prioritize, and organize social media information. Dashboards are often useful for monitoring trends and emerging topics of interest.

Trend-monitoring dashboards and sites may be useful in identifying search terms. They also help in forming a picture of what is not known, something every bit as important as what is actually known. Dashboard coverage may be broad or narrow. Examples of the types of sites that some find useful include:

- **Hootsuite (Social media management, $$$$):** https://hootsuite.com
- **Meltwater (Formerly Icerocket, $$$$):** https://www.meltwater.com/
- **Netvibes (Personal dashboard):** https://www.netvibes.com/en
- **TrendsMap:** https://www.trendsmap.com/
- **Tweetdeck:** https://tweetdeck.twitter.com/.

Google is preeminent in many areas, including no-cost social media search and monitoring tools. Useful tools include **Google Trends** at http://www.google.com/trends/, which monitors topics of interest. There are also Google communications tools and applications designed for production and dissemination of social media content.

Build a Solid Base

Social media research is about connections, discussions, and conversations. But for OSR researchers it is also about pacing. The social media field is vast; it is complex. Most social media searches are time-eaters.

Know the basic social media resources and thoroughly explore all of them, but make careful decisions about how much time or energy should be devoted to any of them.

The Internet changes continually, but some information resources are pillars to build with. Learn the details of a key handful first. Practice how to use those sites effectively. Publishers have put together books on many of the major programs. Reading, and doing while you read the text, is often the quickest path to expertise. Only after you have mastered whatever programs that you selected as the most important to your work is it wise to add additional social media to your repertoire, a single program at a time. Develop an organizational structure within your SOP and create schedules for learning each new medium. Where it applies, create a hashtag cheat sheet you can refer to quickly.

Avoid frustration; choose those social media that you feel will be most advantageous to your research requirements. The first-choice programs obviously depend on your information needs. That choice is yours but many people in the West start with half-a-dozen resources and gain expertise with each before moving on to other social media sites:
- Twitter
- Facebook
- LinkedIn
- YouTube
- Reddit
- Instagram.

***

Project:
Think through the types of commercial tools and online social media you will want to use for your research. List the types and any sites in your SOP.

19. Web 1.5 and 3.0

Humans like to categorize, placing things and concepts in neat boxes. Categorizing is a convenience; it is not always a necessity. But it's not always that easy to definitely or properly classify things. There is a gray area between Web 1.0, Web 2.0, and Social Media that can be best described as Web 1.5.

On a very basic level Web scouts who send information or trade may be considered part of either the Web 1.0 or Web 2.0 experience, as are newsgroups and similar, older, web structures.

Sometimes technologies fall into one category, sometimes into another category, depending on their use at the moment. As an example, news media sites such as the *New York Times* usually provide a one-to-many information pathway, but at other times – such as when readers or viewers of videos comment – the site is interactive and more like a blog from the Web 2.0 era. How any particular technology is used at the given moment may determine whether or not it is part of Web 1.0, Web 2.0 or Social Media

There are a number of techniques and technologies that do not fit conveniently into the simplicity of the Web 1.0-Web 2.0 paradigm. These were developed and even prospered in the older Web but have interactive components.

Discussion resources have long been a part of the Internet. They have some aspects of Web 2.0 but were developed as part of Web 1.0. Some of those resources even display characteristics of the BBS (bulletin board systems) that were popular prior to the creation of the Internet and the Web.

469

Listserves

Listserves are a way of communicating with other people online. They may be looked at as one of the – not old, but ancient – Internet technologies. They were widely developed and immensely popular in the early Web 1.0 era but there are reasons to consider them as Web 2.0 digital communications because of their interactivity.

Listserves are a means of communication that offers a limited, but real, level of interactivity. Listserves function, essentially, in the same way as scouts do – providing information on subjects that the listserve deals with. They are not as popular as they were in the salad days of the Internet but can still be useful to those researchers who are allowed to interact.

They are viable, valuable, resources for the researcher on long-term projects – provided that researcher is aware that they are available for exploitation and exploration.

Usenet Newsgroups

Usenet protocols govern the generation, storage, retrieval and exchange of what the service calls "news articles." Despite the nomenclature, those "articles" actually are more like emails and bear scant, if any, relationship to news reporting.

Usenet and its "newsgroups" are accessed through newsreaders, computer apps that allow researchers to read from and post in this system. The newsreaders are different from programs that allow users to read the Web or email. Although some modern email clients contain the coding to read both email and newsgroup traffic, there are some questions about how well those multi-purpose programs actually function with Usenet posts.

Usenet newsgroups were developed as far back as the end of the 1970s. Reports of Usenet's death have been exaggerated, certainly, but it has been on life support for years. Effective OSR use of

Usenet sites is challenging but, in some cases, when they are used carefully and thoughtfully, Usenet sites can provide usable information.

The Usenet system is often considered wide open. Unmoderated newsgroup postings are usually propagated to users immediately. But some newsgroups are moderated. That is, all posts are reviewed – and must be approved – by site managers prior to being forwarded to Usenet users and sites.

Unmoderated Usenet newsgroups are often magnets for spammers and commercial sex operators. Unmoderated newsgroups can easily be hijacked with a deluge of *non-sequitur* posts. Commercial sex organizations, pill purveyors, or others, begin filling the pages with their come-ons. Users who want to talk about the original subject flee. Eventually the last legitimate posters drift away, leaving behind a shell that no one visits.

Threaded Usenet posts – a user broaches a subject with a comment or question and others respond to the same subject – allow discussions and responses to be followed easily.

Usenet eschews a central server to store its posts, distributing them to a wide aggregation of participating servers. Those individual servers of the Usenet organization "talk" to one another and spread the posts.

In some respects, Usenet is similar to email except that message posters never possess the address list, only the Usenet users' servers know who can access the posts.

Usenet users tend to use their real names, email addresses and, crucially, screen names that can be researched. That often solves tracking and tracing problems.

The challenging complexity of the Usenet system, combined with its decades-old design, prompts many Internet Service Providers to either limit customer's access, eliminate the service entirely, or to offer it through a contracted service. A few providers concentrate wholly on Usenet and offer the services, at a fee, to people whose ISPs do not offer access.

The Usenet, itself, is divided into categories – groups of similar subjects – and then these are subdivided further into individual sites. The "Big Eight" categories of the Usenet are:

- Comp is for computer-related posts.
- Humanities is for subjects such as wide-ranging as philosophy and the arts.
- Misc is for the variety of miscellaneous areas that do not fit neatly into other categories.
- Mediarec covers recreation and entertainment.
- News is only about Usenet, not the news media..
- Sci deals with subjects involving science.
- Soc is about social issues.
- Talk is a category for subjects that are considered controversial.

A popular ninth part, perhaps more important than all the others, is the data-transfer section of Usenet called alt.binaries. It makes up the largest part of the Usenet traffic because of the size of its posts. This is also the most heavily used portion. Music, videos of all kinds, still pictures, and even software move through alt.binaries.

Retention of messages, and the time that different services may save them, is a current and continuing issue related to Usenet research. The longer the retention time the greater the chances that something useful will be found among the messages.

Starting places for Usenet-type sites include:

- **EasyNews ($$$$):** https://members.easynews.com/login/

- **Google Groups:**
  https://groups.google.com/forum/#!overview
- **Newshosting ($$$$):** https://www.newshosting.com/
- **UsenetServer ($$$$):** http://www.usenetserver.com
- **Yahoo Groups:** https://groups.yahoo.com/.

Google Groups is a mashup of Usenet remnants and new groups hosted by Google.

Web 3.0

Unlike what we dubbed Web 1.5 as an interim step in the Internet's development – or even 1.0 and 2.0 – Web 3.0 is a future destination, though a loosey-goosey one.

Web 3.0 remains a somewhat elusive concept. The term differs in meaning to different people. No detailed definition is universally accepted.

Web 1.0 was passive, one to many. There were some elements of interactivity within it, which we can call Web 1.5. Web 2.0 came about when individual users took, or were given, a more active role. User participation in the communication process is the hallmark of Web 2.0, best exemplified by social media.

Web 3.0 is – generally – considered to be the process of giving meaning to all the data on the Internet, harnessing the unstructured facts and data and turning these into structured, usable information. At least, on the surface, it sounds very much like OSR on steroids! The concept that animates Web 3.0 is that computers and artificial intelligence will do the work automatically, speedily, and without friction, using what is literally a web of information resources that stretches around the world.

Web 3.0 would require a common language, not only a common spoken tongue but common computer languages that would allow fast, accurate, interactions.

Web 3.0 is envisioned as the thoughtful web, the web that thinks on its own rather than following the commands of humans at a keyboard.

Web 3.0 is often seen as an amalgam of the semantic web, artificial intelligence, and blockchain technology. The semantic web would personalize information to the individual's meaning, understanding, and needs. Artificial intelligence would make decisions, computing and balancing, acting seamlessly despite different formats, and it would do so faster than humans could. Blockchain technology is needed to store and parcel out needed data points that go into the process, selecting only the facts that are applicable and moving them from their resting place to the attention of the Web 3.0 user.

Digital assistants such as Cortana, Siri, and Alexa are forerunners of Web 3.0, certainly, but a long road remains to be covered before Web 3.0 becomes a reality. "Over-promised and under-delivered" is perhaps the best way to describe Web 3.0 at present.

The as-yet-unfulfilled promise of Web 3.0 is the ability to ask a single question and have the Web respond with a single answer that takes every factor – including the ones you haven't thought of – into account.

Although computer scientists are working on making Web 3.0 a reality, humans need to continue looking for, and finding, the information pieces needed to resolve questions – whether on the Web or off it. Open source researchers have not yet become redundant. Now, today, human thinking is still needed in order to move all the information pieces that people can find to a place where they can be examined and linked together by decision makers.

While members of the computer community are clawing their way forward, and some progress is being made in the direction of Web 3.0, for the foreseeable future humans – including you – will continue using OSR techniques and tradecraft in order to remain at the forefront of information exchanges.

***

Project:
Explore, on the Internet, the uses of such services as Listserves and Usenet, then determine whether or how you would use these resources for your own projects. Include your decision about that in your SOP.

20. Evaluating Your Material

Whatever the field, information is first collected and then analyzed for accuracy. Accuracy is the watchword of OSR.

The open source operator can make assumptions – guesses if you will – during the search phase but has to hew strictly to the findings during the analysis phase.

The output of any particular field, when the collection phase concludes, can be called information intelligence, OSR, OSINT, CaR, IL, CI, OPPO or any of half a dozen other names. But until the information is collected, analyzed, and turned into a comprehensive and vetted product, becoming "insight," it remains just "information" or "data."

Insight is created from linking pieces of accurate information together. You, and your clients, want insight – not because it looks nice on a page, but because it is the best basis for action. Accurate information is the edge that all people need. Factuality is essential to information supremacy.

Analysis and the classification of information must be done carefully. OSR professionals know that their reports must be carefully researched. Reports must be written with the same circumspection and caution that diplomats put into the cables sent to their capitals.

Incorrect or piffling reports are bad for you. That's obvious. And bad or useless information that you pass on is even worse. Anything you use or provide to others has to be both valuable and accurate. It must be accurate in every respect, providing clarity of thought.

Your reputation, or that of your information shop, rides on both the accuracy and truthfulness of others as well as your own ability to determine their honesty and the value of their information.

Analysis paralysis, the inability to act on assessments, should never be a problem in OSR. If you collect the facts and present them in an understandable form the decision makers may be paralyzed and feel constrained to act by the facts. But that is not the problem of the open source collector. That is someone else's problem. All the collector can do is find the pertinent information and tell the truth.

Hierarchy of Truth
There is a hierarchy in matters of truth:
- Factual information
- Mistakes
- Half -truths
- Lies and disinformation
- The Big Lie.

Mistakes happen – but you don't want them tripping you up. Half-truths, lies, and disinformation quickly get you into trouble. "The Big Lie" can start a war, kill people, or steal freedoms and rights.

"The Big Lie" is in a class by itself. It is a state-sponsored untruth. It may be defined by a statement often attributed to Nazi spinmeister Joseph Goebbels: "If you tell a lie big enough and keep repeating it, people will eventually come to believe it. The lie can be maintained only for such time as the State can shield the people from the political, economic, and/or military consequences of the lie. It thus becomes vitally important for the State to use all of its powers to repress dissent, for the truth is the mortal enemy of the lie, and thus by extension, the truth is the greatest enemy of the State."

Disinformation, by many other names, is much in the news today. Confusion over what constitutes fake news, alternative facts, and questions about how to deal with this issue are rife. Disinformation even has supporters. Defenders of fake news – some have financial reasons, others see political or social reasons to approve of it – contend we live in a post-factual period.

Facts don't matter they say. "Lies" are not a word found in their vocabulary unless they are talking about their opposition. When something furthers their cause, or fills their pocketbooks, they term it "alternative truth." Now, more than ever, it is the responsibility of open source researchers and of all information professionals to separate contrivance from reality, eliminating the strands of mythology.

Mythology is Dangerous in OSR

Information is of no value when it is unreliable.

"Facts" that are not factual may be fine in a novel, or emotionally uplifting, but they are never alternatives to actionable information.

"False facts" or alternative truth, whatever people want to call them, are often designed to appeal to emotions or the prejudices of the listener, reader, or viewer. They may make some people feel good. But misleading information usually leads to eventual problems for the person who tries to act on it. Eventually that "good feeling" turns into uncertainty as to "what went wrong" and then morphs into anger over the knowledge of having been royally suckered. In the meanwhile, someone is hurt or damaged.

Few outside safeguards exist to ensure that information found anywhere on the Internet – particularly in social media – is accurate. Anyone can – and will – publish anything on the Web. While the Internet did not create disinformation, Web technology has made the widespread misuse of it increasingly easy and nearly cost-free.

Previously, for disinformation to spread rapidly and be taken seriously it had to appear in newspapers, in books, or over the airwaves – and those media were usually too expensive for most people to set up in order to just spread disinformation.

Legitimate publishers and broadcasters had a financial incentive to make certain they were publishing facts. They hired editors and fact checkers to make certain their reputation, and that of their medium, was unsullied – to assure that their products were indeed correct. If the word got around that their product was really verbal baloney their reputation would be ruined and, more importantly for them, their financial investment in presses or broadcast equipment would be lost.

That has all changed. Technological changes – not all changes can be called advances – now subtly encourage lying. Today the price of spreading disinformation is miniscule. The cost of untruths is small. It is possible to make a living by lying on the Internet, creating false material so outrageous that people will click on it and make money for charlatans through click-bait items. At worst, in most cases, people spreading false information only need to create a new website for themselves if they are caught and exposed.

After Collection Comes Evaluation

Collection is the necessary first step in the OSR process. Without collection there are no follow-on steps.

But it is the vetting, assessment, and interpretation that turn raw information into useful, actionable, knowledge and insight. The evaluation of collected information, the process of turning it into insight, is a tricky, challenging, and convoluted process.

Evaluation was at the heart of Sherlock Holmes' efforts, perhaps more so than information collection. He repeatedly talked about assessment's importance. "It is one of those cases where the art of the reasoner should be used rather for the sifting of details than for the acquiring of fresh evidence" Holmes said in the adventure titled *Silver Blaze.*

Sherlock Holmes revealed his secret of good evaluation when he said in *The Adventure of the Beryl Coronet* that "It is an old maxim of mine that when you have excluded the impossible, whatever remains, however improbable, must be the truth." Analysis is often a matter of exclusion in this Holmesian view, a process of cooking off the fat to get to the meat of the matter.

In *The Adventure of the Sussex* Vampire Holmes he felt the need to add: "One forms provisional theories and waits for time or fuller knowledge to explode them."

The master of intellectual feats also recognized another verity: Sometimes researchers have to work with possibilities rather than hard facts. In *The Hound of the Baskervilles* Sherlock Holmes insisted that probabilities and possibilities must also be taken into account – that proof positive is not always possible. "The probability lies in that direction," he said. "And if we take this as a working hypothesis we have a fresh basis from which to start our construction of this unknown visitor."

If the Holmes of fiction was a keen observer, he was a fanatic about managing and assessing the detailed information he had collected.

Information Management
Information management techniques are essential to OSR.

The collected data must be easily retrieved by the researcher or research desk at every stage of the process. Files and folders must follow a pattern that is understandable to the researcher. Items should be properly named and accessible. Having information that is "right on" is useless if it cannot be found and used.

Analysis is the process in which collected information is evaluated for usefulness and correctness. Pieces of information are integrated with other good information to create a package describing the current or previous situation, or predicting future developments. That is obvious. What is less understood is that the process of analysis, assessment, and interpretation should also identify issues and problems that could impact or change the report. Examples of this could be a focus on the wrong priority, a lack of information, or a lack of assets needed to collect the required information.

There is both positive and negative evidence. Most people are aware of the former; fewer can see that the lack of something can also be indicative in the analysis process.

Sherlock Holmes made that point clear in *Silver Blaze,* during a discussion with Inspector Gregory, who asked "Is there any point to which you would wish to draw my attention?"

"To the curious incident of the dog in the night-time," Holmes said.

"The dog did nothing in the night-time."

"That was the curious incident," said Holmes.

The final OSR product may rely on the process of elimination that Holmes demonstrated.

Always be cognizant that some preliminary analysis actually takes place during collection process, but the final vetting has to be the most intensive analysis, the point where facts are double-checked, any tentative conclusions are reconsidered, and output is reviewed and revised.

All information is not equal. New light may be shed in old work during analysis. Original ideas may have to be revised. Newer research may suggest a rereading and revision of the meaning of previously discovered data. Old information may not have been understood, or even misunderstood, in earlier times.

There are multiple types of analysis.
They include:

- Content analysis, also called information analysis
- Source analysis
- Sentiment analysis
- Trend analysis
- Frequency analysis
- Strategic baselining
- Link analysis
- Geolocation analysis.

Of these, the first two are absolutely essential in all OSR. These are often dealt with during the collection process. The other types of analysis are important in some cases and are worth looking up on the Internet to determine if they apply to your research needs. The last type, geolocation analysis, is essential to those using the Bellingcat research model.

Information or content – and sources – must be carefully evaluated on at least two fronts:

- How believable is the information?
- How believable is the source?

Believability and the quality of the information on hand is the most important issue. After all, bad sources sometimes produce good information and even the best sources are sometimes wrong. Either way, insight never comes from bad information.

As a first step in evaluation, during the collection process always read the "about us" message on any site. A site that says it traffics in "joke" stories or "satire" is probably not a useful source. The "about us" message may provide information that will allow you to quickly wipe a site and its messages off your believability list or give you clues on how to rank the site.

There are many resources which can help you evaluate news sites, but for other media and resources you are pretty much on your own. Analysts have to worm their own way through the assessment thicket. PDF files, databases and slide files often are a better, more reliable, resource than Web pages and news sites. But even these must be assessed carefully.

Fact-check sites are usually not useful to the average researcher. OSR operators seldom deal with the same stories that fact-check sites do. However, sites that provide information on general bias levels and leanings can be highly helpful in any assessment of sources by providing a baseline of believability. They include:
- **Media Bias Chart:** https://www.adfontesmedia.com/
- **Zimdars List:**
  https://docs.google.com/document/u/1/d/10eA5-mCZLSS4MQY5QGb5ewC3VAL6pLkT53V_81ZyitM/mobilebasic.

A relatively quick way to assess a piece – quick ways are useful but should never be relied upon when evaluating essential information – is to go through a short script seeking negative issues. The more red flags that go up during your script search, the more suspicious the information is. But be aware there is no magic threshold number that warns of potential problems. That remains a judgement call.

Quick-and-dirty red flags include:
- Appeals are made to strong emotions such as hope, fear, or anger.
- Excessive punctuation, or all-caps, are used to stress a point, LIKE THIS!!!!
- Discovery of the information was facilitated by some less-reliable means such as emailed links from previously unknown sites or through social media channels.

- Suggestions that a site possesses secret information or information that the government, media, or others want to hide from the public.
- Evidence the writer or information source is unknown or anonymous, or there is a lack of clarity about the original source.
- The "about us" message or other text describes the site as "satirical" or a joke site.
- The "contact us" email differs from the website address, particularly if it is a free address such as Gmail.
- A search of the website name brings up information that questions the reliability of the site or its postings.
- The information is posted without a date.
- The information is unique or is cited only by other sites and sources that are dubious.
- The information lacks hyperlinks or any references to recognized reliable sources.
- Based on reverse-image searches, pictures appear to have been stolen, altered, or fudged.
- Fact-checking sites claim the information is untrue.

While there is no foolproof script that will prove whether something is true, or is a lie, professionals – and smart people – consider these factors when assessing any set of purported facts.

- Accuracy
- Authority, Authenticity, and Competency
- Currency
- Objectivity and Conflict of Interest
- Plausibility
- Coverage or Completeness
- Appearance.

Accuracy may be considered the faithful measurement or the representation of the truth; it is also correctness and precision of the content. Accuracy decisions often depend upon the rigor used in collecting the information. Sloppy collection methods affect the accuracy of the output. Clues to accuracy include:

- Is the information verified by another source?
- Is the information provable fact or is it opinion?
- Origin is important – where did the information originate?
- Was the information carefully collected and scrutinized during collection?
- Does the information seem reasonable or does it clash with information from other sources?
- Have you used the source before with good results?
- Is there any editor or a fact-checker who verifies the information?
- Are the sources for factual information clearly listed so they can be tracked?
- Are there noticeable errors (even with spelling)?

Why might the last point be important? Spelling errors not only indicate a lack of attention and effort, but also can actually produce inaccuracies in information. Even bad typography can produce errors. For instance: "Stern" and "stem" look alike when the type is smudged, but when you talk about ships it makes a great deal of difference if the reader sees an "m" or is presented with an "rn" run together.

Whether any errors stem from carelessness or ignorance, they put both the information and anyone who passes along the bad information in an unfavorable light.

Authority – it is linked to authenticity or competency – is often considered the 800-pound gorilla in the room. Arguments about facts often come down to who really knows what.

It is important to identify whether an information source is authoritative in the given field. Expertise is important. You might take the word of a chicken farmer when it comes to eggs, but when it comes to nuclear weapons you will want a nuclear weapons expert. By the same token, nuclear weapons specialists – unless they also raise poultry as a sideline – are not usually go-to people on egg-layers no matter how smart they are. Facts and ideas found on a site should be linked to an author, or if an organization or business, to the entity involved.

This provides accountability for the facts or ideas. Once the identity of the fact-provider is established it becomes possible to consider additional credibility factors. But until the authority (authenticity or competency) question is answered most reliable assessors look askance at the reliability of any information. Backlinks often help determine authority.

An author's authority is often evaluated on the basis of authenticity, competency, and trustworthiness.
- Authenticity: Is the author who he claims to be? Check domain names and the extension as well as site ownership. Check for academic qualifications (degrees, certificates and formal training) or any non-academic qualifications (history, professional associations, or family connections).
- Competency: "Is the source capable?" is the key question. Direct (personal involvement) vs. Indirect (quality of research and use of sources) enter into this evaluation.
- Trustworthiness: This may involve sourcing such as links to articles or footnotes, the track record of the individual, evidence of apparent bias, and timeliness (dated, overtaken by events).

Other important questions on authority include:
- Does the person, group, or site actually have access or proximity to the type of information presented? Are the sources actually in a position to know this information?
- Is the identity of the source or the authors clear and are they the people who they claim to be?
- Do authors display a bio that can be double-checked?

- Are the author and publication/medium considered by others in the field to be trustworthy, competent, and knowledgeable?
- Does the author have a respected following?
- Does the author have other works available, and if so what are they?
- Are reviews/comments posted or available, and are those credible?
- Do all authors have the degree, certification, credentials, or other academic background to speak on the topic?
- Is there contact information?
- Has the author accurately drawn upon, and correctly represented, all sources cited?
- Does the publication or site have research and publishing guidelines and if so, how strictly are these enforced?

Backlinks – outside sites linking with material on a site you are using – are often considered a possible measure of expertise. Backlinks are also known by other names such as incoming links, inlinks, and inward links. Because the number of backlinks is considered an indicator of a website's value and the authority a site has, some webmasters buy backlinks through companies set up for that purpose.

There are many backlink checkers that will reveal the number of referring domains to a site, including **SmallSEOTools**: https://smallseotools.com/backlink-checker/

Currency is the question of whether something belongs to the present. Is the information timely? It is not unheard of for events that happened years ago to be written about like they just happened, or even as if they are yet to occur. When evaluating currency it is important to:

- Determine when the information was published or posted. Look at the top and bottom of the page to see if the webmasters included a 'last updated' date.

- Read any pages that discuss 'news' or 'press releases.' If no news briefs have been posted on those pages in a couple of years, it could indicate that the rest of the site is no longer current.
- Be aware, acutely aware, that some sites put the current date on an item when a page is displayed, no matter when it first appeared.
- When all else fails, check to see if links on the page are current, expired, or even functional.

Objectivity and Conflict of Interest – is the information uninfluenced by emotions, pecuniary factors, or personal prejudices? That is a vital question. Look carefully to see if the information shows evidence of bias or if the page appears designed to push any particular goals, including those that might financially benefit the information provider.

Bias is a common problem, particularly on the Web. Specialists must judge the level of deception in any source or resource. It is safe to assume there is always some bias. The simple act of selecting one fact over another skews any presentation. This does not make the presentation wrong or the "facts" incorrect, in fact it may point toward the correct conclusion.

Understanding and measuring of the effect of any bias is the important part of effective research.

"Expectation bias" or "confirmation bias" is a serious problem for the investigator. It affects everything from the design of the information search to the conclusion of a report. People find what they expect to find in the places they expect to find it. They seldom seek information in unusual places or look for any information that counters their expectations. Cognizance of the inherent danger of confirmation bias is the first, and perhaps the best, defense against mendacity and fake news.

Confirmation Bias was something that Sherlock Holmes recognized as a researcher's problem when, in *The Boscombe Valley Mystery*, he said: "There is nothing more deceptive than an obvious fact...." Holmes knew!

Cultural and social biases are not always apparent or taken into consideration. But they are always present. They, too, must be taken into account.

Some questions to consider about the source or information include:

- Does it come from a non-partisan research organization or from some advocacy group with a stated agenda?
- Do sites, the page links, and any guestbook comments provide clues to a page's objectivity?
- Is there advertising on the page that relates to the subject of the page?
- Does the 'About Us' page provide clues to any possible bias?
- Does the page provide information on its resources or research methods?
- Does the domain name and type of site – (gov), (com), or (org) – suggest anything about the objectivity?
- Can you corroborate any position you find with similar positions published in other sources, such as periodicals or books? In this way you can discover where a position appears on the continuum.
- Does the tone appear to be what you expect from an objective source? Good information sources have a calm, reasoned, tone. They present information in a balanced manner. Pay attention to, and question the reasoning for, highly emotional writing. Writing that is overly critical, attack-oriented, or spiteful often indicates an unfair, even irrational, presentation rather than a reasoned argument.

Plausibility – put simply, the information makes sense. This can be tricky. Confirmation bias must always be taken into account here, but plausibility should also be considered.

- Is it reasonable?
- Does it appear to be true?
- Is it consistent with other background information?
- Is it reported elsewhere by sources that have a good reputation?

Coverage is the extent or degree to which something is observed, analyzed, and reported. A rule of thumb is that any "unique" fact or report is of dubious reliability.

Someone has to be first, it's true, and everyone wants to "break" a story, but second or third place is not bad. When other reputable resources ignore the information an analyst must ask "why?" Important questions are:

- Is the same information available from reliable sources elsewhere?
- What topics are covered?
- Is the coverage surface vs. in-depth? Ephemeral coverage suggests the source has little information.
- Accessibility (free vs fee) may play a role and needs to be considered.

Appearance – the outward or visible aspect of a person or thing – is sometimes a factor in determining reliability. In many ways this links with spelling errors discussed earlier. This factor should be considered one among many since some fake news sites appear very business-like and quite professional. Factors that are worthy of consideration include:

- Is the site professional-looking?
- Is it easy to use?
- Is the site look well organized?
- Is it as comprehensive as would be expected from the site type or does it have a limited reach?

- Do the links work?
- Does the site appear to be well-maintained?
- Do graphics and multi-media obscure any content?

It sometimes helps to create a matrix to rate each category as one to three (high, medium or low), one to five, or one to 10. You can even add up the numbers of each category for a total score, and weight the categories (since some issues are more important than others). **Warning:** Such an all-inclusive numerical matrix may appear more reliable than it actually is in determining information quality since the assigned numbers are, at best, only guestimates. But in certain circumstances such a matrix is useful.

Ferreting out disinformation and discounting it is always complex. Information assurance always requires careful and time-consuming analysis. Those who aren't willing to spend time and energy to question every scrap of information they receive are going to be fooled. They will be taken advantage of more often than someone who proves thoughtful in the processing of information.

Careful analysis and interpretation of data is the duty laid on us by the age we live in – dubbed The Information Age.

Primary and Secondary Sources

As a general rule, the more "hands" information passes through, the more suspect is its accuracy and reliability. While not necessarily true, the rule of thumb is that information from original or primary sources (people who actually experienced the situation or were observers) is likely to be more reliable than information supplied by secondary sources (people who heard of, or saw, information about the incident).

Primary sources provide first-hand evidence or, at least, testimony. It may be information that is recorded at the time of the event; notes or other raw data may be in this category. Witnesses are original sources. They may record their observations at the time, later in memoirs or autobiographies, or even in oral histories. Primary source information may be in print or some other format, such as an audio book.

The common preference for primary sources must be balanced against other factors. Often primary sources see only their part of the big picture while a secondary source may have a more inclusive view. Primary sources may not notice what is in front of them, may interpret what they see in a way that alters the meaning, or may simply lie about their experience. Primary sources, when their accounts are consistent, are highly valued. But the preference for primary sources should not become a blind faith in them or their accounts. Witnesses to a crime are primary sources, but there is much evidence that their testimony in court can be badly flawed for any number of reasons.

Secondary sources, such as news websites, compile the most important information on a subject and may be more accurate than primary sources who know only the part of an event they witnessed.

Unless a journalist actually witnessed an event, news reports are always considered to be from secondary sources.

Other Vetting Factors

The level of the source, primary or secondary, is only one factor that goes into the assessment of an information item. The type of posted material should be considered. Straight factual reporting, analysis (which generally involves opinions), or re-posting of material from sources that are unidentifiable, all enter into the validation equation. When material is reposted or credited to other sites, the responsible information professional checks those other sites to make certain the repost is accurate, complete, and to make certain the other site and the reported information actually exists. In the age of fake news, false information, alternative facts, and deep fakes, nothing can be taken as a given – not even videos.

Quoted material may never have been said and events may not have happened as described. Many famous quotes are apocryphal; expect any that aren't famous to be equally suspect.

Checklists and scripts are useful for in-depth study of a site, but are often too cumbersome and time-consuming for many uses. The quickest and best response may be to use the strengths of the Web itself to find out what others know or say about the site or resource. At the very least you can get a broad view of both source and content, and often the reasoning for those views, by getting the "group's view" of both. Go off-site, check the Internet for articles about the site, sponsoring organizations, authors, or associated people. Only if a source passes that initial test is it worth investing the time and energy to use a detailed checklist.

Ferreting out fake news can be far more complex than being aware of bias and leaving the work to fact-checking organizations. True information assurance requires careful analysis and interpretation. Researchers have to put their skin, and their time, into the game.

Disinformation is often successful; it spreads rapidly and widely because it confirms ideas the reader already holds. It proliferates when the person will not or cannot put in the effort, thought, and time to analyze the purported "facts."

When evaluating sites it is wise to ignore elements like organization titles, logos, and even posted domain names. These are ephemeral factors which can easily be spoofed. On pages that promote fakes as fact, these elements are often slavishly copied or are designed specifically to lull the unsuspecting into ready acceptance. False news sites, for instance, pattern their page design on the format and "feel" of well-known publications. Footnoting may provide a site an aura of expertise and a pretense of quality that their pages are not entitled to. Undoubtedly you can footnote even the idea of a flat earth. Official-sounding names go far. Site names may mimic those legitimate sites; some fake-artists use logos from agencies or entities that readers have grown to trust.

Importantly, put on your skeptic's hat. Too often people simply, and wrongly, assume that if the search engine provided the information it is probably true. Search engine's returns have become an article of faith to many people; their information may often be unquestioned and unwaveringly accepted. There is sometimes an unspoken assumption that the search engine creators have included some mysterious algorithm that weeds out falsehoods. Nothing could be further from the truth. The information ocean is wider than the Pacific, deeper than the Marianas Trench, and the tall tales told on the Internet reach Mt. Everest proportions.

In OSR you don't want to be anyone's best friend; you want to think like a banker, questioning everything. Assume that everything you find anywhere may be inaccurate, but consider that everything will potentially lead to correct information – even factually incorrect data.

If you plan to use any personal backgrounding websites – and there are many – test their relative reliability with checks on yourself, your family, and friends you know a great deal about. You will get a sense of overall reliability, which is useful, but that never guarantees complete accuracy. Assume, until proven wrong, that all information on such sites is incorrect. It is often more useful to try to prove information wrong than to try to prove it correct.

Credibility and Reliability Ratings

The quality of information passed on to others, its reliability, is a major factor in determining the reputation of the collector. Collectors should provide a client with information on both the validity of any source and the reliability of the information. Whatever the source, materials must be vetted. Their probable level of accuracy and truthfulness should be cited to aid the client in the decision making processes.

Both the source credibility and the reliability of the information itself become part of any rating.

Common source vetting ratings are:
1. **Reliable** - Authentic, trustworthy, or competent resource with a background of unbroken reliability.
2. **Usually Reliable** – While there may be small doubts about some aspects of authenticity, trustworthiness, or competency, the source has historically been reliable.
3. **Somewhat Reliable** – While there is some doubt about the authenticity, trustworthiness, or competency of the resource, it has provided reliable information in the past.
4. **Reliability in question** – There are significant doubts regarding authenticity, trustworthiness, or competency but the source has sometimes provided reliable information previously.
5. **Unreliable** – The source has a track record of providing incorrect information and lacks any reputation for authenticity, trustworthiness, or competency.
6. **Unknown reliability** – For one reason or many, there is no information available with which to properly evaluate a source's reliability.

Determining the source analysis rating on websites can be helped by using such sites as **Website Outlook,** which provides website valuation and stats at http://websiteoutlook.com/. Similar sites may be found using key words such as "analysis" or "analytics."

In addition to rating the source, the particular piece of information must be rated. While both the source and the information from the source are rated, the information rating generally carries the most weight.

A. **Confirmed** – Independent sources have confirmed the information; it is logical and consistent with other information.

B. **Probably True** – While the information is not confirmed by independent sources, it is both logical and consistent with other information.

C. **Possibly True** – While unconfirmed by independent sources, the information is reasonable and is consistent with some information about the subject.

D. **Doubtful** – Unconfirmed by independent sources; it is illogical but possible. Lacks key information about the subject.

E. **Improbable** – Lacks any confirmation, is illogical, or is contradicted by other information.

F. **Misinformation** – Appears to be unintentionally false; is illogical in itself and is contradicted by other confirmed information from independent sources.

G. **Deception** – Appears to be a deliberate falsehood; is contradicted by other information available from reliable, independent sources.

When an (A 1) is listed after a piece of information that would be a top rating. A (G 5) appearing after a sentence or reported fact would indicate a bottom rating. A (C 3) rating would be mid-range.

***

Project:
In the SOP's analysis section indicate what level of analysis you anticipate undertaking, and how you will mark the material submitted to a client.

Project:
Write five to ten sentences In the SOP's analysis section explaining how you anticipate carrying out analysis and what factors you will use in assessing the information you gather.

21. Production

Output is the final, and critical, challenge. No matter how good the OSR search has been, nor how potentially useful the information that you found, the effort is wasted if the information is not disseminated in a usable form to those who need it. As in trig class, you must "show your work."

Readability is important to usefulness, and perhaps as importantly, it is one of the keys to believability. What the product looks like does matter. Information written on a bar napkin may be quite accurate, even highly inventive, but it is nowhere as believable as a well-formatted and documented report.

Reporting Phases
While an OSR report may be a one-off – and many are – long-term projects often require more. There may be as many as three reporting phases:
- Exploitation flash reports
- Interpretation
- Supplementary Interpretation.

The Exploitation flash phase is when the information – the results are often in raw form or without significant interpretation – has been gathered and passed to decision makers so they may make any initial adjustments they deem necessary. Immediate reporting of important information normally takes place within one hour to one day after its discovery. It meets immediate information needs. The selection of facts to be reported is based on significance, important changes, or activity. Timing is the important factor here.

The Interpretation phase report normally will be a day to several weeks after the information was gathered. This second phase weaves all of the most recently collected information in with previous data, explaining in an organized and comprehensive manner what the analyst thinks it all means. This second phase report provides details of events and situations, aggregating all the available facts. It is a view from 30,000 feet. Timing remains important, but this is generally less time-sensitive than the first phase.

The Supplementary Interpretation phase can be considered a final wrap-up of a project or a review of the current state of knowledge about a subject. It take place at the conclusion of a project or when a review of a situation is needed, perhaps at quarterly intervals on ongoing projects. It is an in-depth, detailed, coordinated view and appraisal – an authoritative summing up that is seldom time-bound. It is often a detailed report that may focus on specialized areas.

Version Control

One critical issue too often overlooked is version control. Failure to develop an effective version control system, one that works for the individual researcher, research desk, or the team, can lead to hours spent trying to recreate any work that was previously done – and being only marginally successful at that. Version control is particularly important when more than one researcher is involved in a project, but should be thought through even on one-person projects.

Whatever information professionals do, they need to develop a system that will control their output version, saving older versions but making certain that any needed changes are done on the current version. It's a lot more difficult than it sounds.

Version control often revolves around either saving the latest version by date/time (e.g. "Report 2020-01-3-1700") or name (e.g. Report Name Version 2.5.6). These can be combined by using the year, month, date, and version for the day as in "Report Name 20.1.3-5.6.

This is not a treatise on report writing, or publishing, but a few ideas are worth looking at:

- Printable documents in computer-readable formats should be simple and straightforward.
- All documents should be created with readability in mind, and designed for the particular audience.
- Executive summaries are usually essential.
- When technically possible, there should be a system of indexing and a method of rapid movement to selected items. Tabs and links work.
- Web sites for display of the output can be highly useful, particularly if these are enhanced by maps and/or selected graphics or multi-media items.
- Linking to original sources, or copies of those sources, often help "prove" the product.
- In many cases the date and time that collection ended are important to know, as well as the time period covered; events occurring after collection and analysis can alter the information landscape.

Key Elements

Design and content of a document are best left to the drafter. None-the-less we recommend the inclusion of executive summaries and major pieces of source material, perhaps in an annex. These are essential in EVERY report. Consider developing a word cloud of your own report to determine, or visually confirm, the emphasis of your research results. By the same token, word clouds of the information sources you use in writing a report can become useful "tells" as you write your report.

Web source material can be treated as major footnotes, along with the URL, while the original article, paragraph, or quotation may be listed as an appendix or in an end note. Robust sourcing materials, included as an appendix, allow the user to consider the same material the researcher or research desk used in reaching a conclusion. This allows report readers to decide if they agree with researchers. It often improves buy-in even if the customer never checks the sources.

The best reports make clear any differences between known facts, presumed information, and speculation; they also identify any unknowns.

Source credibility and information reliability ratings should always be given in order to explain the process and bolster the conclusion. This allows readers to review the results and make independent judgments of the weight to assign any critical piece of information. Without the sourcing data any report is at best minimally valuable and there is often an ongoing suspicion of shoddy workmanship.

Users also need to know how and why the information was analyzed – for strategic, operational, tactical, or technical reasons. Sometimes the emphasis and conclusions of the same data will change with the analysis level, interpretation, and reasoning.

Information gaps, and relationships between events and the players, are often worth highlighting.

In-depth reports should be broken into discrete sections that cover a subject thoroughly. Each section should have a summary. This can be limited to a one-paragraph length. Individual summaries should not be concatenated and turned into the report's summary, however.

Reports should identify the author(s) and any reviewers, as well as their qualifications. There should be complete contact information, allowing the report's readers to question the originators about issues they deem unclear or foggy.

Background material should always be available to a customer, often as an appendix of a report. This improves trustworthiness, helps establish accuracy, shows transparency, and provides important baseline information to clients who want to delve further into the issue.

The material that can be useful in a report includes a description of the information, the way it was acquired, and where it resided originally. It often helps to describe the way the information was collected, analyzed and how any conclusions were reached. The supporting materials can be included in the report itself. It is often advisable, in the supporting material as in the report itself, to avoid jargon and include a dictionary of terms as well as a section of caveats.

Supporting documents – explainers – are often written in the first-person plural ("we did so and so"). They may be done in a question and answer format. Videos, sound bites, or visual aids may be included if the format of the report permits.

A complete report will deal with whatever distortion field was found, that part of the information universe which challenges your research. It is important to know and understand what others are thinking.

Some organizations have pre-designed formats which report writers are expected to follow. If a client has set a particular format, that is the one to use. If a required format has not been specified, remember that many word processing programs have format sheets. Some digital research programs have proprietary output capabilities. These can be useful; whatever is available should be explored.

For those who do not use a client's format, computer-aided formats, or production programs, consider these points:
- Always use the paper size most common to the area you are working. American reports are standardized on the 8½ by 11 inch size. Legal documents are longer. Many other countries use a different size paper, so it is important to know who

your audience is and to use a paper size they are most familiar with. Anything else detracts from the message.

- If the report is printed out, remember that plain paper – of some shade of white – is easiest to read. However, too aggressive a bright white distracts from the message.
- There are myriad typefaces and fonts available. Research has shown some fonts are easier to read than others. In English a serif typeface such as Times Roman is best for the body copy written for Americans. Studies show that Americans – who are used to serifs on the type – find Times-Roman or a similar typeface much easier to read in long sentences. In other countries, readers seem to have no trouble with sans-serif body types such as Arial. Anything that detracts from your message, such as typefaces your readers are not used to, should be avoided.
- Headlines and titles should be eye-catching. Arial works well for headlines or titles, even for Americans. To help set headlines and titles apart and bring attention to them consider using a combination of **bold face** and *italic*. That makes the words stand out; the forward-slant suggests that the words are important and racing forward. Anything less than a suggestion that your text is important detracts from your message.
- Too many typefaces are distracting. A report using a wide variety of typefaces ends up looking like a gaudy circus poster. Two or three typefaces, in a couple of different sizes, with their bold and italic fonts, are all you normally need or want. They provide a consistency that a multitude of typefaces cannot. Inconsistency detracts from your message.
- Too many type sizes can also be problematic. Type is measured in "points." Consider routinely using 11 or 12 point type in the body of a report. Those sizes are easy on the eyes, particularly on the eyes of middle-aged adults. Difficulty reading detracts from your message. There is another reason for using a reasonable size. And that other reason is: It takes up more room on the page than smaller

type sizes. Consequently you get fewer words per line. Yes, you can pack more words into a line by using smaller type sizes. That's actually not a bargain. As you read your eye travels across the page, comes to the end of the line, and then dips down one line to pick up the continuation of the text. Studies have shown that somewhere after a line length of about ten to 15 words the eye has a problem picking up the next line. That causes a break in the cognitive process while the brain and eye coordinate to find the start of the next line. Anything that interrupts the smooth flow of an idea detracts from your message.

- The eye needs "white space." Margins should be wide enough so that the text doesn't look cramped and crowded. There should be space between lines so that ascenders of l and d don't interfere with the descenders of j and g. "Gray type" is boring – and something that is boring detracts from your message.
- Headline or title type sizes can vary but should not change in the same report. Consistency suggests competence. It is possible to use type as small as 14 points for headlines, and sometimes as large as 38 points, when using a 12 point body type. The headline type must be visually larger than the body type, but not so large that it overwhelms the type where your message is to be found – in the body of the document. Inconsistency in headline sizes and over-large type distract the reader from the message.
- Fancy initial letters at the start of a paragraph, or pull-quotes in boxes, can be distracting, particularly when they change the line length that a reader has become used to. Such design flourishes are fine for some document styles, but in "strictly business" reports these tend to draw attention away from the substance of the text and dilute the attention your message receives.
- Pictures or visuals can be invaluable or they can be seen as distractions. Choose any pictures carefully. Pictures are intended to be distractions from the text. If they illustrate

something important, they should be used between paragraphs (not at one side of the text so that line lengths vary because of the presence of the picture). Pictures for the sake of pictures, or art for the sake of art, lessen the attention a reader will give to the text. Stock photos seldom add anything important. Artwork of any kind should contribute to the story you want to tell. Link diagrams and other visualizations are often useful and can be created through sites such as **VIS:** https://vis.occrp.org.

- In reports, multiple columns seldom make sense. The "newspaper format" of multiple columns is used for display purposes when there are many stories and because a line of type spread across an entire newspaper page would be impossible for the eye to follow and then pick up the continuation of the line when it returns. In a report there is really only one story and that is your story. When a reader gets to the end of a line in a multi-column format it is too easy for the eye to "bleed" over into an adjacent line of another story. White "gutters" and "black column rules" can help corral any eye travel, but using columns will only make your report text harder to read.

- Ink colors abound; there is always a temptation to set off the report with multiple colors. There is a tendency to do so for the sheer enjoyment of the diversity. The reality is that hundreds of years of experience and experimentation have shown that black ink on a white background is the easiest to read. If you use colors, do so sparingly and with some consistency. Too many colors spoil the message.

- If the pages of your text will be bound, or put in loose-leaf notebooks, leave extra space on the spine side of the page – normally about an extra one-quarter to one-half inch. Words that are hidden, or nearly hidden, in the binding distract from your message and the information you found.

- If the report is sent out in digital form, remove all metadata about you or your search before sending, but keep and possibly highlight any metadata that provides information about search subjects.

∗∗∗

Project:
In the Production section of your SOP write out details of the formats you plan to follow for reports, and any other planned production item.

Afterword

R.A. Norton, Ph.D.

Professor and Director, The Futures Laboratory and Coordinator, National Security Programs, Auburn University Open Source Intelligence Laboratory

Open Source Research (OSR) or as it was once called, Open Source Intelligence (OSINT), has changed dramatically since I first began to discover its power to produce insight, when conducting research on the immense Soviet Biological weapons program known as Biopreparat (Биопрепарат).

The discipline then and now, was as much an art as a science and therefore developed slowly, often lacking the full respect it deserved, because other competing means for Intelligence gathering were successful. Many of the alternate means of gather Intelligence or "INTS" relied heavily on technology, which naturally translated into seemingly endless and limitless federal contracts. In those days of budgetary abundance cost connoted value. "Good things surely can't be inexpensive!" was a common mantra in the halls of the Pentagon.

OSINT in those days was also very labor intensive and could not rely on technology. Hand and mind was used to develop insight. Candidly, many decision makers in the Intelligence Community (IC) and military perceived the classified means of gathering Intelligence as somehow better if for no other reason than they WERE classified, although many gaps, secrets and mysteries remained. To the detriment of building insight, certain decision makers either ignored OSINT or considered it illegitimate. The United States had invested hundreds of billions of dollars, perhaps even more in developing the classified "INTS". Quietly however, behind the scenes and in many parts of the military and IC, OSINT was starting to come into its own.

When I first became acquainted with one of this volume's authors, Mark Monday, we often discussed the power of OSINT in providing the "80% solution". Over the years, OSINT practitioners proved this claim true many times. OSINT could provide insight, sometimes breathtakingly so. OSINT was to be sure not a panacea, but where applicable, could provide foundational Intelligence that drove requirements. OSINT was growing in strength, but quietly. Then that fateful day on 11 September 2001, not only changed the nation, it changed the IC and the Intelligence process. OSINT began to shine.

The authors, Miguel Fernandez, Mark Monday and Dr. Emil Sarpa, all early OSINT practitioners, were like the rest of our small community of professionals tasked by our respective organizations to build its power. An 80% solution was no longer acceptable. The IC and military, our nation needed better. Intelligence professionals tend to rely on proven Tactics, Techniques and Procedures (TTPs). OSINT was again different, in that in many cases we did not have the requisite TTPs, much less a thorough knowledge of where to make insight discoveries.

Development of the tradecraft took time, but as it matured, Mark Monday and Dr. Emil Sarpa began to educate future Military Intelligence decision makers including those who were attending the Army Intelligence School at Ft. Huachuca. Both saw a need to codify some of the tradecraft and successfully did so, in their first book, "What You Don't Know…Your Guide to Achieving "Knowledge Advantage" in the Information Age!" Many Intelligence related academic curricula utilized this important volume as a resource and its use continues today.

One such curriculum is that developed at Auburn University, where I met another contributor to the present volume, Alan Millington. An instructor friend of mine, who worked in the Auburn University English Department, first introduced me to Alan. I had decried for years to my friend the need to find students who could think critically and then most importantly communicate well both verbally and through the written word. These communicators are the future of OSR. Alan quickly proved his analytical skills, which had started years earlier while working as an enlisted member of Marine Intelligence in Afghanistan. During his time working in the Auburn University Open Source Intelligence Laboratory, we dealt with a wide variety of "sporty" analytical challenges, presented to us by military government and business customers. Moving forward on OSR's capabilities for developing insight, we were able to achieve consistently better than an 80% solution and even on occasion a 90% solution or better.

This is where OSR is today. New technologies are making possible capabilities that even a few years ago, were only possible through the classified INTS. Its potential continues to evolve rapidly, so much so that it is difficult to keep up. For instance, currently OSR can perform many of the capabilities previously resident only through Measures and Signatures Intelligence (MASINT). That has happened in the last 2-3 years. Imagery Intelligence (IMINT) is also undergoing a revolution. The future? Sub-meter resolution imagery of the entire earth – updated daily, available commercially. OSR is changing the way we develop Intelligence and the way we fight wars. Several instances where OSR served the warfighter remain highly classified. Those stories are not likely to become public knowledge, considering the OSR techniques are still very much in use today. This brings us back to the current volume.

The authors stress "Knowledge Advantage" throughout the volume. Knowledge, whether rightly or wrongly has become a commodity. It has also become a key domain in warfighting. Discerning fact is essential for knowledge building and development of insight. As indicated by the title of this book, it is "Elementary". Although, some might make accusations of appropriating language, the foundational elements of knowledge advantage are "bricks and mortar', provided by the OSR "Tradecraft". This volume brings together the foundational techniques, but also provides hidden "nuggets" or clues about the future directions of OSR/OSINT. The authors' backgrounds and current linkages to the educational enterprise give some clues about the OSR/OSINT pathways and pathfinders. A highly educated OSR/OSINT workforce is essential to future success in insight development. OSR/OSINT practitioners need to be synthesizers.

The amount of information available is beyond human comprehension and yet still continues to expand. Current and future needs are a workforce capable of drinking from the proverbial firehoses, while also being "critical thinkers"; a term so frequently used to describe needs that is has become almost banal. OSR/OSINT practitioners must be "all source analysts", capable of taking not only the volume, but also variety of available information. Who are these people? Where do we find them and more importantly, how do we develop more of them? The answers lie in part in the backgrounds of the authors here. They have both the vision and understanding of some of the answers.

Miguel Fernandez is currently teaches Freshman composition as a member of the Composition and Literature faculty and Faculty Liaison for Student Veterans at Chandler-Gilbert Community College in Arizona. He also focuses on OSR/OSINT research techniques to detect and decipher bias and fake news. These are critical skill sets for the future of OSR/OSINT. The greatest of OSR/OSINT discoveries mean nothing if analysts are unable to summarize cogently and then communicate in a timely manner to decision makers. OSR/OSR training has to begin early. Emil Sarpa's experience teaching at the High School level provides one possible solution – begin OSR/OSINT training in high schools, perhaps even earlier. Although, the Auburn University Open Source Intelligence Laboratory does not have a huge data set as evidence, we do have a few examples, one spectacular, for the utility of identifying young talent and then nurturing it through college graduation. One of our successes is a young man, identified in high school, who is currently serving as a fellow in a highly prestigious program in one of the three letter agencies.

Mark Monday's former assignment was at the US Army Intelligence Center at Ft. Huachuca. Although I work with all of the services, my estimation is that the most critical needs for better OSR/OSINT reside within the Army. Although, Army leaders have certainly come to understand that OSR/OSINT can help them answer critical strategic and even tactical questions, they have not fully embraced the discipline. That is changing as future Army and larger Military Intelligence leadership is educated of its value. Mark has been driving that effort at Ft. Huachuca. I have had occasion to work with some of the Combat Commands (COCOMs) using OSINT. Those commanders have success stories to tell. Interestingly, but perhaps not surprisingly and as alluded to earlier, US Special Operations Command (USSOCOM) has had some spectacular wins in the dark places of the world, driven in part by OSR/OSINT.

Alan Millington's contribution to this volume illustrate the importance of future technology, the human/machine interface that can and must help automate the OSR/OSINT process towards insight. Alan and I have spent many hours looking at problem sets and discussing technology solutions. Current needs are extensive. Future needs will be massive. Humans will have to have technology that enable faster, quicker, surer discovery of key information. As he and I have both briefed at some of the highest levels of decision-making within DOD, the customer is not in need of the millions of available data points, but rather in the "five key documents" that answer the question, but currently remain hidden in the background noise that is cyber. Automated technology can help immensely with discovery and discernment.

So where should future OSR/OSINT practitioners begin their journey of discovery? A key place to start is mastering the elements presented in this volume. As indicated by the authors, although the links to the resources provided have a shelf life, the underlying principles of how you think and approach OSR/OSINT problems remains relatively consistent. Assuming you the reader become an OSR/OSINT practitioner, you will likely one day need to answer the question posed by a decision-making customer asking how you will develop insight. When asked, hand them this book or the ones likely to come after it (remember OSR/OSINT is ever changing). To many decision makers that answer will be sufficient. For those decision makers educated by Miguel or Mark or Emil, other questions are likely follow. In those cases state simply, "This is our foundation, upon which we will build the OSR/OSINT TTPs, as we better come to understand the problem set. They will understand the wisdom of that approach and will understand better than most that OSR/OSINT will remain a creative process, certainly aided by technology and automation, but still a human process borne of the mind – remaining both an art as a science. Best of luck on your future journey of discovery and insight!

Appendix A.
Internet Basics

Knowledge of basic digital technology is essential for professionals charged with looking for important information nestled in the impossibly vast spectrum of facts that are found in the chaos of the Internet.

No one, you included, can know everything about computers, their use, and the Internet. Much of anyone's needs, when encountering new terms or techniques, can be found through a word search of the Internet.

The size of files impacts time – how long it takes to download data and the time required to go through them. Thus, understanding sizes is essential.

Bit: The bit may be considered the atom of all digital activity. It is both a storage unit and a state of energy; on-off, 0-1, yes-no. This is the way this smallest unit of computer information is often described.

Byte: The byte is a computer storage unit made up of eight bits. A single character in the alphabet is a byte in length.

Kilobyte (KB): If computer language was precise – which it isn't – a kilobyte would be exactly 1,000 bytes. It isn't. A kilobyte is a mathematical rendering of two to the 10th power and is actually made up of 1,024 bytes.

Megabyte (MB) or **(Meg)** continues the imprecision and the mathematical formula – two to the 20th power. It is about 1,000 kilobytes and is in the neighborhood of one million bytes.

Gigabyte (GB) or **(Gig)** is two to the 30th power and moves into the billion-byte range.

Terabyte (TB) takes the equation to the 40th power and moves into the trillion range.

Petabyte (PB) is about 1,000 times larger than a terabyte and continues the mathematical calculation to the 50th power.

Exabyte (EB) moves the calculation to the 60th power and is about 1,152 followed by 15 zeros.

The byte chart continues to ascend by mathematical powers through **Zettabyte, Yottabyte,** and **Brontobyte.**

Avoid confusing kilobits and megabits with the terms kilobytes and megabytes. The first two terms refer to computer communication speeds while the later are measurements of size or storage capacity. One **kilobit** is a thousand bits (1,000 bits) and a **megabit** is a thousand times larger (1,000,000 bits). These terms are used in describing the speed of data transfers, the number of data pulses that can be transferred per second.

The Internet

It's important to remember that the Internet, as an institution, does not exist. There is no single organization called "the Internet." The Internet consists of many independent information nodes cobbled together like strings of Christmas lights. Some network nodes come. Some go. Some are pristine; other nodes are sloppy. The Internet at this hour is not the same as it was an hour ago, nor will it be the same even 30 seconds from now. The Internet is a network of the willing and capable. It constantly changes. No one runs the Internet. Individual nodes are run by someone, of course, but no one is in charge of the entire entity called the Internet.

Understanding the Internet, and how it works, may not be essential in doing research, but it helps make things that happen on the Internet understandable. Internet information is chunked, cut into "packets" and moved out from its location to its destination. The packet header carries the information about where the packet is going and where it came from. Whatever data there is in the message – text, a video, or some other type of file, goes into the body of the packet. Information the computer needs to process the information, to keep the packets together, in the proper sequence, and to route the query and return is included in header information attached to each packet.

If it goes out *en clair* Web information will be sent as http; encrypted packets go out as https – the additional "s" is meant to indicate the message is secure.

Routers forward the packets of material from the original address – the user's IP address – to the destination through a series of other routers. The routers include the IP user's address in the header so that a message can be answered or a file can be brought back to the requestor. That IP address, which also can give a great deal of information about you, the sender of the packet, can be read by the operators of every router the packet passes through, as well as the system operator at the packet's destination.

In normal circumstances http or https packets that are sent to you or that you ask for are a pointer directly to you. But there are ways for you to become less conspicuous, if not anonymous, by making identification of the originating computer problematic.

When messages go out over a Virtual Private Network (VPN) they go initially to the VPN server, which encrypts the entire message – including the IP address – and stores it in another packet that carries its own address in place of your IP address. It then forwards the revised message normally. What router operators along the line, and the system operator at the site you are contacting, see is the IP address of the VPN service as the message sender. The VPN's address is the only address the final site and its server can see or reply to. Any interlopers who gain access to the message see only the VPN's address. Neither do the system operators at intermediate servers know the identity of the original sender.

When the return message comes back to the VPN from the site you communicated with, the VPN knows who you are and forwards the message on to you. That provides some level of obscurity but does not provide for anonymity. The VPN operator, if pressured by such things as a court order or a visit from a government agency, can reveal who sent what and who responded. For that reason check out where any VPN is located. Avoid ones in unfriendly countries or locations known to collect information for blackmail.

Tor, The Onion Router, and similar computer programs use mid-stream servers to obscure the destination of traffic, but break up the IP address in such a way that it and the routers it travels through never have both the message sender's address and the message at the same time. Tor, when used properly with all the security rules in place, drastically reduces your chances of being followed and cannot be pressured to reveal the IP address of the sender of any message or material. To make Tor more secure, users employ Bridges, a program that runs on a thumb drive or disk to access the Web through Tor.

***

Machines – whether they are computers or phones – access the Internet in one of two ways. They are wired or wireless.

Machines connected to the Internet are either servers or clients.

There is no third entity called "The Cloud." The cloud is simply some server somewhere that substitutes for your own machine's memory.

Servers provide services to other machines. Clients are the machines that connect to the servers and seek services from them.

Servers generally deal with a specific type of Internet service. Web servers, email servers, and FTP servers provide services to their respective type of clients. Servers generally have an IP address that does not change. This is different from, say, a computer dialing into the system through a modem.

Any computer that is calling another needs an IP address to operate, so it is assigned one for that online session. An Internet Service Provider (ISP) does not need an IP address for each customer, but only an address for each customer it is supporting at a given time.

Protocols are required to tell servers what to do with the query that a client machine sends. They are the way one node talks to other nodes in an understandable way. Different Internet applications have different formulae for communicating, such as HTTP for Web pages, mailto for email, and others including FTP, and Telnet. The front end of the formulae tell the Internet what applications need to be brought into play. Message – or files – sent over the Internet all have headers which tell the system such things as where the message came from, what it is composed of, and where it is going. Headers are a form of metadata and may be exploited; information can be squeezed from them by people knowledgeable about OSR.

Ports are the location that information goes through on a machine – ports may be systematic or dynamic

***

There are many parts of the Internet but the Web and email are the most used portions. Telnet, Gopher and other parts of the Internet have been largely superseded by the Web. Nonetheless they are still usable.

***

There are four parts of an email address. The user name is first, although that handle may differ significantly from the person's name in real life. The @ sign comes next and is a separator. The next portion identifies the host computer system. A period separates the host computer system name from the type of domain.

***

Internet Universal Resource Locators (URLs) are the "addresses" that the Web uses. They are actually numbers – sets of numbers between 0 and 255 – with periods for separation. People don't remember seemingly-random sets of numbers though computers do fine with them. The Internet system is designed to serve the needs of both humans and machines. A user enters a site name as a Universal Resource Locator (URL) and the Internet system matches the typed-in site name to a numbers-only address, shipping the message, request, or answer on to the correct place. You, as a user, don't see any of that, however.

Domain Name Servers (DNS) are the key to making the Internet work. This is where the directory of domain names is kept and the site names are linked to the numerical IP addresses. Until the numeric identity of a site is established at the DNS, a query cannot go anywhere. While domain names are relatively easy for people to remember and use, computers and other similar machines access websites via numeric IP addresses that are found in the DNS server.

DNS servers get their information on a regular basis from the Internet's Central Registry, where Internet Service Providers (ISPs) and hosting companies send information about the creation of new websites, or the demise of old ones. The central registry information is kept current.

When you type in a URL the DNS server finds the numeric identity, the actual address that the system recognizes, and connects your ISP to it.

It normally takes at least 12, and as many as 36, hours to update the servers worldwide when a new domain name is registered. This is known as the propagation period.

***

Sometimes the Internet doesn't work as you want it to do. Common error messages are:

- 403 – Forbidden
- 404 – Not found
- 500 – Server error (Generalized)
- 503 – System overload (Temporary, in most cases)
- 522 – Connection timed out (Unble to connect to server).

***

Application program interfaces – APIs – are a way of calling up coded information residing in another location, such as applications. Consider, find, and use various APIs as if they are small programs that will provide the researcher or research desk with elegant answers to some of the more difficult techniques.

Appendix B. Your Reference Library

Organize!

A library or repository should be central to the people it serves and by all measures, secure.

Your personal library is likely to consist of machine-readable materials and books or magazines on paper or other fiber-based materials. Your own library should store virtually any type of material, including text, PDFs, images, audio, video, databases, saved Web pages, and non-digital materials.

Researchers are, indeed, part of an information universe, the totality of which we cannot see, the size of which is too large, and the reaches too diverse, to allow expertise in every area. Open Source researchers are somewhat like astronomers, people who can hive off an area for intense study but who never see the whole picture with granularity. Expertise in Red Shift does not make an astronomer a leader in Martian geology.

Your research library should focus on your own field(s) of study but still be extensive enough to answer basic questions about some of the further reaches of the research universe, exploring areas that remain beyond your expertise.

Get and keep a copy of basic reference books that you might need in your field, or at least know where you can access the information quickly.

Your Local Library

You know some resources, but this is a good time to utilize the expertise of your reference librarian. Get to know your local librarians, but remember they are there to help you do your work –

not to do the work for you. Asking librarians: "what reference do you have on (general subject)? I am looking for information on/about (specific issue)" is generally a good way to approach a subject.

As a starter at the library, familiarize yourself with the *New York Times Index, The Wall Street Journal Index,* and *The London Times Index*. These three reference sources provide a good overview of general news about any subject, as reported in the daily media. Then review your subject in the *Reader's Guide to Periodical Literature,* giving you resources in the magazine field, and the subject guide *to Books in Print.* This should give you a basic library grounding on information that is generally available on the subject you are, or will be, researching.

This is a good place to begin building a bibliography of your field. Your bibliography at the start may be as simple as photocopying the applicable pages from these publications. There are bibliographies available in many fields and these are good additions to your own personal bibliography. Check with librarians and others to see if that work has already been done. Remember: Don't reinvent the wheel.

Depending on the subject you are researching, you may want to photocopy applicable sections of organization and trade directories. Often it is useful to have, or know how to get, alumni or other college directories that may show who studied in what areas and who you can call upon for expertise.

You would be well advised to know what publications applicable to your research area may be published by Bowker, Gale Research, Marquis Who's Who, and Wilson. All of these publishers put out in-depth materials that may be useful in your field.

Many of the research publications available in a library are too expensive for the average online researcher or desk to buy for their home or office, but knowing where to look for the information and what information is available is half the solution. Workarounds, such as personal photocopies of the applicable book pages, are useful additions to any personal library.

Your Personal Library

No one should presume to tell you what you need to put in your personal research library, but an hour or two of preliminary thought about its contents may save you a day or a week of research time later. Putting thought and effort into the development of your own research library is worthwhile.

Your personal library should be readily searchable; an index is invaluable. Tag all digital entries. From card files to personal search engines on your computer, whatever works for you is appropriate. Search and filter capabilities are important – you always need to find and retrieve what you put into your library; you must be able to do so quickly and easily.

There is much digital material that will be useful in your library, including reference material on OSR.

If you have not downloaded all of the following books to your digital library, you might want to do so.

Untangling the Web, by Robin Widner, is a US government publication released under the Freedom of Information Act. It is old and many site references are outdated, but it provides a thorough-provoking overview. ***Untangling the Web: a Guide to Internet Research*** (2007) 651 pps.
https://www.governmentattic.org/8docs/UntanglingTheWeb-NSA_2007.pdf

Ben Benavides' Trilogy: Mr. Benavides was an instructor at the Army Intelligence School, teaching Open Source Intelligence. He has produced a number of free digital books to teach people how to use the various techniques of OSINT. All are available at http://phibetaiota.net/2016/09/ben-benavides-desktop-osint-handbook/

- *Desktop OSINT Handbook*. 49 pps.
- *Exploring Social Media Web Sites*. 32 pps
- *2oolkit on the Go*. 255 pps.

NATO OSINT Handbook Trilogy:

- *NATO Open Source Intelligence Handbook*. 57 pps (2001)
  www.au.af.mil/au/awc/awcgate/nato/osint_hdbk.pdf

- *NATO Open Source Intelligence Reader*. 110pps (2002)
  www.au.af.mil/au/awc/awcgate/nato/osint_reader.pdf

- *NATO Intelligence Exploitation of the Internet* 104 pps (2002)
  https://nsarchive2.gwu.edu/NSAEBB/NSAEBB436/docs/EBB-005.pdf

Army OSINT Manual 91 pps (2012) *US Army ATP 2.22-9*. http://fas.org/irp/doddir/army/atp2-22-9.pdf

Verification handbooks Three books, useful in disaster situations to check information reliability from Internet user-generated materials, are available at http://verificationhandbook.com/.

Toolkits

Online or downloadable toolkits (utility packages) can make research easier by concentrating needed programs, api's, and other resources in a single location. Professional information searchers acquaint themselves with the variety of toolkits and find many parts, if not the entire sites and kits, useful.

- **Bellingcat Online Investigation Toolkit:**
  https://docs.google.com/document/d/1BfLPJpRtyq4RFtHJoNpvWQjmGnyVkfE2HYoICKOGguA/edit

- **Maltego ($$$$):**
  https://www.paterva.com/web7/buy/maltego-clients.php
- **OSINT Framework:** https://osintframework.com/
- **SamSpade:** https://sam-spade.en.lo4d.com/

Research Materials Sites

These sites may be useful to bookmark or place in the research library section of your SOP. Consider:

- **American Factfinder (US Census Bureau):**
  https://factfinder.census.gov/faces/nav/jsf/pages/index.xhtml
- **American Heritage Dictionary (Usage notes):**
  https://ahdictionary.com/
- **Answers.com:** http://www.answers.com/
- **AP Stylebook ($$$$):** https://apstylebook.com/
- **AP vs Chicago (Stylebook comparison):**
  http://apvschicago.com/
- **Bartleby.com (Textbook solutions):**
  https://www.bartleby.com/
- **CentralOps (Internet utilities):**
  https://centralops.net/co/
- **CIA World Factbook:**
  https://www.cia.gov/library/publications/the-world-factbook/
- **Collins English Dictionary:**
  http://www.collinsdictionary.com/dictionary/english
- **Conscious Style Guide (Bias and minority issues):**
  http://consciousstyleguide.com/
- **Diccionarios.com (Multiple languages):**
  http://www.diccionarios.com/
- **Dictionarist (Multiple languages):**
  http://www.dictionarist.com/
- **Dictionary.com:** http://dictionary.reference.com/
- **Dictionary for translations (Multiple languages):**
  http://freedict.com/

- **Dictionary Reference:** http://dictionary.reference.com/
- **Digital Public Library of America:** https://dp.la/
- **Diversity Style Guide (Handbooks from minority journalist groups):** http://www.diversitystyleguide.com/
- **Email-checker.com ($$$$, Verify email account):** https://www.email-checker.com/how-it-works/
- **Email Dossier (Investigate email addresses):** https://centralops.net/co/emaildossier.aspx
- **Email Harvester (Bulk email downloads from sites):** https://www.abbulkmailer.com/email-harvester-free.php
- **Email Tracker (Email header analysis)** https://www.iptrackeronline.com/email-header-analysis.php
- **Emailhippo: (Email account verification):** https://tools.verifyemailaddress.io/
- **Encyclopedia Britannica Online ($$$$):** http://www.britannica.com
- **Encyclopedia.com:** http://encyclopedia.com/
- **Factfinder (US demographics):** https://factfinder.census.gov/faces/nav/jsf/pages/index.xhtml
- **Foreign Word (Multiple languages):** http://foreignword.com/
- **Geo-social footprint (Where email originates):** http://geosocialfootprint.com/
- **How Stuff Works:** http://www.howstuffworks.com/
- **InfoPlease (Atlas, encyclopedia, dictionary, thesaurus):** http://www.infoplease.com/
- **Link Everything Online (LEO, German to multiple languages):** http://dict.leo.org/
- **Martindale's:** http://www.martindalecenter.com/
- **Merriam-Webster Dictionary (Citations of use):** https://www.merriam-webster.com/
- **Merriam-Webster Thesaurus:** https://www.merriam-webster.com/thesaurus

- **One Look Dictionary Search:** http://onelook.com/
- **PowerThesaurus (Crowd-sourced):** https://www.powerthesaurus.org/
- **ProQuest (Librarians):** http://proquest.umi.com/pqdweb
- **RefDesk Fast Facts:** http://www.refdesk.com/facts.html
- **Refseek.com:** https://www.refseek.com/
- **Search Systems: (US and foreign public records):** http://publicrecords.searchsystems.net/
- **SymbolHound (Computer code symbols):** http://symbolhound.com/
- **Thesaurus.com:** http://www.thesaurus.com/
- **The Quotations Page:** http://www.quotationspage.com/
- **Time and Date:** https://www.timeanddate.com/
- **Trace Email:** https://whatismyipaddress.com/trace-email
- **Translating Dictionaries (And currency conversion):** http://dictionaries.travlang.com/
- **Verifalia: (Email address validator):** https://verifalia.com/validate-email
- **Visual Thesaurus ($$$$):** https://www.visualthesaurus.com/
- **Wikipedia:** https://www.wikipedia.org/
- **Word Reference and Dictionary Links (Multiple languages):** http://wordreference.com/
- **Yahoo Finance and Currency Converter:** https://finance.yahoo.com/
- **Zanran (PDF content extraction):** http://www.zanran.com/

Over time you will find many of these useful. You will want, and need, additional books and sites. Almanacs, dictionaries, atlases, thesauruses, spelling manuals, glossaries, encyclopedias, and gazetteers are useful in addition to any guides and research books appropriate to your particular searching needs. Digital references are also available at **Infoplease,** http://www.infoplease.com/index.html

You will also want books that explain in detail the programs you use or plan to use, as well as instruction manuals on the techniques of OSR, information intelligence, or whatever name your research field goes by. While many professions use similar research techniques, they may call their particular process different things.

A current almanac and a good atlas or map collection – these may be either digital or fiber-based – are other key edition additions to the libraries of most information professionals.

Important books about your field may be useful additions to your personal research library, both for reference and to assist in finding keywords needed in online searches.

No single book meets every need of a researcher. Some books are new and help the researcher or research desk keep up with changes. Some are older but provide the type of valuable knowledge base that remains valid, even today. Of these latter type, many are out of print and have to be sought out.

When buying books, generally look first to the local suppliers or the larger chains that stock many volumes. ABE Books, which serves as a contact point for book stores, also provides users with volumes that are out-of-stock, used, and new releases.

Everyone's needs are different. For that reason we are reluctant to talk about our own reading list. We have broken some of our library down into general categories that suit our own needs.

You may find that the books – as listed – do not fit your needs. Many of our books are older but provide a valuable baseline. Before purchasing any book we suggest you go to your nearest public library and see if the book is available there. If it is not, you can probably borrow a copy through interlibrary loan to see if it is really worth your investment in both time and money.

General Research Texts
- *How to Become a World Class Investigator,* Julie Clegg, Lionquest Publishing, – , 2018
- *How to Find Out Anything,* Don MacLeod, Prentice-Hall Press, New York, 2012
- *Open Source Intelligence Techniques, Seventh Edition,* Michael Bazzell, CCI Publishing, San Bernardino, CA
- *The Chicago Guide to Fact-checking,* Brooke Borel, University of Chicago Press, Chicago, 2016
- *The Extreme Searchers Internet Handbook, Fourth Edition – a Guide for the Serious Searcher,* Randolph Hock, Cyber Age Books, Medford, New Jersey, 2013

Social Media
- *Social Media Analytics – Techniques and Insights for Extracting Business Value Out of Social Media,* Matthew Ganis and Avinash Kohirkar, Pearson Education Services, India, 2017

Libraries and Searching
- *Knowing Where to Look,* Lois Horowitz, Writer/s Digest Books, Cincinnati, Ohio, 1988
- *The New York Public Library Book of How and Where to Look It Up,* Sherwood Harris, Editor, Prentice-Hall, New York, 1991

Information Literacy
- *From Library Skills to Information Literacy) – a Handbook for the 21st Century;* California School Library Assn.; Hi Willow Research and Publishing; San Jose, CA; 1997
- *Information Literacy) Instruction Handbook*; Christopher N. Cox and Elizabeth Blakesley Linddsay, Editors; American Library Assn; 2008

Organization of Downloads/Digital Librarianship

- *Building Digital Libraries,* Thomas Reese Jr and Kyle Banerjee, Neal-Schuman Publishers, Inc. New York, 2008

- *Organizing Audiovisual and Electronic Resources for Access,* Ingrid Hsieh-Yee, Libraries Unlimited, Inc., Englewood, Colorado, 2000

Computer-assisted Reporting (CaR)/Journalism

- *A Journalist's Guide to the Internet,* Christopher Callahan and Leslie-Jean Thornton, Pearson Education Inc., Boston, 2007

- *Computer-Assisted Reporting – a Comprehensive Primer,* Fred Vallance-Jones and David McKie with Aron Pilhofer and Jaimi Dowdell, Oxford University Press, New York, 2009

- *Computer-Assisted Research – a Guide to Tapping Online Information,* Nora M. Paul, Bonus Books, Inc and the Poynter Institute for Media Studies, Chicago, IL, 1999

- *Winning with Data – Transform Your Culture, Empower Your People and Shape the Future,* Tomasz Tunguz and Frank Bien, John Wiley & Sons, Hoboken, NJ 2016

OPPO

- *Opposition Research Handbook: A Guide to Political Investigations,* Larry Zilliox; Unknown; Unknown; Unknown (Digital)

OSINT

- *The Tao of Open Source Intelligence,* Stewart K. Bertram,IT Governance Publishing, Ely Cambridgeshire, UK, 2015

Maps and Mapping

- *Google Maps Hacks – Tips and Tools for Geographic Searching and Remixing,* Rich Gibson and Schuyler Erle, O'Reilly Media, Inc., Sebastopol, CA, 2006

Sites and Information Resources

- *Find it Online – Third Edition – The Complete Guide to Online Research,* Alan M. Schlein, Facts on Demand Press, Tempe, Arizona, 2003

- *The Manual to Online Public Records – The Researcher's Tool to Online Resources of Public Records and Public Information,* Cynthia Hetherington and Michael Sankey, Facts on Demand Press, Tempe, AZ, 2008

Competitor Intelligence

- *Competitive Intelligence for Dummies,* **Jim Underwood, John Wiley& Sons, Inc; Hoboken, New Jersey, 2013**

- *Perfectly Legal Competitor Intelligence – How to get it, use it and profit from it,* Douglas Bernhardt, Pitman Publishing, London, 1993

- *The Guide to Online Due Diligence Investigations – the Professional Approach on How to Use Traditional and Social Media Resources for Investigations,* Cynthia Hetherington, Facts on Demand Press, Tempe, Arizona, 2015

Security

- *Darknet: A Beginner s Guide to Staying Anonymous Online*; Lance Henderson; Createspace Independent Publishing Platform; United States; 2013

- *Incognito Toolkit; Tools, Apps, and Creative Methods for Remaining Anonymous, Private, and Secure While Publishing, Buying, and Researching Online*; Rob Robideau; Personal Armament; Unknown; 2013

- ***Tor and the Dark Art of Anonymity***; Lance Henderson; Lance Henderson, San Bernardino, CA; 2017

Appendix C. US Government OSINT Operations

There are at least two different views of the Open Source Intelligence (OSINT)/OSR world. They can be categorized as the US government vs. The Rest of the World.

The difference between working for the US government and working in the rest of world is striking. Your abilities are actually more circumscribed in the US government world. Most US government OSINT researchers are restricted to passive observation only. They cannot ask questions or "engage" in any way – they are only allowed to look and listen.

While the common world-view of research allows open source operators to be proactive and contact people for information, most US government practitioners cannot do so. For instance, most people think they could call an expert on a subject or engage in a conversation – even debate – on a subject at a cocktail party, eliciting information or views. They feel able to collect information about US persons – people and corporations. In the US government model those are not only often forbidden; there may be career-ending consequences for anyone who breaks the rules.

For those researchers restricted to passive observation only, the possible pitfalls come early. The questions are many; clear answers are few, but the government version will always be starkly outlined by agency regulations.

US government information collectors using this book, without following the restrictions on collection imposed by their particular agency, would undoubtedly face serious legal sanctions. Restrictions vary from agency to agency, but whatever the rules and restrictions, they will be enforced by that organization.

In the outside world, OSR practitioners use computer programs that mask their identity; many government agencies forbid masking. OSR operators do other things that a professional working for parts of the US government may not do at all or will be severely limited in doing.

Few restrictions are promulgated in this manual, far fewer than in government operations. The overriding one here is "do not break the law." But employer rules, as well as laws, must be followed even if they are seen as self-defeating.

The first and arguably the most important US government rule is simple: OSINT is observation. Strictly speaking, collection is limited to observation. Collectors may not take active roles or even ask questions – that is, elicit information (elicitation) – or engage people in conversation. All dialog with information sources is forbidden.

Total passivity is not required under many other research regimens. Fifth grade students doing their homework are often less constrained than US open source operators. The civilian version of open source research (and the collection practices of many other nations' and groups' intelligence agencies) differ significantly from the US model. Other countries and organizations may allow their collection professionals to "engage," "elicit," or ask questions, but that is not the way OSINT in practiced by most of the US government.

United States government practitioners are also prohibited, in most cases, from collecting intelligence on US Persons – a wide category that includes people, groups, and even corporations.

This restriction is known as Intelligence Oversight. Government-sponsored collectors will want to know how or whether their agency or group is bound by Intelligence Oversight regulations.

The failure to observe Intelligence Oversight rules can easily mean the loss of a career or even legal prosecution. This is another area where non-government US civilians and foreign collectors are not required to follow the strictest rules.

US government rules often prevent use of some computer programs and Internet resources that are commonly used in the civilian world (and by other national intelligence agencies). Programs and apps that civilians often put on their computers and use in their daily searches may well be unavailable to government practitioners.

In US government operations, Operational Security (OPSEC) is often paramount and is the reason given to prohibit the use of many programs and techniques used outside the government. That is not necessarily because the proscribed programs and techniques are inherently insecure. Sometimes they have simply not been formally tested for security and approved for use. In other words, they have not been properly wrung-out. "Too busy" can be invoked as an excuse for not testing out useful programs and techniques. On the chance that there is some security fluke in a program or resource, the government simply puts it off-limits for use.

Those who join professional US intelligence organizations in the future will undoubtedly find that many things allowed in this text are forbidden or severely curtailed by their organizations' regulations and rules.

Red tape handcuffs many government users. Calcified bureaucracy creaks and grinds its way forward rather than advancing seamlessly. Moreover it usually rules with an iron fist. For government people involved in research, the best advice is: Just get used to it! In some quarters there is even an active, heated, and ongoing debate as to whether Open Source Intelligence (OSINT) is actually a separate intelligence area. That debate is for others to decide. It is irrelevant here.

The important point, no matter who you work for, is to scrupulously observe your left and right limits.

Appendix D. Tradecraft of Security

In life there are good decisions, calculated risks, and bad judgement. Calculated risks are gambles that people take when they hope they can get away with it – gambles which turn out to be correct. When gambles turn out wrong they were not calculated risks – they were simply bad judgement.

People sometimes take what they call calculated risks during their research, often about their own security. When a calculated risk turns into bad judgment, it can destroy the research program and damage the researcher.

Open source researchers avoid rolling the dice on their security.

Precautions are a must! The unknown world you are exploring may hide the unexpected that will hurt you. "No one, and no site, is completely trustworthy." Follow that rule of thumb, even if it seems slightly cynical, and you will face far fewer difficulties and dangers.

Whatever you do, wherever you go as a researcher, may interest everyone from nosy neighbors and political parties to governments and criminal groups. Open source research often involves those who may be adversaries or opponents; researchers face many types of potentially hostile activity.

Governments, from China and Russia to the United States, want to collect everything that everybody does anywhere on the Internet. Governments use bulk surveillance and try, with some success, to get program developers to put back doors in programs so they can track anyone at their convenience. Governments actually use only a tiny portion of that power or material, but they want to collect every click, every address, every message, every 1 or 0 that moves anywhere on the Internet. Government bureaucrats often appear prepared to save anything they can collect in perpetuity, hoping that it might somehow be useful later. After all, who knows what will be useful in the year 4040?

Hackers, some of whom are employed by sinister characters or have unworthy motives themselves, also have potential interests in following information professionals and the material they collect. Hackers may work for governments, business, or on their own for their own personal reasons. Even otherwise impeccable sites can be dangerous; uploaded advertisements, which are often unvetted even by otherwise-reliable sites, can contain malware.

Online research isn't an unalloyed service for the good. It can be and sometimes is used maliciously, as in doxxing. Doxxing involves searching out – and publishing – private or identifying information about someone using the Internet, usually with the intent to cause the person harm or distress. Researchers who irritate the people or groups they are studying are vulnerable to doxxing attacks.

Good security can help prevent angry governments, hackers, and would-be doxxers from notching their success against you. If the targets don't know you are studying them or cannot identify you even if they know that someone is studying them, they cannot attack you. That is why your security measures should be in place before you do anything else. It is too late to correct a problem after your security loophole has been discovered and exploited. You can't put the toothpaste back in the tube.

Phishing, Spoofing and Misdirection

Principle ways hackers get private information from you include phishing and spoofing.

Phishing is a way getting people to hand over information. Victims may be asked to provide passwords, Social Security numbers, bank account information or other personally identifiable information (PII). And people do hand it over. Willingly, even cheerfully. Often the phishers simply ask for the PII, saying it is needed for some seemingly legitimate purpose. They specialize in tricking the user. Phishers may use email or other parts of the Internet in their schemes. They may phone and suggest they need information to carry out some otherwise-legitimate activity – and usually their pitch is framed as a way to help you. Spearfishing is a subcategory of phishing that targets an individual; whaling targets the "big fish" or top executives of an organization.

Spoofing allows people with questionable motives to masquerade as someone or something else. It may involve creating a fake email or website that asks the user to click on a link or carry out some action. When users do so, viruses or malware can be installed on the user's computer. The malicious code can be one of several types. It may allow the hacker to get inside your computer and steal information stored there, or even as it is being typed – literally split seconds after it crossed your mind. It may also allow the hacker to encipher your entire disk and demand payment before you will be able to access anything again. The malicious code could allow the hacker to use your computer as part of a botnet that carries out other nefarious activities. It may be used to infect other computers on the system.

Related to spoofing is misdirection. A term from the world of magic, misdirection is a command to "look over here, not over there." Misdirection to other pages can be used for any number of things, including identifying you or even gaining access to your computer system. If a user is identified as being from the wrong area of the world, has an IP address that the system operator doesn't like, or is personally identified as being someone who the system operator does not want looking at the site, the operator can automatically misdirect all future inquiries elsewhere.

In common misdirection schemes the site actually sends you to some other location, a location which may have been designed to provide incorrect information to the researcher. In any event it never gets you closer to the information you are seeking.

Spoofing and misdirection on the Web can often be fought by matching the top address on the browser to the address being loaded, shown at the bottom of the browser. If they are not the same you are being redirected. Or you can hover your mouse over any link to see what it actually connects to: When the typed URL doesn't match the one you are, or will be, sent to you know that something is amiss. You may not know why. Not all redirections are misdirections. In itself, a redirection does not mean anything nefarious is happening, but you need to think through the "whys" of the situation – and the "who's" of the redirection.

Malware and Viruses

Protection against all malware and viruses is a must. It is not uncommon to have pop-ups warn that your anti-virus isn't working properly or is out of date. "You need to clean your machine because you have something bad on it" is the substance of the common ploy. When you click on the link to their ballyhooed answer to "the problem" what actually happens is you may install malicious code. The virus or malware you then mistakenly installed might do anything from logging your future keystrokes and sending the hacker information on everything you do to infecting your computer with programs that continuously, and maddenly, pop up advertising.

In your email program consider disabling web-ready presentations – message presentation in HTML – since malware can easily be spread through that technology.

Hackers, including the just-for-the thrill-of-it type, are a threat to everyone. Hackers are as unpredictable as lightning strikes. They, and all threats, can employ:

- Botnets
- Malware
- Phishing tactics
  - Spearfishing
  - Whaling
- Spyware
- Trojans (Trojan Horses)
- Viruses
- Worms.

Be aware of how your own system can be used to spy on you. Advanced snoopers – they would likely be working for someone but you may be chosen randomly – can use your built-in camera and microphone, and even the headphones on your computer, to gather information about you and your activities. The "bad guys" can literally see and hear you.

Hackers who get into your system can turn on your camera and broadcast your activities back to themselves – or elsewhere. Turning off the camera on your system is no guarantee. If they are able to reach inside your system they probably have the capability to turn it back on. A piece of tape over the camera lens opening won't stop any video feed, of course, but it does blank out any picture. The computer's built-in microphone is likewise vulnerable to hackers. Taped padding over the built-in microphone muffles the sound and reduces the chances that anything useful can be picked up by any snoopers. Even some headphones can be pirated for spying by a script-kiddie who is able to snare you into downloading malware that simply reverses the technology of the headphones. Earpiece membranes are repurposed to act as microphones by the malware. The earpieces pick up any sounds, convert them to electromagnetic signals, and send them back to the snoopers.

While this is not a book on security, you still need some level of protection. Maybe your protection doesn't need to be as stringent as US government rules require, but it must be carefully calibrated to your specific, unique, needs. Further information on all of these threat types is readily available on the Internet by typing in the appropriate term.

Adopt the "need to know" rule. Don't talk to others about anything you have discovered, or how your work is going. People who don't need to know may be prone to talk in order to show how well-connected they are. On occasion money, fear, or blackmail will make your associates talk about things they know, things they really have no need to know, to people who have no right to know. Protect yourself and your associates.

Website Reputation

Even good sites can be used to infect your computer with malware. Advertising they accept and put up is often unvetted and may be a source of infection, but some sites are widely known to be problematic. You want to avoid those sites like the plague because they are designed to infect anyone who ventures there. Malware, unwanted software, or social engineering messages are likely to be downloaded from such sites. Always consider whether you want to check a new, unfamiliar site with website reputation software before going to any site for the first time. While these sites and programs do not all work the same way, nor do they provide similar types of protection, they are worth considering as integral parts of your SOP's security plan:

- **Abuse Blocklist:** https://zeustracker.abuse.ch/blocklist.php?download=domainblocklist
- **Google Safe Browsing:** https://developers.google.com/safe-browsing/?csw=1
- **Joe Sandbox:** https://www.joesandbox.com
- **MalwareFighter:** https://www.malwareurl.com/index.php
- **ScanUrl:** https://scanurl.net/
- **Scumware:** https://www.scumware.org/
- **SucuriSiteCheck:** https://sitecheck.sucuri.net/
- **Threat Crowd:** https://www.threatcrowd.org/

- **Threat Miner:** https://www.threatminer.org/index.php
- **URLVOID:** https://www.urlvoid.com/
- **VirusTotal:** https://www.virustotal.com.

Computer Security

One of the first rules of computer security is "protect your IP address," the address your computer has on the Internet. IP addresses are the digital equivalent of the physical address of your home or office. The IP address is where the various parts of the Internet send information. Protect your IP address as you would a Social Security number because it is much like your Social Security number – it identifies you and can be used to hurt you if it falls into the possession of any antagonists.

Before you even sign on to a computer you will encounter your first security stumbling block. In virtually every case, unless your computer was set up with security foremost in mind, it is probably seriously leaking information about you, information that can be used by adversaries. That often includes your IP address. Use the many checking systems shown in Chapter 5 to determine what information you are leaking and look for way to stem the flood of information by using resources listed in the chapter, including **Panopticlick:** http://panopticlick.eff.org/

Think carefully about your computer systems.... That's right. Systems. Plural. Ideally you will have two systems. That ideal may be rarer than Kryptonite but it is worth talking about even if it is unlikely that most employers will provide a two-system setup. Some people who provide their own setup may be able to use a two-system approach, or maybe one day there will be an epiphany and accountants will say "hey, that's not such a bad idea!"

One of the computers is designated as the Research Computer; it is the one used for going out to the Internet. The Production Computer never touches the Internet and is used to process data, store it, and to write with. These two computers are connected only through Airgapping. Airgapping details are included in the chapter on setting up your system.

Make your Research Computer, in particular, as anonymous as possible. That starts with the naming of the system when it first comes out of the box. Something like "John's Computer" – assuming John really isn't going to use the system – is a far better name for the system than "XYZCompanyUnit123." No system should ever be an arrow pointing back to you, your agency, or any employer.

Always research through a commercial site. Never sign on to the Internet through a home location where any malware you might acquire will blossom across the entire system of an employer. It happens!

Have a professional install all operating system security updates and set secure browser options.

Minimize the program extensions added to the Research system as these often are insecure. Many add-on programs to browsers are not written by people who have security in mind; they just have a "neat idea" and a smattering of coding knowledge. Thoughtless computer settings and problematic extensions aid adversaries.

Encryption

Encryption is basic protection against thieves and snoopers. Encryption makes it **harder** for anyone to read what you wrote, what you have on your computer, or what you are sending to or receiving from some source.

Most modern encryption programs available in the United States are difficult to break; even government agencies are often stymied by some of the modern encryption algorithms.

HTTPS Everywhere is an extension that encrypts communications with websites. It can be downloaded from the Electronic Freedom Foundation at https://www.eff.org/https-everywhere.

Consider using only end-to-end encryption for emails and instant messages. Try PGP for emails and OTR for instant messages. Sites have cropped up to make email communication safer. These include:

- **Hushmail:** https://www.hushmail.com/
- **ProtonMail:** https://protonmail.com/
- **Signal (Whisper Systems):** https://whispersystems.org/
- **Telegram:** https://telegram.org/
- **WhatsApp:** https://www.whatsapp.com/.

Use the encryption available on many programs for Voice over Internet calls.

Encryption is not only for emails. Use full disk encryption for the entire computer: This prevents anyone from taking, copying, or hacking into the hard drive and reading from it. BitLocker, PGP, and TrueCrypt work on Windows machines. FileVault is available for Macs.

For general encryption, consider using Blowfish, Twofish, and Threefish algorithms. Almost any algorithm can be broken eventually, but these present difficult problems. The will slow or stymie any decryption process, even posing difficulties for many governments.

Access Control

One way of locking your computer is to use a thumb drive with programs such as **Predator,** available at https://www.predator-usb.com/predator/en/index.php. The thumb drive becomes an access control device that you can remove from the computer, put in your pocket, purse, or briefcase and walk away. Removing the thumb drive disables the mouse and keyboard and darkens the screen. Inserting the thumb drive back in the computer allows legitimate users to continue their work. A scheduler in the program can also limit the time of day that access is permitted. The program can even be configured so that it takes a picture of anyone who attempts to use your computer keyboard. It can also send intrusion alert messages by email.

Clipboard Control

It is important to clear your computer's clipboard or cache of files before signing on to the Internet, between any visits to sites, and sometimes even during extended visits. Clean clipboards provide no information that antagonists can access and use against you. When antagonists can reach back to your computer they are able see everything on your clipboard. What you have on your clipboard at any particular time may not only help identify you, it may identify your interests or the interests of those you are working for.

Few people think about this rudimentary security practice; even fewer do it.

Instructions on clearing the particular browser clipboard or cache are available online. Extensions to major browsers that make the process easier and faster can be ferreted out by looking for the words "clear cache" with your search engine. One such is **ClearCache** at https://github.com/TenSoja/clear-cache.

Passwords and Pass Phrases

Passwords on your computer and at sites you visit are often your only safety feature. But passwords are irritating and even problematic to many people. You have heard all the injunctions: change your passwords often; each site should have a different password; passwords should be at least eight (or 20) characters long; they should consist of capital letters, small letters, numbers and signs; the password should never be written down; it should not be a recognizable word or words; it must be changed every six months; the same one may not be used again until you have gone through 10 iterations – yada, yada, yada.

Password rules have become so onerous that few people willingly follow all of them. In reality, they should be strong but they also must be memorable. And, yes, each site should have a different password in case hackers make off with that site's password files. You don't want every site that you use to become vulnerable overnight because everything you do, and every place you go, is tied to a single compromised password.

New studies suggest there is a better way, one that is neither so complex nor daunting that no one can possibly follow all the rules. Use a pass phrase or a pass code!

There are thousands of memorable phrases to choose from. Shakespeare or a favorite graphic novel may be your inspiration, but let's take a famous one from the start of WW II as an example. The speech has this famous phrase: "a date which will live in infamy." That could become the pass phrase: adatewhichwillliveininfamy. But is that really isn't secure enough? It's long, but can be cracked – perhaps not easily. but it is vulnerable. Instead capitalize the first letter (or last letter) of every word: ADateWhichWillLiveInInfamy. Or maybe every fifth letter: adatEwhicHwillLiveiNinfaMy. Or how about shortening it to the first (or last) letter of every word: adwwlii. Maybe we want to add some numbers and signs, but also capitalize every second letter aDwWlIi1941!

Or maybe you want to start, not with a phrase from a book, but a home or office address you used five years ago and a phone number from your childhood. The key is to make it possible to remember how to input the password. You know the phrase and how you altered it. You don't need to write it down. It's long and is not easily recognizable.

Or the password may be three or four unaffiliated words – as in cHINA1919HourSays. Consider using programs such as Diceware to create multi-word passcodes.

Password Managers

Password managers are useful for "remembering" your pass codes, but keep in mind that many sites where you are required to have or use a password or pass code also have a "forgotten password" link. A forgotten password may be upsetting, but often it is not critical.

Still, password managers can make life easier. These are alternatives to a written list or memorization of long, random, and complex passwords. Password managers generate passwords that are difficult to remember and hard to break. Some password manager sites will fill in the unique password for you at sites you use. As useful as they are, however, keep in mind that your online existence will be toast if you forget the master password to the password manager.

Some key password managers and generators include:
- **1Password ($$$$):** https://1password.com/downloads/windows/
- **Keeper ($$$$):** https://keepersecurity.com/
- **LastPass ($$$$):** https://www.lastpass.com/password-generator
- **RoboForm ($$$$):** https://www.roboform.com/
- **StickyPassword ($$$$):** https://www.stickypassword.com/.

Favorite Cybercriminal and Spy Attachments

Cybercriminals have found that some types of links and attachments are more useful than others into tricking users to click-and-infect their machines. Emails that purport to come from a friend whose address has been compromised, or messages believed to have come from widely-known organizations, are highly effective tricks and come-ons.

Malicious payloads may give the attacker access to everything on your computer, install keyloggers to record your every keystroke, or run ransomware to lock up your system until you fork over payment. They can spy on you through your own camera or your computer's sound system, add you to their botnet, or take control of your system for whatever purpose.

Generally speaking, Portable Document Files (PDFs) are among the most-used malicious attachments. They are easily disguised as anything written, from ebooks to free offers. Other popular formats that are widely used by cybercriminals include Microsoft Office files such as Word or Excel, or their clones. These can harbor malware macros or scripts. Zipped files are notorious, as are RARs.

The antidote to email scammers is prevention.

Be wary about opening attachments or clicking on links. Delete any message or attachment from sources you don't know or whose identity is foggy. If you do know the source and consider the person reliable, ask the person whether they sent you the message before opening anything. Yes, it takes extra time and is frustrating, but it is not as frustrating and time-consuming as trying to clean an infected machine. A third option – to be used on a limited basis with a coterie of close friends – is to have a passphrase or code included in any message that has an attachment or file. If the codeword isn't in their message you can assume the attachment contains malware.

The last line of defense is, of course, having a complete and recent full system backup – often done at night while you sleep – to allow a quick recovery in case your best prevention efforts fail. As Navy SEALs say, "one is none and two is one."

Social Media and Apps Pose a Threat

Assume that every time you log on to Social Media sites that your email address, gender, birthdate, likes, and every post you make is available to anyone who is willing to pay the provider a few cents for the information. Apps – applications – those small, lightweight programs that do specific things but seemingly are given to you out of the goodness of their creators' hearts, also pose threats. There is no free lunch. If you aren't paying for something, someone else is but needs information about you or from you to make their investment worthwhile. If something is called "free," assume you and your information are being monetized unless – and until – you have proof to the contrary.

Privacy policies in apps and elsewhere generally tell the truth because the law says they have to, but most of the facts you really need are buried deeper than a pirate's treasure stash and the wording is probably more obtuse than any auto dealer's contract. Apps and sites, after screens of legalese that make even attorneys hold their heads in their hands, will come up with some all-inclusive language along the lines of "we may collect, use, transfer, sell and disclose information for any purpose in perpetuity." And you cannot negotiate their terms.

Be cautious about what information an app or program wants to take, or which features it wants to access – if it tells you. When it doesn't need the information it is asking for it is preparing to scam you. Calculator apps don't need access to your camera or location information. See what you are giving away and to whom for what purpose. Remember that you can never assume the reason given is 100 percent accurate; people do lie.

Avoid downloading apps from "alternative," "unofficial," or third-party vendors; all too often their code – or their promised code since they may not even deliver the product you sought – contains malware. Use only official app stores that the particular product or site you are downloading have blessed. And find out what the online community thinks. **CNET** at https://www.cnet.com/ and

Tom's Guide at https://www.tomsguide.com/ are among the useful sites for checking out the suitability of apps and programs. At the very least, use your online ability and seek knowledge and advice from the people of the Internet about anything you put on your computer. Someone undoubtedly knows, and probably has posted, if there is a discernable danger.

Any app or questionnaire which wants more than the most basic information or that seeks what is called Personally Identifiable Information, known as PII, is immediately questionable. Queries about birthdate or place of birth are PII and should be considered suspect, much as a Social Security or driver's license number would be. Always check permissions and save a copy of what, if any, permissions you give. Know what you are giving away, and to whom, for what purpose.

Collection Methods Can Bite You...

Personalization of searches – the ability of sites or people to see what you are searching for or are interested in – can be good or bad. Personalization can help you find useful things; it can also allow people to thwart your searches.

Remember that your own collection methods might reveal critical information about you, your work or your interests. Such indicators may assist those seeking to neutralize your efforts.

Purchasing documents or searching an Internet site are two examples of detectable research and collection techniques that could provide indicators of your interests. Using the same browser for your repeated Internet forays can be used to crack your anonymity. Having, and interchanging, several different browsers helps reduce the ability of any opposition system operators to track you.

Communications Security

For those worried about communicating securely, there is no single answer that works best for everyone. Encryption is the standard answer and is not bad, but encryption of messages almost assures that government agencies will start saving your messages and may try to break the code. Whenever security agencies see messages that you have encrypted you have automatically brought that message to their attention and set alarm bells ringing like Christmas chimes. Assume that any encryption brings unwelcome civic attention.

Sherlock Holmes understood there are dangers of communicating in code. He told his biographer, Watson, that "Your native shrewdness, my dear Watson, that innate cunning which is the delight of your friends, would surely prevent you from inclosing cipher and message in the same envelope. Should it miscarry, you are undone. As it is, both have to go wrong before any harm comes from it," he said *The Valley of Fear.*

There are a variety of coding and cyphering tricks that, together or separately, may improve your security while making your own communication easier.

"Foldering" is a clever method to limit intrusion and prevent snooping into messages. Foddering messages are never "sent" in the conventional sense. This communication method is used by some who open an email account at a site or provider that they deem trustworthy, then write their message in the "drafts" folder. They send the location and log-in details such as the user name and password to the person they want to pass the message to. That person can then go to the drafts account, read the message – and usually erase it or leave any necessary reply. The original sender can check back to the site to receive the reply or the note that the message was read. Since the message was never sent, and technically did not travel through the email system, intercepting it is considered more difficult than usual. "Difficult" is not "impossible," however. Use the technique sparingly since overactive draft boxes invite undue civic attention.

One way to make any communications intercepts more difficult to trace back to you are third-party mail resources. Users write a note at the site; the site generates a URL link which you copy and paste into an email to be sent to the note's intended recipient. When the recipient reads the message, it is erased and the link is no longer active. To improve security the link should be included in an innocuous cover message because a link, by itself, may engender some unwanted attention if anyone is watching your email. There are other types of email security sites as well. Temporary email limits the time any message is available before it disappears.

- **10minutemail (Temporary email):** https://10minutemail.com/10MinuteMail/index.html
- **Nohistoryfy** (Temporary email): https://nohistory.fyi/
- **Privnote (Privacy comms)**: https://privnote.com/#
- **Revealitme (Temporary email)**: https://revealit.me/
- **Safenote (Temporary email):** https://safenote.co/
- **Yopass (Temporary email):** https://yopass.se/#/.

Pastebin can be used in much the same way for communication. But Pastebin-type sites, where text can be stored, are also easily monitored. That should be a search consideration for any researcher.

- **Dumpmonitor (Password and sensitive information monitor):** https://twitter.com/dumpmon
- **PasteLert** (Posting alerts): https://andrewmohawk.com/pasteLert/.

Remailing services like **Anyonymouse** at https://anonymouse.org scrub off return address information that would identify you and run the message through a series of addresses that scramble the source before delivering the message to its destination. That makes hitting "reply" to a remailed message useless, but recipients who are aware of how the system works can use a remailing system to reply.

SecureDrop https://securedrop.org is an email messaging system now used by many media outlets to scupper the eavesdropping efforts of hackers and nosy governments.

Encryption software is relatively easy to locate on the Web and there are some reasonable choices at the right price – free.
- **Cypherix:** http://www.cypherix.com
- **Kruptos**: http://www.kruptos2.co.uk
- **Folderlock:** http://www.newsoftwares.net/folderlock
- **Safehouse:** http://www.safehousesoftware.com
- **Signal:** https://signal.org/.

A simple – that is to say effective, but insecure – way to hide text is to write one or several lines you wish to communicate somewhere within an otherwise innocuous Microsoft WORD file. With your mouse select the text you want to hide. In the WORD program, click on "Home." Launch the font dialogue pop-up by clicking on the arrow that points down and to the right, found at the bottom of the "Font" box. Then check the "Hidden" box. The text you painted will disappear. Send the file. You will have to let message recipients know what area to paint and then uncheck the "Hidden" box, by some sign, code word or mark at the point where you inserted the hidden text. The recipient paints the area that you have indicated contains the hidden information and goes into the "Home" display and unchecks the "Hidden" box. The text will reappear. You can add a bit more security – before you select and hide the text – by changing the font color to white or whatever color the text background may be.

Steganography, or stego, is probably the safest of all clandestine means of communication. It takes a little longer than whipping off an email, but where secrecy is paramount, stego is one of the best solutions.

Stego seamlessly hides a message, or even a complete document, inside a picture or musical piece. Only people who know both where to look for the message or document, and who have been told how to extract the hidden information, are likely to be able to access it. Since people send or post pictures or music all the time, snapshots and songs generally excite no suspicion.

Stego – unlike encryption – leaves no tells. It does not reveal that you are communicating, much less that your communication is secret. When done properly, stego is utterly invisible. Even someone closely watching your email or postings has no idea you are communicating information. If you send a picture directly to a contact someone might wonder, of course, but your own photo of a sunset, with an attached a message, would look quite in place with a photo caption that says "saw a great sunset yesterday" or "what a gloomy sunset we've had." Likewise you could create a web site or YouTube page on sunsets and let those people you want to read the included messages know that only pictures captioned "one of my favorites" contains a message. They also have to know the process and the password to dig out the message before they can read it, so you need to communicate that, securely, in advance.

Exceptionally large files, of course, can be a giveaway. But the files have to be really large to excite suspicion. Even amateurs often get away with putting a stego message inside a photo they have lifted from somewhere on the Internet, but probably the safest way is to use a picture you take – and have scrubbed of EXIF information – so that no one can compare the digital size of the photo you use to the size of one found in the EXIF data. If you encrypt the message inside the stego picture or audio file you can add another layer of security and probably prevent snoopers from finding or reading it over the course of a lifetime. Even sophisticated intelligence agencies lack the capability to uncover, much less decrypt, well-framed stego messages.

Stego programs can be found on the Internet by a simple search for "steganography programs." **Invisible Secrets**, which can be found at http://www.invisiblesecrets.com/download.html, or **OpenPuff**, which is available at https://www.softpedia.com/get/Authoring-tools/Authoring-Related/Puff.shtml, are among the stego programs available on the Internet.

Digital Footprint, Online Persona

You leave an information trail whenever you tramp through the digital forest. Commonly called the digital footprint; the trail is essentially a set of fingerprints. Many people can see and record that fingerprint. Who sees you or your IP on the Internet?

- Administrators of websites you visit
- Security personnel at those websites
- Internet Service Providers (ISPs), who can now sell information about you and your Web activities
- Proxy sites used in the data transfer.

Records about you that can be, and often are, retained by site managers include:

- Computer configuration (e.g. browser and settings, operating system, Internet services)
- A personal profile, one based on surfing habits
- Details of your pattern of searches and subjects of interest.

The online *persona* is your social identity, established in online communities and websites. It identifies where you appear to connect from and who you say you are when accessing sites. It may reveal:

- Your Internet Service Provider's (ISP) name
- Email verification
- Your time zone and location
- Your organizational affiliation
- Cookies you have retained, which is one reason an investigative searcher clears the browser of cookies often.

The digital footprint and online persona, together, are used to identify you. Things most people would not imagine, including the time of day you come online to a site, or the fonts you chose on your browser, are used to create a personal profile that can be matched directly to you and your searches. Profile builders, looking at your browser and other connections, may snare you with such things as leakage of your:

- ISP
- City, state, region, or country
- Time zones
- Various metrics of Windows
- Screen resolution
- Extensions and add-ons.

Your footprint and persona, the browser leakage, identify you as a unique individual among the millions of Internet users. The footprint and persona speak about your computer, where you are from, where you are going, and even your methods of searching. Thoughtful system operators may even be capable of deducing from the leakage items your level of expertise and professionalism.

Maybe you can't prevent yourself from leaving this type of fingerprint but you can smudge it by turning off – or on – features during your browsing to be less of an individual and more of a generic visitor.

It is wise to use several footprint-checking sites to see what information you are leaking before going to any other sites, particularly if you are accessing adversarial sites. Many information professionals use one or even a few checkers to survey themselves for browser leakage before doing any online work. Different types of checkers zero in on different parts of your system.

At the very least, test your own address to get an idea of the wide range of information that others can gather about you, your location and your system. Much depends on the need for secrecy and deniability of the search.

See What the Other Side Can See

To see part of what the other side – including an adversary – may be able to see when you go to a site try some of these:

- **Am I Unique:** https://amiunique.org/fp
- **Browserleak:** https://browserleaks.com/
- **Browserleak Canvas:** https://browserleaks.com/canvas
- **Browserleak Social Media Leak Testing:** https://browserleaks.com/social
- **Browser Mirror:** https://centralops.net/asp/co/browsermirror.vbs.asp
- **Browser Spy:** http://browserspy.dk/headers.php
- **Check Your Persona:** http://navigators.com/cgi-bin/persona.pl
- **DigiCrime:** http://www.digicrime.com/noprivacy.html
- **Evercookie:** https://samy.pl/evercookie/
- **IP-adress:** http://www.ip-adress.com
- **IP Check:** http://ip-check.info/?lang=en
- **IPchicken:** http://ipchicken.com/
- **IP Leak:** https://ipleak.net/
- **IP Leak Privacy Test:** http://ipleak.com/full-report/
- **IP Location:** https://www.iplocation.net/
- **MrWhoer:** https://whoer.net/
- **My IP Info:** http://myipinfo.net/
- **Panopticlick**: http://panopticlick.eff.org/
- **UniqueMachine:** http://uniquemachine.org/
- **What is My IP Address:** https://whatismyipaddress.com/.

Your Security Depends on Anonymity

Loss of online anonymity can compromise security. Always think risk mitigation, rather than risk elimination. Some of the general precautions are:

- Use two computers when possible: Production and Collection, and air-gap between them.
- When collecting, disable non-essential system or browser parts that may record your activity.
- Use masking programs, when possible, to hide your identity and affiliation.
- Use VMware to run a virtual machine, if available.
- Be aware of what your browser discloses about you.
- When possible, use cached copies of sites from search engines first.
- Always try using cached pages when a website won't let you on because of credentialing or sign-on issues; it often works.
- Beware of referring URLs. Type URLs into new windows instead of clicking on them.
- Do *not* click on the titles of your search results
- Vary visits to different times of day.
- Act casual!
- Be discrete, not deceptive.
- Do not use a personal home computer or a computer that has not been security-hardened for research.
- Search the safest resources first; if you find whatever information you need there you will not need to go to adversarial sites.
- Use strong passwords.
- Use a "No Name" operating system (Designate your computer as "New User" or "John's/Jane's computer").
- Regularly update browsers and software.
- Limit your time on high-risk sites and consider using an offline browser.
- Consistently and constantly run virus scans.
- Clear your history often, sometimes after each site visit.
- Adjust Internet options and browser preferences to their safest levels consistent with your search needs.

- Avoid opening shortened URLs.
- In browsers that have it, select "Private Browsing" but do not rely on it.
- Keep all connection details as anonymous as possible and set up the PC as minimally as possible.
- Be careful of all browser extensions.
- Always refer questions you have to security professionals; if you have a question there is a reason to check out the issue.
- Properly dispose of all documents and media.

VPNs

VPNs – virtual private networks – send a different IP address to destination sites, much as Tor does. They hide your address behind their own address. VPNs provide privacy but they do not provide anonymity. The VPN operator knows the user's IP address – after all, they need to forward any pages or information that the user wants to see. Some VPNs will provide user information to governments whenever asked. VPNs are wonderful for privacy, but they can never be counted on to provide anonymity. When used with Tor and similar anonymizing systems, they significantly enhance security. VPNs often cost money. They include:

- **Anonymizer Universal ($$$$):** https://www.anonymizer.com/
- **Anonymouse:** http://anonymouse.org/anonwww.html
- **Anonymouse Email:** http://anonymouse.org/anonemail.html
- **CyberGhost VPN ($$$$):** https://pro.cyberghostvpn.com/
- **Express VPN ($$$$):** https://www.expressvpn.com/
- **HideMyAss ($$$$):** https://www.hidemyass.com/
- **Hotspot Shield:** https://www.hotspotshield.com/free-vpn
- **Ipredator ($$$$):** https://www.ipredator.se/
- **Ironsocket ($$$$):** https://ironsocket.com/
- **JonDonym ($$$$)** https://anonymous-proxy-servers.net/
- **NordVPN ($$$$):** https://nordvpn.com/

- **PersonalVPN ($$$$):** https://www.personalvpn.com/
- **Private VPN ($$$$):** https://privatevpn.com/bestvaluevpn/
- **Private Tunnel ($$$$):**
  https://portal.privatetunnel.com/apps
- **Proton ($$$$):** https://account.protonvpn.com/signup
- **Proxify ($$$$):** https://proxify.com
- **ProXPN ($$$$):** https://secure.proxpn.com/
- **PureVPN ($$$$):** https://www.purevpn.com/
- **SaferVPN ($$$$):** http://www.safervpn.com
- **Strong VPN ($$$$):** https://strongvpn.com
- **Surf Anonymous Free:** http://download.cnet.com/Surf-Anonymous-Free/3000-2144_4-75300270.html
- **SurfEasy ($$$$):** http://www.surfeasy.com
- **Tunnel Bear ($$$$):** http://www.tunnelbear.com
- **Windscribe ($$$$):** https://windscribe.com
- **ZenVPN ($$$$):** https://zenmate.com/.

Consider using multiple VPNs, switching between them to make your search interests even less obvious.

Payments May be Tricky

Many things, including security and anonymity on the Web, come at a price. That price tag may include a loss of anonymity. Providers have to record payments against their records of accounts.

Cash is seldom an answer in the digital world. Anything you put on your own credit card is an arrow stuck in your back, and the shaft points directly at you. Digital currencies or cryptocurrencies such as Bitcoin are one very complicated answer to payment problems.

Grocery store credit cards – the kind of anonymous prepaid credit cards you buy at a checkout counter – can be used to make it more difficult to trace you. If you use this method, always pay for the card with cash and buy it at a supermarket or store you do not shop at – in the next county if possible.

Anonymity can never be assured, but any step creating roadblocks to identification helps preserve your anonymity. Tax deductions for business expenses like this may be legitimate, but they are always unwise.

Tor is Widely Used

Tor, also known as The Onion Router, reaches sites that cannot be accessed through the regular open web. These dark web sites are like top level domains (TLDs) but they are only accessible through Tor's network. While using Onion Router sites it is well to remember that Tor was primarily designed to protect people like site owners, posters, and administrators; protection for those browsing a site is essentially an afterthought.

Tails is a separate communications operating system that can be used alongside Tor. When the communication is completed, the Tails operating system disappears and with it, all evidence of the communications.

Download Tails to a thumb drive or burn a disk and use it from that drive or disk. **Tails** is available at https://tails.boum.org/. **Whonix,** another system for secure access to the Internet using Virtual Box, is available at https://www.whonix.org/download/.

Other Useful Security Tools

I Search From, at http://isearchfrom.com/, simulates a search on Google from different devices or even locations. Changing the type of device and the location helps confuse your identity. It can be a major factor when trying for anonymity.

Privacy Badger can be found at https://addons.mozilla.org/en-US/firefox/addon/privacy-badger17/?src=hp-dl-featured. It is useful to block tracking cookies and spy ads while browsing on Firefox. Privacy Badger is a product of the **Electronic Frontier Foundation** https://www.eff.org.

Have I Been Pwned https://haveibeenpwned.com/ is a service that can help you determine if your address has been compromised in a data breach. It provides information similar to **WeLeakInfo** (**$$$$**): https://weleakinfo.com/

Shouldichangemypassword is a site designed to tell users when their passwords have been compromised. The site can be accessed at https://shouldichangemypassword.com.cutestat.com/. A similar site is **BreachAlarm:** https://breachalarm.com/.

The **Trusted End Node Security System** is not widely known but you may want to see whether this free security system works for you. It is a US government (Air Force) creation, available to the public in PC or Mac versions. It boots a thin Linux operating system from a CD or USB flash drive without using a local hard drive. Administrator privileges are not required; nothing is installed. No trace of work activity (or malware) is written to the computer or the system your computer is on. Everything disappears when you close down. This security methodology was created to address particular cases. The system seems to be updated quarterly but there are no patches. When a new system is available you download a complete new file. The security system can be downloaded from the site at https://www.spi.dod.mil/lipose.htm.

Flagfox, at https://iplookup.flagfox.net/, is a browser extension that displays a country's flag on the web browser, showing the location of the website's server. This gives you a better idea of where you are communicating. The tool also provides features that can be used in evaluating a website.

Legal Issues
Legal issues can quickly become security problems.

You don't have to be a lawyer to know there is a legal thicket just waiting to ensnare the unwary. If you are using material from the Internet in any way, but particularly if it is a commercial use, your information shop needs advice from an attorney to guide you through the legal tangles.

We are not attorneys, but we constantly encounter legal issues with even the most basic questions about open source use, questions that demand speedy resolution.

In the United States, at least, the US Congress, in PL 109-163 § 931, defines open sources as "Publicly available information anyone can lawfully obtain by request, purchase or observation." That seems so simple, but it is not. There may be lines, there may be bright lines to legal questions, but there is always an element of confusion about the most basic question: "Is what I am gathering really Open Source?"

Even attorneys have different views. You need legal counsel to tell you the bright lines, and advise you about the ones that are not as clear; you need lawyers to advise you about your particular situation and how to avoid tripping over those lines.

There are other questions as well.

For some, those working under US government restrictions barring the collection of material on "US persons" – a broad category that includes some corporations – the collection of any material may be highly constrained.

And people working under those restrictions are also prevented from interacting to get information. The legal definition of Open Source allows a "request" for information but other rules that apply to some government researchers technically prevent them from interacting, which they must do to "request" information.

"Observation" seems like such a simple word – but how limiting a term is it and what does it really mean? Those restricted to "observation" in its strictest sense might be left "observing" a blank screen because signing on to many sites (or even buying a newspaper) theoretically involves far more "action" than simple "observation." Cynics could make the argument that even putting words into a search box constitutes action, not observation.

We know that the vast majority of material on the Internet is not even catalogued by search engines, yet a major thrust of Open Source Research is to gather data that search engines miss or have but do not normally report. Does searching for that mountain of hidden mountain of material move beyond observation?

Some moves by both open source researchers and hackers effectively trick computers and servers to give up information that the owners of the information may not have wanted released. Even when searching a site that tells search engines not to grab certain information, there are ways to snare the material. Does that information still meet the definition of open source? Or what about personal, private, information that a hacker has stolen somewhere and posted on the Internet? Is that now fair game? Is it unethical? Is it illegal? Only a lawyer can give you definitive answers.

Open Source information can well be defined in the wording of the law but the true definition of what it is, and the limits a researcher can go to obtain it under the rule of the law, is nothing if not murky. It is also subject to change by courts and legislatures.

What is clear: Avoid computer intrusions unless you have permission and the authority to do so. Any time you sign into a site with someone else's identity or password you are risking a jail sentence.

There are other challenges. Information collection has a mixed reputation. Some consider it a gateway to spying or "hacking." And even "hacking" may be a confusing term. Hacking has two different meanings. Among the *cognoscenti* of the online community the word means a smart, if unconventional, way of solving a problem – a creative work-around or a quick-and-dirty solution to a roadblock. In more general usage it means the unethical, and probably illegal, accessing of a computer or system.

Some research techniques discussed here, other than using a search engine, qualify as hacking in the sense of a "smart way of solving a problem." These techniques are often used legally, as in penetration testing, but some of those same research techniques may also be used illegally – they can be hacking in the second, black-hat, sense of the word. The researcher or research desk has to know where and when the lines turn bright red.

No one can ethically advocate, endorse, or promote any illegal method of obtaining information. "Security" means safety for you and also for the subjects you search. It means avoiding theft, even taking things that don't feel like theft. Despite the widespread belief that anything on the Internet is free for the taking, many Internet materials are no more free than a book published last month.

Stay on the right side of the law; consult an attorney any time you have the slightest doubt about the legality of anything you plan on doing, or information you plan to take. A legal consultation fee is pocket change compared with the costs you would face in either a civil or criminal trial.

Read, understand, and follow the mandates of the US Economic Espionage Act. The portions regarding the protection of trade secrets and national information infrastructure protection are particularly important. Arcane laws are never trivial in their potential impact.

Researchers in the US who do online research should acquaint themselves with Title 18 US Code §1030, a dense section dealing with fraud and related activities as they deal with computers. In fact, it makes sense to read all of Title 18 US Code Chapter 119 to get an idea of how easy it is to cross into problem territory.

Unauthorized access to protected computers is illegal, and even planning a computer break-in with others – even if it is not carried out – could result in conspiracy charges. What is "unauthorized' and what is a "protected computer" are terms of art. It is too easy to cross lines that can cause trouble.

Follow the plain-view rule – if it is in public view it's probably OK. But whenever you are in doubt, or when information is not obviously intended to be public, refer the question to your legal counsel. Look to ethical or code of conduct standards for your organization to keep everyone out of trouble.

The "Terms of Service" or "End User License Agreement" – known as a EULA – is always a potential danger. Almost everything you put on your computer, and every program or application, has an attached EULA – one that you must agree to, and adhere to.

The EULA is a legal contract, spelling out what you can and cannot do. It also spells out what the site or program owner can do with information about you, for how long, and what rights it may have to access your system, monitor your computer or phone, and sell or use your information, etc. Maybe one out 500 users read the typical EULA before accepting its terms. And it is a matter of acceptance. Although a EULA is a legal and enforceable document you have no opportunity to negotiate or renegotiate any part of it. It is written by attorneys in language that is as dense and boring as it is binding. You cannot negotiate over a EULA; you either accept it or don't. And if you don't agree with the wording you cannot use the program, application, or site.

It is quite possible for anyone who has never read the EULA contract on a site to easily violate it and face legal problems; it is equally easy to give away rights you never knew you had – or those you would never give up if you actually knew what was being required of you.

The typical EULA gives away your rights while saddling you with responsibilities. Many people, for instance, use a mail program heavily but haven't read the EULA that describes how the company has the right to read and store your text.

Professional researchers often download a copy of every EULA they encounter and read it, line by line before opening the packaging, downloading programs, or using a site.

Acceptance of a EULA's terms – and they may indeed be onerous ones – can be triggered almost by looking at the program or packaging. The more likely the results will be bad for the user, the more stringent the terms will be and the more rights you give away.

Remember, EULAs are never, ever, designed to protect you.

Download and save every EULA or "terms of service" agreement you are asked to accept. These are contracts and you should have a copy of what permissions you have given and what you have agreed to. Even better, actually read the terms of service before you "sign" them. Dated copies of EULAs can and should be saved in some section of the SOP set aside for that purpose in case you or your attorney have to refer to what you actually agreed to.

For many the same reasons. read and download privacy policies on a site – they also tell you what a site's owner can do and how it can use your information.

Copyright, and copyright violations, are specialties in law. Many attorneys make their whole career – and a fine living – over the issue of what can, and cannot, be used and by whom. We do not presume to give any advice beyond "please be very careful."

Virtually every word or picture you find on the Internet, or in fiber documents, has some type of copyright attached.

Fair Use rules in the United States allow certain uses of copyright material without payment or permission. Those Fair Use rules may or may not apply to you. These same rules may not be applied by copyright authorities in other countries. For an extensive review of **Fair Use**, and your obligations under it, refer to the warnings and advice provided by Stanford University at: http://fairuse.stanford.edu/overview/fair-use/four-factors.

Finally, protect yourself and your work. Ensure the finished product always includes a "Fair Use" statement where that is applicable and complies with any additional specific legal guidance. Consult your attorney or legal counsel to draft a Fair Use statement appropriate to your needs. A common fair use statement looks somewhat like this: *"In accordance with Title 17 U.S.C. Section 107, this material is distributed without profit to those who have expressed a prior interest in receiving the included information for research and educational purposes.*

"Inclusion of stories, links to websites or other items does not indicate an endorsement of them and does not indicate agreement with the content. We are not responsible for either the veracity or the accuracy of the content. These materials are selected and presented as a means of showing 'what is being said' with the belief that readers will find the information useful or interesting. We have no affiliation whatsoever with the originators of these articles nor are we endorsed or sponsored by the originator. All original content and/or articles and graphics in this message are copyrighted, unless specifically noted otherwise. All rights to these copyrighted items are reserved. Articles and graphics have been placed within for educational and discussion purposes only, in compliance with 'Fair Use' criteria established in the Copyright Act of 1976.

"The principle of 'Fair Use' was established as law by Section 107 of The Copyright Act of 1976. 'Fair Use' legally eliminates the need to obtain permission or pay royalties for the use of previously copyrighted materials if the purposes of display include 'criticism, comment, news reporting, teaching, scholarship, and research.' Section 107 establishes four criteria for determining whether the use of a work in any particular case qualifies as a 'fair use'. A work used does not necessarily have to satisfy all four criteria to qualify as an instance of 'fair use'. Rather, 'fair use' is determined by the overall extent to which the cited work does or does not substantially satisfy the criteria in their totality. If you wish to use copyrighted material for purposes of your own that go beyond 'fair use,' you must obtain permission from the copyright owner. For more information go to: http://www.law.cornell.edu/uscode/17/107.shtml"

Appendix E. Capturing Contents

Capturing key material and saving copies as proof is essential to the research process. It is not enough to look up information; it must be available for later use and referencing.

Capturing text is fairly easy, capturing other media is not.

Usually text can be saved simply by a "save as" command. Easy as pie! But saving the entire page, including pictures and other parts of the page, is more problematic.

Screen captures are one of several possible answers. Capturing the screen, or part of it, is a basic and useful technique for saving a picture or whatever is being displayed. Place the cursor on the picture or the entire screen you want to save. Holding down the control key while pressing the print screen key (often abbreviated and located in the top row of computer buttons) usually copies the item. Windows places your copy of the screen on the clipboard, although it is invisible to you.

You can save the screen picture to a graphics file (go to programs such as Paint) or it can be saved in a number of other file program types, including some word processing and even spreadsheet files. Place the cursor in whatever location you want to save the screen or picture and do a mouse right click (if you have a right-hand mouse) and select the type of paste you want to do. You can, alternatively, place the cursor where you want to locate the captured screen or picture and simultaneously do a Ctrl-V.

Screen capture copies what is visible on the screen, but it captures all of it. That includes things that show on the screen that are not essential or even wanted. A useful alternative is to use a snipping tool. Snipping tools have the advantage of being able to collect the portion of the page you want rather than the whole page. Snipping tools allow you to exclude the parts of the page you do not want to save. The **Free Snipping Tool** is one that is available to users at https://download.cnet.com/guides/snipping-tool/ or search online for "snipping tools."

Alternatives include such programs as CloudApp, Cobra Snipping Tool, Evernote Web Clipper, FastStone Capture, SnagIt, Free Online Screenshot, Jing, Greenshot, LightShot, Nimbus Screenshot, PicPick, ShareX, Shutter, and TinyTake. Some programs are free; some are free to use for a short time and then require a payment for continued use, while others require immediate payment.

Alternatives that offer a variety of ways to capture not only what shows on the screen, but even parts of the page that are not visible, include:

- **Nimbus Screen Capture (Add-on):** https://addons.mozilla.org/en-US/firefox/addon/nimbus-screenshot/
- **ShareX (Full Web page capture):** https://getsharex.com/.

Turning the web page into a pdf file is another alternative that some find useful at problem time. Programs such as **Fireshot ($$$$)** at https://getfireshot.com/ or the **Printfriendly** browser extension at https://www.printfriendly.com/, may help solve some of the page-saving problems.

To capture several pages or even an entire website you might use an off-line browser. **HTTrack's** copier at https://www.httrack.com/ is one of such sites. Such programs can be found by entering terms such as "website copier" or "off-line browser" in your search engine's box.

Different off-line browsers work differently, so there is always a learning curve for users. Off-line browsers will save pictures in the file.

Webmasters, of course, don't relish the idea of people copying their entire website and try – some with success – to thwart the use of offline browsers. While they won't work for a researcher every time, an offline browser is a useful implement in the toolbox.

When webmasters seem to make it impossible to download and save by any of the routine routes, either save as a print-out or save the material by using video programs such as CamStudio, Movavi Screen Recorder, or Replay Video Capture. These will save copies of pictures on a page but you will need to transcribe any text or other information before it can be used by a word processor. Scroll down, or go from page to page. With video capture programs leave about 10 seconds or more between each screen that you capture. The 10-second delay gives you the opportunity to pause the playback of each new section while reading, and typing out pertinent parts. These are not the easiest or best ways to save what you see, but they are workarounds when you are stymied using all other methods.

Always check, before you leave a page you want to keep, that the page or the material indeed has actually been saved to your computer.

It also makes sense, in many cases, to save and search the source code for information and details that are not visible on the page that is presented to viewers.

Archive sites are also useful but the material is stored off of your own computer. These sites include **Archive.today:** http://archive.is and **Archive.org (aka Wayback Machine):** https://archive.org/.

Hunch.ly ($$$$): https://hunch.ly/ is a Web-capture plug-in to Google Chrome that captures, stores, and annotates all webpages visited during a research session.

To save material for later use may require you to get inventive. But there is undoubtedly some way, if something is shown on your screen, to download a permanent record of it.

Appendix F. Search Strategies and SOPs

No strategy or search script comes with a golden guarantee. Despite the tub-thumpers who promise unfailing results with their system, nothing is written in stone. Knowledge of the research field and intelligent guesses may be equally responsible for positive final reports. But sometimes nothing you do, no amount of luck, can garner the information you seek. Neither perspicacity nor promise is guaranteed to turn into performance; the prospect of failure always looms in any search.

However, there are best practices that make success far more likely.

Know what you are searching for – that's the first thing. Then figure out where the information is, who has it, and how you can obtain it.

If you have been following a particular subject for some time and collecting documents in your library, you may already have the information and either forgotten it or didn't notice it when you first collected the information. Never overlook obvious sources, including your own resources and the material you have collected in the past.

Spend some time – even if it is minimal – strategizing. Leave no stone unturned. Nonetheless recognize – accept – that limitations such as time and resources may prevent you from achieving the gold standard of research, from being able to report with absolute certainty. Sometimes you will have to accept any progress, however incomplete, as achieving the goal. When you can achieve the gold standard, good on you. But keep in mind that the perfect is the enemy of the good. There are limits; there are rock faces that cannot be climbed and heights where the air is too thin to support your wings. Always opt for progress, even while hoping for perfection.

Determine the best search strategies, tools, and the most likely sites that will have the information you need. Always read instructions and help files that are posted on a site. Plan to use more than one browser for security reasons, but also change browsers in the event that a page doesn't display properly. Use two or more search engines to see if they produce different results.

Outline a tentative search plan that includes techniques, sites, and probable key words. When appropriate, include useful non-digital resources such as city directories in the search.

Give some thought to where, on the hidden web, information might be located. Databases and any other sites closed to search engines can be major resources for some searches.

If necessary, make a guess about URLs that might reveal information. Change the URL address endings (e.g., .gov to .com) to test for possible pages.

Start – and keep up to date – logs of where you went, what you did, and the search words or techniques you used. These will be useful to you and help your clients understand how the search was conducted. Your logs will note highlights of the search.

There might be sections in your logs that analyze techniques, tools, procedures, any problems including equipment and system failures, explanations of any deviations from the planned search, and – of course – the inevitable "other" that does not drop conveniently into any section.

Begin searches with terms you know; add new ones as you see them pop up in your results.

Plan to use the most obscure search terms first, where possible, in order to limit the number of returns. But when using more than one search term do a second search that puts the most important – read likely – search term first because many search engines often give extra weight to the word that is in first place.

Search using singular terms rather than plural forms because many search engines do not find singular terms when you use a plural word, but most will find plural terms when you search for the singular.

In multi-word searches, plan to use quotation marks and do "exact wording" probes. Consider whether you want to do "similar word" searches using a thesaurus.

When searching for a person or entity plan to initially concentrate your search in the physical area of your target. Think locally! Utilize regional services, databases, and directories where possible, searching in the predominant language of that area.

If the search is in a country or area with a different language – in Canada, for instance, English and French get equal treatment – search in all probable languages. In countries where English is not spoken as a first language always search for pages in the native tongues. Avoid limiting yourself or your search by insisting on being an Anglophile. Be conversant with the local alphabets, languages and writing systems. Use them in your Internet searches. At the very least, learn the terms most likely to appear on any local Web page such as "search' or "links" so you can effectively use those pages.

Follow the "look around rule" on any page you visit or believe might be useful; make at least a cursory test of every link. Run "link:" searches where possible to see who else might be linking to the page.

Consider and test for possible misspellings or typing errors – for instance where a forward slash has been changed into a backslash or "foreign" is misspelled as "foregin."

When on a page that is deep in a site, start removing the last entry in the URL and continue moving backward until you reach the home page. It takes little time but you never know what you will ferret out.

Use advanced search techniques where appropriate. On any site where their use is permitted, advanced searches will invariably help you drill down.

Create, and save to your SOP, a basic search script you can turn to immediately. Alter your script and SOP in any way that makes it more usable for your own searches.

***

When looking for online information about people it is important to determine where they are now, or were active, as well as how they identify themselves.

Picking people out of the pack is essential.

Outside of the Internet, people often identify themselves by their name, and on important documents the Social Security number or driver's license may be used. These, and dates of birth, mother's maiden name, place of birth, and other information is often useful in tracking people.

Many people have the same name. There are at least 3,600 people named William Brooks in the US – and that doesn't count several hundred more named Bill Brooks. Of course each has a discrete social security and driver's license number – but those are legally difficult to obtain and are not routinely used for most purposes.

But on the Internet, email addresses and user names are widely used for many purposes. Email addresses and user names, also called "handles," are critical "first-search" Internet resources.

User names are often derived from their email addresses. The email billbrooks123abcxyz@gmail.com becomes billbrooks123abcxyz as a user name when the rest of the address is chopped off. The user name is an important, and often unique, means of identification. In some searches it is far more important than the person's name.

Most people have more than one user name for reasons of security, or because of differing requirements of particular sites for the size or the construction of user names. While security rules dictate that user names and login passwords should be different on every site, few people follow that rule. With small variations where they are needed to meet site requirements, most people use the same or similar user names, sign-ins. and passwords across the Internet. Johnsmith as a username may become Johnsmith567 when more than 10 digits, or numbers, are required in a site login. People often add ABC, 123, a repeat of their name, or their birthdate to fill in any extra spaces on log-ins. It's something they can remember. On companion sites, sites such as Google's YouTube and Gmail, the log-in information will almost always be identical.

Running searches on a known username or login through a couple of the larger search engines may, or may not, produce usable information but is always a wise test. When you have username data, try using it on different services to see if the person has an account anywhere.

When postings on Social Media platforms may have been deleted, remember they may have been deleted on the site but they may have been saved elsewhere. While there are no guarantees, work-arounds for that problem are worth trying when time permits. These include cached pages of major search engines (often click on down arrow), and archive sites (http://web.archive.org).

When searching for information on individuals also try to identify birth dates, addresses of the past and present, phone numbers, email identities, as well as the names of friends and relatives. These are common search starters you can plug into several quality search engines or search surrogates such as Facebook.

People often change their names, particularly on social media where they may maintain multiple profiles on different sites that cater to different interests, but they seldom change their birth date. This is one of first questions asked during many account registrations and people reflexively fill in that information. When trying to track down a person their birthdate can be important information, as can a school name.

Email addresses tend to be steady. Often they will lead to more locations where a person posts, both by searching directly for the address or exploring whether part of the address is possibly a screen or user name. Handles are searchable clues on name check sites such as:

- **Checkusernames:** https://checkusernames.com/
- **EmailSherlock (Reverse search):** https://www.emailsherlock.com/
- **Knowem:** https://knowem.com/
- **Namecheckr:** https://www.namecheckr.com/
- **User Search:** https://www.usersearch.org/.

Select two to five search engines for a "quick and dirty" run through of the handle, name or birth date. Check the lists in the Search Engines chapter or choose them from the list below. Some basic ones might include:

- **Ask (Also directory):** https://www.ask.com/
- **Bing:** http://www.bing.com
- **Dogpile:** http://www.dogpile.com/
- **DuckDuckGo (Does not track user):** http://www.DuckDuckGo.com
- **Google:** http://www.google.com

- **Google Advanced Search:**
  https://www.google.com/advanced_search
- **Lycos:** http://www.lycos.com
- **Yahoo!:** http://www.yahoo.com
- **Yahoo (Advanced):**
  https://search.yahoo.com/web/advanced
- **Yamli (Arabic search engine):** http://www.yamli.com
- **Yandex (Russian-European):** http://yandex.com
- **Yippy:** http://yippy.com/.

Build your search; start with the basics such as name, birth date, address, phone number, email address, and online "handle," then move up the scale. Knowing these elements will provide a solid basis for all person searches.

Sites such as **Black Book Online**, used thoughtfully, can provide some of the basics: https://www.blackbookonline.info/.

Proper nouns are an important means of searching because they tend to be limiters.

Reverse engineer any facts you have about a target.

Develop a standard search process and script – one you feel you can rely on to provide due diligence, but always avoid limiting yourself to the four corners of that search SOP.

Always consider the context of your search every time you use a search script.

If you are not restricted to "observation only" you can seek out people who knew, and might talk about, your subject. Neighbors and school chums may provide new details which lead to additional search threads.

Understand the need for "due diligence" and what that means when balanced against any required time lines.

Your basic search SOP might include:

- Search of several different, likely, search engines by full name(s), including any handles, usernames and initials, current and previous location or residence, as well as organization, employer, or groups in which people are members. This is common and provides good results. It is generally the go-to-first methodology.
- Then put quote marks around the various terms you have used previously, narrowing the search.
- Find and use birthdates, with and without names.
- Anything with numbers, such as phones and addresses, should be searched.
- Look for old accounts.
- Understand that many popular sites have sister accounts that may be linked automatically – even without the knowledge of the user. Check for any cross-pollination of sites with common ownership.
- Cross-site triangulation of an individual can produce large amounts of useful information. Look for family and friends listed on a site; they will have information about your subject even when that person is careful about what, where, and even if they post about themselves. Think in terms of a network of people and groups. Intersects – where people or things share some commonalities – are important.
- City directories of current and former residences are often a valuable resource; they may provide contact information on neighbors, who might be a good source.
- College or university alumni groups or publications and yearbooks potentially have information from the present as well as the past.
- School records and graduation information, either from the school itself or the **National Student Clearinghouse**, at http://studentclearinghouse.org/, may be useful.

- Check directories at the person's workplace if you know that. Search the website of the person's workplace, or that of any groups the person is known to be affiliated with, for any mentions. Gather some basic information about all businesses or organizations the person is involved with or belongs to.
- Rummage through rosters of any groups the subject might be a member of; you never know what connections or background will be revealed.
- Check biographical directories; Many people who are not well-known are listed in resources such as WhosWho. Look at Internet sites the person might be using, such as newsgroups.
- Dating or "hook up" sites may provide an unlooked-for picture of the research subject. People may lie on these sites (always valuable to know) so any photos are highly suspect. On the other hand, people seeking intimacy may also be overly-truthful when they use sites like Ashley Madison, eHarmony, Farmers Only, Grindr, OkCupid, Our Time, Plenty of Fish, and Tinder. Users sometimes throw caution to the winds when emotions and hormones click in. Postings may reveal user names that are traceable elsewhere. And in almost all cases they provide some truthful location information, even if it is only a zip code.
- Search online commercial sites that claim to provide address, phone, or email information. Double-check and triple-check any and all information you obtain from these commercial "people finding" sites as these often mistake people of similar names and confuse identities. Such sites are useful, but their word is far from gospel.
- Voter registration records may prove beneficial.
- Assessor sites provide information on property ownership, including boats and aircraft. Check values, co-owners, and previous owners. Those might provide clues.
- Secretary of State sites can be searched for any businesses owned, or evidence about board members of companies.

- Licenses are generally required for businesses and some other activities; check issuing agencies.
- Professional licensing boards, where that is appropriate, potentially have important information ranging from complaints to background information.
- DMV records are sometimes useful.
- Charities searches (such as through ProPublica) and political contribution records may reveal some of the real interests of the subject.
- If you know the person's hobbies or interests, check any specialized websites that the person may be linked to.
- Searches of all available archives such as The Wayback Machine https://archive.org/web/, the Newspaper Archive https://newspaperarchive.com, and Google News Archive http://news.google.com, can be useful.
- Criminal, Civil, Divorce and other court records can be revealing. It is wise to search:
  o Local courts in the current area
  o Local courts in areas of the previous residence
  o Federal courts in the current area
  o Federal courts in areas of the previous residence.
- Offender and sex offender lists can be surprising.
- Tax records and liens in government files are worth a look.
- Audits and financial disclosure documents may be revealing.
- Filings of public companies and lists of board members are a baseline record when the subject is a business. They may also be useful when a person is known to be closely associated to company leadership.
- Regulator records, orders, and consent decrees often provide useful information.
- Corporate filings or Uniform Commercial Code (UCC) reports can provide helpful information.
- Records of Trademarks/Patents may also provide useful knowledge.
- Government contract records should not be overlooked.

- Wedding license and birth records may be worthwhile.
- Obituaries of family and friends can lead to some useful information.
- Military service records, if appropriate, may be revealing.
- Search for, and document, any personal or business websites of the subject.
- Search social networks applicable to your subject and create a record of all postings using screenshots, offline browsers, or a video scroll of the site. Sites that are associated with work and professional standing are likely to have contact information. Many social media sites also have information on, or links to, friends, associates, plans and activities. Search likely social media sites using the person's name, any "handle" or sockpuppet identity you have discovered, or phone number. Look for:
  o Friends and relationship information
  o Messages and postings
  o Employment information
  o Links or pictures of interest.
- Check photo and video sites carefully for any presence of the person, making certain that pictures are indeed those of – or posted by – the person. Picture searches should include a search for similar pictures and all pictures should be checked for EXIF and tag information.
- Look for metadata on any posted social network activity or pictures.
- Common verbal social constructs in any society will also be used online. Phrases and speech patterns that are common to a group or society may be useful in searches. In the US "was a member of" or "joined" are others.
- Search the Deep Web and Dark Web for your subject.
- For long-term projects create appropriate "Alerts" on Google and other sites.

When you have identified any website with information about your subject do a "site:" search of the entire website.

If time permits repeat all searches with a second or even third search engine to help establish your due diligence; it may turn up additional material.

If a website is closely linked to your subject, or is the subject of the search, a competition analysis overview through such sites as **Alexa.com** is a good bet.

Perform file-type searches on every name, whether individuals, businesses and organizations as above, looking particularly at files in:

- Text (txt, rtf, docx, doc, odt, odg, ods, wp)
- PowerPoint (ppt, pptx etc.)
- Portable Document Format (pdf)
- Spreadsheet (xls, xlsx, csv etc.)
- Databases (mdb, db, etc.

The Fagan File Finder at http://www.faganfinder.com/filetype/ may be helpful. **Find-PDF-Doc** at http://www.findpdfdoc.com/ may also be useful.

Look carefully at all files that have been found for any "hidden" information. It is not unusual for the creators of many file types to "hide" slides or other parts of the file – and the hidden portions may contain what you are looking for.

If direct searches for people, businesses, or anything with a name do not prove profitable, stop for a minute. Think who might be in their circle: family, friends, and organizations. Concentrate on the people and groups around your target. Your targets may be canny enough to remain off the radar but those around them probably are not trying to do so. Look at the collected information and search names of associates and relatives, collecting information on those people using the same methods you used to search about the person.

Foreign Searches

Foreign searches about persons present special difficulties; overseas subject and issue searches can be equally problematic. Always conduct foreign searches in the predominant language of the area.

Country-specific search engines or subject directories, guides and portals are potentially useful starting points for foreign searches.

In many cases if you don't know where else to start, begin your search with the US State Department or government sites, the United Nations, other diplomatic sites, or sites of university-level educational institutions in the foreign country. If nothing else you will assure yourself nothing is available.

Remember that many nations of the world were colonies of European countries; there is often a connection between former colonies and mother countries that can help guide your research.

Non-profit or charitable organizations are often useful information resources in many less-developed nations.

Second "Speed" Search Plans

In addition to having a regular search plan in your SOP, it often helps to have a shorter generalized "speed search" plan that you can modify as the time needs require. A shortened search plan outlines, but does not define, much of what you will want to track and methods you will want to use. It is the "50% solution" that you can tailor to fit your specific needs of the moment.

Best practices and planned searches sometimes have to be set aside in a speed search. Consider how you would alter your normal search plan – such as the one above – to turn it into a "quick and dirty" procedure to fit your unique needs. Speed plans really are individualized ones, created with the understanding that they have to be completed within a set, and always short, period time.

Professionals often develop speed plans suitable for one hour, four hour, and eight hour increments.

Remember to always balance the speed and completeness of any search. Completeness is the ideal but sometimes your search will be overtaken by events.

Time will NEVER stretch and deadlines are deadlines; an LTIOV warning really means "the last time information is of value." When events are fast moving, the balance of an information search is weighted toward speed. Eventually – probably sooner rather than later – you will face "the tyranny of the urgent." The demand for speed means thoughtful planning and your normal SOP has to be replaced by a previously designed format that "sort of" fits. Having and using an emergency format allows better on-the-fly decisions when there is little time for deep thought. It may not be perfect, but it is better than staring at the keyboard and wondering "What do I do now?"

Appendix G. Basic Search Plan Format

Name(s) of Researcher(s):

_____

_____

Client:

_____

_____

Priority – Is time more important than detail level?

_____

_____

Product format:

_____

_____

WENTK – Who else needs to know:

_____

_____

LTIOV – Last Time Information of Value:

_____

Date of Start:

_____

Tentative search timeline, including drafting and review:

_____

_____

_____

_____

_____

Scope and Focus:
_____
_____
_____

Original Question:
_____
_____
_____

Question to be researched:
_____
_____
_____

Who, What, When, Where, Why, and How elements:
_____
_____
_____
_____

Context of the question. The user's actual need:
_____
_____
_____

What does requestor already know; and doesn't know
_____
_____
_____
_____
_____
_____
_____
_____
_____

Search technique:
- Hunter-Focused
- Gatherer-Broad
- Mixed

What must be found out:

_____

_____

_____

_____

_____

What resources, tools and methods will be used:

_____

_____

_____

_____

Assets I already have (knowledge/capabilities):

_____

_____

_____

_____

Assets needed (refinement/tools/help):

_____

_____

_____

_____

Information I can get in time (deadline):

_____

_____

_____

_____

Likely location(s) (Physical area of search):

_____

_____

_____

Languages to be used:

_____

_____

_____

Product format desired: _____

Identify what is known and who knows it:
- How much do I know about the subject?
- Has this question been addressed previously?
    - If so, by whom?
    - If so, where is that information?
    - If so, can I get it there?

_____

_____

_____

_____

_____

_____

_____

_____

Resource types to be used in collection (Circle all to be used):
- Alert services
- Audio-visuals
- Blogs
- Books and magazines
- Chatrooms
- Corporate sites/materials
- Databases

- Directories
- Email
- Forums
- Games
- Government sites
- Gray material and ephemera
- Libraries
- Listserves/discussion lists
- Meta-search engines
- News media
- Non-Internet resources
- Observation
- Photos or satellite views of important sites
- RSS feeds
- Search engines
- Social media
- Subject matter experts
- The Dark Web
- The Hidden Web
- The Open Web
- Think tanks or subject matter experts
- Usenet groups
- Wikis
- Other resources:_____
  _____
  _____
  _____

Browsers and Search Engines to be used

_____
_____
_____
_____
_____

Location(s) To Be Saved To:

_____

_____

_____

_____

_____

Security Plan Outline:
- o Own Critical Information: _____
- o Possible Threats:_____
- o Vulnerabilities: _____
- o Risks:_____
- o Countermeasures:_____

Keywords: Found in question researched and from searched items:

Example Word	Similar	Broader	Narrower	Related Words
Smoking	Smoke, smoker	Tobacco	Cigarettes, Cigars	Nicotine, Lung cancer

Names, handles, personal identifiers:

_____

_____

_____

_____

_____

Family Members:

_____

_____

_____

_____

_____

Groups, Organizations, Associates:

_____
_____
_____

Government and Court Searches:

_____
_____
_____

Venues to be Searched (Name/Date):

_____
_____
_____
_____
_____
_____
_____
_____

Sites where information found:

_____
_____
_____
_____
_____
_____
_____
_____
_____
_____
_____

Sites Devoid of Useful Information:

_____
_____
_____
_____
_____
_____
_____
_____
_____

Actual Browsers Used/Date-Time:

_____
_____
_____
_____
_____
_____
_____

Actual Search Engines Used:

_____
_____
_____
_____
_____
_____
_____
_____
_____
_____
_____
_____

Vetting and Validation of Sources Methods

_____
_____
_____
_____
_____
_____
_____
_____
_____
_____
_____
_____

Researcher Comments:

_____
_____
_____
_____
_____
_____
_____
_____
_____
_____
_____
_____
_____
_____
_____
_____
_____
_____
_____

Appendix H: Sockpuppets – Alternative Identities

While this book is designed to help you collect information, there is also a contrarian side – the side involving your own privacy or secrecy, the side designed to prevent others from collecting information from and about you.

As you learn what and how much information you are able to collect and use, you may also become alarmed at those things that everyone from stalkers and businesses to Internet providers and central governments can collect and then stuff into a character study file about you and your online activities. The world is getting more digitally invasive.

Smart people, geeks, businesses, stalkers, governments, spies, and heaven knows who else push the boundaries constantly. They build on new techniques. They look for weak spots, both old and new. They don't always follow the left and right limits that you set for yourself in OSR.

You cannot effectively opt out of the digital world. Even if you never touched a computer keyboard or a smart phone screen, others are probably posting about you. Friends and family may post pictures or social media comments about Thanksgiving dinners you attended. Government agencies post things about you and your family, from home and aircraft ownership to political contributions and data about your business and the licenses you hold.

Information about you is out there. Birth records to death records – they are all online. Thousands of groups and governments scrape up every factoid they can about every breathing person. Information collectors are scouring the web for information about you even as you read this.

Opting out of the digital world is not feasible for anyone, even if it were possible. But this is particularly problematic for anyone doing OSR.

Identity counts for everything. Perhaps it is impossible to prevent anyone from seeing what you are doing on the Internet, but there are ways to prevent anyone from linking any activity that can be readily seen to your identity.

Sockpuppets, when allowed by employers or others, are one of the many ways to obscure identity. Sockpuppets are "another you." They act as a separate identity, another "person." They are simply covert accounts.

Depending on clients, personal or business needs, and a variety of other factors you may need to use several different versions of "you" to be a properly protected user.

Sherlock Holmes didn't invent sockpuppets, but he knew that alternative identities were useful, sometimes essential, to him and other investigators.

Holmes did not hesitate to use false identities when – and as – needed. *The Adventure of Black Peter* has Watson revealing that "… my friend had been absent so often and so long from our lodgings that I knew he had something at hand. The fact that several rough-looking men called during that time and inquired for Captain Basil made me understand that Holmes was working somewhere under one of his numerous disguises and names with which he concealed his own formidable identity. He had at least five small refuges in different parts of London, in which he was able to change his personality."

Sockpuppets are the alternative – OK, fake – identities used on the Internet. The "other you" may be as simple as calling yourself

"John Smith" on a social media site or as complex as creating an entirely new "life" on the Internet.

Sockpuppets are not identity theft. Legal sockpuppets are not based on a real person; they are, however, "whole cloth."

Many government agencies and private concerns forbid employees to create or use sockpuppets. Some employers frown – with great frowning – upon staff members using sockpuppets. Many online sites prohibit sockpuppets under their terms of use. Using a sockpuppet can put the users in legal, financial, or employment jeopardy.

Nevertheless, sockpuppets are useful to information professionals. At the very least, if your information shop has no significant prohibition against using an alternative identity, consider whether you need to create at least a bare-bones email sockpuppet – an alternate name and email address only. Many sites unnecessarily require you to sign in with a name, password, email, or phone number. And you can be assured that shortly after you enter any email address you, will be inundated with advertisements, pitches, and messages from people you never knew. The site you signed on to makes its money by selling your identity and contact information.

While many sites require you to fill in personal information, for the most part your truthfulness is not really critical when doing many elements of OSR. Fake identities are every bit as useful as your real identity for most research needs.

When you are required to give a phone number to sign up to a site or service many people use a burner phone, or one of the temporary phone services available online. You won't be bothered with as many robocalls. And the lack of automated digital birthday greeting messages from an insincere sysop you never met probably isn't going to knock the bottom out of your existence either.

When you develop a sockpuppet you can, and probably should, write down the details of any different *personas*, refreshing your memory any time you go online with any alternate identity. Create and refer to a written character study of every sockpuppet you use.

Successful sockpuppet users never adopt an alternate *persona* like an actor. They use the identity as if it is real; they live the role they have created for the sockpuppet when using one.

Sockpuppets are, of themselves, neither good nor bad. There are often good reasons for open source researchers to use a sockpuppet. But on the Internet the bad reasons for using a sockpuppet often predominate.

Sherlock Holmes used his false identities for good, but he knew that they also make life difficult for the researcher trying to separate fact from fiction. Holmes was willing to use fake identities, but he didn't want others to do so. "'No, no; the real name,' said Holmes sweetly. 'It is always awkward doing business with an alias,'" the great detective is quoted as saying in *The Adventure of the Blue Carbuncle.*

Whether you create and use one or not, if you spend much time on the Internet, and particularly if you spend much time on social media, you are likely to encounter sockpuppets.

Being able to identify a sockpuppet is important to analysts. Secure researchers must understand how sockpuppets are developed and used, even if they themselves do not create one for themselves.

When developing a sockpuppet, some people utilize websites that create false identities. **Fake Name Generator** is one such site, at http://www.fakenamegenerator.com/. These sites are easy to find by using terms like that in any search engine. Some sockpuppet name sites provide additional life "details." That may include phone numbers, address, age, mother's maiden name, birthdate, and even the sign of the zodiac.

Fake name generators may not be useful for some, but for everyone they are important to visit at least once to see the variety of "facts" and information that a good sockpuppet might eventually need to have available.

Effective sockpuppets are reliably consistent – perhaps their creators use a notebook that contains the elements of the "legend" or made-up story. The ability to refer back to the sockpuppet's "legend" prevents the "silly to dilly" mistakes that can unmask a sockpuppet. Because many Internet users are sharp-eyed, deviations from past statements are immediately spotted.

Memory is a poor substitute for written records, as Conan Doyle proved by a major slip of his own making. In *A Scandal in Bohemia*, Holmes fleetingly calls his long-time landlady Mrs. Hudson by the wrong name – Mrs. Turner. That slip of his prodigious memory, perhaps, is an example of why details should be written down rather than left to memory.

Likewise, when you are trying to determine if someone is using a sockpuppet a written record helps. It is a good idea to snatch all the postings of a questionable target and put the revealed "facts" of the poster into a database or spreadsheet similar to the one below. Comparisons of statements over time – and it may be a short time – can help uncover a sockpuppet's misstatements.

	Person 1	Person 2	Person 3
Name(s)			
Email address			
Password			
Location, physical address			
Age/Birthdate			

Sex			
Height			
Weight on date			
Color hair			
Color eyes			
Picture			
Marks/scars/distinguishing features			
Special Abilities			
Disabilities			
Work-present and past			
Talents			
Hobbies			
Parents/grandparents			
Spouse/significant others			
Children			
Siblings			
Co-workers			
Friends			
Enemies			
Schooling			
Appealing traits			
Repugnant traits			
Food preferences			
Favorite music			
Favorite authors(s)			
Favorite shows			
Clothes/wardrobe			
Housing descriptions			

Room descriptions			
Motivators of person			
Favorite phrases			
Vacations & travel			
Miscellaneous			

Problems often arise when researcher cannot identify a sockpuppet for what it is – a fakement.

Many good sockpuppets hew close to the truth about themselves, at least some elements of the truth. The "legend" and claimed skill sets of the sockpuppet often mirror those of the sockpuppet creators or those around them. This creates a feeling of "naturalness."

Even people who have developed an otherwise-quality sockpuppet may use their actual birthdate. That is often one of the first questions asked by many sites in registration and in their rush to complete the site's form people often just answer with the truth. They sometimes list themselves under the schools they actually attended, another common security mistake that wary researchers can use against targets.

Particularly over a long term – where there are many data points to consider – legends are often revealed as the fabrications they are. For that reason sockpuppet users often maintain a stable of fake identities for use in case one identity is outed. That happens often.

Using a notebook outlining the "facts" of a particular sockpuppet is almost required when the user creates more than one false identity. It is too easy to confuse the attributes of one personality with those of another fakement.

Female sockpuppets appear to receive less scrutiny than male ones, but many males have a difficult time slipping into a female *persona*. Anyone who can do so, however, has a good success rate.

To create a sockpuppet of any utility the user must have two things: a name or Internet handle and a Web address.

Both the names John Smith and John Wayne are problematic as sockpuppet names, yet each has positive aspects. John Smith is so general and generic that anyone trying to trace a posting or contact information is going to be overwhelmed with false positives. John Wayne as a name is very specific, and hardly generic. For different reasons it will be difficult to cut through the many articles about the actor to research the person behind the sockpuppet name. In either case a researcher is going to be overwhelmed with either possibilities or information about the wrong person. But importantly both names are likely to be tagged as questionable, probably sockpuppets, by many sites on social media, where signing on with false credentials is prohibited. Sockpuppet identities should never be obviously fictitious.

A good approach is to go to a site such as **How Many of Me:** http://howmanyofme.com/ and carefully experiment with names to find an identity where there are between 1,000 and 2,000 people of the same name. In most situations the name will be common enough that it will not be easy to trace, but neither will it normally excite the disbelief of site managers who are intent on only allowing only real people, with actual identities, to use their site.

It is important to decide on an age and date of birth. Under no circumstances use Jan 1, or the current date, as that sets off alarm bells. Also avoid using your own birthdate. Choose the birth year and age to match the general age of anyone your sockpuppet is likely to converse with.

Most people creating their own sockpuppet probably have little choice but to use "free" email sites when setting up an email. These include:
- **33Mail:** https://www.33mail.com/
- **GetNada:** https://getnada.com/

- **Gmail:**
  https://support.google.com/accounts/answer/27441?hl=en
- **GMX:** https://www.gmx.com/
- **Mail.com: https://www.mail.com/**
- **Outlook:** https://outlook.live.com/mail/
- **Proton Mail (Encrypted)**: https://protonmail.com/
- **SafeMaily:** https://safemaily.com/
- **TemprEmail:** https://tempr.email/en/
- **TenMinuteMail:** https://10minutemail.com/
- **Tutanota:** https://tutanota.com/
- **Yahoo Mail**: https://overview.mail.yahoo.com/.
- **AOL Mail**: https://help.aol.com/products/aol-mail.

Sockpuppets, whether yours or others', often use covert email addresses from "free" sites, making that an important element to consider when checking whether someone's online presence is actually a sockpuppet. While email addresses from free webmail sites are hardly determinative of a sockpuppet, they are an important data point, prompting a knowledgeable person to delve further into the actual identity of people on the Internet. A working email address from something other than a free webmail site provides excellent "cover" for a sockpuppet.

It is also important, in some cases, to have a phone number. In the modern world few people live without a phone. Anonymous phone contact, but tied to your sockpuppet's identity, can be achieved with a variety of tools and junk accounts, including Google Voice.

The truly good sockpuppet also has dimensionality and a presence on the Web, primarily on social media. The not-so-good ones lack any presence other than an email, or if they do have a Web presence their sparse postings lack emotions or they will have a cardboard personality.

Good sockpuppets live somewhere, a home they can describe inside and out, room to room, driveway to backyard fence, stairway to kitchen appliances. Housing descriptions may be based on pictures from real estate or photo-mapping sites. These allow sockpuppets to paint a picture of "their" home and "their" neighborhood like a real resident.

Sockpuppet users may claim to be from anywhere – but anyone who claims to be from, or in, a location that is not their own has some formidable steps to climb in making their artificial world seem real and reasonable.

Sockpuppet users must digitally "live" in their claimed location. Employment, social happenings, news of local events, holidays and vacations, even the prevailing sense of local humor may have to be displayed through the sockpuppet. Vagueness about location excites suspicion but detailed information also invites inspection. Someone on the Internet inevitably lives in any neighborhood that the sockpuppets claim as their own.

Religious, ideological, and political affiliations need to be brought up over time. An Internet "person" lacking any such background stands out as a cardboard creation. To a great extent any sockpuppet character needs a back story – without that they were "born yesterday." And a believable sockpuppet must also have a future, a story that includes hopes, dreams, fears, and prospects.

Sockpuppets have favorite foods. They have relatives. Long-term sockpuppets need friends and enemies. A sockpuppet has the same types of interactions that everyone experiences daily. Are their conflicts passive or active? Things like this and a person's passions are found in good sockpuppets. They are missing from the poorer ones.

Timing of messages and Internet availability is crucial. Every person has some way of making a living. Hours and days must be set aside for that. Somewhere along the line work will come up – issues will range from the commute to events at work and the bosses there. If a sockpuppet's messages appear to have been posted during the work hours specified in the legend, the sockpuppet must have a good explanation for that discrepancy.

Well-crafted sockpuppets socialize and reveal, in some way, why they want to interact with others. Their messages display mood swings, highs and lows. Habits will become apparent in the best ones, even some commentary on diet and drinks will appear.

Sockpuppets must be kept up. It not enough to simply develop one and leave it for the time when it is needed. That kind of sockpuppet stands out as a fake.

Any overlooked detail may be used to unmask the sockpuppet. One of the most important European spies in World War II, in one report, claimed to be drinking wine with shipyard workers in Scotland. Wine? Scottish shipyard workers? Yeah, right! But such a massive clue that Juan Pujol Garcia had made up the whole story was missed; he went on to create a group of informants who never existed, developing a pre-computer sockpuppet spy circle that successfully misinformed the Nazi war machine regarding the timing and location of the Normandy invasion.

Better sockpuppets often do a lot of "liking" of other people's posts on social media as this tends to create a sense of community and often results in getting "likes" in return. That, in its turn, affirms the "humanness" of the sockpuppet and affirms that this is indeed a real person. Sockpuppets follow people, and thus pick up followers in return.

Some transient subjects – weather, local happenings, and unusual natural or political events – are found in the posts of good long-term sockpuppets but will be absent from the writings of cardboard creations.

Sockpuppets often post pictures or videos. A lack of pictures is often another a telltale sign that some social media connection is actually a sockpuppet. A picture of a pet, a car, or other abstraction seems to work almost as well as a portrait picture in "proving" any Internet profile is legitimate. While there are many pictures of people on the Internet that could be stolen and used to authenticate a sockpuppet, one of the first steps in unraveling any false identity is determining where the picture was stolen from. For that reason photos or other pictures used in sockpuppet posts should be original and must never have appeared on the Internet.

Cultural differences, even down to language and the slang used in the area the sockpuppet claims to live, will be reflected in the better fakements. Every bit as important as displaying the correct cultural norms is the adoption of subcultural behaviors and language. A lack of knowledge about group thinking, behavior, and terminology can be the clue that unravels a sockpuppet. Things are simple as whether a sockpuppet calls a soft drink "soda" or "pop" may be instrumental in outing a faker; regional language variations may be clues.

Effective sockpuppets require serious thought in their creation and judicious use. Exposing one calls for careful thought as well.

Appendix I: Advanced Tools and Toolkits

Many of the tools, sites, programs, and techniques useful to hackers and spies also are valuable to the information professionals who are willing to sidle up to – but always stay on the right side of – legal and ethical lines.

Some techniques and procedures of OSR can be either powerful tools or deadly weapons, depending on who uses them, why, and how.

Some advanced resources automate the information gathering process, provide graphical displays, collect metadata and link pieces of information together in a more understandable way. Many of these resources require an advanced knowledge of computers and the Internet for effective employment.

Properly used, these toolkits and resources can reveal:
- Confidential files
- Differences in files of same name
- Email or IP addresses and phone numbers
- Geo locations
- Metadata
- Open ports
- Server information
- Social networking postings and connections
- Websites.

Some advanced tools and toolkits that each researcher or research desk should evaluate for their own uses, many used by white hat hackers, include:
- **Awesome OSINT:** https://github.com/jivoi/awesome-osint
- **Bellingcat's Online Investigation Toolkit:**

https://docs.google.com/document/d/1BfLPJpRtyq4RFtHJ
oNpvWQjmGnyVkfE2HYoICKOGguA/edit
- **BlackWidow:**
  https://github.com.cnpmjs.org/1N3/BlackWidow
- **Central Ops (Internet utilities):**
  https://centralops.net/co/
- **Citizen Evidence Lab (Bellingcat-type tools):**
  https://citizenevidence.org/toolbox/
- **Datasploit:** https://github.com/DataSploit/datasploit
- **DiffNow:** https://www.diffnow.com/compare-clips
- **ElevenPaths FOCA (Document metadata):**
  https://github.com/ElevenPaths/FOCA
- **EXIF (Jeffrey's Image Metadata collector):**
  http://exif.regex.info/exif.cgi
- **FOCA (Document metadata):**
  https://filehippo.com/download_foca/
- **Freeality:** http://www.freeality.com/
- **Hunchly ($$$$, Web capture):** https://hunch.ly/
- **Maltego ($$$$):** https://www.paterva.com/web7/
- **Metagoofil (Metadata collector):**
  http://www.edge-security.com/metagoofil.php
- **OSForensics:** https://www.osforensics.com/tools/
- **OSINT Framework:** https://osintframework.com/
- **OSINT Tools Comparison:**
  https://docs.google.com/spreadsheets/d/18U1qcaPaqIF8ER
  VLI-g5Or3gUbv0qP_-JUtc0pbEs0E/edit#gid=0
- **OSIRT (Law enforcement only):**
  http://www.osirtbrowser.com/
- **Recon-ng (Reconnaissance tool):**
  https://bitbucket.org/LaNMaSteR53/recon-ng
- **Sam Spade 1.14:** https://sam-spade.en.lo4d.com/
- **Shodan (IoT):** https://www.shodan.io/
- **Spiderfoot**: https://www.spiderfoot.net/download/
- **Splunk ($$$$):** https://www.splunk.com/
- **StartMe:** https://start.me/p/wMdQMQ/tools

- **ToolboxToolbox (Everything for everybody):** http://www.toolboxtoolbox.com/
- **YouGetSignal (Multiple testing tools):** https://www.yougetsignal.com/

All these sites should be reviewed. Explore the list above and use the relevant parts of it when creating your SOP and search plan.

To create a highly-secure system, immediately, consider combining the VM Ware search machine described in Michael Bazzell's Seventh Edition of *Open Source Intelligence Techniques* with Justin Seitz' **Hunch.ly** program: https://hunch.ly/.

While we do not have a financial interest in either of these, we believe the two – put together – could provide a firm base on which to build your own research process and individualized SOP.

The instruction and details contained in Michael Bazzell's Seventh Edition of *Open Source Intelligence Techniques* will help researchers build a secure operating system that is tailored for open source research. It will hinder, and probably prevent, the subjects of your research from identifying you and your interests. Using the detailed techniques and links will provide you with advanced abilities to do in-depth research on subjects of your choice.

Justin Seitz's Hunch.ly program also provides security but most importantly sets up a way to actually collect, easily find in your system, and then use, the captured information in reports.

Those capabilities, along with your own SOP and the techniques and resources of this book, should provide you with a viable triad that you can use as you begin developing your own information program – whether for yourself, your family, or your employer.

It is that elementary.

Index

453, 461, 465, 472, 485, 505,
557, 573, 575, 587, 601, 610,
612
planning, 11, 14, 22, 24, 37, 40,
44, 67, 92, 97, 129, 141, 142,
143, 144, 147, 154, 157, 158,
164, 190, 279, 338, 405, 415,
424, 463, 464, 569, 590
plausibility. *See* vetting
practitioner. *See* collector
privacy-aware search engine,
203, 204
production system, 104, 119,
120
proxy, 114, 203, 558, 562
research system, 54, 78, 102,
103, 120, 166, 167, 546
reverse image search, 390, 437
robots.txt, 264, 265, 273, 284,
336, 337
scouts, 249, 250, 256, 469, 470
search engine, 21, 27, 30, 37,
44, 49, 50, 63, 64, 78, 80,
112, 131, 159, 163, 167, 169,
170, 173, 174, 178, 179, 183,
185, 191, 192, 193, 194, 195,
196, 197, 198, 199, 200, 201,
202, 203, 204, 205, 206, 207,
208, 209, 210, 211, 212, 214,
216, 217, 218, 219, 220, 221,
224, 225, 226, 227, 228, 229,
230, 231, 232, 233, 237, 238,
239, 240, 241, 242, 243, 245,
246, 249, 251, 252, 253, 254,
255, 256, 261, 263, 264, 265,
266, 268, 269, 281, 296, 336,
337, 338, 340, 345, 350, 351,
353, 360, 368, 377, 384, 387,
389, 390, 391, 394, 395, 403,
423, 437, 448, 455, 456, 460,

495, 525, 548, 561, 567, 568,
574, 578, 579, 581, 582, 583,
584, 588, 589, 595, 599, 604
search script, 27, 55, 577, 580,
583
security, iv, 2, 11, 13, 25, 34,
37, 43, 45, 46, 47, 48, 52, 63,
74, 76, 92, 94, 96, 99, 102,
103, 104, 106, 107, 111, 112,
115, 116, 117, 120, 121, 127,
128, 129, 130, 131, 132, 133,
134, 135, 136, 137, 138, 139,
144, 164, 165, 166, 167, 171,
172, 175, 179, 180, 188, 189,
192, 193, 203, 205, 211, 216,
217, 228, 242, 270, 271, 272,
275, 285, 291, 348, 358, 370,
371, 372, 374, 375, 376, 377,
378, 380, 388, 393, 403, 404,
405, 440, 450, 458, 509, 518,
533, 537, 539, 540, 543, 544,
545, 546, 548, 553, 554, 555,
556, 557, 558, 560, 561, 562,
563, 564, 565, 568, 578, 580,
581, 596, 607, 614, 615
semi-controlled media, 313, 315
Sherlock Holmes, 7, 8, 9, 14,
30, 37, 40, 41, 61, 69, 70, 71,
74, 75, 87, 99, 129, 141, 150,
177, 188, 250, 257, 269, 288,
292, 357, 360, 385, 424, 426,
441, 448, 480, 481, 482, 490,
554, 602, 604
social media, 5, 20, 23, 43, 46,
48, 50, 55, 64, 66, 75, 77, 81,
82, 100, 133, 146, 147, 163,
204, 222, 237, 245, 249, 290,
324, 328, 354, 357, 358, 360,
379, 383, 385, 388, 392, 393,
396, 412, 430, 435, 436, 437,

Coming soon!

*Join Us to Explore More of
The Wide World of Information
at:*

opensourceresearch.net